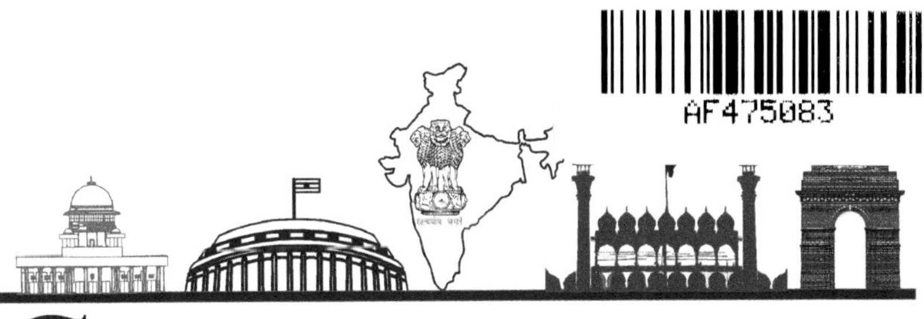

Government and Politics in India

For
Bachelor of Arts [BA]

BPSE-212

Useful For

Delhi University (DU), IGNOU, Berhampur University (Odisha), University of Kashmir, Sambalpur University (Odisha), University of Kalyani (West Bengal), Gurukula Kangri Vishwavidyalaya (Uttarakhand), Himachal Pradesh University, Cooch Behar Panchanan Barma University (West Bengal), Ranchi University, University of Culcutta, Pune University, University of Mumbai, Andhra University, School of Open Learning (DU), Gondwana University (Maharashra), Babasaheb Bhimrao Ambedkar University (Lucknow), Dr. Babasaheb Ambedkar Marathwada University (Aurangabad), University of Madras, Netaji Subhas Open University (Kolkata), Odisha State Open University, all other Indian Universities.

GULLYBABA PUBLISHING HOUSE PVT. LTD.

ISO 9001 & ISO 14001 CERTIFIED CO.

Published by:

GullyBaba Publishing House Pvt. Ltd.

Regd. Office:
2525/193, 1st Floor, Onkar Nagar-A,
Tri Nagar, Delhi-110035
(From Kanhaiya Nagar Metro Station Towards Old Bus Stand)
Ph. 011-27387998, 27384836, 27385249

Branch Office:
1A/2A, 20, Hari Sadan,
Ansari Road, Daryaganj,
New Delhi-110002
Ph. 011-23289034
011-45794768

E-mail: hello@gullybaba.com, Website: GullyBaba.com

New Edition

Price:

Author: GullyBaba.Com Panel

ISBN: 978-93-82688-92-1

Preface

In the 66 years, since India achieved independence in its "tryst with destiny", the strength and stability of the nation have been tested many times. India has become democratic republic with a system of government. The central government is also known as the union government, and its structure is much like the British parliamentary system, with distinct, but interrelated executive, legislative, and judicial branches. State governments are structured much like the central government, and district governments exist in a variety of forms.

This GPH book ***"Government and Politics in India (BPSE-212)"*** looks back over the years since independence and examines India's experience with democratic political institutions, and its efforts to establish itself as a power in South Asia and the world.

This book is written specially in question & answer format to provide students the instant gratification of a correct answer. We have tried to solve all possible questions from the exams' point of view. Sample question papers have also been included to help students to understand the unique examination structure. We hope that this book would not only be a favourite study material for the students but also can be a nice resource for teaching.

An attempt has been carefully made to present this book more useful and meet the requirement and challenges of the course prescribed by IGNOU University.

We wish you a successful and rewarding career ahead. Feedback in this regard is solicited.

– GPH Panel of Experts

Acknowledgement

Our compliments go to the **GullyBaba Publishing House (P) Ltd.,** and its meticulous team who have been enthusiastically working towards the perfection of the book.

Their teamwork, initiative and research have been very encouraging. Had it not been for their unflagging support, this work wouldn't have been possible. The creative freedom provided by them along with their aim of presenting the best to the reader has been a major source of inspiration in this work. Hope that this book would be successful.

– GPH Panel of Experts

Publisher's Note

The present book BPSE-212 is targeted for examination purpose as well as enrichment. With the advent of technology and the Internet, there has been no dearth of information available to all; however, finding the relevant and qualitative information, which is focused, is an uphill task.

We at **GullyBaba Publishing House (P) Ltd.,** have taken this step to provide quality material which can accentuate in-depth knowledge about the subject. GPH books are a pioneer in the effort of providing unique and quality material to its readers. With our books, you are sure to attain success by making use of this powerful study material. Provided book is just a reference book based on the syllabus of particular University/Board. For a profound information, see the textbooks recommended by the University/Board.

Our site **gullybaba.com** is a vital resource for your examination. The publisher wishes to acknowledge the significant contribution of the Team Members and our experts in bringing out this publication and highly thankful to Almighty God, without His blessings, this endeavor wouldn't have been successful.

– Publisher

Topics Covered

Contents

Question Papers

1 Historical Background

An Overview

English East India Company constituted to promote trade with India was firmly established its domination in India by 1600 AD when the Mughals were at the height of their power and glory.

Within a century, the Mughal power became degenerated and disintegrated. The Britishers took advantage of this situation, tightened their grip over India with a series of legislations.

The British built in India the largest colonial empire. But it was a different kind of colony from most others. Different sections of the society responded to colonialism in India. Their responses depended on the nature of issues relating to them and the impact of colonialism on them. Independence was the conclusion of a long struggle against colonialism.

The colonialism was very decisive in the making of modern India. It radically changed the face of Indian society. It also resulted in a churning within that society.

Q1. Briefly discuss the concept of Colonialism.

Or

Define Colonialism.

Ans. Colonialism is the establishment, exploitation, maintenance, acquisition and expansion of colonies in one territory by people from another territory. It is a set of unequal relationships between the colonial power and the colony and between the colonists and the indigenous population.

Fig. 1.1: Colonialism

Colonialism normally refers to a period of history from the 15th to the 20th century when people from Europe built colonies on other continents. The reasons for the practice of colonialism at this time include:

- Economic benefits to the colonising power, which may or may not benefit the colony.
- To expand the power of the colonizer.
- To escape persecution in the colonizer.
- Obtaining military advantage, such as the creation of a buffer state or the removal of a threat.
- To convert the indigenous population to the colonists' religion.

It may be driven by economics, religion or militarism.

Some colonists also felt they were helping the indigenous population by bringing them religion and civilisation. However, the reality was often subjugation, displacement or death.

There are four common characteristics of colonialism:

- Political and legal domination over an alien society;
- Relations of economics and political dependence;
- Exploitation between imperial powers and the colony;
- Racial and cultural inequality.

Q2. Discuss the nature and stages (phases) of colonialism.

Ans. Nature of Colonialism

Colonialism produced a society, which was neither capitalist as in Britain, nor was it pre-colonial or pre-capitalist. Thus, for example, India under British rule neither resembled capitalist Britain nor was it basically similar to Mughal India. The development of agrarian relations in the colonies- in India, or Egypt, or Indonesia makes this aspect quite clear. For example, landlordism in both *zamindari* and *ryotwari* areas of British India was something new; it did not exist in Mughal India. It was the creation of British rule. It was the result of the colonial rulers' efforts to transform Indian agriculture. Indian agriculture was not capitalist but it had many capitalist elements; for example, property relations were capitalist; land was now a private property, which was freely bought and sold on a large scale. Infact, we can say that the colonial societies under-went a fundamental transformation under colonialism. They were made an integral part of the world capitalist system. For example, colonialism in India was as modern a phenomenon as industrial capitalism in Britain the two had developed together since the middle of the 18th century.

Capitalism was, by its very nature, a world-system—that is, it must cover the entire world; but it does not cover the entire world in the same way. It has one face in the metropolis and another in the colonies. It develops the metropolis as a modern industrially developed country. The same capitalist process, which produces economic development in the metropolis and makes it an advanced capitalist country produces and maintains underdevelopment in the colonies and transforms them into colonial societies. Colonialism uproots old society and economy, but the new colonial society and economy are as much a barrier to modern economic development as are the old, pre-capitalist economy and society.

Stages of Colonialism

Colonialism may be divided into three distinct stages, which were related to distinct forms of exploitation or surplus appropriation. Consequently, each stage represented a different pattern of subordination of colonial economy, society and polity and therefore, different colonial policies, political and administrative institutions, ideologies and impact as also different responses by the colonial people.

(1) First Stage of Colonialism: First stage is described as the Period of Monopoly Trade and Direct Appropriation or the Period of East India Company's Domination, 1757-1813. During the last half of the 18-century, India was conquered by a monopoly trading corporation — the East India Company. The Company had two basic objectives at this stage:

(a) The first was to acquire a monopoly of trade with India. This meant that other English or European merchants or trading companies should not compete with it in purchase and sale of Indian products. Nor should the Indian merchants do so. This would enable the East India Company to buy Indian products as cheaply as possible and sell them in world markets at as high a price as possible. Thus, Indian economic surplus was to be appropriated through monopoly trade.

(b) The second major objective of colonialism at this stage was to directly appropriate or take over governmental revenues through control over state power. The East India Company required large financial resources to wage wars in India and on the seas against European rivals and Indian rulers and to maintain naval forces, forts and armies around their trading posts, etc. East India Company did not possess such resources and the British Government neither possessed them nor was it willing to use them to promote the Company's interests. The much needed financial resources had, therefore, to be raised in India from the Indian people. This provided another incentive to make territorial conquests in India.

This lack of change was also reflected in the ideology of the rulers. No need was felt to criticize traditional Indian civilisation, religions, laws, caste system, family structure, etc. for they were not seen as obstacles at that stage of colonial exploitation. The need was to understand them sympathetically so that political control and economic exploitation could proceed smoothly without arousing opposition from Indians on religious, social or cultural grounds.

This period witnessed large-scale drain of wealth from India. This wealth played an important role in financing Britain's industrial revolution. Drain of Wealth from India constituted 2 to 3 per cent of Britain's national income at the time.

(2) Second Stage of Colonialism: The second stage was a period of exploitation through trade and is also termed as Colonialism of Free Trade during the 19th century. Immediately after the East India Company became the ruler over most parts of India, an intense struggle broke out in Britain to determine whose interests would the newly acquired colony serve. Britain was after 1750 undergoing the Industrial Revolution. The newly developing industrial capitalists began to attack the East India Company and the forms of its exploitation of India. They demanded that colonial administration and policy in India should now serve their interests, which were very different from those of the East India Company. They did not gain much from a monopoly trade in Indian products or from the Company's control over Indian revenues. They wanted India to serve as a market for their ever-increasing output of manufactured goods, especially textiles. They also needed from India exports of raw materials, especially cotton and food grains. Moreover, India could buy more British goods only if it earned foreign exchange by increasing its exports. Increasing exports were also needed to enable dividends of the East India Company and profits of British merchants and earnings and pensions of British officials to be transferred to Britain.

The British were for years not willing to let India's textiles be imported into Britain and later their export was no longer economic, these exports from India could consist only of agricultural raw materials and other non-manufactured goods. In other words, to suit the convenience of British industrial capitalists, British colonialism in India must enter its second stage. India must become a subordinate trading partner of Britain, as a market to be exploited and as a dependent colony to produce and supply the raw materials and food-stuffs Britain needed. India's economic surplus was to be appropriated through trade based on unequal exchange. As a result, Britain increasingly produced and exported goods which were produced in factories using advanced technology and less labour and in which level of productivity and wages was high. On the other hand, India produced agricultural raw materials through backward methods of production using great deal of labour leading to low productivity and low wages. This international division of labour was, moreover, not only highly unfavourable to India but was unnatural and artificial and was introduced and maintained forcibly through colonial domination.

The beginnings of the change occurred with the passing of the Regulating Act of 1773 and Pitt's India Act of 1784, which were primarily the result of intense struggle within the British ruling classes. The East India Company was saved and given a reprieve by the French Revolutionary Wars after 1789. However, the Company gradually lost ground. By 1813, when another Charter Act was passed, the Company had lost most of its political and economic power in India; the real power being wielded by the British Government which ruled India in the interests of the British capitalist class as a whole.

Modern education was now introduced basically with the objective to man the new, vastly expanded administration. However, it was also expected to help transform India's society and culture. This transformation was needed for two reasons; it was expected to,

- create an overall climate of change and development and,
- generate a culture of loyalty to the rulers.

It is to be noted that it was around this period that many Indian intellectuals like Raja Ram Mohan Roy began to work for social and cultural modernisation for different reasons, mainly as part of national regeneration.

If India's socio-economic structure was to be radically transformed, its existing culture and social organisation has to be declared unsuitable and decadent. Indian culture and society were now subjected to sharp criticism. No racialism was, however involved in this criticism for it was simultaneously maintained that Indians could gradually be raised to the level of Europeans.

The earlier forms of surplus extraction continued during this phase. This, plus the costly administration, plus the efforts at economic transformation led to a steep rise in taxation and in the burden on the peasant. Because of the constant needs of colonial administration for funds to maintain military and civil administration and for construction of railways and its large reliance on taxation of land, which had its own limits, colonial administration suffered from constant financial constraint.

(3) Third Stage of Colonialism: The third stage of colonialism is described as the Era of Foreign Investments and International Competition for Colonies. A new stage of colonialism was ushered in India from about 1860s. This was the result of several major changes in the world economy:

(a) Spread of industrialisation to several countries of Europe, the United States and Japan with the result that Britain's industrial supremacy in the world came to an end.

(b) There was intensification of industrialisation as a result of the application of scientific knowledge to industry. Modern chemical industries, the use of petroleum as fuel for the internal combustion engine and the use of electricity for industrial purposes developed during this period.

(c) There was further unification of the world market because of revolution in the means of international transport.

The new industries in many industrialised countries consumed immense quantities of raw materials. Rapid industrial development also led to continuous expansion of urban population, which needed more and more food. There now occurred an intense struggle for new, secure and exclusive markets and sources of agricultural and mineral raw materials and foodstuffs.

Moreover, the development of trade and industry at home and extended exploitation of colonies and semi-colonies produced large accumulations of capital in the capitalist countries. Simultaneously there occurred concentration of capital in fewer and fewer corporations, trusts and cartels and merger of banking capital with industrial capital. Outlets had to be found for this capital. This led to large-scale export of capital. Once again, the developed capitalist countries began a search and compete for areas where they could acquire the exclusive right to invest their surplus capitals.

Thus, in their search for markets, raw materials and fields for capital investment, the capitalistic countries began to divide and re-divide the world among themselves.

Colonialism at this stage also served important political and ideological purpose in the metropolitan, that is, imperialist countries. Chauvinism or aggressive nationalism based on the glorification of empire could be used to tone down social divisions at home by stressing the common interests in empire. The British, for example, raised the slogan that "The Sun never sets on the British Empire" to spread pride and a sense of contentment among workers on whose slum-houses the Sun seldom shone in real life. The French talked of their "Civilising Mission", while Japan talked of Pan-Asianism and claimed to be the champion of the Asian people.

During this stage, Britain's position in the world was constantly challenged and weakened by the rival capitalistic countries. It now made vigourous efforts to consolidate its control over India. Reactionary imperialist policies now replaced liberal imperialist policies. This was reflected in the viceroyalties of Lytton, Dufferin, Lansdowne and Curzon.

The strengthening of colonial rule over India was essential to keep out the rivals, to attract British capital to India and to provide it security. After 1850, a very large amount of British capital was invested in railways, loans to the Government of India, trade and to a lesser extent in plantations, coal mining, jute mills, shipping and banking in India.

India also performed another important role for Britain. Its army — men and financial resources — could be used to fight Britain's rivals in the struggle for the division and re-division of the world. In fact, the Indian army was the chief instrument for the defence, expansion and consolidation of British empire in Africa and Asia. The result was a costly standing army that absorbed nearly 52 per cent of the Indian revenues in 1904.

Politically and administratively, the third stage of colonialism meant renewed and more intensive control over India. Moreover, it was now even more important than ever before that colonial administration should reach out to every nook and corner of India. The administration now became more bureaucratically tight efficient and extensive than earlier. Railways were built at even a faster rate.

A major change now occurred in the ideology of colonialism. All talk of training the Indian people for self-government died out. (It was revived in the 20 century after 1918 as a result of pressure from the Indian national government). Instead, the aim of British rule was declared to be permanent 'trusteeship' over the Indian people. Indian people were declared to be a permanently immature, a child people, needing British control and trusteeship. Geography, race, climate, history, religion, culture and social organisation were cited as factors, which made Indians permanently unfit for self-government or democracy. Britain had, therefore, to exercise benevolent despotism over them for centuries to come.

Efforts at the transformation of India continued during this stage, though once again with meagre results. This was partly because of the financial constraints and also because of the rise of the national movement. Even the limited changes produced an intelligentsia, which began to oppose colonialism and analyse the mechanism of colonial exploitation. The British administrators increasingly assumed a neutral stand on social and cultural questions and then began to support social and cultural reactionaries in the name of preserving indigenous institutions.

Q3. Describe and analyse the impact of the first phase of British colonialism in India.

Ans. While the British retained much of the Mughal revenue system, they made some drastic changes of detail within its overall structure. The first, though a minor one, was they raised the share of revenue collected enormously. It has been estimated that the total revenue collected from the Bengal Diwani in the first few years of British rule doubled whereas for the last 100 years it had remained the same. This was a huge increase. It is important to remember that this led to severe famines, a third of the population perished, but it is important to note that the revenue collected continued to grow. As an aside, it is important to remember that under the Mughals a part of the revenue collected was reinvested to help the economy and the growth of local product but very little came back under the British.

They made various changes in what they retained of the Mughal revenue system. One fundamental change they made was to make the revenue calculable on the total land entitled to cultivate rather than the land actually cultivated. This was crucial. For example, under the Mughal, if the peasant was entitled to cultivate, for instance, 100 acres of land but actually cultivated only 55 acres, the revenue collected was only for 55 acres but the British assessed and collected the revenue for the entire 100 acres of land. Now imagine the enormous burden it may have put on the peasants because barring a few nobody cultivated the entire land one was entitled to cultivate. In other words, the assessment under the Mughals can be said to be based on the produce and not on holdings and therefore there was a flexibility in-built into the system. Secondly, it has also been noted by many that the actual rent in full was not always collected and considerations were given to the difficulties of the peasants. Thirdly, under the Mughals, the revenue was calculated in cash but more often it was collected in kind so the peasant did not have to go for distress sale. Finally, and very significantly, the failure to pay in time or repay other kinds of debt did not lead to the loss of land under the Mughals. The British forced the auction of land in case of failure to pay the revenue or other debts and for the first time allowed non-peasants to buy up land.

Earlier land could be transferred only to another peasant. Non-peasants could not alienate peasant lands. So some transfer used to take place within the peasantry.

It should be obvious from the above that the system introduced by the British was inflexible in relation to the vagaries of agrarian economy in conditions like those prevailing in our tropical climate dependent on monsoon. It gave rise to the beginning of the conversion of land into a commodity like entity, even though land cannot become a commodity in the way cloth can be.

Nevertheless, massive alienation of land became a feature of the agrarian relations. A repercussion of this was, one, the ability of the superior holders or the money-lenders to confiscate the land of the peasants for realisation of arrears due to whatever reasons and, two, even the land of the superior holders, like *Zamindars*, could be taken over the moneylender for failure to repay debt and the interest accumulated on it. The consequence was the emergence of absentee landlords as a sizeable proportion of land owners who then would let out land on back breaking rent or share-cropping.

This was not confined to the Diwani of Bengal and the system of land tenure introduced there. However, this was a common feature for the whole of India under the British administration, whichever land tenure system we look at. In the Permanent Settlement created by Cornwallis in Bengal, the government gave over the right of revenue collection to a small number of large *Zamindars* who had powers over cultivators now reduced to tenants. The *Zamindars* had to pay to government fixed amount, which was fixed forever but no restriction on rent rates till late in the 19th century. The book you can believe most – GPH Book.

Q3. Describe and analyse the impact of the second phase of British colonialism in India.

Or

How did de-industrialisation affect the agrarian economy?

Or

What was the impact of second stage of colonialism on Indian political economy?

Ans. This stage of colonialism had a two-fold impact on the Indian political economy, namely damaging and developmental.

The Damaging Role: Prior to the British arrival in India, the industry was large and widely spread with secondary manufactures. These pre-capitalist manufactures were spread all over the country with mutually beneficial links between them agriculture and manufacturing. However, after the first half of the 19th century there was no growth of new industries in India in a process called de-industrialisation. In the first decade of the 19th century one-way free trade was introduced (i.e. exports from Britain were exempt from custom duties in India). Cotton textiles for instance made a large portion of India's exports. Within a few decades cotton textiles vanished from India's export list. This was because the British discouraged manufacturing in India and pushed for extraction of raw materials. At the same time there were massive imports of cheap textiles from England thus demand for local produce declined. Britain had then become a top producer of cotton textiles in the world. Cotton goods produced in India had to pay a higher duty than those of Britain's. This became the reality for other manufactures such as silk goods whereby the British forced the weaver under its control to give up weaving and replaced it with the production of raw silk as it was more profitable in Europe. Britain also monopolised the sale and manufacture of salt, opium, indigo, etc. By the second half of the 19th century, de-industrialisation was complete. Its effect on agriculture was damaging. Workers tossed out of secondary manufactures were thrown into agriculture for direct sustenance. The land had to support so many more people that it did before. This exacerbated an already impoverished peasantry. Relations of peasants with landlords worsened as the number of landless agricultural labourers increased. This condensed into absolute reduction in workers' wages in agricultural operations and secondly rent was increased (rack-renting became common) which facilitated easy eviction of the tenants as share-croppers. Poverty, not in a relative sense but of an absolute kind was wide-spread. Under an Indian administration, income from government service would have contributed to the local progress and not to foreigners. The diversion of upper-class income into the hands of foreigners hindered the development of local industry for it placed purchasing power into the hands of people with a preference for foreign goods, thus boosting imports. The amount of money that went to foreigners could have been used to raise income levels in India.

The Developmental Role: Beginning in the 19th century, the British had set up a modern administrative apparatus and subsequently a judicial system and together with merchantile firms. Large number of Indians was needed to run it. To allow for this, by the 1830's a complete shift to English both in administration and education was effected. Consequently, a new class of Indians well versed in English emerged. They established a monopoly first over the jobs and then over professions like lawyers, doctors and engineers. The upper stratum of this was the new Indian elite. Their power extends to current times causing resentment among lowers castes like the Dalits and the Muslims. Another significant form of development was railway constructions. By 1914, 34,000 miles of railways were constructed linking all major areas in India. Railways made mobility of goods and people across India easier and enormously contributed to trade and capital development. It brought about the integration of various local economic zones. On the otherside, railways also contributed to a greater integration of Indian economy into the metropolitan one thus augmentating India's economic exploitation. This was because of the route alignment and fare-structure. Apart from the trunk, routes linking the main the cities to the capital, railroads primarily were aligned so as to link interiors to port cities from which finished goods were imported into India while raw materials were exported to Britain. Fares for goods were higher if transported between two interior places but much lower if the same were to move from interior to the port cities. This was to discourage internal trade and facilitate external trade with Britain. Such were developments that freedom fighter Dadabhai Naoroji called 'drain theory'. Irrigation networks were another significant form of development. Construction of vast irrigation networks was took place, but confined to areas as neglection of traditional irrigation works like wells and village ponds occurred. The earlier traditional system was under the farmers control so they could regulate crop mixture and rotation of crops. Modern networks put the peasants at the mercy of landlords who controlled the government public works like canals. More power was given to landlords and moneylenders at the expense of the peasants. Investment in irrigation caused great disparities among various regions in India. Investment went into two or three areas with the higher production potential, like Punjab. These areas experienced significant productivity growth cultivated by more labour and capital investments. Irrigation also led to changes in the cropping pattern. It facilitated the growth of exportable food grains and commercial crops. These new export food grains marginalised the production of millets (a cereal requiring little water which was the staple food of the poor) and the pulses (the chief and only source of protein for the poor). By 1914, 25 per cent of the total cropped area came under the cash crops. By 1880's a fairly sizeable Indian capitalist class was emerging, mostly concentrated around port-towns; marking the early beginning of capitalism under Indian entrepreneurship. The British contributed to public health by establishing Western medicine and training, and also establishing quarantine procedures. Consequently death rates fell.

Q4. Describe and analyse the impact of the third phase of British colonialism in India.

Or

What led to the growth of modern industry in India?

Or

What is "import substitution" industrialisation?

Ans. In the last decades of the 19th century, the nature of colonialism was transforming. There was intense competition among capitalist countries to export capital to and establish industries in colonies like India. According to liberal economist Hobson and revolutionary Lenin, capitalism had entered a new phase called Imperialism. India at the time had developed a number of industries such as the cotton textiles, steel and sugar. This was boosted after the First World War. Indian capitalists who had accumulated large capital through trade started establishing industries of their own. They gained large concessions from Britain to start industries and also pushed it to modify the one-way free trade, with the aim of protecting the Indian industrialists. Britain was forced to grant protective tariff to protect them. Indian capitalist assets started to grow faster than those of the British. By Second World War India had extensively achieved self-sufficiency. Much of what was imported from Britain was now being produced with the country itself; this pattern of industrialisation has been referred to as 'import-substitution industrialisation'. The colonial mode of development imposed serious disjunction as pointed out by Bagchi between industry and agriculture. Most areas that developed industry remained agriculturally backward whilst those that were agriculturally advanced like Punjab remained industrially backward. As a result, agricultural areas became hinterlands for the industry. Areas that constituted of mainly Muslim populations developed no industry and remained hinterlands. Thus, this contributed to Muslim separatism, which as we know led to the partition of the country and the creation of Pakistan. Upon gaining independence, India was the most developed outside the advanced capitalist countries. It had the largest capitalist class well versed in influencing politics as well as the largest and accomplished middle class. It paradoxically also had the highest incidence of poverty both urban but especially rural seen through undernourishment, poor health, illiteracy and lack of shelter.

Q5. Discuss the reaction of peasants and tribes against the colonial rule.

Ans. Reaction of Peasants

In the areas occupied by the British new land revenue systems, such as the Permanent Settlement in Bengal and the Ryotwari system in other areas, were introduced. Both these were-alien to the subcontinent, and implied the superseding of the traditional rights of the village community over their land.

Two forms of property now came into being. In Bengal where the Permanent Settlement was implemented, *Zamindars* became the intermediaries between the state and the peasants. In other areas, the peasants were directly burdened with very high taxes.

The company began to extract revenue with a vengeance. In Bengal alone, the total revenue collected doubled from ₹63.4 lakh in 1762-63 to ₹147.0 lakh in 1765-66. R.C. Dutt, who studied the impact of colonialism on the Indian economy, estimated the extraction to have increased from ₹2.26 crore in 1765-66, to 3.7 crore in 1769-70. Even the severe famine caused no decline in the taxation reflecting the unscrupulous greed of the new rulers. This created a severe crisis for the old *Zamindars,* who were now reduced to the status of revenue farmers. The new land revenue arrangements also affected the/class of people dependant on State patronage, such as traditional scholars, fakirs, artists, etc. The revolts of the *Zamindars* and other dispossessed people formed the earliest responses to colonial power.

The peasantry was the worst victim of the new system. The peasants reacted in the form of protest against the colonial oppression. The peasant reaction came in many forms. Titu Mir's (1782) rebellion was one such early response to the British rule. Titu Mir led the poor peasants near Barasat in 24 Parganas (Bengal) against the *Zamindars,* both Hindus and Muslims. He instructed his followers to follow pure and simple Islamic practices. The movement began to spread into the adjoining districts of Nadia and Faridpur. Its popularity finally forced the colonial authorities to kill Titu Mir and suppress his movement. In November 1831 Titu Mir's headquarter at Narkulbaria in Barasat district was destroyed. He and fifty of his followers were killed, and several hundreds of his followers were arrested. The more widespread Farazi movement of Haji Shariatullah (1781 - 1840) in eastern Bengal followed this. Shariatullah asked his poor peasant followers to strictly observe the duties (far'iz, hence far'izi) enjoined by the Quran and Sunna (Islamic law), and to maintain God's unity. He stressed that so long as the British rule Bengal the congregational prayers on jumma and Id should not be performed, as according to tradition they must only be performed in a misr aljami (a town where an amir and a qazi, properly appointed by an independent Khalifa are stationed). This was one of the strongest indictments of British rule. Under his son Duda Mian (1819-1862), the impoverished and landless peasants, artisans and weavers joined the

Farazi ranks. The Farazis attacked both the landlords in the area, who incidentally were Hindus, as well as the British Indigo factory owners. The colonial authorities tried very hard to suppress the Farazis and to rescind Shariatullah's indictment of British rule. It was finally in the last decades of the nineteenth century that the movement's new leaders asked the population to extend loyalty to the British. The anti-British felling was so strong that people were not allowed to seek redressal of grievances in the British courts without permission from the Farazi leaders.

In 1859-60, the peasants in Nadia district of Bengal heard that the new Lt. Governor was sympathetic to their condition. They refused to accept the advance paid by the indigo planters coercing them to grow indigo. The movement spread through the delta region. Indigo planters were attacked and soon the entire system began to collapse. As a result of this revolt, the indigo cultivation system came to an end in the area. In the 1870s, there were protests in Pabna (Bengal). The peasants organised themselves into agrarian leagues here. In 1873, a large-scale movement of the peasantry in Pabna and the adjoining areas was another strong indictment of colonial rule.

In the Ryotwari areas, the peasantry came under increased pressure of revenue demanded in cash. The situation was aggravated with the introduction of commercial crops such as cotton. This further increased the monetary requirements of the peasant; at the same time, it diminished his self-sufficiency.

The moneylenders in Bombay Presidency were mostly outsiders in the local peasant communities. They began approaching law courts for the settlement of debts. This resulted a massive alienation of peasantry from their lands. Community bonds among the peasantry against the moneylenders strengthened, and they rose against the moneylenders in 1875 in the districts of Ahmednagar and Poona.

The Tribal Response: A significant number of people in the subcontinent for centuries lived in socio-cultural and economic worlds different from other social formations based on caste or other principles of hierarchy. The word tribe, an import from the European language and knowledge systems, was used to describe these people. The relationship between the two formations varied from context to context. Colonialism created spaces and conditions for non-tribal outsiders to move in large numbers into the habitat of the tribal people. The colonial rule brought about other fundamental changes in the life of tribals.

Living in relative isolation, the tribal population had, over the centuries, evolved social, cultural and political patterns differently. The colonial state facilitated penetration of revenue farmers, forest contractors and Christian missionaries in a large number into the tribal habitat. The British with little knowledge of the communities living in forests and hilly terrain like Chhota Nagpur and Santhal Parganas acknowledged the outsiders who had established themselves in the area as the ruling potentates over the tribal lands too. They entered into revenue arrangements with them. The latter in turn transformed their customary gifts and tributary relationship with the tribals into a compulsory revenue relationship. The new legal system forced this relationship on the tribal people, with the colonial masters as the supreme revenue lord. Thus, the tribal people were deprived of their traditional rights over the land, forest and all that they were familiar with for centuries. With little knowledge of the new legal system, which had no notion of the rights of tribal people, the latter found no sympathy with the rapidly penetrating agricultural communities too.

The central Indian tribes, particularly those living in the Chhoota Nagpur and Santhal Parganas area, were the worst sufferers in the new situation. When the British began penetrating the Jangal Mahals and Chhota Nagpur after 1780, thekedars and other intermediaries also entered into the system. The heightening of certain internal differences within the tribes in the colonial perception precipitated these changes. The colonial system and the outsiders began treating individuals within tribes like the Pahan (priests) or the Munda (leader) or the Munda tribe, whose status was that of one amongst equals, as landlords or political and social leaders. This attached the relatively egalitarian structure of communities such as that of the Mundas and the Oraons in Chhota Nagpur. The coming of the missionaries and the large scale conversions, particularly in the last decades of the nineteenth century, also created new inter and intra-tribal differentiation. The arrangements evolved over centuries between the tribal differentiation. The arrangements evolved over centuries between the tribal population and the neighbouring communities were also distributed. The Ghatwals in the Jangal Mahals were traditionally the police force of the local ruling potentates in Chhota Nagpur. The abolition of this arrangement resulted in the famous Chuar rebellion of the Chatwals in the 1790s. Similarly, the reservation of forestland for colonial purposes altered the tribals relationship with the forest and his habitat. However, the most radical change came in the shape of the large-scale intrusion of the outsiders.

The most powerful expression against the outsiders, who mostly came as moneylenders, revenue contractors, lawyers and landlords, was the famous Hul rising of the Santhals in Damni-I-koh (modern day Santhal Pargana district). In 1855 under the leadership of Sidho and Kami, the Santhals attacked the colonial authorities as well as outsiders whom they called dikus. In 1832-33, the Bhumiji in the Jangal Mahals revolted against the colonial authorities, while in the 1850s, the tribal leaders called Sardars in Ranchi district revolted against the rapid land alienation.

The Christian missionaries in the Chhota Nagpur area provided a helping hand to the exploited tribal people. They not only opened hospitals and schools, but also enlightened the colonial authorities about the tribals and their problems, taking up their cause with the administration. On the question of land, however, neither the colonial authorities nor the missionaries had any intention of intervening. A large section of the tribal people in Chhota Nagpur, therefore, began to see the missionaries as no different from the colonial matters. It is in this context that Birsa Munda and his Ulgulan (the great tumult) emerged in Ranchi district in 1899-1900. The followers of Birsa attacked all visible symbols of colonial authority like police stations. The entire tribe participated. When Gaya Munda and his men returned from an attack on the Khunti police station, the Munda women gave them a traditional welcome reserved for men returning from a hunting expedition.

Assam came under British rule only in 1826, and the colonial penetration in the Naga hills and in the Manipur area was relatively late. In Assam, Vaisnavism had exerted a great influence on the local population over the centuries. Contact with Calcutta opened the area to new influences. One such influence was an alternative to the available mode of Hinduisation. Kalicharan Mech of Dhubri was inspired by a Hindu sanyasi of Calcutta and started a new faith, eschewing the expensive rituals attached to the prevailing hinduising modes in the area. The new converts, called Brahmas, engaged themselves in the eradicating illiteracy of their tribes. There was also a move towards abstinence from rice, beer, meat, etc.

The forces of change were too large and too rapid for the tribal people to adjust. For inspiration, therefore, they looked back to their past. All their revolts were characterised by a conscious invocation of a lost but golden past. Sidho, Kanu and Birsa Munda, all of them painted a glorious picture of their tribe in a bygone age, Satjug, *vis-a-vis* the tribe's present suffering Kalijug. Birsa blamed the white fathers, the black fathers (the converted tribals), and the colonial authorities for the miseries of his tribe, which had lost its land and religion and had become a victim of overall degeneration. This consciousness provided the ideological basis for solidarity behind all these movements. Attempts to revive community memories of the pre-Christian days by those who were disturbed by the growing divide between the Christian and non-Christian world-views.

This was combined with an attack against the outsiders and British rule in the last decades of the 19 century. The Khasi tribe made such an attempt.

The ongoing national movement influenced the tribal movements in the early decades of 20 century. The Tana Bhagat movement of Gumla in Ranchi district, and the Zeliangrong movement in the Naga hills were two such instances. Jadonang (1905-1931), who set up the Haraka religious cult with three basic objectives started the complex Zeliangrong or Haomei movement in 1925. The first aimed at reformation of the tribes, particularly the Zemi, Liangmei and Rangmei, to enable them to face the onslaught of Christianity. Secondly, the overthrow of the exploitative colonial laws by attacking British rule and third, establishment of the Naga Raj. The movement was also aimed against the Kuki tribe, the "outsider". From 1927 onwards, influenced by Gandhi, Jadonang began a civil disobedience movement in the area. On 13 June 1931, Jadonang was arrested and sentenced to death, and finally hanged on 29 August 1931. Gaidinliu, a teenage girl, took over the leadership of the movement. In March 1932, the entire village of Bopugoanmi in the Naga Hills was burnt down by the government forces, in retaliation to the attack on the Assam Rifles outpost by Gaidinliu's followers. Finally, the seventeen-year-old leader, called Rani Gaidinliu by Nehru, was arrested on 17 October 1932, and sentenced to life imprisonment. Thus, when she was set free in 1947 on Nehru's personal insistence, she had already spent all her youth in jail.

Q6. In which way the middle class/intelligentsia was different from the peasantry and tribals?

Or

In which way did the middle class/intelligentsia respond to colonialism?

Or

How did the intelligentsia generate public debate?

Ans. The intelligentsia is a social class of people engaged in complex mental labour aimed at disseminating culture.

The colonial rule saw the emergence of a few class whose members came mostly from the newly educated sections and the professionals created by the colonial establishment. This class was not attached to any royal court or religious establishment and was entirely on its own, except that it depended on the new colonial economy for its sustenance. Well versed in their own traditions, this class encountered the full blast of the new ideas shaping the west, equipping them to view their own society and its institutions on their own merit. They found that-infanticide, polygamy, sati, practice of untouchability, prohibition of female education and widow remarriage, and absence of any critical knowledge system characterised their society. Further, religious and social practices were inseparable, thus, legitimising all inhuman practices through recourse to religion. Education in the classical mode imparted in Sanskrit, Arabic or Persian was devoid of any critical component. It was also based on caste and gender discriminations-non-Brahmins and women were not allowed Sanskrit education. The first generation of intellectuals and reformers, particularly the father of the Indian reform movement Raja Ram Mohan Roy (1772-1833), realised their unusual predicament very early in their Careers. While they had to defend the societies, religions and traditions of India against the evangelical and utilitarian attacks, they also had to eradicate the evil and inhuman practices that prevailed in the society. The evangelists had been criticising Hindu and Muslims practices and institutions as inhuman, and had presented Christianity as the means of deliverance. The educated class was the first to face this onslaught on their religion and society. A large section of the educated was converted to Christianity. Those like Raja Ram Mohan Roy who did not think conversation was the answer, worked towards reforming their own society. Their vision of a new society was informed by the ideas of freedom, equality and fraternity and a religious universalism, which advocated a common core among the world's religions.

The Ideas and Vision of New Class

The ideas and vision of this new class was articulated best in the work, of Raja Ram Mohan Roy. With sound knowledge of Persian Arabic, Sanskrit, Hebrew and several European and Asian Languages, Ram Mohan Roy acquired a deep insight into different religious traditions. He was well versed with the movement of ideas taking place in Europe. He realised that a critique of tradition was necessary for removing wide spread illiteracy, ignorance and practice of inhuman and cruel practices like widow burning, infanticide, excessive ritualism, polygamy, and prohibition on remarriage of Hindu windows. These practices were legitimised by invoking religious texts and traditions. Ram Mohan Roy and later Vidyasagar in Bengal, Veershalingam in Andhra and Krishna Shastri Chiplunkar in Maharashtra studied the shastras themselves to prove that the Hindu religion never sanctioned such practices, which were based on the wrong and often false interpretations of the Brahmins. They were also clear that tradition had to face the test of reason and social good. In addition, that social good was to be based on notions of equality, liberty and fraternity. Ram Mohan Roy was the forerunner in this.

Social Reformers and Public Debate

The reformers never rejected traditions but rather put them to critical evaluation. Such a critique required engagement of an informed and critical mass of people. Thus, the reformers made it a point to engage in public debate through newspapers and journals, as Ram Mohan Roy did through Mirat-ul-Akhbar, Keshub Chandra Sen through Indian Mirror and Sulabh Samachar, Bal Shastri Jambhekar through Darpan (1832). Almost all issues related to social reforms were debated publicly, reflecting a core democratic principle, which came to fruition during the national movement, gaining ground during this time. A significant result of these literary outpourings was that the vernacular languages were enriched. Bengali, Assamese, Marathi, Gujarati, Tamil, Telgu and other major languages were enriched by this. The reformers indirectly contributed to the growth of linguistic communities, which was recognised clearly in the 1890s and in the long-run contributed to the demand for a separate Orissa, Andhra, etc.

The reformers also realised that to defend their society against missionary and colonial criticism and also for permanent reform, it was important that education be imparted not only to all sections of men, but to women too. They campaigned for a critical and scientific education system. What India required was "not the revival of Sanskrit learning", Ram Mohan Roy argued, "but promotion of a more liberal and enlightened system of instruction, embracing Mathematics, Natural Philosophy, Chemistry and Anatomy with other useful subjects." It was Lord Macaulay, the Law Member in the Viceroy Council, whose decisive intervention was crucial in winning the case for English education. However, Lord Macaulay's intention was to produce a class of Indian in colour but British in taste, yet Ram Mohan Roy and others wished to bring the fruits of new knowledge into India and infuse Indians with these new ideas and spirit. For excellent score, read GPH book.

Q7. Briefly explain reforms movements under colonial rule.

Ans. Reform movements are movements, which are organised to carry out reforms in some specific areas. Usually such movements use legitimate means within the larger framework of the society and without disturbing the existing framework.

The reforms for which Ram Mohan Roy stood were eradication of the kulin system (marriage of young girls to higher subcaste Brahmins, often much older, resulting in the practice of polygamy), stopping the sale of young girls in marriage, abolition of cast system, introduction of widow remarriage and abolition of sati. Sati was a prevailing practice among the high caste Hindus where the widow had to die, at times forcibly, along with the dead husband on the latter's funeral pyre. Ram Mohan Roy considered this cruel practice to have no sanction in the shastras. He and his friends led an agitation, which finally resulted in Sati being banned by Legislative Council Act of 1928.

Ram Mohan Roy also engaged the Christian missionaries in public debates over their attacks on oriental religions. He criticised the missionaries for presenting a caricatured version of Christianity and distorting its essence. This attack was from the standpoint of religious universalism. He established the Brahmo Samaj in 1828 to provide space for all those who believed in non-sectarian religion. He did in 1833 in Bristol, England. The Brahmo Samaj became the nucleus of reform activities in Bengal and throughout India.

Ishwar Chandra Vidyasagar, who became the principal of Sanskrit College, opened the gates of Sanskrit learning to non-Brahmin students. He worked tirelessly for widow remarriages and education for the girls. It was through his efforts that in 1856 widow remarriage was made legal. Keshub Chandra Sen, one of the most gifted successors of Ram Mohan Roy, took the latter's message across the country. His visit to Bombay and Madras in 1864 and N.W.F.P in 1868 resulted in the formation of Prarthana Samaj in Bombay Maharashtra, with a strong tradition of reforms dating back to the days of the Bhakti saints in the medieval period, produced Bal Shastri Jambhekar and Gopal Hari Deshmukh who assumed the name Lokahitawadi. They criticised the privileges of the Brahmins, and the devaluation of women and lower castes from a rationalist viewpoint. Gopal Ganesh Agarkar and Krishna Shastri Chiplunkar, a Sanskrit pandit with an extremely critical perspective on the challenges facing Hindu religion and society, joined them. The Scientific and Literary Society formed in Bombay in 1848 and the Prarthana Samaj (1864) became the centers of the reform movement.

The new ideas soon swept the Parsi community of Bombay Presidency. Cursetjee Nusserwanjee Cama, Nowrojee Furdonjee and Sorabjee Shapoorjee Bengalee took the lead in this. The emphasis was on the status and education of women. Cursetjee Cama started regular schools for girls and Sir Jamshetjee Jeejibhai opened four schools for Parsi girls, which were taken over by the Parsi Girls Association in 1856. Furdonjee's Gujarati periodical Vidyasagar and Bengalee's Jagatmitra and the Dyan Prakashak Mandali disseminated new social and literary ideas.

Dadabhai Naoroji's journal Rast Goftar (1851), best reflected the reforming trends within the community.

Engulu Veerswamiah in Andhra wrote in 1857 that there was no recognition of untouchability in the shastras, and conversions to Christianity were taking place due to this practice. Samineni Murthoonarsimiah Naidoo of Rajamundry wrote Hitasoochanee in which he focussed on the social inequities related to marriage and female education. It was however, kandakri Veereshalinan (1848-1919) who gave the reform process in Andhra in organised and dynamic form. His journal Vivekdrdhini, (1974) criticised the orthodoxy by taking fairly rationalist stance, and also attacked caste inequities and the disabilities of women in society. He started a number of schools for women, in addition to those of the Christian missionaries. From 1883, he began to publish Satihitabodhini, which addressed issues concerning women, inaugurating an era of women's journals in Andhra. Meanwhile, Keshub Chandra Sen's Visit in 1864 and establishment of the Brahmo Samaj boosted the efforts of the reformers. Chembeti Sridharalu Naidu of Cuddalore became the first Anusthanic Brahmo (1869) in south India when he began officiating Brahmo ceremonies in Kakinada. The raja of Pitharpur set up schools for girls.

In Assam, attacks were directed against kulinism and the practice of sati. Jadrum Barua propagated widow remarriage, himself marrying a widow. Gunaviram Barua and Hem Chandra Barua later attacked these practices with renewed vigour. In Bibhaha Paddhati and Tin Ghaini, Hem Chandra Barua attacked polygamy and its associated evils, while his Bahire Rang chang Bhitare Koa Bhaturi exposed the irreligious acts of the priestly class.

Assumption of power by the British affected the Muslim aristocracy in northern India the most. The aforementioned British land revenue system impoverished the Peasantry in Bengal, who were predominantly Muslims. The responses in different regions, therefore, were varied. The earliest response was one of extreme antagonism towards the British rule. The lack of an anti-colonial critique led to its expression on religious terms as exemplified by the Jahabi movement of Syed Ahmed of Rai Bareilly (1786-1831) and Farazi movement of Shariarullah.

The mutiny and the retribution meted out to sections of the Muslim aristocracy in northern India brought a change in attitude. Reconciliation to British rule rather than antagonism was thought to be prudent to bring reforms to Muslim societies. In Bengal, Syed Abdul Lateef (1828-1893) and

Ameer Ali (1849-1928) made efforts to impart English education to the Muslims. It was Syed Ahmed (1817-1898) who realised that any reform within the northern Indian Muslim communities required addressing the changed circumstances of the Muslim aristocracy. He felt that the aristocracy needed to be equipped with a modern education to regain their sense of confidence and leadership. In 1875, he started the Mohammedan Anglo-Oriental College in Aligarh, as the harbinger of reforms of the Muslims in India. The women in Muslim communities were better placed because they were never denied literacy like their Hindu or Parsi counterparts. The recitation of Quran provided them with elementary literacy, but it was only in the first decades of the 20th century that efforts were made to bring Muslim women into schools outside the home. Begum Rokeya Sakhawat Hussain (1880-1932) of Bengal established a Girls school in Calcutta in 1911. The effort of the families of Badruddin Tyabji and H.S. Bilgrami, and the royal family of Hyderabad is worth mentioning in this regard.

In all the attempts to reform societies, efforts were made to engage critically with tradition. However, there also existed a stream of thought, which attacked existing traditions in toto arguing that traditions actually legitimize oppression and unequal social relations. Therefore, they tried to present alternative social vision based on equity and social justice. In Poona, a gardener's son Jyotiba Phule (1827-90) having personally experienced caste oppression, presented in alternative history of the community he termed the Bahujan Samaj. He saw the Brahmins as the outsiders who captured the land of the Bahujan and reduced them to the status of untouchables and lower castes. He criticised all traditions, including Bhakti saints like Ramdas as legitimising these inequities. Ambedkar later developed this powerful stream of thought. Pandita Ramabai's (1858-1922) 'The High Caste Hindu Woman' focussed on the strong patriarchal character of Brahmanical orthodoxy, and engaged with larger question of the sanctity of tradition and perpetuation of caste and gender inequalities. In Madras, Ramaliagnaswami represented a very powerful rationalist line.

Q8. Write short notes on the following:

(i) Reform vs. revival under colonial period.

Ans. There were perceptible changes in the intellectual life of the subcontinent during the second half of the nineteenth century. The writings of Bankim Chandra Chatterjee, Akshay Kumar Sarkar, Rajendra Lai Mitra, Bhudev Mukherjee in Bengal, and Vishnu Shastri Chiplunkar,

Balgangadhar Tilak and Bhandarkar in Maharashtra displayed a new sense of confidence, culminating in Vivekananda's championing of Vedanta. It was the confidence of a society over the rediscovery of its glorious past. It was also a reaction to the racial arrogance displayed by the British after the mutiny. The revivalist reaction was aimed at reforming society on the basis of the glorious Hindu past, and hence critical of reforms inspired by western ideas. Vishnu Shastri Chiplunkar, whose father Krishna Shastri Chiplunkar was one of the early reformers, espoused such revivalism. Another stream opposed any state or legislative involvement in the matter of social reform. Ram Mohan Roy had to face opposition from Radhakanta Deve, one of the early proponents of this stream.

Revivalists were not necessarily against reforms. While the early intellectuals retained a critical relationship with the ancient past, it was replaced now by the revivalists' sense of assertion of the past. Dayananda Saraswati, born as Moolshankar in Kathiawar, made the social arrangements in the Vedas as the basis for reform. He tried to counter western criticism against the iniquitous Hindu society, and do away with many unnecessary and cruel practices in Hinduism itself. To propagate reform based on these ideas, he established the Arya Samaj in Bombay in 1875. The Theosophical Society also espoused the greatness of the religious traditions of India, and posited these against western traditions. Vivekananda emphatically proclaimed the superiority of the Vedantic religion.

(ii) Critique of colonialism

Ans. The descriptions and explanations of the apparent lack of growth and development in the Indian economy produced during the colonial period itself were dominated by the nationalist critique of British rule and the imperial response to it. This debate, which has continued to haunt the modern literature as well, was political in origin, revolving around the question of whether India had suffered or benefited from British rule. In economic terms, it focussed attention on the evident poverty of the mass of the Indian people in the late nineteenth century, and the prevalence of famine in the 1870s and late- 1890s, which seemed to suggest that agriculture could not support the population. The nationalist argument, put forward most forcefully by Dadabhai Naoroji, a Parsi businessman and founder of the Indian National Congress, who was elected to the House of Commons to speak for Indian interests in the 1890s, and by Romesh Chandra Dutt, who resigned from the Indian Civil Service to pursue his attacks on the revenue administration of Bengal, focussed on the distortions to the Indian economy brought about by British rule, and the impoverishment of the mass of the population through the colonial 'drain of wealth' from India to Britain over the course of the nineteenth country.

The central theme of the nationalist case was the way in which Indian resources were drained off to Britain by the mechanism of imperial rule. India had long appeared to be a major asset for Britain: yet as early as 1772, when a financial crisis in Bengal prevented the East Indian Company from paying a dividend and required it to ask the British Government for assistance, London was forced to face up to what became the great riddle of the Raj—whether India was Britain's foremost asset or its greatest liability. By the last quarter of the nineteenth century India was the largest purchaser of British exports, a major employer of British civil servants at high salaries, the provider of half of the Empire's military might, all paid for from local revenues, and a significant recipient of British capital. The crucial point for the nationalists was that British rule brought about a 'drain of wealth' as India met a large deficit in goods and services with Britain, plus interest charges and capital repayments in London.

Q9. What was the outcome of the realisation by Indians about the exploitative nature of colonial rule?

Or

What according to the early nationalists was the contribution of the colonial administration, their exploitative and discriminatory nature?

Ans. The Indians for a long time bore the brunt of the British rule. Gradually, the educated Indians realised that allowing the British to settle in India had been harmful to the interest of the Indians. They then enlightened the masses about the exploitative British colonial rule.

The writings of Dadabhai Naoroji, Badruddin Tyabji, K.T. Telang, Gopal Krishna Gokhale, R.C. Dutt and M.G. Ranade clearly laid the responsibility for the growing poverty and unemployment among the people on the colonial state. They also criticised the colonial authorities for not associating Indians with the country's administration. When Surendra Nath Banerjee (1848-1925) was disqualified from joining the civil services on a flimsy ground, he travelled across the country and educated his countrymen regarding the discriminating nature of colonial rule. In 1883, the Illbert bill attempted to empower an Indian judge to preside over the trial of European. The vehement and organised protests of the British and European public against the bill, which they thought was subverting the racial hierarchy, opened the eyes of a large section of Indians to the essentially racial character of the state. It made them conscious of their position as subject people, and as not entitled to the equality promised in the Queen's proclamation (1858), or which they had hoped to acquire through education.

As a result of this realisation, the Madras Native Association, Poona Sarvajanik Sabha (1870), Indian Association (1877) in Bengal, and Madras Mahajan Sabha (1884) were formed. They demanded increased Indian representation in the Legislative bodies and viceroy's Executive Councils, and increasing the age of eligibility for Civil Service examinations and the government budget on education and other developmental activities. Newspapers like Amrita Bazar Patrika, The Bengalee, The Hindu, and the Tribune were started, to express the concerns of the people. The Indian National Congress organised by Allan Octavian Hume (1829-1912), which was a product of this need, held its first conference in Bombay from 25-28 December 1885, to take up issues of national importance.

Early Nationalists like Firozshah Mehta, Gopal Krishna Gokhale, M.G. Ranade, Surendra Nath Banerjee, P. Ananda Charulu, and S. Subramaniam Iyer strongly believed that the common interests and well being of Indians were being thwarted by the exploitative acts of the colonial state, such as the draining of resources from India. They, however, stressed that the colonial state was amendable to reasons, and once cognisant of its mistakes it would ultimately give Indians their due. They were also conscious of the existence of heterogeneity of community and society in India. It was the measures of the British administration, new communication channels and English education that made it possible to unite people into a collective community called nation. But this consciousness was not equally developed and strong among all segments of the population. Thus, while demand for reforms was to be articulated for the nation, simultaneously, efforts were needed to concretise and collectivise disparate sections into the fold of the nation. The nationalists tried to inform public opinion along these lines.

Q10. What were modes of protest suggested by the extremist leadership?

Or

Write a note on extremist phase of nationalism.

Or

Write an essay on the nature of extremist nationalism in colonial India.

Or

Discuss extremist nationalist phase.

Ans. At the end of the 19th century, a few leaders like Lokmanya Bal Gangadhar Tilak, Bipin Chandra Pal and Aurobindo Ghosh imparted a new vigour to the nationalilst struggle because they had a radical outlook and advocated active resistance to British imperialism. The extremists condemned the British Rule in India as reactionary and held it responsible for the country's economic downfall and cultural degeneration. They called upon the people of India to suffer and make sacrifices for the sake of their country.

Tilak said, "Political rights will have to be fought for. The Moderates think that these can be won by persuasion. We think that they can only be obtained by strong pressures."

Another school of militant nationalism was that of the Terrorists, who aimed at turning the British out of India by revolutionary and violent means.

In India, Annie Besant, Rajendralal Mitra, Bal Gangadhar Tilak, Bankim Chandra Chatterjee and above all Vivekananda asserted the superiority of the Indians and their gloriou past. This new confidence was represented by a fresh generation of leaders; Bipin Chandra Pal, Aurobindo Ghosh and Ashwini Kumar Dutt in Bengal; Ajit Singh and Lala Lajpat Rai in Punjab; Bal Gangadhar Tilak in Maharashtra; and G. Subramaniam Iyer, N.K. Ramaswamy Iyer, C. Vijayaradgavachariar, T. Prakasham and M. Krishna Rao in Madras. They criticised the moderate tone of the Congress leaders; Instead of prayer and petition, they advocated passive resistance, boycott, adoption of Swadeshi and national education as new modes of protest.

The solidarity of the Indians was shown when Bengal was partitioned in 1905, and east Bengal was amalgamated with Assam to create a new province. It was said that Bengal was too large and unwieldy for efficient administration. However, the regular pronouncements of different officials since 1930 made it known that the real reason behind the partition was to weaken the growing nationalist sentiments in Bengal, particularly those of the 'Bengali babus'. The protest against the partition soon took an organised shape, and finally the Swadeshi Movement officially commenced from 7 August 1905. Boycott of foreign goods and government schools became the prime modes of protest. National schools and Swadeshi manufacturing units were opened. On 16 October 1905, when partition was to become operative, many people in Bengal fasted, and at Tagore's suggestion tied Rakhi on each other's wrist as a mar of solidarity. Processionists around the cities sang songs written by Rabindranath Tagore and others. The Swadeshi movement spread to other parts of the country, and provided the first spurt of nationalist activity in Assam, Orissa and Punjab.

The new leaders demanded a more assertive Congress, which the early nationalists saw as disastrous not only for the Congress but also for the reform process initiated by the Congress. Their political vocabulary did not include faith in public agitation and movements. However, this was not because they belonged to the educated or middle class. It was more due to their different perception of the colonial state and their lack of understanding of the current political mood.

At the annual session in Banaras in 1905, the new leaders succeeded in making the Congress adopt Swadeshi, boycott and national education as its policies. In 1906, achievement of Swaraj in terms of Dominion status within the British Empire was adopted as the goal of the Congress. The new extremist leaders tried to push the moderates out of the Congress. This disastrous move finally led to the split in Congress at Surat in 1907, where the extremists were pushed out of the party. The colonial state, taking advantage of the situation, suppressed the extremist leaders with heavy hands. Tilak was imprisoned and sent to Mandalay jail in Burma. Moderate leaders began losing popular sympathy, and henceforth lived with the hope that they were leading the country towards liberation through constitutional reforms.

The Swadeshi movement brought into the national movement new forces like students and urban youth, and places like Assam and Orissa into the mainstream. Bengal, Punjab and Maharashtra, however, remained the centre of activities. Individual acts of terrorism, displaying a high sense of patriotism and sacrifice, by Khudirarh Bose, Aurobindo and Barindra Ghose, Rashbehari Bose and Sachin Sanyal, Ajit Singh and Madanlal Dhingra, and Damodar Savarkar, captured the imagination of the country's youth. Khudiram Bose and Prafulla Chaki who hurled a bomb at the Muzzafarpur Magistrate Kingsford's carriage but unfortunately killed two innocent ladies (1908), became household names when Khudiram was hanged. Rashbehari Bose and Sachin Sanyal (1912), in a state procession, threw a bomb that hurt the Viceroy Lord Hardinge who was seated on an elephant.

Notwithstanding their unalloyed sense of patriotism, the extremists used cultural symbols like Shivaji, Ganesha or Goddess Kali for organisational and inspirational purposes. They also lacked concern for the peasantry, and the absence of any social programme later acted as an impediment both to its own ideological development and to the growth of the movement.

Q11. Discuss the following:

(i) Ghadar Movement

Ans. In 1913 AD the Indian emigrants organised a party known as the Hindustan Ghadar party in the USA to work for the liberation of their motherland. This aim could be achieved only by an armed national revolution in India. Baba Sohan Singh Bhakna was elected as its President and Hardyal as Chief Secretary. The other prominent members were Kanshi Ram, Karim Bakhash, Ajit Singh, Munshi Ram and Ram Chandra. The party also started a newspaper called "Ghadar" which carried a strong anti-British propaganda among the Indians. Lala Hardyal was appointed as its editor. Soon a large number of branches of Ghadar Party were opened in Canada, European Countries, China, Japan, Fiji and Malaya States. The Ghadarites wanted to start an armed rebellion in Indian against the British as in 1857 AD They felt that as the British were engaged in the world war, it would be easy to inspire the soldiers and common people to join them in revolt. The Ghadar revolutionaries, mostly the Sikhs, were sailing to India in large numbers not only from Canada and the USA but also from Far Fast Countries. The Government of India took elaborate measures to prevent the infiltration of Ghadar trained territorists in India. Inspite of all that, by the beginning of December 1914 AD, nearly 3000 Ghadarities had come back to India. The returned emigrants started a campaign of loot and murder to equip themselves with necessary funds to fight the alien rule. However, their plot to organise a rising in the army failed. A large number of Ghadarities were arrested and sentenced to various terms of punishment. The movement failed because the leaders of the party and their followers did not prove sincere to their cause till the end. Secondly, the lack of men and money, arms and ammunition contributed to the failure of movement. Thirdly, the revolutionaries did not keep their plans of action secret. Their organisation was inefficient and weak. Fourthly, the remarkable efficiency of the British intelligence was no less responsible for the failure of the movement. It was due to the information supplied by them that the government captured a large number of revolutionaries on reaching the Punjab. Lastly, the stem measures taken by the Government of India and the brutal methods of Punjab police also helped to crush the revolutionaries. Most of the Ghadarites were arrested and cases were instituted against them. Some of them were sent to gallows. Majority of the martyrs and the imprisoned were the Sikhs. Men like Kartar Singh Sarabha laid down their lives. He was the youngest in age among those active revolutionaries who had come back to India.

Although the Ghadar movement failed to do any serious damage to the British Government, it was a remarkable movement in the history of struggle for freedom of India. It was the first secular movement, which aimed to liberate India by force of arms. It attracted all the important communities of India, the Hindus, the Muslims and the Sikhs. The example set by the Ghadarites inspired the World War II efforts of Netaji Subhash Chandra Bose. The Ghadar movement had tremendous effect on the Sikhs in the Punjab and elsewhere. It brought a change in the attitude of the Sikhs against the British. Many Ghadarites later joined the Gurdwara Reform Movement. This gave a radical aspect to the Babbar Akali movement. Some Ghadarities played an important role in the establishment of Kirti Kisan party, a union of agricultural labourers. This party was later amalgamated with the Communist Party of India.

(ii) Home Rule Movement

Ans. The First World War also gave impetus to the Indian national movement. In the beginning, the Indians in general remained loyal and cooperative in return for which they expected that the Government would fulfill their demand for Swaraj. However, the war led to increased misery among the poor classes of the Indians. There was heavy increase in taxation and prices of daily necessities of life. The people were getting ready to join any national political agitation. In such circumstances in April 1916 AD, Lokmanya Tilak formed in Poona a Home Rule League to raise public support for the attainment of Swaraj. In the September of the same year, another association with the same title was started in Madras by Mrs. Annie Besant. The two leagues worked together and pushed forward a strong propaganda for Home Rule in the country. It was during this agitation that Tilak gave popular slogan "Swaraj is my right, and I will have it". Pandit Moti Lal Nehru and Deshbandhu Chittaranjan Dass also gave support to the movement. Mrs. Besant popularised the idea of Home Rule among the masses through personal contact and through the two newspapers New India and Common Weal. In order to suppress the movement, the Government arrested important leaders of the Movement. Mrs. Besant was looked upon as a dangerous person by the British Indian Government and even kept in internment for some time in 1917 AD

(iii) Non-Cooperation Movement

Ans. Under the leadership of Mahatma Gandhi, the Congress decided to start the Non-Cooperation Movement against the British Government. It aimed to

- support the Khilafat Movement.
- compel the government to compensate for the atrocities committed by it on the people at Jallianwala Bagh and during the martial law in the Punjab.

To achieve the goal of Swaraj, the following programmes were adopted:

- Boycott of the elections under the Government of India Act, 1919 AD
- Boycott of government schools and colleges.
- Boycott of the law courts.
- Boycott of foreign goods.
- Surrender of titles and honourary offices.
- Refusal to attend government Darbars.

The constructive side of the programme consisted of:

- Establishment of national schools and colleges.
- The use of private arbitration courts in the place of government courts for litigation, etc.
- Use of Swadeshi cloth on a large scale.
- Revival of hand spinning and hand weaving.
- The removal of untouchability.

The movement was to be completely non-violent.

Progress of the Movement

The movement captured the imagination of the people from the very start. The whole nation rose as a one man. Many distinguished lawyers like C.R. Das, Pandit Moti Lal Nehru, Jawaharlal Nehru, Lajpat Rai, Vitthal Bhai, Vallabh Bhai Patel and Dr. Rajendra Prasad gave up their practice to join the movement. Many prominent Muslim leaders like Ali Brothers, Dr. Ansari and Maulana Abdul Kalam Azad came forward as non co-operators. Many students gave up studying in the government schools and colleges. Many national education institutions like Gujarat Vidyapith, the Bihar Vidyapith, Bengal National University, Jamia Millia of Delhi, the National College of Lahore, etc. were started. The Swadeshi cloth became popular. The Takla and Charkha appeared in every home and became the symbols of movement. Liquor shops and foreign cloth shops were often picketed. In the Punjab, Non Co-operation Movement was headed by Lala Lajpat Rai. The Gurdwara Reform Movement—which was being carried in the Punjab, was linked with Non-Cooperative Movement. Mahatma Gandhi called the Gurdwara Movement as the first decisive battle for freedom.

Suspension of the Movement

The Non Co-operation Movement brought the common people in the political struggle of the country. It created among them a spirit of self-confidence and self-reliance. When the movement was in full swing in 1922 AD, there was a strange and unexpected development. Gandhiji suddenly decided to call of the campaign. The reason, which prompted this action, was that an angry mob had attacked and burnt a police station at Chauri Chaura, a village in the Gorakhpur district of UP in which 22 policemen were killed. Gandhiji took a serious view of this incident. He announced that the Indian people were not yet ready to wage a non-violent struggle.

The suspension of non co-operation movement greatly shocked the younger leaders of Congress like Subhash Chandra Bose and Jawahar Lal Nehru. The common people had lost enthusiasm to continue the movement. It gave an opportunity to the Viceroy, Lord Reading to strike hard. The government arrested Mahatma Gandhi on March 22 and sentenced him to six years imprisonment on the charge of sedition. He was, however, released from prison in the beginning of 1924 AD By this time, the people of Turkey rose under the leadership of Mustafa Kamal Pasha, deprived the Sultan of his political power, Kamal Pasha abolished the office of Khalifa. The new constitution of Turkey provided for the separation of religion and politics. As a result, the question of Khilafat had also been closed. But soon the political condition in India took a new turn and the Congress intensified the struggle for the achievement of complete independence or Poorna Swaraj in place of the Swaraj.

(iv) The Simon Commission

Ans. The terrorist activities gave great impetus to the freedom struggle. The Government felt the need of a fresh review of the political situation in India. In 1927 AD, it appointed a commission under the leadership of Sir Simon to review the progress made by the Indians after the implementation of the reforms of 1919 AD and to recommend measures for further constitutional changes in the country. The Congress decided to boycott the Commission. Demonstrations, black flags and loud slogans of 'Go Back Simon' greeted the commission wherever it went. The Government resorted to suppress the people with an iron hand. At Lahore, the police mercilessly lathi charged a peaceful boycott procession in which

Lala Lajpat Rai received lathi blows. He died of his injuries after a month in November 1928 AD At Lucknow, Pandit Jawaharlal Nehru and Pandit Govind Vallabh Pant also received injuries in an assault while leading a procession. The Commission, however, continued its work and its report formed the basis of the Government of India Act 1935 AD

(v) Civil-Disobedience Movement

Ans. Under the leadership of Gandhiji, the Civil Disobedience Movement was launched in AD 1930. It began with the Dandi March. On 12 March 1930, Gandiji with some of his followers left the Sabarmati Ashram at Ahmedabad and made their way towards Dandi, a village on the west coast of India. After travelling for twenty-five days and covering a distance of three hundred and eighty-five kms, the group reached Dandi on 6 April 1930. Here, Gandhiji protested against the Salt Law (salt was a monopoly of the government and no one was allowed to make salt) by making slat himself and throwing up a challenge to the British government. The Dandi March signified the start of the Civil Disobedience Movement.

The movement spread and salt laws were challenged in other parts of the country. Salt became the symbol of people's defiance of the government. In Tamil Nadu, C Rajagopalchari led a similar march from Trichinopoly to Vedaranyam. In Gujarat, Sarojini Naidu pretested in front of the slat depots. Lakhs of people including a large number of women participated actively in these protests.

The Civil Disobedience Movement carried forward the unfinished work of the Non-Cooperation Movement. Practically the whole country became involved in it. Hartals put life at a standstill. There were large-scale boycotts of schools, colleges and offices. Foreign goods were burnt in bonfires. People stopped paying taxes. In the North-West Frontier Province, the movement was led by Khan Abdul Ghaffar Khan, popularly known as 'Frontier Gandhi'. For a few days, British control over Peshawar and Sholapur ended. People faced the batons and bullets of the police with supreme courage. No one retaliated or said anything to the police. As reports and photographs of this extraordinary protest began to appear in newspapers across the world, there was a growing tide of support for India's freedom struggle.

(vi) Quit India Movement

Ans. In August 1942, Gandhiji launched the Quit India Movement ("Bharat Chhodo Andolan"). A resolution was passed on 8 August 1942 in Bombay by the All India Congress Committee, declaring its demand for an immediate end of British rule. The Congress decided to organise a mass struggle on non-violent lines on the widest possible scale. Gandhiji's slogan of 'Do or Die' ('Karo ya Maro') inspired the nation. Every man, women and child began dreaming of a free India.

The government's response to the movement was quick. The Congress was banned and most of its leaders were arrested before they could start mobilising the people. The people, however, were unstoppable. There were hartals and demonstrations all over the country. The people attacked all symbols of the British government such as railway stations, law courts and police stations. Railway lines were damaged and telegraph lines were cut. In some places, people even set up their independent government. The movement was most widespread in Uttar Pradesh, Bihar, Bengal, Bombay, Odisha and Andhra Pradesh. Places such as Ballia, Tamluk, Satara, Dharwar, Balasore and Talcher were freed from British rule and the people there formed their own governments.

The British responded with terrible brutality. The army was called out to assist the police. There were lathi-charges and firing at the unarmed demonstrators. Even old men and children were shot dead while taking part in processions. Protestors were arrested and tortured and their homes raided and destroyed. By December 1942, over sixty thousand people had been jailed.

The few leaders who had escaped arrest went into hiding and tried to guide the mass movement. Among them were Jai Prakash Narayan, S M Joshi, Aruna Asaf Ali, Ram Manohar Lohis, Achyut Patwardhan and Smt Sucheta Kripalani.

The Indians suffered greatly throughout the Second World War. There was a terrible famine in Bengal in AD 1943 in which over thirty lakh people died. The government did little to save the starving people.

Q12. What was the result of Gandhi's participation in the peasant movement in Champaran?

Ans. In 1917, Indians witnessed the first test of Gandhi's methods of agitation at Champaran in Bihar, where the European indigo planters forced the peasants to pay illegal rent and other exactions. When Gandhi reached Champaran, the District Commissioner ordered him to leave the district, which he refused. It was a new event in the history of the national movement. Gandhi and his associates recorded the exact and detailed camplaints of the peasants, and placed these before the government. The government unable to ignore the enormous facts finally forced the planters to return 25 per cent of the illegal exaction to the peasants. This destroyed the planters prestige and the peasants' fear of them. Gandhi also led the workers in Ahmedabad against the mill owners, and the Kheda peasants against the colonial administration. By the end of 1918, he had established himself through his unique protests against exploitation and injustice. His simple and austere life led the common masses to identify with him.

Muhammad Ali, Shaukat Ali, Abdul Kalam Azad and sections of ulama particularly from Firangi Mahal, Lucknow, were at this time engaged in the Khilafat agitation. When they approached Gandhi, they found him sympathetic to their cause. Gandhi appealed to the Congress to side with the Khilafists against what was a serious breach of trust by the British.

Q13. Write a short note on protest against the Rowlatt Act.

Or

Why did the British government pass Rowlatt Act?

Ans. Before Gandhi entered national politics in 1919, all of India was ignited by an anti-British extremist zeal. Reacting in sheer fear and panic, the British government appointed a commission, presided over by Justice Rowlatt, to investigate all seditious activities; the recommendations of the commission, approved by Rowlatt in July 1919, became a law notoriously called "The Rowlatt Act." This by far was one of the most repressive British acts, which introduced extreme and severe measures in which any Indian could be arrested anytime on even the slightest suspicion of terrorist involvement; he or she could be imprisoned without the right to appeal and without open trial. It enforced wartime measures in the absence of war.

Gandhi suggested formation of Satyagraha Sabhas to protest against this draconian law. An all India hartal was planned for 30 March 1919, which was put off till 6 April 1919. Hartal was observed in Orissa, Assam, Madras, Bombay and Bengal. On the Baisakhi day of 13 April 1919, the police under General Dyer opened fire on a peaceful gathering at Jallianwala Bagh in Amritsar, and killed an official estimate of 379 unarmed and defenceless people. Subsequently, martial law was clamped, and people were even made to crawl of their belly before Europeans. The Jallianwala Bagh incident incensed the country. Rabindranath Tagore returned the Knighthood conferred by the British crown. Instead of questioning General Dyer, the British people presented a purse to him. The Hunter commission inquiring into the incident published, in the words of Gandhi, "page after page of white wash."

Q14. What were the basic differences between Gandhi and Ambedkar?

Or

Write a note on Gandhi–Ambedkar debate.

Ans. The issue of reserved seats for scheduled castes brought out certain differences between Ambedkar and Gandhi. Gandhi launched his biggest social movement against the practice of untouchability. He argued against the notion of occupational hierarchy, which gradually had come to define the varna system. Because some works were considered inferior, the performer of those essential jobs came to be regarded as untouchable. He wished to destroy this notion of hierarchy, so that the varna system regained its pure and indiscriminate form. Ambedkar opposed Gandhi, and argued that untouchability was legitimised by the varna system. Unless the caste system itself was abolished, caste oppression would not go. Gandhi, however, did not agree because the institution of caste had endured for centuries, and it was merely its cancerous growth that needed to be removed. Both argued vehemently, but true to the democratic ethos of the national movement, respected each other's opinion and tried to convince each other of the' merit of their respective positions. Temple entry movements at vaikom and Guruvayur in Kerala using Satyagraha as the weapon and the countrywide movement for the upliftment of lower caste people were the direct result of Gandhi's constructive programme.

Q15. What was the most important reason for the rise of communalism?

Ans. The stagnant economy of India during the British rule was an important factor for the growth of communalism in India. It was deeply rooted in and was an expression of the interests and aspirations of the middle classes in a social set up in which opportunities for them were inadequate. The communal question was, therefore a middle class question par excellence. The main appeal of communalism and its main social base also lay among the middle classes.

It is, however, important to note that a large number of middle class individuals remained, on the whole, free of communalism even in the 1930s and 1940s.

According to Bipan Chandra communal politics till 1937 was organised around government jobs, educational concessions and the like as also political positions - seats in legislative councils, municipal bodies, etc - which enabled control over these and other economic opportunities.

According to him, communalism developed as a weapon of economically and politically reactionary social classes and political forces. Communal leaders and parties were in general allied with these classes and forces. The vested interests deliberately encouraged communalism because of its capacity to distort and divert popular struggle, to prevent the masses from understanding the real issues.

Q16. Write a note on The Indian National Army.

Ans. After the war was over, the leaders were freed in July 1945 and an election was declared. Meanwhile, the Indian National Army (INA) had captured the popular imagination. Mohan Singh and others of the British India Army, who were made Prisoners of War by the Japanese, formed it in 1940. Subhash Chandra Bose leaving the country in a dazzling display of courage, took the lead in organising the army afresh. Facing all sorts of discrimination at the hands of the Japenese army, the soldiers braved the difficult terrain and reached the Kohima border. But soon the Japanese reversal began, the INA's hopes of hoisting the Indian flag atop the Red Fort were shattered. The INA soldiers were taken prisoners by the British and tried for treason in 1945. The first trial began in November in the Red Fort. In November 1945 and in February 1946, the entire country angrily protested against the trials and sentences of these heroes of Indian Independence.

It was amidst this nationalist wave that elections to Provincial and Central legislatures were held. Though the right to vote was limited to a small section of the population, the election was a test of the ideologies of nationalism and its opponents. Congress candidates won unprecedented victories, while the Muslim League won all Muslim seats. This vindicated its claim of being the sole representative of the Indian Muslims. Large number of Pirs and Sajjadanashins canvassed for the League in Punjab and Sindh. The body of ulamas, Zamaitul-ulama-I-hind, which opposed the Pakistan demand, openly supported the Congress. The Hindu Mahasabha, which claimed to be the sole representative of the Hindus, was badly routed, with its leader Syama Prasad Mukherjee getting only 146 votes against his opponent's 6,000 in the Calcutta seat.

Q17. Discuss the factors leading to the emergence of new classes during colonial period.

Ans. The emergence of the social classes in India was the direct consequence of the establishment of a new social economy, a new type of state system and a state administrative machinery, and the spread of new education during the British rule.

These classes were unknown to past Indian society, since they were primarily the offspring of the new capitalist economic structure, which developed in India because of the British conquest and the impact on her of the British and world economy. The India people were reshuffled into new social groupings, new classes, as a result of the basic capitalist economic transformation of India society.

The process of the rise of new social classes in different parts of the country and among various communities was, however, an uneven one. This was due to the fact that the new social economy spread, both in time and tempo, unevenly, since this spread depended on the growth of political power of Britain in India. The conquest of India by Britain resulting in the economic transformation, which it led to, was not a single simultaneous event. India was subdued by Britain by installments and through stages. Different parts of the country became more or less economically transformed on the new capitalist basis in sequence of their political subjugation. Hence, new social classes came into being earlier in those zones, which came under British influence earlier. Bengal was among the first prizes which fell to Britain and where the British Government created, for the first time in Indian history, private property in land in the shape of Zamindari. Therefore, it was in Bengal that two of the new social classes, the zamindars and the tenants, came first into existence. It was also in Bengal and Bombay that the first industrial enterprises such as jute and cotton factories were started leading thereby to the emergence of such new classes as industrialists and proletariat. Further, it was for the same reason that in these provinces Britain established a complex, well ramified, administrative system and introduced new educational institutions imparting knowledge in modern sciences such a modern medicine, law, etc. thereby leading to the growth of the professional classes first.

However, as the British conquest of India finally enveloped the entire country, the new social economy, administrative system, and modern education spread all over India and gave rise to new social classes on a national scale.

The process of the rise of new social classes among different communities was also an uneven one. This was due to the fact that certain communities were engaged, in the pre-British period, in definite economic, social, or educational vocations. For instance, in pre-British society, mainly the banyas were traders and Shroffs, and the brahmins, the custodians of education among the Hindus. In the new social environment, the banyas were among the first groups (another being the Parsis) to take to modern capitalist commerce and banking and develop into new social classes, namely the commercial and financial bourgeoisie. Similarly, the Brahmins were among the first to study and assimilate the modern education introduced by the British government and project a modern intelligentsia and an educated middle class. The upper strata of the Muslim community in the pre-British period, were, on the whole, divorced from medieval trade or money-lending and were mainly engaged in military and administrative careers. Further, they predominantly resided in Northern India, which came under the British rule much later. The vast Muslim population of Bengal mainly belonged to the poorer classes. Hence a modern intelligentsia, a modern educated middle class and a bourgeoisie, on a substantial scale, sprang from within the Muslim community later than from with the Hindu community.

Q18. Write a brief note on 'old classes in a new milieu'.

Ans. India had undergone a transformation on the capitalist line under the British rule but this transformation was not as thorough as it was in France, England or the United States of America. This meant stunted industrial development. Consequently, some of the old classes continued to survive. The classes of village artisans and urban handicraftsmen were such classes. However, the context within which they were functioning had changed because of the development of capitalist economy. Now village artisans unlike in the past were no more servants of the village community. They started sending goods manufactured by them to the market. The urban handicraftsmen who had earlier worked for nobles, princes or wealthy merchants now started selling their products in the market. Another important class for the pre-British period, which managed to survive, was that of the princes they ruled over nearly one third of Indian Territory. They survived because after 1857 the British had abandoned the policy of annexation because largely the princes had remained loyal to the British during the revolt of 1857. However, for the survival the princes had to accept the British paramountcy. All the vital powers of these states were surrendered to the paramount British power. Through Residents the British started, interfering in the internal affairs of these states. The condition of the general people was miserable in these princely states. Democratic liberties were almost non-existent. The land revenue and taxation were very high and most of the revenue raised was spent on luxurious life styles of the princes. The introduction of the new economy gave opportunity to the princes to invest in commercial, industrial and financial ventures at times even outside the territory of their princedoms. From the nobles of the medieval times they had transformed into capitalists bound with national capitalist economy.

Q19. Comment on the following:

(i) Zamindars: their interest and organisation

Ans. The class of zamindars had been largely the creation of the British government. N.N. Ghosh writes: "The zamindars with whom the

Permanent Settlement was made, were an aristocracy manufactured by Lord Cornwallis. They were entirely the creatures of the state." Due to such genesis, the zamindars, on the whole, always supported the British government and opposed it only when their Zamindari rights were in any way encroached upon. The British government, on its part, counted upon them as a reliable loyal force and treated them with favour. "Sir Lawrence showed the Talookdars all the attention and consideration in his power." Lord Lytton frankly stated that the conservative forces of the India society including the landed aristocracy should serve as the support of the British rule in India. In various reforms and constitutional schemes introduced by the British government, the zamindars were given special representation and the political weight of this class was thrown on the side of the British government, either in the struggle of the latter in legislatures or outside against the nationalist forces.

The landed aristocracy almost always supported the government when the Indian National Congress, under Liberals, Extremists or Gandhi, put forth demands for democratic rights, administrative reforms or Swaraj, and organised struggles, parliamentary or extra-parliamentary, to back up these demands. This was due to the fact that the landed aristocracy apprehended that any democratic transformation, social, political or economic, would jeopardise its class interests and even class existence.

The zamindars were, on the whole, conservative and unenterprising. They formed their principal organisation, the British Indian Association, in 1851. E. S. Montague described this organisation in his Indian Diary, published in 1930, thus: "The British Indian Association (is) more or less a conservative body headed by the Maharaja of Burdwan, the best type of conservative Indian. He has a fierce love of the British connection—not a passive acquiescence, but a firm belief in it. He is a large and very rich zamindar, and wishes to be made an independent chief."

The Indian princes were the first to be associated with the state apparatus established by Britain in India. In 1862, the Maharaja of Patiala and the Raja Benares were nominated to the Governor-General's Legislative Council. The next group of nomination consisted of zamindars. About this, K. B. Krishna writers: "A group of nominations can be drawn as it were beginning with the rajas, zamindars, retired officials, merchants and professional classes."

The zamindars took, on the whole, an anti-democratic stand, on vital questions affecting the life of the Indian people. BC Pal writers: "To protest against the Press Act of Lytton, the Indian Association convened a public meeting of the inhabitants of Calcutta at the town hall. The British Indian Association, representing the Bengal Zamindars, refused to join the meeting. But, the educated middle class, not only of Calcutta and Bengal but practically of the other provinces also, fully supported this protest of the Indian Association."

Since the zamindars appropriated a good proportion of income from land, the economic condition of the mass of tenants in the Zamindari zones steadily deteriorated. While the latter were increasingly impoverished, agriculture also, for lack of proper manure, seeds, etc., increasingly decayed. The nationalists as well as British statesmen recognised the precarious position of agrarian economy in the Zamindari area and the alarming poverty of the tenant population.

(ii) Tenants: their interest and organisation

Ans. The permanent settlement did not give birth to the class of zamindars alone. It also created a class of tenants in the countryside. They were subjected to exorbitantly high rent. Those who failed to pay rent even due to reasons beyond their control faced ejectment. The zamindari arrangement resulted in general impoverishment of the tenants. The Bengal tenancy acts of 1859 and 1885, which aimed at the improvement in the condition of the tenants, could not deliver much and their condition continued to deteriorate. In course of time, the tenants became politically conscious which manifested in the formation tenants unions in UP, Bihar, Bengal and other areas. The tenants also came under the influence of the Kisan Sabha started by N.G. Ranga and Swami Sahajanand. In UP these were mobilised Baba Ram Chand. These were not only critical of the British rule they were also critical of the Indian National Congress for showing leniency towards the interest of zamindars. Their main demands included reduction of rent, abolition of illegal dues collected by the zamindars. The kisan sabha opposed the zamindars and the zamindari system.

(iii) Peasant-proprietors

Ans. In south and south central India where the Ryotwari settlement was introduced, there emerged a class of peasant proprietors. In these areas, the cultivators were recognised as the owners of their plots in return to their payment of land revenue. The general condition of this class worsened mainly because of excessive land tax, fragmentation of the size of holding and heavy indebtedness. The condition of some of the peasant proprietors improved and they joined the ranks of rich peasants but most of them fared miserably and joined the rank of poor peasants and tenants of the absentee landlords. Some of them even joined the class of land labourers. The peasant-proprietors became politically conscious much ahead of the tenants. It was because they were in direct contact with the foreign ruler while in Zamindari areas the Zamindars mediated between the government and the tenants. The peasant proprietors did not have difficulty in recognising their enemy, the British rule. The tenants saw the Zamindars as their enemy not the British rule. The consciousness of the tenants was also blunted because of the Gandhian approach of class harmony. Gandhi emphasised the need of unity between the Zamindars and the tenants for the achievement of Swaraj. The leaders of kisan sabha like N.G. Ranga and Sahjanand pressurised the Indian national congress to formulate a programme of the demands for the tenants. They also held that the congress was aligning with Zamindars against the interest of tenants in some areas.

(iv) The Kisan movement, main landmarks

Ans. The formation of the UP Kisan Sabha in February 1918 marked a watershed development in the history of peasant movements in India. Around this time, the kisans started exhibiting political consciousness. They began taking part in nationalist struggles. Their organisations emerged under their own leadership for the achievement of their programmes and objectives. It does not mean that before 1918 there were no peasant movements. In fact, there were many. However, these movements had narrow and local aims and were devoid of any proper understanding of colonialism or any conception of an alternative society. A conception that could unite people in a common struggle on an all India basis and sustain any long-term political movement was absent.

Among the major peasant movements of the nineteenth century was the Indigo Revolt of 1859-60. Indigo was used as a dye for the cotton clothes manufactured by factories in England. Almost all the indigo planters were Europeans and they forced the peasants to grow indigo on the best part of their land. Most of the magistrates were also Europeans and in case of any dispute they used to side with the planters. The indigo revolts enveloped all the indigo-growing districts of Bengal by 1860. The peasants joined together to raise funds to fight court cases filed against them. The planters succumbed to combined pressure and closed their factories. The role of intelligentsia in the indigo revolt was to have a lasting impact on the nationalist intellectuals. Din Bandhu Mitra's play Neel Darpan became famous for its vivid description of the exploitation by the planters.

Between 1870 to 1880, large part of East Bengal witnessed agrarian unrest caused by efforts of zamindars to enhance rent beyond legal limits. This they were doing to prevent the tenants from acquiring occupancy rights under Act X of 1859. To achieve this objective, they used coercive methods like forced eviction and seizure of crops. In May 1873, an agrarian league was formed in Pabna district to resist the demands of the zamindars. The tenants refused payment of enhanced rent and raised funds to challenge the zamindars in courts. Many of the disputes were settled partly due to government pressure and partly due to zamindar's fear of being dragged into long drawn legal battle by the united peasantry. The 1885 Bengal tenancy act was an attempt to address the worst aspects of the zamindari system.

Poona and Ahmednagar districts of Maharashtra became theatres of major agrarian unrest in 1875. In these areas, cotton prices had gone up in 1860s due to American civil war. When the civil war ended cotton prices crashed. A fifty per cent increase in rent by the government and a series of bad harvests further compounded the woes of the peasants. The peasants had no option but to go to the moneylenders. The moneylenders used this opportunity to tighten their grips on the peasants and their lands. The peasants organised a complete social boycott of the moneylenders. They attacked the houses of the moneylenders and also burnt the debt records. In response to this unrest, the government brought the Deccan Agriculturists Relief Act in 1879. Among other important peasant movements in other parts of the country in the nineteenth century were the Mappila outbreak in the Malabar region and the Kuka revolt of Punjab.

Peasant movements in the twentieth century were distinct from those of nineteenth century. Now both the peasant movements and the freedom struggle started influencing each other. Three major movements emerged in the second and third decades of the twentieth century. The kisan sabha and Eka movement in the Avadh area of UP, the Mappila rebellion in the Malabar region and the famous Bardoli Satyagraha in Gujarat. In UP, the peasants were faced with the problems of exorbitant rent, illegal levies, begar [unpaid labour] bedakhli [ejectment]. The hefty increase in the prices of essential commodities after the war had further added to their problems. The UP kisan sabha was formed in 1918 and by June 1919 it had set up 450 branches in the province. An alternative Avadh kisan sabha was set up in 1920, which succeeded in integrating all the grassroots Kisan sabhas of Avadh. This Avadh kisan sabha appealed to the kisans to refuse to till bedakhli land and not to do begar. The Avadh rent act of 1921 attempted to address to some of these demands. Towards the end of 1921, another movement grew in some areas of Avadh under the name of Eka [unity] movement. The main cause of discontent was that the rent in these areas of Avadh was 50 per cent higher than recorded rent. Severe repression by the government brought this movement to an end. The Malabar area of Kerala, which had witnessed disturbance even in the nineteenth century in August 1921, witnessed rebellion by Mappila [Muslim] tenants. Nambudri Brahmins landlords exploited the Mappila tenants. This rebellion had started as an antigovernment anti-landlords affair but acquired communal colours. It was crushed ruthlessly by the government. Another important struggle of the peasantry broke out in 1928-29. A thirty per cent increase in rent was recommended in the Bardoli taluka of the Surat district in 1926. The peasantry fought under the able leadership of Sardar Patel. The peasants fought and forced the government to withdraw the increase in rent.

The 1930s witnessed a countrywide awakening of Indian peasants. The economic depression of 1929-30 and consequent drastic fall in prices of agricultural commodities had badly hit the income of the peasants. However, the government and the Zamindars refused to bring down tax and rent. There was a spurt in peasant movements in UP, Andhra and Bihar. The left ideology propagated by J.L. Nehru, Subhash Bose and the communists was gaining in influence. The leftists underlined the need of an independent class organisation of peasants. The All India Kisan Sabha was formed in 1936 with Sahjanand, the founder of Bihar Kisan Sabha as president and N.G. Ranga, the founder of Andhra kisan movement as secretary. The birth of an all India organisation representing the aspirations and common demands of peasants from all over the country was a development of great significance.

The Indian national congress shied away from raising the issues concerning the peasants more particularly the tenants living in the zamindari areas. According to Bipan Chandra, Congress did not want to weaken Indian nationalism by dividing our people in political groups based on different economic interests. In 1930, the eleven-points submitted to the British government by Gandhi did not include the main demands of the peasants like reduction of rents and redemption of agricultural indebtedness. The formation of the Congress ministries in a majority of the provinces raised the expectations of the peasants. These ministries brought many legislations aiming at debt relief, restoration of land lost during depression and security of tenures to the tenants. These steps did not affect the conditions of peasants belonging to lower strata. Many kisan leaders were arrested and their meetings banned. The congress was accused of being anti-peasant. The radical elements within the kisan sabha accused the congress of siding with the capitalists and zamindars.

After the end of world war second when independence appeared imminent the peasants started asserting their rights. The demand of zamindari abolition was raised with a great sense of urgency. In Telangna the peasants organised themselves to resist the landlord's oppression and played an important role in the anti Nizam struggle. In 1946, the Bengal provincial Kisan Sabha led the movement of the share croppers who wanted to pay only one third and not half share of their crop any more to the jotedars. This movement came to be known as Tebhaga movement.

(v) Rise of Modern Indian Intelligentsia

Ans. In India, a modern intelligentsia developed decades before modern industries were established and the industrial bourgeoisie came into existence. Raja Ram Mohan Roy and his group constituted the first group of intelligentsia who studied western culture and imbibed its rationalist and democratic doctrines, conceptions, and spirit. The number of educated Indians was small in the first decades of the nineteenth century. It was only after the British government established more and more schools and colleges, private effort of the missionary groups and enlightened Indians reinforcing this growth, that a big class of educated Indians developed during the second half of the nineteenth century, projecting from it a large section of intelligentsia.

The role of the intelligentsia in the history of modern Indian nationalism was decisive. They integrated, to a great extent, the Indian people into a modern nation and organised various progressive socio-reform and religio-reform movements in the country. They were the pioneers, organisers and leaders of all political national movements. They brought ideas of nationalism and freedom to wider sections of the Indian people, through educational and propaganda work, which involved great self-sacrifice and suffering. They created rich provincial literatures and cultures, trying to impregnate them with the spirit of nationalism and democracy. They produced great scientists, poets, historians, sociologists, literatures, philosophers and economists. In fact, the progressive intelligentsia, which assimilated modern western democratic culture and comprehended the complex problems of the incipient Indian nation, were the makers of modern India.

Between 1851 and 1884, the professional classes had formed three organisations in the country, namely the Madras Native Association, the Bombay Association, and the Indian Association. These organisations pressed the government to Indianise the services on the ground that the state machinery of a country must be staffed by its own nationals and not by foreigners. The demand also corresponded to their own sectional interests.

With the establishment of Universities in the country after 1857, the numerical strength of the educated Indians rapidly increased. The educated Indians were the first to acquire national consciousness in Indian. Outstanding members of the Indian intelligentsia backed up by a commercial and incipient industrial bourgeoisie founded in 1885 the first national political organisation of the Indian people, the Indian National Congress. The language adopted by the Congress was English. The intelligentsia thus became its first leaders. The important thing to note, however, is that in all its phases of development, the nationalist movement was led by the intelligentsia—whichever section of it led it and however different its ideology, methodology and programme were, from those of other sections. During the Liberal phase, the nationalist movement was led by such outstanding Liberal intellectuals as Gopal Krishna Gokhale, Dadabhai Naoroji, S. Bannerji, Mahadev Govind Ranade, Pherozshah Mehta, and others, who were the product of modern education introduced in India by the British government. In its next militant phase, the movement was guided by such great and sacrificing leaders as Bal Gangadhar Tilak, Bipin Chandra Pal, Aurobindo Ghose and Lala Lajpat Rai who themselves belonged to the modern English-knowing intelligentsia. Even the terrorist movement, which, as a minority current, grew in the country, was initiated and led by educated middle class youths who had studied the Irish terrorist and Russian nihilist movements. After 1918, when the nationalist movement, due to a number of historical reasons, acquired more or less a mass basis, its leadership was provided by members of the intelligentsia such as Gandhi, C. R. Das, Motilal Nehru, Vithalbhai Patel, C. Rajagopalachri, Rajendra Prasad, Jawaharlal Nehru, Subhas Bose and other socialist and communist intellectuals.

The various social reform and religious reform movements among the Hindus, the Muslims and other communities, were organised by the members of the intelligentsia of those communities. For instance, B. R. Ambedkar, a member of the intelligentsia, led a movement of social reform and political education among the depressed classes. In fact, almost all progressive social, political, and cultural movements, which took place during the British rule, were the work of the intelligentsia who had imbibed the new western education and culture. The intelligentsia has been the organiser and leader of all progressive movements in all countries in the modern world. In countries like China, India and others, where the general mass of population has been illiterate and ignorant, the intelligentsia has been playing a particularly important role, since the illiterate and ignorant masses of these countries are not in a position to take even a minimum initiative in self-organisation and self-enlightenment. It was the educated Indian who, having studied the history of trade union and peasant movements in other countries, gave a lead to the Indian workers and peasants and helped them to form their class organisations and movements. If the Indian masses had been literate, they could have known by study, the trade union and other movements in other countries, and would have, on their own initiative, formed such organisations. Similarly, the educated Indians who had assimilated modern ideas of democracy and freedom and who knew about the social, cultural, and scientific achievements of other peoples, spread this knowledge among the illiterate Indian masses.

The educated middle class was the product of the new system of education inaugurated by the British government in India. It was composed of lawyers, doctors, technicians, professors, journalists, state servants, clerks, students and others. The educated middle class steadily grew in number in the second half of the nineteenth century and after, as a result of the increased establishment of modern educational institutions in the country.

The Council Act of 1861 "was a concession to the educated aristocracy." "The Council Act of 1892 was another index to the growth of the professional classes and to the concessions given to these classes."

The growth of modern education in India was not paralleled by a proportional economic development of the country. Industrial development guarantees a general economic development of the society, thereby increasing its wealth and general prosperity and by creating an ever increasing number of jobs and other avenues of income. This was slow in India due to a number of factors, of which the economic policy of the British government was an important one. As a result of this disparity, by the end of the nineteenth century, unemployment among the educated class had already assumed serious proportions. Political discontent that rose out of the economic suffering due to unemployment among the educated middle class was an important factor in the growth of the political current of militant nationalism of which Bal Gangadhar Tilak, Lala Lajpat Rai, Bipin Chandra Pal, and Aurobindo Ghose were the principal leaders. It also led to the growth of the terrorist movement.

As the educated middle class grew in the country in the subsequent decades and became more conscious of its own sectional interests, its various groups began to form their own organisations and formulate their own demands. Thus, there came into existence, in increasing numbers, organisations of these groups over and above their general organisations such as Youth Leagues, Volunteer organisations. This process became particularly swift after 1930. A number of unions and associations of such groups as teachers, lawyers, engineers, emerged to defend and organise struggles for getting redress of their grievances. These organisations were similar to trade unions or kisan sabhas, which protected the sectional and immediate interests of workers and peasants. The rapid growth of students' organisations and unions, particularly after 1934, all over India, culminating in the formation of all-India students organisations, was also notable.

(vi) The Capitalist Class

Ans. The emergence of the capitalist class was the result of the opening up of the Indian economy to the world capitalist system, the process of industrialisation and the growth of the banking sector. Thus, the mercantile, industrial and financial capitalists were born. The accumulation of sufficient savings in the hands of Indian merchants, princes, zamindars and moneylenders provides the basis for the emergence of the Indian industries. The industrialisation of the country started with the setting up of cotton textiles, jute and coal mining industries in 1850s. However, most of these industries were owned by the British capitalists because investment in India offered them the prospect of high return due to availability of raw material and labour at cheap rate. Besides, they could count on an obling colonial government and bureaucracy. However, the Indian capitalists had to suffer hostile trade, tariff, taxation and transport policies of the government. In its infancy, Indian industries needed protection for rapid growth. All other industrialised countries had protected their infant industries by imposing heavy customs duties on imports from foreign countries. A policy of free trade was imposed upon India to suit the interest of British industries because India was not a free country.

From the beginning most of the cotton textiles industry was owned by the Indians. The Swadeshi and Boycott movement launched by the Indian National Congress in 1905 gave a fillip to the expansion of the Indian industries. The period of the first world war [1914-1918] proved to be a boon for the Indian industries. The diversion of shipping to the war needs had made imports difficult. Therefore, to cater to the war needs many industries were established. Between 1914 to 1947, the Indian capitalist class grew at a faster pace and encroached upon areas of European domination. Towards independence, Indian capitalist class owned around seventy per cent of the market and eighty per cent of deposits in the organised banking sector.

The rising capitalist class had become quite powerful and conscious by 1905. This class supported the Swadeshi and Boycott movement launched by the Indian National Congress because the objective of the movement suited their class interest. After the First World War and more particularly after 1919-20, the influence of this class started increasing in the nationalist movement and the Indian national congress. According to Bipan Chandra it is true that the congress accepted funds from the capitalist class but inspite of this the congress maintained its independent position on, policy and ideological matters. According to A.R. Desai, the capitalist class was attracted towards congress because of Gandhi's leadership, his theory of social harmony, his opposition to the idea of class struggle and his concept of trusteeship.

The capitalist class was aware of the contradiction the interest of the colonial government and their own independent growth. They realised that a national government would provide better atmosphere for their growth. The Indian capitalists were making efforts since 1920s towards forming a national level organisation of Indian commercial, industrial and financial interests. These efforts culminated in the formation of the Federation of Indian Chambers of Commerce and Industry in 1927. The F.I.C.C.I. was very soon recognised as national guardian of trade commerce and industry. It pledged its support to the Indian freedom struggle since its inception.

During the 1930s, the congress was getting increasingly radicalised under the leadership of Nehru and the socialists. The fear of radicalisation did not push the capitalist class to align with the imperialists. The Post War Economic Development Committee set up by the capitalists in 1942 drafted the Bombay Plan, which attempted to accommodate socialist demands like equitable distribution of property, partial nationalisation and land reforms without capitalism surrendering its basic features.

(vii) Growth of working class movements

Ans. Though as an organised movement, the Indian labour movement began only after the end of the World War of 1914-18, there had been, before that, episodic activity of Indian labour. This activity was, however, of a sporadic and spontaneous character and was not animated by any definite conscious class purpose.

The Amalgamated Society of Railway Servants was founded in 1897. Its membership was, however, composed only of salaried upper staff of the railways, mostly Anglo-Indians. A few unions like the Printers' Union in Calcutta and the Postal Union in Bombay were also formed in the first decade of the twentieth century. These unions were, however, weak in membership and lacked a proper theoretical or programmatic basis. The period before 1918 witnessed a few industrial strikes also. They were mostly spontaneous, unorganised, and not animated by any clear trade union consciousness.

Politically also, the Indian working class remained almost unconscious and passive till 1918, the only exception being the political general strike of the Bombay textile workers in 1908 on the occasion of the incarceration of B. G. Tilak, the popular nationalist leader. It was 'the only political action' of the Indian workers and was greeted by Lenin as the symptom of their growing political awakening.

It was, however, after 1918 that the Indian working class took to the road or organisation on class lines and increasingly developed trade union and political consciousness. This transformation is described in the Report of the Whitley Commission as follows:

"Prior to the winter of 1918-19 a strike was a rare occurrence in Indian industry. Lacking leadership and organisation, and deeply imbued with a passive outlook on life, the vast majority of industrial workers regarded the return to the village as the only alternative to the endurance of the hard conditions in industry. The end of the war saw an immediate change. There were some important strikes in the cold weather of 1918-19; they were more numerous in the following winter, and in the winter of 1920-21, industrial strikes became almost general in organised industry. The main cause was the realisation of the potentialities of the strike in the existing situation, and this was assisted by the emergence of the trade union organisers, by the education which the war had given to masses, and by the scarcity of labour arising from the expansion of industry, and aggravated by the great epidemics of influenza."

The economic crisis following the war, entailing suffering for the workers, the repercussion of such events as democratic revolutions in Germany, Austria, Turkey and other countries and the socialist revolution in Russia, among the Indian people including the working class, and the general ferment in the country, were also some of the causes of the beginning of the organised movement of the Indian working class after 1918.

The years 1918 to 1920 were marked with the outbreak of a series of strikes throughout the country, in a number of industrial centres including Bombay, Cawnpore, Calcutta, Sholapur, Jamshedpur, Madras, and Ahmedabad. It was the first time that such numerous and extensive strike actions took place. In addition to these economic strikes, workers in Bombay and a number of other industrial towns went on a political strike as a protest against the Rowlatt Acts, demonstrating thereby their growing political consciousness. It marked the entry of the working class in the nationalist movement.

It was during this period that the first attempts to form trade unions in various industries took place in a number of centres, such as Bombay, Madras, and others. Soon, a number of trade unions sprang up in the country.

In 1920, as a result of the efforts of N. M. Joshi, Lala Lajpat Rai, and Joseph Baptista, the All-India Trade Union Congress was founded. Its declared aim was to co-ordinate "activities of all organisations in all the provinces of India, and generally to further the interests of Indian labour in matters economic, social, and political."

The formation of the All-India Trade Union Congress was a landmark in the history of Indian labour. For the first time, the growing trade union movement found an all-India expression.

The leadership of the A.I.T.U. Congress remained for almost a decade, mainly in the hands of liberal politicians like N.M. Joshi. Nationalists like V. V. Giri and C. R. Das, in course of time, also associated themselves with it. The nationalist and reformist ideology of the leadership determined the propaganda carried on among the workers. The A.I.T.U. Congress, however, had a very small numerical base.

After 1927, a left wing leadership developed within the trade union movement, mainly, composed of left nationalists, socialists and communists, which steadily began to displace the earlier leadership. Since 1922, socialist and communist ideas had been spreading among the Indians resulting in the crystallisation of socialist and communist groups in the country. These groups realising the significance of the working class for the success of the nationalist movement organised Workers' and Peasants' Parties. The members of these parties gained increasing influence in the Trade, Union Congress. Their declared object was to base the trade union movement on the principle of class struggle and also draw the workers into the orbit of the nationalist struggle with a programme of national independence to be secured by the method of direct action.

The left wing succeeded in becoming the leader of the A.I.T.U. Congress, the old leadership of the Joshi group becoming a minority force within the Congress. In 1929, a sharp difference of views occurred between the two wings over such questions as the boycott of the Royal Commission on Labour and representation at the International Conference at Geneva. It led to a split resulting in the secession of a number of trade unions which formed the Indian Trades Union Federation under the leadership of the Joshi group. A further split in The A.I.T.U. Congress took place in 1931. The two sections, however, united in 1935.

In 1938, both the A.I.T.U. Congress and the Indian Trades Union Federation achieved unity resulting in the re-emergence of a strong All-India Trade Union congress in country. The All-India Trade Union Congress had an advanced programme which included such objects as the establishment of a socialist state in India; socialisation and nationalisation of the means of production, distribution and exchange, as far as possible; amelioration of the economic and social conditions of the working classes; securing for the workers civil liberties like freedom of speech, press, association, assembly and strike; participation in the national struggle for freedom from the point of view of the working classes, and abolition of privileges based on caste, creed, community, race or religion. This was an advanced democratic and socialist programme.

The total membership of the All-India Trade Union Congress, which comprised trade unions in various industries, stood at 3,37,695 in 1942. This was a small per cent of the total number of workers. The low membership of the trade union organisations in India was mainly due to such reasons as the poverty and cultural backwardness of the workers, danger of victimisation at the hands of the employers. During the period of strikes, however, trade unions had maximum influence among the workers and gained in membership.

It was after 1927 that the Indian working class entered the phase of considerable activity in the sphere of both economic and political struggle. During the years 1928-30, some of the biggest economic strikes including that of the Bombay textile workers took place. After 1927, the Indian working class began to constitute itself as an independent political force, evolved its own flag and independent class programme, and its considerable section followed its own leadership in the united nationalist movement. The workers joined the demonstrations organised by Indian

National Congress as a protest against the Simon Commission, mostly under their own flag, with their own slogans, and under their own leadership. The government considered this development as dangerous and a result of communist agitation. It, therefore, enacted the Trades Dispute Act and issued as an Ordinance the Public Safety Bill in 1929. The former restricted the freedom to strike and the latter armed the government to deport undesirable aliens. It also arrested a number of labour leaders belonging to the left wing and started their trial,—the famous Meerut Conspiracy Case. Sections of the working class also participated in the Civil Disobedience Movement of 1930-33.

The great success of the Congress candidates at the elections held in 1937 was due to the enthusiastic support of the workers to whom the Election Manifesto of the Congress had appealed. They felt, however, disillusioned about the Congress governments. They accused them of not fulfilling their pledge to improve their living and working conditions and also blamed them for enacting undemocratic pro-capitalist legislation like the Bombay Trades Dispute Act, for police firing on the strikers in Bombay, banning labour meetings and imprisoning labour leaders.

After 1938, there was a rapid growth of trade union organisations in the country. This growth was reflected in the increase in the number of trade unions affiliated to the All-India Trade Union Congress. This new social class was acquiring increasing importance in the nationalist movement.

The main aim of GPH book is to provide knowledge as well as good marks in exams.

2 Philosophy of Indian Constitution

An Overview

The constitution of a country is a set of written rules that are accepted by all the people living in a country. It is a body of rules that determines the organisation of government, the distribution of powers to the various organs of the government and the general principles on which these powers are to be exercised. The constitution defines the relation between the states and the individual. It closely connects the laws of a country to its deeply attached moral values. It highlights the value and morals connected with a nation. Thus, the constitution of a country not only provides a legalistic documentation, it even highlights the political philosophy of a state.

Q1. Write short notes on the following:

- **Constitutional Government**

Ans. Constitutional government is defined by the existence of a constitution—which may be a legal instrument or merely a set of fixed norms or principles generally accepted as the fundamental law of the polity—that effectively controls the exercise of political power. The essence of constitutionalism is the control of power by its distribution among several state organs or offices in such a way that they are each subjected to reciprocal controls and forced to cooperate in formulating the will of the state. In the contemporary world, however, constitutional governments are also generally democracies, and in most cases they are referred to as constitutional democracies or constitutional-democratic systems.

- **Constituent Assembly**

Ans. A constituent assembly (sometimes also known as a constitutional convention or constitutional assembly) is a body composed for the purpose of drafting or adopting a constitution. As the fundamental document constituting a state, a constitution cannot normally be modified or amended by the state's normal legislative procedures; instead a constituent assembly, the rules for which are normally laid down in the constitution, must be set up. A constituent assembly is usually set up for its specific purpose, which it carries out in a relatively short time, after which the assembly is dissolved.

Unlike forms of constitution-making in which a constitution is unilaterally imposed by a sovereign lawmaker, the constituent assembly creates a constitution through "internally imposed" actions, in that members of the constituent assembly are themselves citizens, but not necessarily the rulers, of the country for which they are creating a constitution. As described by Columbia University Social Sciences Professor Jon Elster:

"Constitutions arise in a number of different ways. At the non-democratic extreme of the spectrum, we may imagine a sovereign lawgiver laying down the constitution for all later generations. At the democratic extreme, we may imagine a constituent assembly elected by universal suffrage for the sole task of writing a new constitution. And there are all sorts of intermediate arrangements."

Q2. What was Cabinet Mission and what was its plan?

Or

What was the proposal of the Cabinet Mission Plan on the Interim Government?

Or

What was the relationship of the Muslim League with the Constituent Assembly?

Ans. The Cabinet Mission comprising three members–Lord Pathick–Lawrence (Secretary of State for India), Sir Stafford Cripps (President of the Board of Trade) and AV Alexandor (First Lord of the Admiralty), came to India on March 19, 1946. It could not reach any agreement about the formation of an interim Government and the machinery for formulating the Constitution, after discussions with the congress and Muslim League. Thereupon, the Cabinet Mission issued a Statement on May 16, 1946 formulating a plan for the future Government of India. According to it, there was to be a Union of India, embracing both British India and the Indian States, with control over foreign affairs, defence, and communications, and the power to raise the money required for such purposes. All other subjects were to be vested in the Provinces and the States, but the provinces were to be free to form groups for common action. India was to be divided into three groups of provinces–Group A consisting of Madras, Bombay, Central provinces, United provinces, Bihar, and Orissa; Group B of the North–West Frontier Province, the Punjab, Sindh and Balochistan; and Group C comprising Bengal and Assam.

The Cabinet Mission also recommended a scheme for formulating constitution which provided that the Union Constitution was to be framed by a Constituent Assembly, the members of which were to be elected on a communal basis by the Provincial Legislative Assemblies and the representatives of the States joining the Union. The Constitution of the Provinces in each group was to be drawn up by the representatives of the three Groups of Provinces meeting separately. The Cabinet Mission suggested the establishment of an interim Government having the support of major political parties by a re-constitution of the Viceroy's Executive Council in which all the portfolios including that of War Member' were to be held by Indian leaders enjoying full confidence of the people.

The Cabinet Mission Plan was not considered satisfactory by any section of the Indian people and with its rejection the last opportunity to avoid the partition of India was lost. However, to begin with all of them sought to utilise it for their own interests. The Muslim League accepted it on June 6, 1946 in as much as the basis and foundation of Pakistan were inherent in the Mission's Plan by virtue of the compulsory groupings of the six Muslim majority provinces in Groups B and C. The Congress on June 25 decided to join the proposed Constituent Assembly with a view to framing the constitution, but did not agree on the proposal for an interim

Government. The Cabinet Mission left India on June 29, and the Viceroy formed a caretaker Government comprising nine officials.

Q3. Discuss the following:

(i) Parties in the constituent assembly

Ans. Partition, in fact, reduced the strength of the Constituent Assembly of India by about a third. All parties lost their members though the Congress strength was proportionately increased. A few more members were later added following arrival of refugees from Pakistan. Most of the representatives of the princely states joined the Constituent Assembly of India.

Congress Dominance

In this Constituent Assembly, Congress had an overwhelming majority. However, the Congress party had nominated several members from outside the party's fold. Many of them were legal experts and leading legislators in the previous British Indian legislatures. Several brilliant officials of the British Indian government, led by Sir B.N. Rau, were drafted for the work of the Constituent Assembly. Experts from outside were frequently consulted. Precedents of the foreign Constitutions were carefully studied.

Leadership of the Constituent Assembly

There were two broad types of leadership in the Constituent Assembly: (1) political and (2) technical. Because of the predominance of the Congress party, the political leadership naturally vested in its leaders. The top of this leadership consisted of Pandit Jawaharlal Nehru, Sardar Vallabhbhai Patel, Maualana Abul Kalam Azad and Dr. Rajendra Prasad. Granville Austin calls the Nehru-Patel-Azad-Prasad team 'the oligarchy.'

Below this level there were the cabinet ministers at the centre, provincial prime ministers, former Congress presidents like Pattabhi Sitaramaiya and important Congress leaders like K.M. Munshi, Thakurdas Bhargava, A.V. Thakkar and Sri Prakasa.

Outside the party's pale there were the legal luminaries of the time and statesmen of the liberal tradition like Alladi Krishnaswami Ayyar, N. Gopalaswami Ayyangar, B.R. Ambedkar, K.M. Panikkar, Pandit Hriday Nath Kunjru (who was not a member of the constituent Assembly) and, in the early days, B.L. Mitter. Of these leaders K.M. Munshi within the Congress and B.R. Ambedkar from outside combined their technical brilliance with statesmanship as did some Congressmen like K. Santhanam and T.T. Krishnamachari whose association with the party was not long.

Krishnamachari, a critic of some aspects of the Draft Constitution, was actually included in the Drafting Committee in late 1948.

The Opposition in the Constituent Assembly

The shape of the opposition in the Assembly was, however, unstable. The Cabinet Mission had divided the Indians into three communities-the General, the Muslims and the Sikhs. The Congress party overwhelmingly dominated the 'General' section and had come into an agreement with the Sikh *Akal* Panth. It also had nominated a few nationalist Muslims like Abul Kalam Azad and Rafi Ahmed Kidwai.

The strength of the Muslim League had been drastically reduced after partition. To cap it all, after Gandhiji's assassination, the Muslim League in India dissolved itself and most of its members joined the Congress Party. Sir Mohammad Saadullah, among them, was included in the Drafting Committee of the Constituent Assembly. Only the Madras provincial unit of the Muslim League decided to retain its identity and acted as a consistent but negligible opposition.

The only, Communist member of the Constituent Assembly, Somnath Lahiri, lost his membership after the partition of Bengal. So did B.R. Ambedkar, leader of the Scheduled Castes Federation, who had first been elected to the Constituent Assembly from Bengal. He was nominated by the Congress from Bombay in the vacancy created by the resignation of the liberal Hindu Mahasabhaite, M.R. Jayakar. He later became Chairman of the Drafting Committee.

The Fence-Sitters

The Congress had nominated not only two Hindu Mahasabha leaders—M.R. Jayakar and Syama Prasad Mukherjee—but also two socialists and two Forward Bloc members. In early- 1948 in Socialists and the Forward Bloc severed their connections with the Congress and directed its members to resign from the Assembly. The members declined and continued in the Constituent Assembly.

Such people, as several Congressman, were critical of several aspects of the Constitution, but could not be called consistent 'oppositionists'. At the end of the Constituent Assembly's work most of them expressed satisfaction. Some Muslim Leaguers and the Akali member, Sardar Hukum Singh, however, remained strong critics of the Constitution for its denial of political status of the minorities to the Muslims and the Sikhs.

(ii) Work of the constituent assembly

Ans. The Constituent Assembly set up a large number of committees on procedural and substantive matters. Some of the Committees consulted outsiders besides discussing issues thoroughly. After preliminary works were completed and the reports of the committees were discussed in the Constituent Assembly, they were forwarded to the Drafting Committee for incorporation of the recommendations in the Draft Constitution. The Draft Constitution was moved in the Constituent Assembly. There were three readings of the Draft Constitution in the way all legislations have. Some of the draft provisions were discussed again and again. The debate was thorough and intensive. After nearly three years of work, the Constituent Assembly of India produced the world's biggest written Constitution. It was authenticated by the Chairman of the Constituent Assembly, Dr Rajendra Prasad, on 29 November 1949 and came into force on 26 January 1950. Meanwhile, 554 princely states merged with a republican India.

(iii) Status of the Constituent Assembly

Ans. This authentication of the Constitution by the Chairman of the Constituent Assembly had a great legal significance. The Constituent Assembly had been set up not as a-sovereign body. It was expected to draft a Constitution for enactment by the British Government. Partition was a result of the British refusal to treat the Constituent Assembly as a sovereign body. The Indian Independence Act, 1947, authorised the Governor-General of India to give assent to the Constitution. The Constituent Assembly did not do even that and got the Constitution authenticated by its own chairman. It was an assertion of the sovereign authority of the Constituent Assembly.

Q4. Write a note on Government of India Act, 1935.

Ans. The Government of India Act, 1935, can be treated as one of the vital milestones of constitutional development in India. This is due to two reasons; firstly, it was a response to various demands and recommendations for a new constitution of India, and secondly, it became an important source for the Constitution of India.

The Act of 1935 drew from a large pool of available reports and recommendations. These included the Report of the Simon Commission (1930) as discussed and finalised by the Round Table Conferences (1930 to 1932), the White Paper examined by the Joint Select Committee (1932), the Nehru Report (1928) and the Lothian Report, which examined electoral provisions for India. It is said that Lord Lothian, while deliberating on electoral provisions, had spoken about democracy 'as not a gift to be conferred, but a habit to be acquired'.

Federal Structure: The Act of 1935 introduced an All-India Federation with the Provinces and the Indian States as units. All previous Government of

India Acts had treated India as unitary. However, the accession of the India States was conditional on their acceptance of the terms. Practically, a federation could not be established as the Indian States opted out of it. However, between the Central and the Provincial governments, the relationship became federal. Thus, instead of an All-India Federation, a partial federation came into being. The Provinces were granted autonomy. Carrying forward the legacy of the 1919 Act, the 1935 Act divided the legislative powers between the Centre and the Provinces. Three lists–a Federal Legislative List, a Provincial Legislative List, and a Concurrent Legislative List–were devised. While the federal government was authorised to make laws for the whole or any part of British India (excluding the Indian States), the Provinces had limited jurisdiction. Concurrent subjects, as the name suggests, were open to legislation at both levels. Residuary powers were reserved by the Governor-General. Though the scheme of division of powers qualified as federal, the feature of residuary powers reserved by the Governor-General was unique. This, combined with the primacy of the federal law when federal and provincial legislation clash, gave it a quasi-federal nature. In fact, the scheme of division of powers into three lists (Federal, Provincial and Concurrent) appears in the Constitution of India. Though there is no parallel to the phenomenon of 'reserved power', the Indian federation after independence enjoys several unitary features, which has prompted experts such as K. C. Wheare to designate the Indian state as 'quasi-federal' in nature.

Provincial Autonomy: Autonomy was granted to the Provinces. They were declared autonomous units of administration instead of being wholly subject to the Central government, as was the case previously. Provincial autonomy was effected from April 1937. The Governor of a Province was to act as the constitutional as well as executive head of that Province. Certain 'special responsibilities' were also to be carried out. The administration of the Province was to be carried out by the Governor on the advice of a Council of Ministers appointed by him from among the elected members of the Provincial Legislature. In the discharge of special responsibilities, the Governor remained under the control of the central government and under the direction of the Governor-General. Further, in legislative matters, federal supremacy remained unquestioned.

Bicameral Legislature: Like the Act of 1919, the Act of 1935 kept the federal legislature bicameral with a Council of States (Upper House) and a Federal Assembly (Lower House). In six provinces (Madras, Bombay, Bengal, the United Provinces, Assam and Bihar), a bicameral legislature was introduced by the Act of 1935, with a Legislative Council (Upper House) and Legislative Assembly (Lower House).

Dyarchy at the Centre: The 1919 Act had provided for a responsible government at the provinces by introducing dyarchy, in which subjects were divided between the Governor and the Ministers for administrative purpose. The Government of India Act, 1935, replicated the same scheme at the centre. The executive authority vested in the Governor-General was divided into two parts; matters in which he had 'discretion' and others in which he acted on the 'advice' of the Council of Ministers. The former included subjects such as defence, external affairs, ecclesiastical affairs and tribal affairs, while the latter included other subjects. However, even in the latter category of subjects, the Governor-General was not bound by the advice of the Council of Ministers if the discharge of his 'special responsibilities' so demanded. Dyarchy at the centre did not become operational and the Governor-General's Executive Council provided under the 1919 Act remained in effect until Independence.

Electoral System: The 1935 Act did not deviate from the time-tested British policy of divide and rule. In line with the Montagu-Chelmsford, Minto-Morley, and Ramsay MacDonald tradition, it formalised the system of separate electorates and provided separate constituencies to various sections of people on communal lines. The electoral system reflected the Communal Award of MacDonald (1932) and the results of the Poona Pact (1932), as applicable to Scheduled Castes. The Poona Pact was the result of Dr Ambedkar's insistence on including safeguards for the Scheduled Castes.

Federal Court: The Act provided for a Federal Court with original and appellate jurisdictions. However, the Privy Council in London remained the final Court of Appeal.

If we look at the arrangement and scheme of federation and government at the federal and provincial levels, it is apparent that the Government of India Act, 1935, provided the philosophy and basic structure of a federal and democratic government, which became the rallying point of the post-Independence federal and governmental systems. The important features of this include the following:

(a) Federal system with division of power between the Union and the States.

(b) Bicameral legislature at Union and States.

(c) Responsible government with collective ministerial responsibility to the legislature.

(d) Locke and Madison's ideal of separation of powers between the three organs of the government, namely, the legislature, the executive and the judiciary, with built-in checks and balances.

However, the proposed arrangements and system of government and federation under the Act of 1935 could not become fully operational. For example, the All India Federation was implemented partially, as the Indian States did not agree to it. Jawaharlal Nehru and Vallabhbhai Patel carried out the task of the integration of the Princely States within the Indian Union with great effort. The system of dyarchy meant to introduce some sort of responsible government at the centre also failed to come to effect. Most of all, the separate electorates remained a sore point for several leaders of the nationalist movement. The Act was a major disappointment to even those who had asked for Dominion Status, let alone complete independence. Jawaharlal Nehru amply voiced dissatisfaction with the Act when he called it an 'unwanted, anti-democratic and anti-national' constitution. Jinnah denounced it equally, and describing it as 'thoroughly rotten, fundamentally bad, and totally unacceptable.'

A significant outcome of the introduction of provincial autonomy was the first general elections held in 1936-37 in the provinces. It resulted in Congress-majority governments in six provinces. These were Bombay, Madras, Central Province, United Province, Bihar and Orissa. In Assam and the North West Frontier Province, the Congress formed the government with the support of other members. Over two years of congress rule (July 1937-October 1939) provided an opportunity to operate governmental affairs and train leaders for the future governance of the country. From the point of view of constitutional development in India, the Act of 1935 was the final one that the Westminster model could concede.

Q5. List out the essential features of the Indian Constitution.

Ans. Every constitution is supposed to have a basic structure that cannot be altered. Our Constitution was written based on laws framed by members of the Constituent Assembly. As Dr Ambedkar observed, 'One likes to ask whether there can be anything new in a Constitution framed at this hour in the history of the world. More than hundred years have rolled when the first written Constitution was drafted. It has been followed by many other countries reducing their Constitutions to writing. The only new things, if there be any, in a Constitution framed so late in the day are the variations made to remove the faults and to accommodate it to the needs of the country. The Constitution of India is remarkable for many outstanding features that make it unique and one of the in world.

The essential features of the constitution of India are as follows:

Sovereign, Democratic, Republic

The 'Preamble' to the Constitution declares that the people of the country are the sovereigns. In other words, 'sovereignty' rests in the people and is exercised through the institutions that have been created for that purpose. The sovereignty of the country cannot be pledged, i.e., India cannot be turned into a colony or a dependency of another country. The entire course of the Freedom Movement was on this quintessential principle of sovereignty.

In the Preamble, it is also stated that the country shall be a Republic and shall adhere to a democratic form of government. In a Republic, there is no scope for a Monarch to reign over the people, but the people themselves rule the country through their elected representatives.

Union of States

An important feature of the Constitution is that it has constituted India as a Union of States (Art 1). There is also scope in the Constitution to create new States as well as to admit new ones. Notable examples of these are the formation of States, for the first time after in 1956 by bifurcating some of the then existing States on a linguistic basis-Andhra Pradesh, Tamil Nadu, Karnataka and Kerala. Through the bifurcation of the Bombay State Maharashtra and Gujarat were formed. More recently, in the year 2000, three new States-Uttaranchal, Chattisgarh and Jharkhand-were created. An example of the admission of new States into the Indian Union is the admission of Sikkim, in 1975, till then a protectorate of India, into the Union. The provision for admitting new States should also be understood in the context that some of the Princely States were yet not ready by the time the Constitution would come into force to become part of India. 'The Nizam's State of Hyderabad is one such example. And, besides, there were French and Portuguese colonies-Pondicherry and Goa that remained to be integrated with India.

The Constitution, thus, provides for creating new States and admitting new territories. Once they become part of India, they do not have the right to secede.

Fundamental Rights

Our Constitution gives us some other rights, which are known as Fundamental Rights. These rights cannot be taken back in normal times. The Constitution gives us six fundamental rights. The following are the fundamental rights given by our Constitution:

- ***Right to Freedom:*** Right to freedom is an important fundamental right. Everyone is free to express his thoughts and ideas through speeches, writing or through newspapers. He is free to criticise and speak against the policies of the Government, if he does not agree with them. He is free to move about and carry on any trade or business in any part of India.
- ***Right to Freedom of Religion:*** The State has no religion. It does not favour any religion. All religions are equal before the law. Every citizen is free to practice, propagate and worship any religion he likes. The State does not interfere with anybody's faith.
- ***Right to Equality:*** All citizens are equal before the law. There is no discrimination between the rich and the poor, high or the low. There is no discrimination of caste, creed, religion, sex or place of birth. Every citizen can get the highest office for which he has the ability and the required qualifications
- ***Right to Education and Culture:*** Every child is tree to receive education in any educational institution without distinction of caste, creed, religion and sex. He is free to receive education up to any level. The minority groups are free to preserve their own language and culture. They are free to give education to their children in any school.
- ***Right against Exploitation:*** It means nobody can be forced to do work without wages. Nobody can take a beggar. It also prohibits taking work from anybody against his wishes and the children below 14 years of age to work in factories, mines and other risky occupa-tions.
- ***Right to Constitutional Remedies:*** This right is the most important right and protects all the fundamental rights. When someone feels that his fundamental rights are being harmed in any way or he is being denied the fundamental rights, he can approach any court of law to seek justice. Supreme Court is the highest court of the country and is the guardian of our fundamental rights.

Directive Principles of State Policy

Part IV of the Constitution contains the Directive Principles of State Policy. It shall be the duty of the State to follow these principles both in the matter of administration as well as in the making of laws. They embody the objective of the nation to establish a 'welfare state'. The socialistic pattern of our society assures equal opportunity to all citizens through suitable means like ensuring adequate means of livelihood and just distribution of wealth. Though these Principles are not enforceable by law like the Fundamental Rights, they strive towards establishing a just society.

Fundamental Duties

The Chapter of Fundamental duties was inserted in our Constitution by 42nd Amendment of the Constitution in 1976. By 42nd Amendment after Part-IV of Constitution, Part IVA and Article 51-A is inserted in the Constitution, which lays down Fundamental Duties of the citizens. Fundamental Duties of the Indian Citizens are as following:

(a) It is the duty of every citizen to abide by the constitution and respect its ideal and institutions, the National Flag and the National Anthem.

(b) It is the duty to cherish and follow the noble ideals, which inspired our national struggle for freedom.

(c) It is the duty to uphold and protect the sovereignty, unity and integrity of India.

(d) It is the duty of every citizen to defend the country and render national service when called upon to do.

(e) It is the duty to promote harmony and the spirit of common brotherhood amongst all the people of India transcending religious, linguistic and regional or sectional diversities to renounce practices derogatory to the dignity of women.

(f) It is the duty of every citizen to value and preserve the rich heritage of our composite culture.

(g) It is the duty to protect and improve the natural environment including forests, lakes, rivers and wild life and have compassion for living creatures.

(h) It is the duty of the citizen to develop the scientific temper, humanism and the spirit of inquiry and reform.

(i) It is the duty of every citizen to safeguard public property and to abjure violence.

(j) It is the duty of every citizen to strive towards excellence in all spheres of individual and collective activity so that the nation constantly rises to higher levels of endeavour and achievements.

The Union: Executive, Legislature and Judiciary

There are three organs or branches of government, i.e. legislature, executive and judiciary. A harmonious functioning among the three is vital for the furtherance of a country.

• **Legislature**

At its Independence, India chose to adopt a parliamentary form of government. In such a form of government, the President is the Head of the State while real executive power is exercised by the Head of Government, the Prime Minister, in association with his Council of Ministers, all of who are collectively responsible to Parliament.

• **Executive**

In India, the legislature and the executive are drawn from one another, while the judiciary is an independent body. The legislature comprises of the House of People (Lok Sabha), Council of States and the President of India. A member of the Union Council of Ministers has necessarily to be a member of either of the lower house, the Lok Sabha or the Upper house, the Rajya Sabha.

• **President**

Both the houses of Parliament and the legislatures in the States elect the President by means of a 'single transferable vote'. The Office of the President, its functions, powers tenure, method of election and re-election, impeachment, and the qualifications required to hold the office are enunciated in Articles 52 to 62. All activities of the state are carried out in the name of the President as the executive power is vested in the President (Art 52). As in the United States, in India, too, the President is the Supreme Commander of the Armed Forces. The President summons both the houses of Parliament and addresses its joint sessions. He has the power to remit sentences and grant reprieve. He appoints all the important functionaries of the state such as the Prime Minister and the Council of Ministers, Judges of the Supreme Court and High Courts, the Attorney General, Governors of States, Chairpersons of Commissions like the Election Commission of India and heads of organisations like the Comptroller and Auditor General of India (C&AG).

• **Prime Minister and Council of Ministers**

The Prime Minster is the Head of Government and presides over the meeting of the Union Council of Ministers. It needs to be kept in mind that there is a difference between the Cabinet and the Council of Ministers; the Cabinet is composed of Ministers of Cabinet rank and Ministers of State, while the Council also includes the Deputy Ministers. The Council of Ministers is collectively responsible to Parliament. Activities of the Ministries are brought under scrutiny by the opposition during the two-hour long Question Hour at the beginning of each day of the Session in Parliament. The Council of Ministers makes recommendations to the

President, in what is called 'aids and advises', in the affairs of the country. Important among the recommendations that we should be aware are those relating to dissolution of the Lok Sabha, declaring war or declaring a 'state of Emergency'.

- **Legislature/Parliament**

The Indian Parliament is the supreme law-making body of the country. It is a bicameral legislature as in the United Kingdom, the United States and several other countries. The upper house is known in Hindi as the Rajya Sabha and in English as the Council of States. It comprises the Chairman, who is also the Vice-President of India, the elected members and 12 nominated members, each holding a term of six years, with one-third of its membership retiring every two years.

A significant aspect and point of difference between the Rajya Sabha and its equivalent, the American Senate is that the membership of each State in it is proportional to its population, whose legislative assembly elects the members of the Rajya Sabha. Thus, all States of the Indian Union do not send an equal number of representatives. The lower house of Parliament is the House of the People, better known as the Lok Sabha. Its members are elected for single term of five years or less directly by all eligible voters by means of 'universal adult suffrage' from territorially delimited constituencies.

The Rajya Sabha has little power over money bills. These cannot be introduced in the Rajya Sabha. It has to return such bills to the Lok Sabha with its recommendations within 14 days, and it is for the Lok Sabha to accept or reject any of its recommendations. In case of a deadlock over a non-money bill between the Lok Sabha and the Rajya Sabha, the President convenes a joint sitting of the two houses to debate and vote on the bill.

A bill takes the form of an Act only after the President gives his assent to the same. The President is empowered to withhold assent to a bill passed by both houses of Parliament or refer it to Parliament with his suggestions. There have been very few occasions when the President withheld his assent, but of course, on the premise that the bill ran in contradiction with 'public opinion'. One such instance was the Postal Bill that was thought to be infringing on the privacy of the people.

- **Judiciary**

The third and very important organ of the government is the Judiciary. The highest court of appeal is the Supreme Court. The Supreme Court has both appellate and original jurisdiction, as do the High Courts in the respective States.

The Supreme Court is the custodian of the Constitution. Laws enacted by the legislature can be declared invalid by the Supreme Court, if it is of the opinion that they are not in conformity with the provisions of the Constitution. This power is known as the power of 'judicial review'. Besides, the Supreme Court and the High Courts can also issue writs to the government and its agencies. A well-known example is the Writ of Habeas Corpus. By pleading for the issuance of such a Writ an applicant asks the Supreme Court to direct the concerned police authorities to present before the court a person who is missing and is believed to be under their custody.

The President of India appoints all Judges of the Supreme Court and High Courts and the Chief Justices. The Constitution also clearly lays down the procedure for impeaching the Judges and Parliament alone can impeach a Judge of the Supreme Court. The instance of initiating the impeachment of a Supreme Court Judge occurred just once, when Justice K Ramaswamy was sought to be impeached, but the motion failed to succeed.

The Supreme Court and Parliament have on occasion entered into a tug. This was finally resolved with the constitution Amendment Act stating that the Supreme Court has the power only to state whether an Act was in contravention of the provisions of the Constitution or not.

Q6. Discuss the emergency provisions of the Indian Constitution.

Ans. The Constitution of India is federal in nature having a unitary bias. On the one hand, it has all the characteristic features a federation, while, on the other hand the Centre is more powerful than the States.

When the Constitution of India was being drafted, India was passing through a period of stress and strain. Partition of the country, communal riots and the problem concerning the merger of princely states including Kashmir. Thus, the Constitution-makers thought to equip the Central Government with the necessary authority, so that, in the hour of emergency, when the security and stability of the country is threatened by internal and external threats. Therefore, some emergency provisions were made in Constitution to safeguard and protect the security, integrity and stability of the country and effective functioning of State Governments.

Emergency Caused by War, External Aggression, etc.

Provisions have been made in the Constitution for dealing with extraordinary situations that may threaten the peace, security, stability and governance of the country or a part thereof. There are three types of extraordinary or crisis situations that are envisaged. First, when there is a war or external aggression has been committed or there is threat of the same, or if internal disturbances amounting to armed rebellion take place; second, when it becomes impossible for the government of a State to be carried on in accordance with the Constitution, and third, if the credit or financial stability of the country is threatened. In each case, the President may issue a proclamation with varying consequences.

Proclamation of National Emergency (Article 352)

The Constitution of India has provided for imposition of emergency caused by war, external aggression or internal rebellion. This is described as the National Emergency. This type of emergency can be declared by the President of India if he is satisfied that the situation is very grave and the security of India or any part thereof is threatened or is likely to be threatened either (i) by war or external aggression or (ii) by armed rebellion within the country. The President can issue such a proclamation even on the ground of threat of war or aggression. According to the 44 Amendment of the Constitution, the President can declare such an emergency only if the Cabinet recommends in writing to do so.

Such a proclamation of emergency has to be approved by both the Houses of Parliament by absolute majority of the total membership of the Houses as well as 2/3 majority of members present and voting within one month, otherwise the proclamation ceases to operate. In case the Lok Sabha stands dissolved at the time of proclamation of emergency or is not in session, it has to be approved by the Rajya Sabha within one month and later on by the Lok Sabha also within one month of the start of its next session. Once approved by the Parliament, the emergency remains in force for a period of six months from the date of proclamation. In case it is to be extended beyond six months, another prior resolution has to be passed by the Parliament. In this way, such emergency continues indefinitely. However, if the situation improves the emergency can be revoked by another proclamation by the President of India.

The 44 Amendment of the Constitution provides that ten per cent or more members of the Lok Sabha can requisition a meeting of the Lok Sabha and in that meeting, it can disapprove or revoke the emergency by a simple majority. In such a case emergency will immediately become inoperative.

National Emergency has been declared in our country three times so far. For the first time, emergency was declared on 26 October 1962 after China attacked our borders in the North East. This National Emergency lasted till 10 January 1968, long after the hostilities ceased.

For the second time, it was declared on 3 December 1971 in the wake of the second India-Pakistan War and was lifted on 21 March 1977. While the second emergency, on the basis of external aggression, was in operation, third National Emergency (called internal emergency) was imposed on 25 June 1975. This emergency was declared on the ground of 'internal disturbances'. Internal disturbances justified imposition of the emergency despite the fact that the government was already armed with the powers provided during the second National Emergency of 1971, which was still in operation.

Effects of National Emergency

The declaration of National Emergency has far-reaching effects on both the rights of individuals and the autonomy of the states in the following manner:

- The most significant effect is that the federal form of the Constitution changes into unitary. The authority of the Centre increases and the Parliament assumes the power to make laws for the entire country or any part thereof, even in aspect of subjects mentioned in the State List.
- The President of India can issue directions to the states as to the manner in which the executive power of the states is to be exercised.
- During this period, the Lok Sabha can extend its tenure by a period of one year at a time. However, the same cannot be extended beyond six months after the proclamation ceases to operate. The tenure of State Assemblies can also be extended in the same manner.
- During emergency, the President is empowered to modify the provisions regarding distribution of revenues between the Union and the States.
- The Fundamental Rights under Article 19 are automatically suspended and this suspension continues till the end of the emergency. However, according to the 44th Amendment, freedoms listed in Article 19 can be suspended only in case of proclamation on the ground of war or external aggression.

From the above discussion, it becomes quite clear that emergency not only suspends the autonomy of the States but also converts the federal structure of India into a unitary one. Still it is considered necessary as it equips the Union Government with vast powers to cope up with the abnormal situations. The exigencies of the situation prevailing in the period 1975-77 necessitated certain changes in the Constitution regarding emergency provisions. Therefore, the 44th amendment was passed on 30th April 1970 to strengthen the democratic features of the Indian Constitution and to protect citizens' rights even during the national emergency.

Emergency due to Failure of Constitutional Machinery in a State

It is the duty of the Union Government to ensure that governance of a State is carried on in accordance with the provisions of the Constitution. Under Article 356, the President may issue a proclamation to impose emergency in a state if he is satisfied on receipt of a report from the Governor of the State, or otherwise, that a situation has arisen under which the Government of the State cannot be carried on smoothly. In such a situation, proclamation of emergency by the President is called 'proclamation on account of the failure (or breakdown) of constitutional machinery.' In popular language, it is called the President's Rule.

Like National Emergency, such a proclamation must also be placed before both the Houses of Parliament for approval. In this case, approval must be given within two months, otherwise the proclamation ceases to operate. If approved by the Parliament, the proclamation remains valid for six months at a time. It can be extended for another six months but not beyond one year. However, emergency in a State can be extended beyond one year if—

- A National Emergency is already in operation; or if
- The Election Commission certifies that the election to the State Assembly cannot be held.

This type of emergency has been imposed in most of the States at one time or the other for a number of times. It was in 1951 that this type of emergency was imposed for the first time in the Punjab State. In 1957, the Kerala State was put under the President's Rule. There have been many cases of misuse of 'constitutional breakdown'. For example, in 1977 when Janata Party came into power at the Centre, the Congress Party was almost wiped out in North Indian States. On this excuse, Desai Government at the Centre dismissed nine State governments where Congress was still in power. This action of Morarji Desai's Janata Government was strongly criticised by the Congress and others. But, when in 1980 (after Janata Government had lost power) Congress came back to power at the Centre under Mrs. Gandhi's leadership and dismissed all the then Janata Party State Governments. In both cases, there was no failure of Constitutional machinery, but actions were taken only on political grounds.

In 1986, emergency was imposed in Jammu and Kashmir due to terrorism and insurgency. In all, there are more than hundred times that emergency has been imposed in various States for one reason or the other. However, after 1995 the use of this provision has rarely been made.

Effects of Imposition of President's Rule in a State

The declaration of emergency due to the breakdown of Constitutional machinery in a State has the following effects:

- The President can assume to himself all or any of the functions of the State Government or he may vest all or any of those functions with the Governor or any other executive authority.
- The President may dissolve the State Legislative Assembly or put it under suspension. He may authorise the Parliament to make laws on behalf of the State Legislature.
- The President can make any other incidental or consequential provision necessary to give effect to the object of proclamation.

The way President's Rule was imposed on 'various occasions has raised many questions. At times, the situation really demanded it. However, at other times, President's Rule was imposed purely on political grounds to topple the ministry formed by a party different from the one at the Centre, even if that particular party enjoyed majority in the Legislative Assembly. Suspending or dissolving assemblies and not giving a chance to the other political parties to form governments in states has been due to partisan consideration of the Union Government, for which Article 356 has been clearly misused.

In view of the above facts, Article 356 has become very controversial. In spite of the safeguards provided by the 44 Amendment Act, this provision has been alleged to be misused by the Union Government. Thus, there is a demand either for its deletion or making provision in the Constitution to restrict the misuse of this Article. The Sarkaria Commission, which was appointed to review the Centre–State relations, also recommended that Article 356 should be used only as a last resort. The Commission also suggested that the State Legislative Assembly should not be dissolved unless the proclamation is approved by the Parliament. It further suggested that all possibilities of forming an alternative government should be fully explored before the Centre imposes emergency in a State on grounds of breakdown of Constitutional machinery. The Supreme Court held in the Bommai case that the Assembly may not be dissolved till the Proclamation is approved by the Parliament.

On a few occasions such as when Gujral Government recommended use of Article 356 in Uttar Pradesh, the President returned the recommendation for reconsideration. The Union Government took the hint and dropped the proposal.

Financial Emergency

The third type of Emergency is Financial Emergency provided under Article 360. It provides that if the President is satisfied that the financial stability or credit of India or any of its part is in danger, he may declare a state of Financial Emergency. Like the other two types of emergencies, it has also to be approved by the Parliament. It must be approved by both Houses of Parliament within two months. Financial Emergency can operate as long as the situation demands and may be revoked by a subsequent proclamation.

Effects of Financial Emergency

The proclamation of Financial Emergency may have the following consequences:

- The Union Government may give direction to any of the States regarding financial matters.
- The President may ask the States to reduce the salaries and allowances of all or any class of persons in government service.
- The President may ask the States to reserve all the money bills for the consideration of the Parliament after they have been passed by the State Legislature.
- The President may also give directions for the reduction of salaries and allowances of the Central Government employees including the Judges of the Supreme Court and the High Courts. For excellent score, read GPH book.

Q7. Write the significance of a written constitution.

Ans. Following are the significance of a written constitution:

(1) Constitution as a Positive Law

A constitution derives its authority from itself. It is, therefore, future-oriented. As a body of supreme laws, the Constitution takes precedence not only over all other laws but also over all customs, traditions and faiths. Such customs and traditions, etc.s are valid as long as they do not conflict with the Constitution. In other words, no provision of the Constitution can be challenged on the plea that it is inconsistent with the tradition, belief and faith inherited from the past.

(2) Its Contractual Nature

Further, a democratic Constitution is a kind of contract among the people or, at least, the bulk of the people. It is based on consensus-a product of bargain among several persons and groups. Such a contract cannot satisfy all persons fully. However, it does satisfy most of them partly. In other words, it is a kind of common minimum programme of a majority of the people, which does not harm the minority interests.

(3) Philosophy of a Constitution

Every democratic Constitution has a philosophy and a vision, which can be summed up as growth with stability. These two concepts are inter-related. Without growth, no stability can be ensured and without stability no growth can be achieved.

(4) Constitution and Justice

Integrally connected with the concept of growth with stability is the concept of justice. No unjust system can make people happy. And an unhappy people cannot work either for stability or for growth of a country.

Q8. What are the differences between Fundamental rights and directive principles to state policy?

Ans. Following are some differences between fundamental rights and directive principles to state policy:

- **Justiciable, Not Justiciable:** Fundamental rights are justiciable, i.e. if these rights are violated, then legal remedy is available through courts. However, directive principles are non-justiciable, i.e. they cannot be enforced in court of law.
- **Negative, Positive:** Fundamental rights are negative in nature, as these prohibit the government from doing things, which impinge the fundamental rights. These act as limitation on the activities of state. Directive principles are positive in nature, as these require the state to perform activities for promoting economic and social welfare of the people.
- **Supremacy:** Fundamental rights are superior to directive principles. In case of conflict between the two, fundamental rights will supersede directive principles.
- Fundamental rights provide civil liberties to citizens while directive principles promote economic and social justice.

Q9. Write a note on the Preamble to the constitution.

Ans. The Constitution of every country has a guiding philosophy, which is usually described in the Preamble to that Constitution. The American

Constitution of 1784, the Swiss Constitution of 1874, the Irish Constitution of 1937, the Japanese Constitution of 1946, the West German Constitution of 1949, the Communist China's Constitution of 1954, the French Constitution of 1958 and the Constitution of Bangladesh, 1973 all begin with a Preamble. The Indian Constitution is no exception. The Preamble to the Indian Constitution reads:

"WE THE PEOPLE OF INDIA, having solemnly resolved to constitute India into a SOVEREIGN SOCIALIST SECULAR DEMOCRATIC REPUBLIC and to Secure to all its citizens:

- JUSTICE, social economic and political;
- LIBERTY of thought, expression, belief, faith and worship;
- EQUALITY of status and opportunity; and to promote among them all
- FRATERNITY assuring the dignity of the individual and the unity and integrity of the Nation;

IN OUR CONSTITUENT ASSEMBLY this twenty-sixth day of November, 1949, do HEREBY ADOPT, ENACT AND GIVE TO OURSELVES THIS CONSTITUTION."

Q10. How did the vision of social transformation develop in India?

Ans. The vision of Social transformation is embedded in popular aspirations. It develops historically. The vision of the Constitution of the United States of America, for instance, developed out of the War of Independence of 1776, which, in turn, sprang from the liberal democratic environment of the eighteenth century.

The Anti-Imperialist Legacy

In India, this vision developed out of her struggle against the British Empire and was nourished by the liberal democratic thinking in the developed world. It was first expressed by the critiques of colonial rule in the late nineteenth century by people like Dadabhai Naoroji, M.G. Ranade and R.C. Dutt. End of imperialism was seen to be the basic pre-condition of India's progress. In the twentieth century, such critiques grew into the freedom movement.

Movements for Social Justice

Side by side with this broad anti-imperialist struggle grew the demands for social justice. Jyotiba Phule enlarged the social reform agenda of the earlier nineteenth century thinkers and activists like Ram Mohan Roy, Iswar Chandra Vidyasagar and Dayananda Saraswati.

The Nationalist Programme

The Indian National Congress was born through a moderate effort to unify all sections of Indians though, initially, it was elitist. In the twentieth century, its anti-imperialist content was gradually unfolded. Simultaneously, it tried to stress not only communal unity but also the need for social and economic justice in the Indian nation, Indian nationalism was a product of all these forces.

Q11. Identify the limitations in the realisation of the vision of social transformation.

Ans. In the realisation of such a vision, however, there were two limitations:

Clash Character of the Indian National Congress

The Indian National Congress, which dominated the Constituent Assembly of India, was not a socialist party nor was it a party of social reform devoted to the abolition of caste system. Such ideas were subsidiary to the primary concern of the Indian National Congress, which was political freedom.

Stress on Politics

The Constituent Assembly of India was engaged in preparing a Constitution for the governance of India. That Constitution, essentially, was to be a political document. In fact, when two members of the Constituent Assembly (Syed Hasrat Mohani, a Muslim Leaguer, and K.T. Shah, a Congressman) moved for incorporation of the term 'socialist' in the preamble to the Indian Constitution, the Drafting Committee turned it down on the plea that a Constitution need not enshrine a social philosophy. Dr B.R. Ambedkar, Chairman of the Drafting Committee, voiced the same opinion on the floor of the Constituent Assembly.

Q12. Comment on the broad ideas of the Indian National Congress about the constitution.

Ans. The broad ideas of the Indian National Congress about the Constitution could be summed up as:

(1) The Parliamentary Tradition

The tradition of parliamentary government had been developing ever since the introduction of the Montague-Chelmsford reforms in 1919. Though the Congress did not take part in it, the Liberals did. There was even an indirect participation in them by the Congress through the Swarajya Party in 1923 even though the Swarajya Party never accepted office. The Muslim League had similar experience with the 1919 reforms.

Both the Congress and the Muslim League of course accepted office under the Government of India Act, 1935. By that time, the Liberals had lost their influence and mostly joined the Congress. In the Constituent Assembly, very few members desired a presidential system of government.

Federalism

The idea of a federation sprang from the devolution of powers by the Government of India Act, 1935, too. The All-Parties Conference of 1928 had earlier suggested a federal form of government to manage the religious and linguistic diversities of the country. The Partition weakened the case of federalism on religious ground. However, the Congress was as committed to linguistic provincialism since at least 1920. The federal idea, therefore, was not given up.

Welfarism

The Indian freedom movement was a mass movement and required the participation of the broadest section of the masses that were made up of poor, uneducated and backward people. The idea of a mass welfare, however, varied from person to person and section to section of the political leadership. Here lay the major ideological differences.

Q13. What were the goals mentioned in the "Objectives Resolution"?

Ans. The Constituent Assembly took almost 3 years (2 years, 11 months and 17 days to be precise) to complete its historic task of drafting the Constitution for Independent India. During the period, it held 11 sessions covering a total of 165 days. Of these, 114 days were spent on the consideration of the Draft Constitution. On 13 December 1946, Pandit Jawaharlal Nehru moved the Objectives Resolution, which stated:

- This Constituent Assembly declares its firm and solemn resolve to proclaim India an Independent Sovereign Republic and to draw up a Constitution for her future governance;
- Wherein the territories that now comprise British India, the territories that now form the Indian States and such other parts of India as are outside British India and the states, as well as such other territories as are willing to be constituted into the Independent Sovereign India, shall be a Union of them all;
- Wherein the said territories, whether with their present boundaries or with such others as may be determined by the Constituent Assembly and thereafter according to the law of the Constitution, shall possess and retain the status of autonomous units, together with residuary powers and exercise all powers

and functions of government and administration, save and except such powers and functions as are vested in or assigned to the Union, or as are inherent or implied in the Union or resulting therefrom;

- Wherein all power and authority of the Sovereign Independent India, its constituent parts and organs of government, are derived from the people;
- Wherein shall be guaranteed and secured to all the people of India, justice; social economic and political; equality of status of opportunity and before the law; freedom of thought, expression, belief, faith, worship, vocation, association and action, subject to law and public morality;
- Wherein adequate safeguards shall be provided for minorities, backward and tribal areas and depressed and other backward classes;
- Whereby shall by maintained the integrity of the territory of the Republic and its sovereign rights on land, sea and air according to justice and the law of civilised nations;
- Whereby this ancient land attains its rightful and honoured placed in the world and make its full and willing contribution to the promotion of world peace and the welfare of mankind.

Q14. Discuss the structural limitations of constitution.

Ans. A Constituent Assembly can only give shape to a transformation that has been brought about by a social or political revolution. A Constituent Assembly cannot make a revolution.

Besides, a liberal democratic constitution cannot itself provide for radical social transformation. It merely provides for a democratic political structure.

Neither was it in the powers of the Constituent Assembly nor was it its intention to set up a socialist state. It was argued that a Constitution does not lay down an economic system. However, it could permit the creation of a certain socio-economic order. In fact, it was realised by the leadership that the social objectives of the Constitution remained unfulfilled. Dr Rajendra Prasad, Dr B.R. Ambedkar and others warned that if these objectives were not soon achieved the political structure created by the Constituent Assembly would not be stable.

Q15. What do you mean by citizenship?

Ans. It is not easy to give a simple and straight definition of citizenship. Since ancient times, some differences have been observed among the ideas put forth by different people about citizenship. The dynamic character of the political conditions of the world is mainly responsible for the difference of ideas about the definition and duties and responsibilities associated with citizenship. Citizenship as an abstract concept refers to the qualities of the citizens. Thus, in the words of Laski "Citizenship is the contribution of one's instructed judgement to the common good."

In ancient Greece, citizenship meant the capacity to participate in the affairs of the state. In fact, Aristotle and some other philosophers considered only those people who had the right to take part in legislative or judicial activities of the state as citizens. Thus, they had a very narrow view of citizenship. In modern states, it is not possible on the part of every individual to take part in the management of the state. Hence, allegiance to the state is regarded as the essence of citizenship. The concept of citizenship is inseparable from the citizens; and for the understanding of the former, one must first know what is signified by the latter, i.e. citizens.

Q16. Comment on the following:

(a) Citizenship and Individualism

Ans. It was, however, the French Revolution and the 'Declaration of the Rights of Man and Citizens' that established the notion of the citizen as a 'free and autonomous individual' entitled to take part in making decisions that all are required to obey, combining thereby the classical notions of citizenship with individualism. With the development of capitalist market relations and the growing influence of liberalism in the nineteenth century, the notion of the citizens as individuals with private and conflicting interests gradually gained primacy. The ideas of citizenship as a primarily civic activity, public spiritedness and active political participation in a community of equals were now being seen as belonging to the past.

(b) Citizenship and Multi-culturalism

Ans. In much of liberal theory till most of the twentieth century, the bias in favour of the individual citizen continued and citizenship was seen as a legal status indicating the possession of rights which an individual citizen held equally with others. The dominant liberal model of citizenship has, however, been criticised precisely on these grounds. The idea that the (individual) citizen can enjoy rights independent of the community to which s/he belongs, has been questioned. Given that modern societies are multicultural, the specific contexts, cultural, religious, ethnic, linguistic, etc., of citizens are being seen as determining citizenship in significant ways. In most western societies, ethnic, religious and racial communities have pressed for rights, which would look at their special needs and would thereby substantiate the formal equality of citizenship. There is a growing effort to redefine citizenship by giving due importance to cultural differences among individuals and strike a balance between the numerous cultural, religious, ethnic, linguistic identities while constructing a common political identity of the citizen of the nation. A notion of 'differentiated citizenship' has therefore gained currency to accommodate the needs of specific cultural groups.

Q17. According to the Constitution of India, who are the citizens of India?

Ans. The Indian Constitution, like the Canadian, provides for a single citizenship. All persons residing in different parts of the country enjoy only Indian citizenship (Article 5). The birth or residence in a particular State does not confer any separate status as a citizen of that state. The Constitution, however, did not intend to lay down permanent law relating to the Indian citizenship but has left the matter entirely to legislation by Parliament. It only described the classes of persons who would be deemed to be citizens of India at the date of the commencement of the Constitution. The following three categories of persons are entitled to citizenship as per the Articles 5-8 of the Constitution.

(1) Domicile: A person domiciled in India at the commencement of the Constitution of India is a citizen of India, provided:

(a) he was born in India;
(b) either of his parents was born in India; and
(c) he has ordinarily been resident in India for the last five years immediately preceding the commencement of the Constitution.

(2) Immigrants from Pakistan: Any person who has migrated to India from Pakistan is a citizen of India provided he or either of his parents or grand-parents were born in undivided India; and

(a) if he migrated before July 19,1948, he has been ordinarily resident in India since the date of his migration.
(b) if he had migrated on or after July 19, 1948, he has been registered as a citizen.

(3) Migrants to Pakistan: A migrant to areas now forming Pakistan after March 1, 1947 is not a citizen of India. However, if he returned to India under a proper permit for resettlement or under the authority of any law and is duly registered, he is a citizen of India.

(4) Residents in Foreign Countries: Any person ordinarily residing in any country outside India is deemed to be a citizen of India if he or either of his parents or any of his grand-parents was born in the undivided India, provided that he is registered as a citizen by a diplomatic or consular representative of India. To get success in your studies, read only GPH book.

Q18. How is the citizenship acquired?

Ans. According to the Citizenship Act, 1955, the citizenship could be acquired through any of the following five methods:

(1) By Birth: All the persons born in India on or after 26th January, 1950 are treated as citizens by birth. However, the children born to foreign diplomats, posted in India are not entitled to Indian citizenship.

(2) By Descent: A person born even outside India shall be treated as citizen of India by descent if at the time of his birth, his father is a citizen of India.

(3) By Registration: A person can acquire citizenship of India by registration with the appropriate authority. The persons who could acquire citizenship by registration include (a) persons of Indian origin who have ordinarily been resident in India for six months, immediately before making an application for registration. A person is deemed to be of Indian origin if he, or either of his parents, or any of his grand-parents, was born in the undivided India; (b) persons of Indian origin ordinarily reside outside India; (c) women married to Indian citizens; (d) minor children of persons who are citizens of India; (e) persons of full age and capacity who are citizens of Commonwealth countries or Republic of Ireland.

(4) By Naturalisation: A person can acquire citizenship of India by naturalisation if he fulfils the following four qualifications:

(a) He belongs to a country where the citizens of India are allowed to become subjects or citizens of that country by naturalisation;

(b) He renounces the citizenship of his country in accordance with law of that country and intimates the renunciation thereof to the Government of India;

(c) He has been residing in India or serving the Government of India for at least 12 months immediately preceding the date of application;

(d) He possesses workable knowledge of an Indian language.

The Act, however, vests the authority in the Government of India to waive any or all of the conditions above in favour of a person who has rendered distinguished service in the cause of philosophy, science, art, literature, world peace, etc. It may be further noted that a person acquiring citizenship by naturalisation has to take an oath of allegiance to the Constitution of India.

(5) By Incorporation of Territory: In the event of certain territory being added to the territory of India, the Government can specify the persons or categories of persons who shall be entitled to Indian citizenship, by reason of their connection with that territory.

Q19. How has the community been recognised in India's citizenship framework?

Ans. The defining parameters of relationship between nation-states and their individual members was constituted by equality and freedom. Equality hinted at an identity and sameness as against iniquitous systems based on ascriptive hierarchies of race and caste. Freedom read with equality would then imply a freedom to pursue individual aims and aspirations to the best of one's capacities in conditions where social differences have been negated or minimised. The citizen in liberal theory was thus the 'floating individual' shorn of all characteristics of his/her social context. It may be pointed out, however, that these defining principles of citizenship were not seen as commensurate with the kind of social relations which existed in non-western societies, e.g., India, where religion and caste were seen as the basis of social life. This so called 'difference' in the organisation of the social structures in the West and East was sought by the colonisers as a justification for subjecting the colonised population(s) to imperial rule. We also saw that liberal theory in the eighties is increasingly seeking ways to accommodate itself to multicultural societies in the West and the realisation that community membership forms a significant determining factor of the individual member's needs and capacities.

If one reads carefully Part III of the Constitution of India enumerating the Fundamental Rights of the citizens of India, one notices that both the individual and the community have been made the subjects of these rights. One can say therefore, that there exists two languages of rights in the constitution, one catering to the individual citizen and the other to the community. By and large Articles 14 to 24 appear to give to individual citizens the various rights of equality and freedom while Articles 25 to 30, seem to cater to the specific needs of religious-cultural communities. A closer reading of the Articles would, however, show that there is in fact no compartmentalisation and some seemingly individual-catering rights are interwoven with a commitment to community rights. If, for example, one looks at Articles 14 and 15, one sees that they assure equality before the law for every citizen and seek to substantiate this equality by prohibiting discrimination based on caste, religion, race etc., thus mitigating differences provided by social contexts. The articles, however, also reserve for the state a commitment to community-ship, in other words, allowing for certain rights in favour of Scheduled Castes, Scheduled Tribes and Other Backward Classes. Thus, Article 15 lays down that 'The State shall not discriminate against any citizen on grounds only of religion, race, caste, sex, place of birth or any of them' and then in clause (4) reserves for the state the right to make 'any special provision for the advancement of any socially and educationally backward classes of citizens or for the Scheduled Castes and Scheduled Tribes'. Similarly Article 16 which guarantees equality of opportunity for all citizens in matters of public employment, also provides for compensatory discrimination in favour of certain communities. Article 17 abolishes untouchability, a debilitating condition imposed on the Scheduled Castes. Articles 25 to 30 concern themselves with freedom of religion and minority rights assuring freedom of conscience, the freedom to religious communities to establish and maintain religious institutions and to 'manage their own affairs in matters of religion', to acquire and administer property, impart religious education, preserve their language, script, culture, etc. This cluster of rights deals explicitly with the rights of religious and cultural communities and minority groups and also forms the basis of the rights of religious communities to administer themselves in civil matters by their own 'personal laws'. A significant factor in this cluster of rights is the scope given to the Indian state to regulate, reform and in some cases administer these communities and institutions. Thus, while the (individual) citizen of liberal theory persists as a subject of rights, the Constitution gives significance to the community as a relevant collective unit determining the circumstances of the lives of individuals. The Indian Constitution has thus made community membership a relevant consideration for differentiation among citizens, so that equality among citizens could be made more substantive. It has introduced thus a 'differentiated-citizenship' to assure that Communities (e.g. Scheduled Castes or Dalits) which had in the past been victims of social discrimination and continue to be disadvantaged, were able to compete on equal terms with the rest of society. Social equality was also substantiated by assuring that while the claims of each community to be culturally difference could be preserved, there would at the same time be an assurance of sameness or equality among communities. The rights of the various communities to preserve their cultural heritage was therefore recognised in the Constitution and the state was to assure non-discrimination. Thus, social and religious communities were given the right to be culturally different and the state was to assist them in preserving their difference. At the same time, the notion of social equality also required that historical disabilities were compensated and equality was made substantive by assuring equality of opportunities. Thus, caste communities were compensated for past discriminations and segregation by including them in the body politic as equal citizens. This equality was assured by giving them special provisions to overcome circumstantial disabilities.

Q20. What are the constitutional rights of the citizens of India?

Ans. Citizens of India have the following rights under the Constitution, which aliens shall not have:

- Some of the Fundamental Rights belong to citizens alone, such as Article 15, 16 and 19.
- Only citizens are eligible for certain officers, such as those of the President, Vice-President, Judges of the Supreme Court or of High Courts, Attorney General, etc.
- The right of suffrage for election to the Lok Sabha and the Legislative Assembly of every State and right to become a Member of Parliament and of the Legislature of a State are also confined to citizens.

Q21. Discuss the various duties of citizenship.

Ans. The constitutional provisions of citizenship and rights might lead one to believe that citizenship is only about a legal status, defining who are the citizens of India and what are their rights or the conditions in which these rights might be enjoyed. A growing body of scholarship believes, however, that such a legal-formal conceptualisation of citizenship as status, is at best a passive notion, answering the question, who is a citizen, only partially. They would want us to move beyond these 'basic structures' (of equality and social justice) which the Constitution seeks to establish, to concentrate also on the notion of citizenship as a function of 'responsible' participation. Citizenship then, would transcend its passive connotation to become also a measure of activity. The basis of a citizen's sense of belonging to the national community, would come then from the attitudes and qualities of responsibility and virtues which distinguish her/him as a 'good' citizen. Responsible participation would manifest itself in diverse social situations viz. how citizens view or act amidst potentially competing forms of national, regional, ethnic, or religious identities; their ability to tolerate and work together with others who are different from themselves; their desire to participate in the political process in order to promote the public good and hold political authorities accountable; their willingness to show self-restraint and exercise personal responsibility in their economic demands and personal choices which affect their health and environment, etc. Such citizenship qualities, it is said, make a democracy stable and governable. Various voluntary institutions and organisations within society including schools, environmental groups, unions and associations are regarded as inculcating these virtues of citizenship. By an amendment (42nd Amendment Act, 1976) a list of Fundamental Duties of Citizens of India was inserted in the Constitution in the form of Article 51A in Part 1VA. The legal status of Fundamental Duties, which are addressed to the citizens is quite like the Directive Principles, which are addressed to the State, in the sense that there are no provisions for their direct enforcement. It may be pointed out here, however, that the Supreme Court has held the Fundamental Duties to be obligatory in nature and although there is no provision in the constitution for their enforcement, any law seeking to implement them may be 'reasonable' under the law. The list of duties, which are 10 in number, nonetheless, gives an insight into what might be seen as constituting 'good' citizenship. Some of them enjoining citizens to strive towards 'excellence' and developing 'scientific temper' or safeguarding 'public property' appear generally to instill sincerity and responsibility. A general slant is, however, towards imbibing a sense of national commonality. It is thus a duty of every citizen of India to respect symbols of national unity like the national flag, the Constitution and the National Anthem and sources of common heritage like the 'national struggle for freedom' and the tradition of 'composite culture'. Citizens are also expected to preserve the 'sovereignty' and 'unity' of the country not only by pledging to 'defend' the country and offer 'national service' but also by spreading a feeling of 'common brotherhood'.

Q22. What are the areas of tensions in citizenship?

Ans. It has often been pointed out that the Preamble, Fundamental Rights and Directive Principles embody the value of freedom and equality, made complete and substantive by ideals of economic and social justice. Criticisms coming from various quarters point out, however, that the nature of citizenship in the Indian Constitution and the manner in which it has unfolded over the years, have shown that the values of freedom and equality have been largely elusive. Studying the nature of empowerment of citizens within the Constitution, A.R.Desai, a Marxist scholar points out the precarious nature of rights in the Constitution. He emphasises that not only are rights not reserved to the people, there is no preservation of the Fundamental Rights already guaranteed to them. The Constitution itself permits and provides the procedure for their amendment and over-riding by the State. Further, the Directive Principles are not addressed to the people, which mean that the people cannot move the courts to instruct the government to provide conditions in which their rights could be made more meaningful. Again, asserts Desai, while there does not appear to be any explicit system of accountability for the State, the people are given some 'fundamental duties'. Desai feels that in the absence of any similar obligations for the State, the provisions relating to Fundamental Duties could be used to abridge the basic rights of citizens. Finally, the fact that certain basic rights such as the rights to work, shelter, education and medical amenities are not Fundamental Rights indicates the class and gender biases of the Constitution-makers. Under such conditions large sections of 'toiling' citizens, i.e. the socially and economically underprivileged, including women, are forced to live in conditions in which their empowerment as citizens remains unrealised.

Citizenship and Gender

A major lacuna relating to the citizenship rights of women lies in the fact that a crucial provision relating to the removal of discrimination against women, conditions in which substantive citizenship rights can be enjoyed by women are listed only as Directive Principles. Article 39 for example provides that the State shall 'direct its policies towards securing', (a) that the citizens, men and women equally, have the right to an adequate means of livelihood; and (b) that there is equal pay for equal work for both men and women. Although the courts have in certain cases intervened to provide equal pay for equal work, substantive economic equality for women remains elusive.

Legally too, women face numerous disabilities. The provisions of Article 44 of the Directive Principles advising the State to 'secure for the citizens a uniform civil code throughout the territory of India' have been particularly in focus in recent years. Various women's groups have demanded that this directive be implemented to rectify women's subordinate position in matters pertaining to marriage, dowry, divorce, parentage, guardianship, maintenance, inheritance, succession, etc. which are presently determined by the 'personal laws' of specific religious communities. While there is a diversity of opinion among women's groups, they have by and large, demanded a system of gender-just laws which would help them realise their potential as citizens.

3 Institution Framework

An Overview

India, a union of states, is a Sovereign Socialist Secular Democratic Republic with a Parliamentary system of Government. The Republic is governed in terms of the Constitution, which was adopted by Constituent Assembly on 26 November 1949 and came into force on 26 November 1950.

The President is the constitutional head of Executive of the Union. Real executive power vests in Council of Ministers with the Prime Minister as head. Article 74(1) of the Constitution provides that there shall be a Council of Ministers headed by Prime Minister to aid and advise President who shall, in exercise of his functions, act in accordance with such advice. The Council of Ministers is collectively responsible to the Lok Sabha, the House of the People.

In the states, the Governor is the head of Executive, but real executive power vests with the Chief Minister who heads the Council of Ministers. The Council of Ministers of a state is collectively responsible to the elected legislative assembly of the state.

The Constitution governs the sharing of legislative power between Parliament and the State Legislatures, and provides for the vesting of residual powers in Parliament. The power to amend the Constitution also vests in Parliament.

The Union Executive consists of the President, the Vice President and Council of Ministers with the Prime Minister at the head to aid and advise the President.

Q1. What do you mean by parliamentary democracy?

Ans. Parliamentary democracy is a democratic form of government in which the party (or a coalition of parties) with the greatest representation in the parliament (legislature) forms the government, its leader becoming prime minister or chancellor. Executive functions are exercised by members of the parliament appointed by the prime minister to the cabinet. The parties in the minority serve in opposition to the majority and have the duty to challenge it regularly. The prime minister may be removed from power whenever he loses the confidence of a majority of the ruling party or of the parliament. Parliamentary democracy originated in Britain and was adopted in several of its former colonies.

Q2. Trace the evolution of parliamentary system of government.

Ans. Unlike American federalism or presidentialism, parliamentary government was not the product of deliberate institutional design. Rather, it gradually evolved in Britain over several centuries.

Norton (1981: 12) identifies 1688 as the beginning of parliamentary dominance, when Parliament prevailed in its conflict with King James II, who was forced to flee the country. Parliament was then in 1689 effectively able to select the new King, William of Orange, and to impose significant constraints on his powers.

According to Lowell (1896: 3), the roots of parliamentary government can be traced back to 1693, when the King first appeased the House of Commons by appointing a government out of the party (the Whigs) that enjoyed a majority there. Important further developments occurred in the late eighteenth century, when William Pitt the Younger, based on solid support in the House of Commons, established the leading role of the cabinet vis-à-vis parliament and, in conducting its daily business, vis-à-vis the monarch. At that time the cabinet was still that of the Crown, though as a rule cabinets were appointed that could count on the support of the House of Commons. Yet, the Commons was still dominated by the King and the aristocracy, who controlled access to the vast majority of seats.

In 1830, however, the House of Commons forced Wellington to resign over his unwillingness, due to a deep split among the Tories, to engage in parliamentary reform. Earl Grey's subsequent Whig Cabinet persuaded the King to dissolve Parliament and then won the general election on the issue of parliamentary reform. The reform passed the House of Commons but was held up by the House of Lords. Grey then asked the King to create enough new peers to force the reform through the Lords. When the King refused, Grey, backed by the Whigs, tendered the cabinet's resignation. The King unsuccessfully tried to install a new Wellington cabinet but eventually had to invite the Whigs back into office and accept their terms. In the end, the House of Lords pre-empted the appointment of many Whig peers and passed the reform bill—The Representation of the People Act—which eliminated or reduced the weight of small boroughs, where elections were often corrupt, and created new seats in towns and cities. The electorate increased from 220,000 to more than 500,000. By 1866, increasing wealth had swollen the ranks of voters to more than one million. After the 1832 Reform Act, the Crown appears to have had scant influence over cabinet appointments or deliberations—and thus became the 'dignified part' of the British Constitution (Bagehot 1963 [1867]). The House of Commons, on the other hand, criticised and could dismiss the cabinet and in most cases also determine cabinet appointments. Over the subsequent decades, party government was established, and the cabinet came to dominate the House of Commons. According to Gary Cox (1987), this was an indirect response to heightened electoral competitiveness. Members of Parliament (MPs) became more active because their re-election increasingly depended on their visibility and constituency service. Yet, while parliamentary activism was individually rational, it was collectively self-defeating. Too many active and ambitious MPs seeking position-taking and credit-claiming opportunities threatened to overburden the parliamentary agenda and induce institutional paralysis. Hence, those procedural rights that had been abused by visibility-seeking MPs were abolished and the cabinet's agenda control strengthened.

Parliamentary behaviour also became more party-based as the larger constituencies required both a different kind of campaigning and greater activity in Parliament. This process accelerated with the electoral reform acts of 1867 and 1884, which enfranchised a much larger electorate. Now the fate of cabinets was no longer decided on the floor of the House of Commons, as it had been in the 'golden age' of parliamentary government (1832–67), but by the general electorate. 'Members of Parliament were gradually relegated to being representatives of that opinion, and their freedom of parliamentary action was correspondingly diminished' (Norton 1981: 16). Consequently, cabinet members and MPs began to address the general electorate rather than the House of Commons. Procedural reform continued and led to the evolution of a government-managed parliament (Norton 1981: 19–20).

Q3. Write the features of parliamentary system of government.

Ans. Parliamentary form of government is the most favourable system in the entire world and its brilliant attributes are as under:

Formation of Cabinet

In the very first proceeding of legislature, the PM nominates his cabinet members keeping in view certain factors. In Pakistan, one forth ministers are always take from senate. The list is presented before the president, for his approval. They are commonly taken from the party's leadership. Well experienced and learned members are given preference and it is because of the nature of the parliamentary system.

Team work

In this system, all ministers work in a team spirit. They must agree on an issue before the cabinet or in-case of different opinion, the minister concerned must resign and all such differences must be kept secret. They either swim together or sink together. All cabinet members are like the stars.

Supremacy of the Prime Minister

In ministerial system, the prime minister is of prime importance and has too much power. In legislature, he is the leader of the house while in executive he is the leader of the council of ministers. He supervises the activities of his minister and acts as a bridge between the cabinet and the president. On his resignation, the council of ministers must resign. S/he is like a shining moon among the stars.

Political Responsibility

Cabinet is collectively responsible before the legislature. Activity of the cabinet can be questioned and checked by the legislature. Ministers remain in office as they enjoy confidence of the legislature. In case of no confidence in a single minister, cabinet must resign and it so called "collective responsibility". In fact, they are responsible before the people through their representatives. People can forward their grievances through their representative and the ministers are accountable.

Term of Government

Term of the cabinet is not rigidly fixed. A minister may be removed or changed any time. Parliament can be dissolved during the national crises. If parliament is dissolved, government no longer remains in office. Parliament, through no-confidence movement against any particular minister, prime minister or against the whole cabinet, can compel the government to leave the office. Although constitution fixes a specific term but government may go before the expiration of the fixed term.

Q4. Write in brief about parliamentary system in India.

Ans. As independence approached, it was most of the leaders in India, for many years had been steeped in the principles of liberal democracy; and what we call it today as socialist democracy. There had been only two leaders namely Subhash Chandra Bose and Gandhi, who tried to look for some other principles on which to lay the future of Indian states. Gandhi brought forth a few ideas, but failed to provide and fashion an alternative principle.

Naturally, the educated Indians learned the principles of parliamentary democracy, even through the British rule in India never practiced any democracy in India. On the other hand, even the Englishmen denied, they considered a Parliamentary system either suited to or desirable for India. Even when this system was under attack by several Asian countries; the leadership in India reaffirmed their faith in the parliamentary democracy.

In independent India, a parliamentary form of government was adopted as the institutional device through which the democratic spirit was sought to be realised. The institutional set up is headed by the President who is the head of the state and the executive, functioned through the Prime Minister, who is the head of the government, and the judiciary, by the Supreme Court, while the Parliament is entrusted with the exercise of legislative powers. These institutions function within the framework of parliamentary government based on the union of the legislative and the executive wings of the government. The executive, the Council of Ministers headed by the Prime Minister, comes from the legislature and is collectively responsible to it. In other worlds, it is through the members of parliament that the people of India exercise control over the executive.

The main principle of this form of democracy was the presence of a popular check upon the government through periodic elections based on adult franchise; granting of liberties to its citizens; and the presence of an independent judiciary to safeguard those liberties. The government is not irremovable and is periodically open for anybody who gets the support of the people and enters it as an individual or as a member of some party. The method of election is affected through persuasion, conversion, change of mind, and change of opinion performed through secret ballot. Moreover, the underlying assumption of our parliamentary democracy is the faith on liberal democratic and individualistic principles.

The process of making this elaborate parliamentary structure functional depends upon the political parties, which constitute the crucial elements in any parliamentary form of government. However, the presence of political parties of all hues and ideologies in the polity, sometimes with antagonistic and diverse conceptions of socio-economic order, renders the functioning of our parliamentary processes difficult. Thus, questions about the feasibility of parliamentary democracy in a country with no stable conventions or rules to regulate the relationship between the various offices created by the constitution and the inability to function as a welfare state under conditions of economic depravity are being increasingly raised. These questions are being buttressed with proposals for alternative forms of government like the presidential system replacing the cabinet form of government. However, we must remember that in choosing the 'Westminster model' with some modifications, the framers of the constitution were motivated by the need for a responsible government to that of a stable government to be found in the Presidential system of government.

Though ideally any democratic executive must satisfy the conditions of stability and responsibility, in practical circumstances a balancing of both has been difficult. A non-parliamentary government is not dictated by its dependence on a parliamentary majority for continuing in office. By assuring a fixed tenure, a non-parliamentary system tends to value stability rather than responsibility. The government's dependence on parliamentary majority makes it incumbent upon the parliamentary government to be responsible in its functions. In our parliamentary democracy, the parliament plays a vital deliberative role as a forum for national debate thereby constituting a popular check upon governmental authority and functions. The individual members of parliament and the opposition during question hour, amendment processes and general debates, have amply demonstrated the deliberative importance of the parliament. Furthermore, the restraint upon government activities and policies is maintained through the introduction of no-confidence motions, cut motions, adjournment motions and calling attentions. Thus, a popular authority of the parliament in our political system is reinforced both through the continuous and periodic assessment of governmental responsibility. It is continuously assessed by the members of the parliament and periodically by the people during general elections. This is unlike the feature in presidential systems where this assessment is only periodic and is limited by the tenure of the executive, making the legislature literally ineffective during normal times. Thus, any assessment of the effectiveness of our parliamentary system must take cognisance of the wishes of the framers to value responsibility over stability.

The parliamentary structure has also been replicated at the level of the states that respects their autonomy and the federal spirit that legitimises the unity of the Union. Consequently, at the level of the states we have elaborate structures that pursue the parliamentary spirit in choosing their leaders and administering government activities by the adoption of parliamentary system to the requirements of large federal states means that the legislative powers of the parliament are limited. Since the federal and the state governments have separate law-making authorities that is derived from the constitution, the Indian situation is characterised by constitutional supremacy rather than parliamentary supremacy. The supremacy of the constitution is further reinforced by constitutional provision of guaranteeing fundamental rights and empowering the judiciary with the power to act as a custodian of these rights.

In short, in our parliamentary democracy, the legitimacy to rule is vested in the parliament, which it derives from the willing consent of the 'people' who make up the electorate. It is the collective personality of the parliament that imposes a code upon the conduct of both, individuals and political parties; the parliament is the protector of individual liberty and the foundation of Indian laws.

An important feature of our parliamentary system, like other parliamentary democracies, is that it clearly demarcates the position and powers of the head of the state and the head of the government, thereby, in a sense establishing dual executives. The head of the government is appointed from the party or a coalition of parties that enjoys majority in parliamentary seats. This Council of Ministers, headed by the Prime Minister is collectively responsible to the Parliament. This principle of collective responsibility puts the idea of accountability in the government and restricts governments from taking decisions that it cannot justify before the Parliament. This not only indicates that the hallmark of parliamentary system is a government that is collective but also implies that executive powers are collegiate in nature helping the maintenance of pluralism of opinions that forms the bulwark against authoritarianism. Moreover, unlike the Westminster model, the head of the state in India is elected and exercises his powers within the express provisions of the constitution. He is also not merely a titular head. The constitution empowers the parliament to impeach the President for the violation of the constitution. This implies that the President is empowered to discharge certain functions on his own for which he is liable. The President is also an integral part of the Parliament and is vested with powers by the constitution that helps to check parliamentary impropriety in case of the inability of political parties to secure parliamentary majority or its loss at any given time. The importance of presidential authority was exhibited on numerous instances of crisis that was confronted by the Parliament. For example, in 1979, the President rejected the request of Morarji Desai to form a government after having resigned as Prime Minister. It was in 1979 that the President insisted that Charan Singh, the successor to Desai seek confidence of the Parliament. The failure of Charan Singh to gain that confidence subsequently resulted in elections. Though these acts of the President were mired in controversies, it is asserted by eminent jurists and writers that the President acted in a manner consistent with parliamentary conventions. Similarly, in 1987, the President used his constitutional authority to return the Indian Post Office (amendment) bill to the Parliament. Thus, the President of India is a potential political counterweight to the Prime Minister, the Council of Ministers and the elected leadership.

In the Indian parliamentary system, as in other parliamentary systems, the government governs in and through the Parliament thereby fusing the legislative and executive branches. The Indian constitution in Article 75(5) emphasises this peculiar fusion by maintaining that if a minister is not a member of any house within a period of six months he shall cease to be a minister. In other words, only a member of the Parliament, which is the legislative body, can become a minister of the government or a member of the executive. The Council of Ministers is, therefore, said to be the hyphen that links the legislative branch of the state to the executive branch.

In a parliamentary system, which is sometimes referred to as the 'Prime Ministerial form' or 'Cabinet form' of government, the Cabinet comprising of a few leading ministers headed by the Prime Minister makes all important policy decisions. The members of the Cabinet are allowed to play important political roles in rendering policy directives but under the overall supervision and authority of the Prime Minister. However, since the time of Lal Bahadur Shastri, the Prime Minister's Office or the PMO has emerged as an important alternative source to the power of the Cabinet. The authority of the PMO was subsequently re-enforced under Mrs. Indira Gandhi and its role enlarged in actual decision-making. This authority of the Cabinet or the PMO has to some extent encroached upon parliamentary prerogatives and its legislative process most notably through the frequent passage of legislation by Ordinance issued in the name of the President. Today, the PMO is a significant centre of authority in the political structure, which not only emphasises it authority in actual decision-making but also in monitoring and co-ordinating policy implementation by the other ministries of the government.

However, governance is not merely dictated by the institutional structure that is established but is dialectic of the interaction of the institutions and the political culture with each having an impact on the other. Immediately after independence, the presence of a single dominant political party with very little opposition had undercut the principle of political pluralism that formed the basis of any parliamentary structure. In a situation where the government had majority control in the Parliament, the legislature was reduced to little more than a 'talking shop'. Parliamentary processes were clouded by the charisma of Jawaharlal Nehru who according to Ashish Nandy had himself become the opposition criticising his ministers for lapses or extolling them to implement policies for development. However, during this period, the authority of the Prime Minister attained supremacy and position of primacy in the Indian political system, the essence of parliamentary democracy and needs of a federation functioned well with state and central politics remaining largely autonomous. During this period, according to political scientist Paul Brass, a strong central government coexisted with strong states in a mutually bargaining situation. Furthermore, during this phase, the firm grip of civilian control over the military was strongly asserted and a political executive responsible to the Parliament provided clear and effective policy guidance.

After the death of Nehru and the power struggles within the Congress, a party enjoying pre-eminent dominance in Indian politics, there was erosion in the values associated with parliamentary democracy and the federal spirit was undermined. The Congress party's efforts to retain that dominant position led to centralising tendencies within the party and even to the imposition of what may be termed as 'elective dictatorship' under the government of Mrs. Indira Gandhi. However, during this period as well the importance and need of the parliament was demonstrably justified. The crisis and power struggle in the Congress party resulted in a vertical split of the party in 1969 over the Congress nominee for the Presidency of India and the election of Mrs. Gandhi's candidate, V.V. Giri, as President. Mrs. Gandhi was expelled from the Congress party, but this expulsion did not affect her position as the Prime Minister since she retained her support in and among the members of the parliament. Thus, a leadership crisis in the party having majority in the parliament did not affect the functioning of the government effectively reflecting the importance of the parliamentary processes. This importance of the parliamentary process was again demonstrated in 1979, when a section of the Janata Party members in the parliament expressed dissatisfaction with Morarji Desai, resulting in his resignation.

However, parliamentary legitimacy and sanctity suffered tremendous challenges during the regime of Mrs. Gandhi. In 1973-74, for example, food shortages, rising prices coupled with the highly personalised and authoritarian style of functioning by Mrs. Gandhi resulted in major political demonstrations in many parts of the country. This was precipitated by a court verdict holding Mrs. Gandhi's 1971 election as invalid. Mrs. Gandhi responded in a manner that undermined parliamentary democracy. The fundamental principles of parliamentary democracy like freedom of expression, enjoyment of civil liberties, a free press and opposition were gagged through the imposition of emergency under Article 352. Furthermore, the argument of parliamentary supremacy was used to justify the undermining of parliamentary norms and procedures. This was done through the passing of new electoral laws superseding the laws under which the Allahabad High Court declared Mrs. Gandhi's election as invalid. This act of the Parliament had the effect of undermining the process of judicial review that was meant to act as a bulwark against parliamentary authoritarianism. This excessive executive power and undermining of judicial independence continued during this period with the choice of Chief Justices and Judges committed to the ruling political party without respect for established norms and procedures.

In fact, the electoral reversals suffered by the Congress party led by Mrs. Gandhi in the 1977 general elections reflected the firm and deep roots of parliamentary democracy in India. The 'people' of India have reflected enough maturity in exercising their franchise periodically by reversing their mandate and trust vested in a particular party. For example, Rajiv Gandhi, who led the Congress party to a massive victory, securing nearly 80 per cent of the seats in the Parliament in 1985, suffered a humiliating defeat in 1989.

The Indian parliamentary system saw its breakdown for a brief interregnum in 1975, restored in 1977, survived the fall of the Janata government in 1979 and the return to power of Mrs. Gandhi. The unprecedented majority won by Rajiv Gandhi in 1985 was followed by the defeat of the Congress and the installation of the V.P. Singh government in 1989 and later that of Chandrasekhar in 1990. The 1991 general elections saw the return of the Congress government under P.V. Narasimha Rao, which survived its term through methods that are now being examined by the judiciary. The consequent bribery trial has thrown up challenges for our parliamentary processes with questions as to whether acts within the parliament are subject to judicial interpretation or not.

The fractured verdict of the 1996 general elections led initially to the installation of a 13 days government of Atal Bihari Vajpayee, the 13 months government of Devegowda and the installation of I.K. Gujral government in 1997. The general elections in 1998 again resulted in a fractured verdict, leading to the formation of the Vajpayee government that lost its majority soon, after a coalition member withdrew support. In the event where no other political party was able to stake claim for the formation of the government, parliament was dissolved and general elections were notified. The 1999 general elections reflected the polarised psyche of the electorate and the inability of any party to secure absolute majority in the parliament. This led to the formation of the National Democratic Alliance (NDA), a coalition of thirteen different parties under the leadership of Vajpayee and its claim to form the government.

However, though all these instances led to instability in governmental functioning, it did not have any negative effect upon the transition of political power. The instability in government functioning did not lead to instability or assertion of radical political claims for the usurpation of parliamentary authority by the other organs of the government or the imposition of any form authoritarianism. This shows that the parliamentary spirit has been deeply embedded in the political consciousness of all the actors in our polity thereby enhancing the necessity and importance of our parliamentary democracy.

The Indian parliamentary structure thus matured through these trials and tribulations, from being an institution dominated by a single party to the emergence of a fractured polity with highly polarised political opinions and mandate. Though we as a parliamentary polity underwent numerous crises with unstable and frequently changing governments, the authority and legitimacy of our parliamentary structures have only matured in the process. Though demands for restructuring the political structure have gained momentum due to these unstable moments, it has been met with immense opposition. This opposition is justified on the basis of claims that any change in the political set up might augment the process of authoritarianism, which will not only harm the effective functioning of political pluralism but will affect the basis of our tolerance respecting diverse religions, ethnic, tribal or other affiliations.

Q5. Trace the historical background of Indian legislature.

Ans. Indian Parliament did not emerge overnight; it evolved gradually during the British rule, particularly since 1858 when the British Crown assumed sovereignty over India from the East India Company. By the Government of India Act of 1858, the powers of the Crown were to be exercised by the Secretary of State for India assisted by a Council of India. The Secretary of State, who was responsible to the British Parliament, governed India through the Governor-General, assisted by an Executive Council consisting of high government officials. There was no separation of powers; all the powers—legislative, executive, military and civil—were vested in this Governor-General in Council.

The Indian Council Act of 1861 introduced little bit of popular element as it included some additional non-official members in the Executive Council and allowed them to participate in the transaction of legislative business. The Legislative Council was neither deliberative nor representative. Its members were nominated and their role was limited only to the consideration of legislative proposals placed by the Governor-General.

Indian Councils Act of 1892 made two important improvements. First, non-official members of the Indian Legislative Council were henceforth to be nominated by the Bengal Chamber of Commerce and the Provincial Legislative Councils, while the non-official members of the Provincial Councils were to be nominated by certain local bodies such as universities, district boards, municipalities. Secondly, the Councils were empowered to discuss the budget and address questions to the Executive.

Indian Councils Act of 1909, based on Morley-Minto Reforms, for the first time, introduced both representative as well as popular features. At the Centre, election was introduced in the Legislative Council though the officials still retained the majority. However, in the Provinces, the size of the Provincial Legislative Council was increased by including elected non-official members so that the officials no longer constituted the majority. This Act enhanced the deliberative functions of the Legislative Councils and provided them opportunity to move resolutions on the Budget and any other matter of public interest barring certain specified subjects, such as the Armed Forces, Foreign Affairs and the Content Digitised by India States. The Government of India Act of 1915 consolidated all the previous Acts so that the executive, legislative and judicial functions could be derived from a single Act.

The next phase of legislative reforms emerged out of the Government of India Act of 1919 brought further legislative reforms in the form of responsible government in the Provinces. At the Centre, the legislature was made bicameral and elected majority was introduced in both the Houses. However, no element of responsible government was introduced at the Centre. The Governor General in Council continued to be responsible as before to the British Parliament through the Secretary of State.

The Government of India Act of 1935 came into being after several parleys between the Indian national leaders and Britain. It contemplated a federation consisting of British Indian Provinces and native states. It introduced bicameral legislatures in six Provinces. It demarcated legislative power of the Centre and the Provinces through three lists; the Central List, the Provincial List and the Concurrent List. However, the Central Executive was not made responsible to the legislature. The Governor General as well as the Crown could veto bills passed by the Central Legislature. The Governor-General besides the Ordinance-making powers had independent powers of legislation or permanent Acts. Similar limitations existed in case of Provincial Legislatures existed as well.

The international political scene and the conditions in India and Britain led the British government to an unequivocal acceptance of India's claim to freedom. The Indian Independence Act of 1947 was passed setting up two independent dominions, India and Pakistan. The legislature of each dominion was to have full legislative sovereignty. The powers of the legislature of the dominion were exercisable without any limitations whatsoever by the Constituent Assembly formed in 1946. This Constituent Assembly adopted the Constitution of India, which received the signature of the President on 26 November 1950.

Q6. Briefly comment on union legislature of Indian constitution.

Or

What are the qualifications and conditions for election as president?

Or

Write the election procedure, term of office, and different powers of President.

Or

Describe the composition, qualification, election procedure, duration, presiding officers and different powers of the Lok Sabha and the Rajya Sabha.

Ans. The Parliament of India together with the President and the two Houses forms the Union Legislature. The Lower House is called the House of the People or the Lok Sabha, while the Upper House is known as the Council of States or the Rajya Sabha.

The President is an integral part of the Parliament though he does not sit in the Parliament. Without his assent, no Bill passed by the Parliament can become a law.

The President

The president is the constitutional head of the republic of India.

Qualifications and Conditions for Election as President

To be eligible for election as President, a person

(i) must be a citizen of India;

(ii) must have completed the age of 35 years;

(iii) must be qualified for election as a member of the Lok Sabha;

(iv) must not hold any office of profit under the Government of India or the Government of any State or under any local authority subject to the control of any of these Governments.

Election Procedure

The President of India is elected indirectly by an electoral college consisting of

- The elected members of both Houses of Parliament; and
- The elected members of the Legislative Assemblies of States in accordance with the system of proportional representation by means of single transferable vote.
- Value of vote of an MP =

$$\frac{\text{Value of votes of total MLAs of 28 states and two UT's}}{\text{Total elected members of the Parliament}}$$

- Value of vote of an MLA =

$$\frac{\text{Population of the state}}{\text{Total elected members of the state legislature}} \times \frac{1}{1000}$$

Term of Office

The President holds office for a period of five years. He is eligible for re-election under Article 56-57.

This term may terminated earlier by (I) resignation in written addressed to the Vice President (II) by removal for violation of the Constitution by the process of impeachment (Article 56).

Powers of President

The President is the Executive Head of the State. He holds the supreme command of India's defence forces and has the power of declaring war and peace. The President of India has to perform the following functions:

Executive Powers

The Constitution vests the executive power of the Union in the President who exercise these powers directly or through officials subordinate to him.

- The President of India has the power to appoint and remove Governors of States, Ambassadors and other diplomatic representatives, Chief Justice and Judges of the Supreme Court and High Courts, Attorney-General, the Chairman and members of the Union Public Service Commission and members of various Commissions like the Election Commission, the Finance Commission.
- President also makes the appointment of the Prime Minister and on his advice other ministers of the Union Government.
- The President has the power to nominate 12 members of the Rajya Sabha and not more than two members of the Anglo-Indian community to the Lok Sabha.

Legislative Powers

The President of India is an integral part of the Parliament but he himself is not a member of Parliament.

- The President has the power to summons and prorogues either House of Parliament, calls joint sitting of the two Houses, when necessary, and dissolves the Lok Sabha.
- No Bill passed by the Parliament can become an Act without the President's assent.
- Previous sanction of the President is necessary for introducing certain Bills in the Parliament such as a money Bill, a Bill for the formation of a new state or altering the boundaries existing states, any Bill relating to states, any Bill relating to a particular languages.
- The President has veto power. He can veto any Bill except money Bill passed by the Parliament. His veto power is a combination of absolute, suspensive and pocket veto.

Judicial Powers

He may grant pardon, reprieve, respite or remission of punishment or may suspend, remit or commute the sentence of any person convicted of any offence

- where the punishment or sentence is by a court-martial;
- where the punishment or sentence is for an offence against any law relating to a matter to which the executive power of the Union extends; and
- in case where the sentence is a sentence of death.

Martial Powers

He is the Supreme Commander of the Defence Forces of India.

Emergency Powers

The emergency powers of the President are enormous. The Constitution provides for three kinds of emergencies, proclamations for which have to be issued by the President as and when necessary. The satisfaction of the President in issuing proclamation for emergency is non-justiciable.

Three types of emergencies:

- war, external aggression or armed rebellion threatening the security of the country;
- failure of constitutional machinery in the States, and
- Financial Emergency.

The Rajya Sabha

The Rajya Sabha is the Upper House of the Parliament. It is elected by the elected members of the Legislative Assemblies of the States and of the Union Territories.

(a) Composition: The Rajya Sabha consists of not more than 250 members. Of these, twelve are nominated by the President for their special knowledge of or experience in Literature, Science, Art and Social Service. The remainders, that is, 238 are the Representatives of the States and the Union Territories elected by the method of Indirect Election. The number of representatives of the States to the Rajya Sabha varies from one (in Nagaland) to 34 (in Uttar Pradesh).

(b) Qualifications for membership of the Rajya Sabha: To be eligible seeking election to the Rajya Sabha, a person

- must be an Indian citizen, over 30 years old.
- should be of sound mind.

- must not be insolvent, i.e., unable to pay his debts or fulfil financial commitments.
- should not be a government employee.

(c) Election: Its members are elected by the elected members of the Legislative Assemblies of the States. Thus, they are elected indirectly. Twelve members are nominated by the President.

(d) Duration: The Rajya Sabha is a permanent House, as it cannot be dissolved. Each member enjoys a six-year term. Only one-third of its total numbers retire after every two years and elections are held to fill the vacancies. Thus, the Rajya Sabha continues to exist permanently, though its members may retire.

(e) Presiding Officers: The Vice-President of India is the ex-officio Chairman of the Rajya Sabha and as such presides over its meetings. He cannot vote on any issue discussed in the House as he is not its member. However, in case of a tie, he exercises his casting vote. The Rajya Sabha elects a Deputy Chairman from among its members. In the absence of the Chairman, he performs all his functions and duties.

Powers and Functions of Rajya Sabha

- The Rajya Sabha secures representation to the several state units.
- After the passage of a Bill through the Lok Sabha, it is sent to the Rajya Sabha and vice versa. No Bill can become a law unless and until it has been passed by the Rajya Sabha.
- The Members of the Rajya Sabha have the right to vote for the election of the President and the Vice-President of India.
- The approval of the Rajya Sabha is necessary for the continuation of the proclamation of emergency beyond a period of two months.
- In matters affecting States or subjects in the State list, a two-third majority of the Rajya Sabha has to approve a measure before the Lok Sabha can legislate upon it.
- Except a Money Bill, the Rajya Sabha can initiate any bill. In the financial field, the position of the Rajya Sabha is weak. It can discuss the Budget but it cannot vote on it. It must pass a money bill within 14 days otherwise it is deemed to have passed it.
- In the Case of other bills, the Rajya Sabha can delay a bill for six months. This is a safeguard against hasty legislation by the Lok

Sabha. If there is deadlock between the two Houses, there is a joint meeting of both Rajya Sabha and the Lok Sabha.

The House of the People (Lok Sabha)

(a) Composition

- The Lok Sabha consists of not more than 550 members. Of these, not more than 530 have to be chosen by direct election from the states. (The seat for Arunachal Pradesh is filled by a person nominated by the President).

  Each state is allotted a number of seats on the basis of its population.
- The Union Territories elect not more than 20 representatives.
- The President has the Power to nominate 2 members of the Anglo-Indian community, if in his opinion that community is not adequately represented in the Lok Sabha.
- Seats are reserved for the Scheduled Castes and Scheduled Tribes. Thus, the bulk of the members are elected directly by the people on the basis of adult suffrage. The Lok Sabha is more powerful because it is elected directly by the people.

(b) Qualifications for Election to the Lok Sabha

- He should be an Indian citizen, at least 25 years old.
- He should not be insolvent, i.e., he should not be in debt and should have the ability to meet his financial commitments.
- He should not hold an office of profit under the government.
- He should not be a proclaimed criminal.
- He should have his name in the electoral rolls in some part of the country.

(c) Election: The members are elected directly by common voters on the basis of adult franchise.

(d) Duration: Ordinarily the Lok Sabha has duration of five years, but it may be dissolved earlier by the President. During a proclamation of Emergency, the Parliament can extend its own life by one year at a time and a maximum of six months thereafter.

(e) Presiding Officers: The Lok Sabha chooses two of its members to be respectively Speaker and Deputy Speaker to preside over its meetings.

Powers of the Lok Sabha

(a) Legislative Powers

The Lok Sabha has more powers over the Rajya Sabha in matters of Legislation.

- The Parliament can enact laws on any matter in the Union and Concurrent lists.
- It can also legislate on any matter in the state list when an emergency has been declared.
- It can enact laws on matters in the state list provided it is declared necessary in the national interest by a resolution of the Rajya Sabha by a two-thirds majority.
- After its passage through the Lok Sabha, a bill is sent to the Rajya Sabha. If it is a Money Bill, the Rajya Sabha must pass it within 14 days, otherwise it is deemed to have been passed.
- In case of any other Bill, if the Rajya Sabha does not pass it within 6 months; there is a joint session of the two houses. The numerical strength of the Lok Sabha is double that of the Rajya Sabha. Thus, the Lok Sabha has a majority and it is therefore, the Bill of the Lok Sabha that prevails.

(b) Financial Powers

A Money Bill can be introduced only in the Lok Sabha, which is the final authority in financial matters.

- It has the power to pass the annual budget.
- It can sanction expenditure on contingencies.
- It has the power to appropriate money out of the Consolidated Fund of India.
- It can impose, abolish or alter any tax.

(c) Power to control the Executive

The Council of Ministers (Executive) is collectively responsible for its policies and programmes to the Lok Sabha. The Lok Sabha controls the Executive by its power to control money grants. If the Lok Sabha refuses to pass the grants, the Ministry has to resign.

Q7. What are the special powers of Rajya Sabha? Discuss.

Ans. The Rajya Sabha has hardly any control over the ministers who are individually and jointly responsible to the Lok Sabha. Though it has every right to seek information on all matters, which are exclusively in the domain of Lok Sabha, it has no power to pass a vote of no-confidence in the Council of Ministers. Moreover, the Rajya Sabha has not much say in matters of money bills.

Nevertheless, the Constitution grants certain special powers to the Rajya Sabha. As the sole representative of the States, the Rajya Sabha enjoys two exclusive powers, which are of considerable importance.

First, under Article 249, the Rajya Sabha has the power to declare that, in the national interest, the Parliament should make laws with respect to a matter enumerated in the State List. If by a two-thirds majority, Rajya Sabha passes a resolution to this effect, the Union Parliament can make laws for the whole or any part of India for a period of one year.

The second exclusive power of the Rajya Sabha is with regard to the setting up of All-India Services. If the Rajya Sabha passes a resolution by not less than two-thirds of the members present and voting, the parliament is empowered to make laws providing for creation of one or more All-India Services common to the Union and the Sates.

Thus, these special provisions make the Rajya Sabha an important component of Indian Legislature rather than just being an ornamental second chamber like the House of Lords of England. The constitution makers have designed it not just to check any hasty legislation, but also to play the role of an important influential advisor. Its compact composition and permanent character provides it continuity and stability. As many of its members are "elder statesmen" the Rajya Sabha commands respectability. For excellent score, read GPH book.

Q8. Write a note on Speaker of the Lok Sabha.

Or

Briefly discuss the functions/roles of the Speaker.

Ans. Each House has its own presiding officers. The Lok Sabha elects two of its members to act as Speaker and Deputy Speaker to preside over its meetings

- The Speaker must be a member of the Lok Sabha. He may be from any party but once he is elected Speaker, he has to be impartial in his decisions.
- He can resign whenever he likes.
- He can also be removed by a resolution of the majority of members of the Lok Sabha giving 14 days notice stating the intention to move such a resolution.
- The Speaker's salary and allowances are fixed by the Parliament.

- The Speaker holds office during the term of the House but when the House is dissolved, he does not vacate his office until the newly elected House meets and elects its Speaker.
- With respect to the discharge of his powers and functions, he is not answerable to anyone except the House. No court of law can go into to merits of ruling given by him.

The office of the speaker is important and a member feels honoured if he is elected as the Speaker of the Lok Sabha. He occupies a position of great authority and responsibility. He has very wide powers to maintain discipline in the House.

Functions or Roles of the Speaker

- The Speaker maintains disciple in the House and conducts the proceedings (debates, questions and answers and the voting) in accordance with parliamentary rules.
- He adjourns (stops) or suspends its meeting if there are insufficient members present.
- He can suspend a Member from the House for misconduct.
- He makes an agenda for the House and allocates times to various items on the agenda.
- He recognizes members on the floor of the House and allots them time to speak.
- He can order a member to yield the floor to another member, i.e., he can ask a member of the House to stop speaking and let another speak.
- He appoints the Chairman of the various Committees.
- When a Money Bill is sent from the Lower House to the Upper House, the Speaker has to endorse on the Bill his certificate that it is a Money Bill.
- He has a casting vote in cast of a tie over an issue.
- He gives ruling on the controversial points of procedure. These rulings are final.
- His decisions to admit notices of question, motions, resolutions, bills, amendments, etc. are final.
- He is the medium of communication between the Members of the Lok Sabha and the President.
- He is the spokesman of the Lok Sabha and he represents it on all ceremonial occasions.

- He is the guardian of the rights and privileges of the members of the House.

Deputy Speaker of the Lok Sabha

The Deputy Speaker acts as a Speaker in the absence of the Speaker. In the absence of both the Speaker and Deputy Speaker, one of the six members of a panel chosen by the Speaker presides over the meetings.

The Deputy Speaker is elected by the Lok Sabha from amongst its members in the same manner in which the Speaker is elected by the House.

Q9. Write a brief note on Chairperson of Rajya Sabha.

Ans. The Vice-President of India is the ex-officio chairperson of the Rajya Sabha; but during any period when the Vice President acts a President or discharges the functions of the President, he does not perform the duties as a presiding officer of the Rajya Sabha. The Vice-President is elected by the members of both the houses of Parliament assembled at a joint meeting, in accordance with the system of proportional representation by means of single transferable vote and the voting at such elections is by secret ballot. The Vice President is not a member of either house of Parliament or of a house of legislature of any State. He holds office for a term of five years from the date on which he enters upon his office or until he resigns his office or is removed from his office by a resolution passed by a majority of members of the Rajya Sabha and agreed to by the Lok Sabha. The functions and duties of the Chairperson of the Rajya Sabha are the same as those of the Speaker of the Lok Sabha.

Q10. Discuss the legislative procedure in Indian parliament.

Ans. Introduction and Passing of Bills

The initiative for substantial legislation comes primarily from the Prime Minister, cabinet members, and high-level officials. Although all legislation except financial bills can be introduced in either House, most laws originate in the Lok Sabha. A legislative proposal may go through three readings before it is voted.

After a bill has been passed by the originating House, it is sent to the other House, where it is debated and voted. The second House can accept, reject, or amend the bill. If the bill is amended by the second House, it must be returned to the originating house in its amended form. If a bill is rejected by the second House, if there is disagreement about the proposed amendments, or if the second House fails to act on a bill for 6 months, the President is authorised to summon a joint session of Parliament to vote on the bill. Disagreements are resolved by a majority vote of the members of both Houses present in a joint session. This procedure favours the Lok Sabha because it has more than twice as many members as the Rajya Sabha.

When the bill has been passed by both Houses, it is sent to the President, who can refuse, assent and send the bill back to the Parliament for reconsideration. If both Houses pass it again, with or without amendments, it is sent to the President a second time. The President is then obliged to assent to the legislation. After receiving the President's assent, a bill becomes an act in the statute book.

Special Procedure with respect to Money Bills

The legislative procedure for bills involving taxing and spending–known as Money Bills–is different from the procedure for other legislation. Money bills can be introduced only in the Lok Sabha. After the Lok Sabha passes a money bill, it is sent to the Rajya Sabha for recommendations. The upper house has 14 days to act on the bill. If the Rajya Sabha fails to act within 14 days, the bill becomes law. The Rajya Sabha may send an amended version of the bill back to the Lok Sabha, but the latter is not bound to accept these changes. It may pass the original bill again, at which point it will be sent of the President for his signature.

Q11. Write a short note on parliamentary privileges.

Ans. For free and efficient functioning of the members of Parliament, it is important that they be granted some privileges. There are two types of privileges for the members of Parliament; enumerated and unenumerated. The important privileges a member enjoys under the enumerated category are: (i) Freedom of speech in each House of the parliament; (ii) Immunity from proceedings in any Court in respect of anything said or any vote cast; (iii) Immunity of liability in respect of publication by or under the authority of either house of Parliament of any report, paper, votes or proceedings; (iv) Freedom from arrest in civil cases for duration of the session for a period of 40 days before and after the session; and (v) Exemption from attending as a witness in a Court.

In the unenumerated category fall similar privileges and immunities which are granted to the members of the House of Commons of British Parliament. Like the House of Commons, the Indian Parliament has power to punish a person, whether a member or a non-member, in case of contempt of Parliament.

Q12. What do you understand by parliament committees? Explain.

Ans. The Parliament is assisted by a number of committees to help it in discharging its duties. These committees comprise of various groups and parties, and the proceedings of these committees are conducted in the same manner as that of the Parliament. Since, the functions of Parliament are not only varied in nature, but considerable in volume and the time at its disposal is limited, it cannot make very detailed scrutiny of all legislative and other matters that come up before it. A good deal of its business is, therefore, transacted in committees. Both Houses of Parliament have a similar committee structure, with a few exceptions. Their appointment, terms of office, functions and procedure of conducting business are also more or less similar and are regulated under the rules made by the two Houses under Article 118(I) of the Constitution.

Types of Committees

Broadly, parliamentary committees are of two kinds–standing committees and *ad hoc* committees. The former are elected or appointed every year or periodically and their work goes on, more or less, on a continuous basis. The latter are appointed on an *ad hoc* basis, as the need arises, and they cease to exist as soon as they complete the task assigned to them.

(1) Standing Committees

***Financial Committees*:** Among the standing committees, there are three financial committees: (i) Committees on Estimates, (ii) Public Accounts, and (iii) Public Undertakings. These constitute a distinct group and they keep an unremitting vigil over government expenditure and performance. While members of the Rajya Sabha are associated with Committees on Public Accounts and Public Undertakings, members of the Committee on Estimates are drawn entirely form the Lok Sabha.

Non-Financial Committees: Besides these three financial committees, the Rules Committees of the Lok Sabha recommended the setting up of 17 department related standing committees. Accordingly, 17 such committees were set up on 8 April 1993. The functions of these committees are (i) to consider the demands for grants of various ministries/departments of the Government of India, and make reports to the Houses; (ii) to examine such bills as are referred to the Committee by the Chairman of the Rajya Sabha or the Speaker of the Lok Sabha, as the case may be, and make a report thereon; (iii) to consider Annual Reports of ministries/departments and make reports thereon; and (iv) to consider policy documents presented to the Houses, if referred to the Committed by the Chairman of the Rajya Sabha or the Speaker of the Lok Sabha, as the case may be, and make reports thereon.

Other standing committees in each House, divided in terms of their functions are:

(a) Committees to Inquire: (i) the Committee on Petitions examines petition on bills and on matters of general public interest and also entertains representations on matters concerning Central subjects, and (ii) the Committee of Privileges examines any question of privilege referred to it by the House or Speaker/Chairman.

(b) Committees to Scrutinise: (i) Committee on Government Assurances keeps track of all assurances, promises, undertakings, etc., given by ministers in the House and pursues them till they are implemented; (ii) Committee on Subordinate Legislation scrutinises and reports to the House whether the power to make regulations, rules, sub-rules, byelaws, etc., conferred by the Constitution or Statutes is being properly exercised by the authorities so authorised; and (iii) Committee on Papers Laid on the Table examines all papers laid on the table of the House by ministers, other than statutory notifications and orders that come within the purview of the Committee on Subordinate Legislation, to see whether there has been compliance with provisions of the Constitution, Act, rule or regulation under which the paper has been laid.

(c) Committees relating to the day-to-day business of the House: (i) Business Advisory Committee recommends allocation of time for items of government business, and other business to be brought before the Houses; (ii) Committee on Private Members' Bills and Resolutions of the Lok Sabha classifies and allocates time to bills introduced by private members; recommends allocation of time for discussion on private members' resolutions and examines Constitution amendment bills before their introduction by private members in the Lok Sabha. The Rajya Sabha does not have such a committee. It is the Business Advisory Committee of that House that recommends the allocation of time for discussion on the stage or stages of private members' bills and resolutions; (iii) Rules Committee considers matters of procedure and conduct of business in the House and recommends amendments or additions to the Rules; and (iv) Committee on Absence of Members from the Sittings of the House of the Lok Sabha considers all applications from members for leave or absence from sittings of the House. There is no such committee in the Rajya Sabha. Applications from members for leave or absence are considered by the House itself.

(d) Committee on the Welfare of Scheduled Castes and Scheduled Tribes members of both houses serve in this committee. It considers all matters relating to welfare of SCs and STs, which come within the purview of the Union Government, and keeps a watch on whether the constitutional safeguards in respect of these classes are properly implemented.

(e) Committees concerned with provision of facilities to members: (i) General Purposes Committee considers and advises the Speaker/Chairman on matters concerning affairs of the House, which do not appropriately fall within the purview of any other parliamentary committee and (ii) House Committee deals with residential accommodation and other amenities for members.

(f) Joint Committee on Salaries and Allowances of Members of Parliament: Constituted under the Salary, Allowances and Pension of Members of Parliament Act, 1954, apart from framing rules for regulating payment of salary, allowances, and pension to Members of parliament, it also frames rules with respect to amenities like medical, housing, telephone, postal, constituency, and secretariat facility.

(g) Joint Committee on Offices of Profit: Examines the composition and character of Committees and other bodies appointed by the Central and State governments and union territory administrations and recommends what offices ought to or ought not to disqualify a person for being chosen as a member of either House of Parliament.

(h) Library Committee: It consisting of members from both Houses, considers matters concerning the Library of the Parliament.

(i) Committee on Empowerment of Women: On 29 April 1997, this committee was constituted with members from both the Houses with a view to securing, among other things, status, dignity, and equality for women in all fields. On 4 March 1997, the Ethics Committee of the Rajya Sabha was constituted.

(2) *Ad hoc* Committees

Such committees may be broadly classified under two heads:

(a) Committees that are constituted from time to time, either by the two Houses on a motion adopted in that behalf or by the Speaker/Chairman to inquire into and report on specific subjects (e.g. Committees on the conduct of certain members during President's address, Committees on Draft Five Year Plans, Railway Convention Committee, Committee on Members of Parliament Local Area Development Scheme, Joint Committee on Bofors Contracts, Joint Committee on Fertiliser Pricing, and Joint Committee to enquire into irregularities in securities and banking transactions, etc.).

(b) Select or joint Committees on Bills, which are appointed to consider and report on a particular bill. These committees are distinguishable from other *ad hoc* committees in as much as they are concerned with bills and the procedure to be followed by them is as laid down in the Rules of Procedure and Directions by the Speaker/Chairman.

Q13. Briefly comment on state legislature of Indian constitution.

Ans. A **state legislature** is a legislative branch or body of a political subdivision in a federal system.

Structure

The State Legislature consists of the Governor and one or two Houses, as the case may be. If the state has only one House, it is known as Legislative Assembly. The other is the Legislative Council. The states having one house are called unicameral and the states having two houses bicameral.

Bicameral States

At present only five states have bicameral legislature, namely, Bihar, Jammu and Kashmir, Karnataka, Maharashtra, and Uttar Pradesh. All other states have only house.

Legislative Council (Vidhan Parishad)

It is also known as the Upper House. Like Rajya Sabha it is also a permanent house and cannot be dissolved.

Strength

The total strength does not exceed one-third of the strength of the Legislative Assembly, subject to a minimum of 40 members. The strength varies as per the population of the concerned state.

Tenure

The Legislative Council enjoys a term of 6 years with one-third of its members retiring every 2 years.

Qualification for Membership

To become a member of the Legislative Council, a person should possess the same qualifications as required for Lok Sabha membership, except the minimum age limit, which has been fixed at 30 years.

Election of Members

One-third of the members of a Legislative Council are elected by local bodies, one-third by the Legislative Assembly, one-twelfth by university graduate with at least 3 years standing, a similar proportion by teachers with at least 3 years standing and one-sixth are nominated by the Governor from among those persons who distinguish themselves in literature, science, or social science.

Chairman

The Council elects a Chairman and a Vice-Chairman from among its members.

Revival and Abolition of the Legislative Council

The Legislative Council can be abolished or revived by the Parliament on the recommendation of the Legislative Assembly. Some time ago, the

Legislative Assemblies of Andhra Pradesh and Tamil Nadu recommended the abolition of Legislative Councils in their respective states and the Parliament enacted necessary laws for the abolition. Recently, the Legislative Assemblies of Andhra Pradesh and Tamil Nadu passed a resolution and sought the revival of the Council. The Parliament enacted a necessary law for their revival. It is for the first time that the State Legislative Assemblies have recommended the creation or revival of the Legislative Council.

Legislative Assembly (Vidhan Sabha)

Also known as the Lower House, it is similar to the Lok Sabha at the Centre.

Strength

Each State Legislative Assembly consists of not more than 500 members and not less than 60 members. The strength varies according to the population of the concerned state. However, the Legislative Assembly of Sikkim has only 32 members.

Constitution

It consists of directly elected representatives of the people.

Tenure

The Legislative Assembly has a term of 5 years but it can be dissolved earlier by the Governor. Its term can also be extended by 1 year during national emergencies.

Elections

Members are chosen by direct election form the territorial constituencies of the state. The candidate should possess the same qualification as are fixed for the Lok Sabha or Legislative Council. The minimum age for becoming a member is 25 years.

Functions

The Council of Ministers is collectively responsible to the Assembly. The Assembly chooses its own Speaker and Deputy Speaker, who can be removed by the Council of Ministers. The Chief Minister of the state is the leader of the House, which is responsible for the administration, executive and legislative policies of the state. A member holding office as a Speaker of an Assembly (a) shall vacate his office if he ceases to be a member of the Assembly; (b) may at the time by writing under his hand addressed, if such member is a Speaker, to the Deputy Speaker, and if such member is the Deputy Speaker, to the Speaker, resign his office, and (c) may be removed from his office by a resolution of the Assembly passed by a majority of all the then members of the Assembly; Provided that no resolution for the purpose of clause (c) shall be moved unless at least fourteen day's notice has been given to the intention to move the resolution; Provided whenever the Assembly is dissolved, the Speaker shall not vacate his office until immediately before the first meeting of the Assembly after the dissolution. For excellent score, read GPH book.

Q14. What is Question Hour?

Ans. Every sitting of both the Houses of Parliament starts with Question Hour. In this first hour, questions relating to government are asked and problem facing the country are brought to the notice of the government in order to expose administrative excesses or to redress to the problem. The questions asked are of the following three types: (i) Starred Questions—to be answered orally on the floor of the House and are marked with an asterisk. During the oral answering, supplementary questions can be put by the members. The Speaker decides if the questions asked should be answered orally or otherwise. One member can ask only one starred question on a day; (ii) Unstarred Questions—to be answered in written form and are not marked with an asterisk. No supplementary questions are allowed. A mandatory notice of 10 days is required to register the question to be asked during a sitting of the House of Parliament; and (iii) Short Notice Questions—are the questions asked on matters of utmost urgency, with regards to public importance. They do not need 10 day notices and so are called short notice questions.

Q15. What are the reasons responsible for the Decline of the Legislature?

Ans. In the twentieth century, the power of the legislature is on its decline. The reasons are as follows.

- **The Concept of Welfare State:** The two World Wars, economic depression and complex problems of modern life converted all states into welfare states. The concept of social welfare has strengthened the hands of the executive. The executive has become a multi-functioning organ. The rise in the power of the executive has led to corresponding decline in the powers of the legislature.
- **Development of Science and Technology:** The development of science and technology has made the society complex. Therefore, complex laws are necessary to tackle social problems. The modern legislature, being composed of amateur politicians, lacks scientific and technical knowledge. Therefore,

it makes laws in broader principles and delegates some legislative authority to the executive.

- **Rigidity of the Party System:** The party whip has increased day by day. Rigid party discipline has curtailed the independence of the ordinary members of the legislature and reduced the debate to a mechanical level. On the other hand, the party whip has strengthened the hands of the executive.
- **Delegated Legislation:** Legislatures lack the time and technical competence to deal with the ever-increasing volume of legislation in a modern state. As a result, the legislature passes the laws in broad outline and delegates the power of making details of laws to the executive. By this delegated legislation, the civil servants enjoy enormous power and influence. In the welfare states of today, the executive has gained leadership in the matter of governmental operation.
- **Meeting Emergencies and Crisis Situations:** Modern states are faced with several crises and emergencies. War, financial crisis, natural disasters like earthquakes, cyclones and floods demand immediate response and that can be done only by the executive. The legislature, being a large body of motley crowd, cannot rise to the occasion. As a result, its importance has declined.

Q16. How is the prime minister of India elected?

Or

Who appoints the prime minister? What is his/her tenure?

Or

Discuss the position, appointment, powers, and actual position of the prime minister.

Ans. The **Prime Minister of India**, as addressed to in the Constitution of India, is the chief of government, chief advisor to the President of India, head of the Council of Ministers and the leader of the majority party in parliament. The prime minister leads the executive branch of the Government of India.

(1) Position of the Prime Minister

The Constitution of India provides for the council of ministers to be headed by the prime minister. The prime minister is the head of the union government, while the president of India is the head of the state. India follows the Westminster model of governance, which empowers the prime minister to oversee the day-to-day functioning of the union government.

The prime minister in his job is assisted by the council of ministers, which includes the cabinet ministers, ministers of state with independent charge, ministers of state who work with cabinet ministers, and deputy ministers.

(2) Appointment of Prime Minister

The prime minister is appointed by the president of India. The president appoints the leader of the party or alliance, which enjoys the majority in the Lok Sabha as the prime minister. If no party or alliance has a majority, the president can appoint the leader of the largest single party or alliance as the prime minister, provided s/he secures a vote of confidence in the Lok Sabha. It is important to note that the prime minister can be a member of either the Rajya Sabha or the Lok Sabha.

(3) Power of Prime Minister

(a) As the head of the Union Government

The prime minister is the head of the union government.

- The president appoints the ministers on the advice of the prime minister. S/he can also appoint a non-member as minister, provided that such a non-member becomes the member of any house within six months.
- The prime minister decides the ranks of his ministers and distributes various departments. S/he is empowered to retain important ministries with himself/herself.
- S/he is the head of the cabinet and presides over the meeting of the council of ministers.
- Though the ministers remain in the office at the pleasure of the president, it is the prime minister who decides on the removal of a particular minister.
- In case the prime minister resigns, the entire council of ministers resigns with him/her.
- Some of the decisions require the prime minister's personal attention.
  - ✓ Important defence-related issues
  - ✓ Decorations, both civilian and defence, where presidential approval is required
  - ✓ All important policy issues
  - ✓ Proposals for appointment of Indian heads of missions abroad and requests for grant of agreement for foreign heads of missions posted to India

- ✓ All important decisions relating to the cabinet secretariat
- ✓ Appointments to state administrative tribunals and the central administrative tribunal, UPSC, election commission, appointment of members of statutory/constitutional committees, commissions attached to various ministries
- ✓ All policy matters relating to the administration of the civil services and administrative reforms
- ✓ Special packages announced by the prime minister for states are monitored in the PMO and periodical reports submitted to prime minister
- ✓ All judicial appointments for which presidential approval is required

(b) **Link between the President and Cabinet:** The prime minister acts as the link between the president and the council of ministers. S/he keeps the president updated on the decisions of the cabinet regarding administration of the union. The president summons and prorogues the Parliament on the advice of the prime minister.

(c) **Supervisory Functions:** The prime minister supervises the working of each department. S/he can advise any minister at any time and the ministers, in doubt, have to consult the prime minister. The prime minister is also the chairman of the Planning Commission Of India.

(d) **Co-ordinating Functions:** The prime minister co-ordinates the functioning of various ministries to ensure the proper growth of the country. S/he may interfere in the functioning of any department in order to maintain inter departmental co-ordination.

(e) **As the Leader of the Parliament:** The prime minister is the leader of the majority party or alliance in the Lok Sabha. The president summons and prorogues the Houses on his advice. The presidential speech, delivered during the joint session of the Parliament, is actually the speech of the prime minister and his/her government. All the important statements relating to the policy of the government is announced by him/her. The Lok Sabha can be dissolved on his/her advice. The prime minister can intervene in any debate in the Lok Sabha.

(f) **As the Leader of the Nation:** The prime minister is the leader of the nation. S/he is the chief spokesperson of the country. S/he represents the country internationally. As the leader of the nation, the prime minister represents our nation at all international conferences like the Commonwealth Summit, summit of the Non-aligned Nations and SAARC nations. S/he can sign treaties and is empowered to commit the nation to certain international obligations.

(g) **Actual Position of the Prime Minister:** The prime minister enjoys a wide range of powers. The government of India is widely referred to as the prime ministerial form of government rather than the parliamentary form of government. However, there are several limitations on the power of the prime minister.

- The prime minister has to always win the confidence of his party and acquire the co-operation of all the distinguished members of his/her party.
- S/he has to face the criticisms made by the opposition party for his/her policy decisions.
- In the case of the coalition government, the power of the prime minister is dependent on the mercy of the allied partners.
- His/Her authority is often checked by the press and public opinion.

Q17. Discuss the composition of the council of minister.

Or

What does a minister promise when he takes the path of secrecy?

Or

What is the size of the council of the ministers?

Or

Define three categories of ministers.

Or

How does a cabinet secretariat work?

Or

State the differences between the cabinet and council of ministers.

Ans. Council of Ministers

After the elections, the president of India, on the advice of the prime minister, appoints the council of ministers. Sometimes a non-member of the parliament too may be appointed. However, he must get elected to either of the Houses of the Parliament within a period of six months.

(a) Oath of Office

Every minister of the government has to take an oath of office and secrecy affirming to be faithful to the Constitution of India; to uphold the sovereignty and integrity of the nation; and to discharge his duties faithfully and fearlessly. The ministers also promise not to reveal the matters that may be brought under their consideration.

(b) Size

The Article 75 of the Constitution of India restricts the number of the council of ministers including the prime minister to fifteen per cent of the total members of the Lok Sabha.

(c) Categories of Ministers

There are three categories of ministers.

(i) **Cabinet Ministers:** They are the most important ministers of the council. They hold the important portfolios such as defence, finance, external affairs and home. These ministers are the only ministers entitled to attend the cabinet meetings. The decisions they take decide the policies and programmes of the government.

(ii) **Ministers of State:** These ministers belong to the second category of ministers in the council. They are not a part of the cabinet. They either assist the cabinet ministers or in some cases hold independent charge of less important ministries. Since they are not a part of the cabinet, they are not entitled to attend cabinet meetings. However, they may be asked to attend a cabinet meeting by the prime minister.

(iii) **Deputy Ministers:** They are the lowest ranked ministers in the cabinet. They assist the cabinet ministers and the ministers of state. They do not participate in the meetings of the cabinet.

(d) Term of Office

The council of ministers, according to the Constitution, holds office at the president's pleasure. However, the president has very limited say in this matter, as the council of ministers are responsible to the Lok Sabha. They may continue in the office as long as they enjoy the confidence of the lower House. The entire council resigns if the Lok Sabha passes the no-confidence motion against them. The president can dismiss an individual minister on the advice of the prime minister.

(e) Salaries and Allowances

The Parliament from time to time, determines the salaries and allowances of the ministers. The ministers, however, are entitled for the constituency allowances as member of the Parliament.

(f) Cabinet Secretariat

The cabinet secretariat works under the charge of the prime minister. It is headed by the cabinet secretary, who is also the ex-officio chairman of the Civil Services Board. The secretariat prepares the agenda of the cabinet meetings, provides information and materials required for such meetings, interacts with various departments to find out the progress made on the decisions taken by the cabinet, etc.

(g) Cabinet Committees

The cabinet committees are decision-making bodies that help the prime minister and the cabinet to function properly. Some of the important cabinet committees include defence committee, foreign affairs committee, political affairs committee, etc.

(h) Cabinet and Council of Ministers

The council of ministers is a wider body than all other categories of ministers. The cabinet is only a part of the council. It consists of the most important ministers of the government and is always consulted by the prime minister. The prime minister may or may not consult all the ministers of the council on every matter. However, all the decisions taken by the cabinet are binding on the entire council.

Q18. What do you understand by ministerial responsibility?

Ans. The ministers in the council are responsible to the Lok Sabha for every action they take. The ministerial responsibilities are of two types:

(1) Collective Responsibility

The term collective responsibility indicates that all ministers of the council are collectively responsible to the Lok Sabha. The Article 75(3) of the constitution clearly states that the council of ministers are collective responsible to the House of the people. The cabinet members swim and sink together. All decisions in the cabinet are taken collectively by the ministers. The cabinet ministers support the decision without any hesitation. The entire ministry is bound to resign if a no-confidence motion is passed against even one minister.

(2) Individual Responsibility

A minister holds office at the pleasure of the president. It means that the president has the power to dismiss a minister for violating the terms of the constitution or carrying out any undesirable activities. The member of the Parliament are entitled to question a minister on the policies adopted by him in the administration, If a department fails to fulfil the expectations, the concerned minister may be dismissed by the president on the advice of the prime minister.

Q19. Describe the relationship between President and Prime minister in the India political system.

Ans. Prime Minister acts as the link between the Cabinet and the President. All key decision of the Cabinet are communicated to the President through the Prime Minister. It is the duty of Prime Minister to furnish such information regarding the affairs of the Union as the President may ask for. It is on the advice of Prime Minister that the President summons and prorogues the Parliament, dissolves Lok Sabha and appoints and removes high officials. The President can refer back the decision of the Cabinet once for reconsideration. However, a reconsidered decision will have to be approved by the President. The President, therefore, acts on the advice of Council of Ministers headed by the Prime Minister.

According to conventions of the parliamentary system, the President is only a constitutional head. He acts in accordance with the aid and advice of Council of Ministers headed by the Prime Minister. Doubts have been expressed by constitutional experts about the controversial relationship between the two offices. Article 78 of the constitution stipulates in the duty of the Prime Minister to communicate to President all the decisions of the Council of Ministers relating to the administration of the Union and proposals for legislation. This makes Prime Minister a link between President and the cabinet and chief advisor of the President. This also gives President the right to information. The Prime Minister is bound to forward to the President such information as the president may demand, regarding the affairs of the Union. The President may even send a decision back for reconsideration by the Council of Ministers.

It was in this context that there was a convention of Prime Minister meeting the President once a week to exchange notes. The first two Presidents Dr Rajendra Prasad and Dr S. Radhakrishanan took active interest in the decisions of the day and wrote letters to Prime Minster Nehru. They however did not create any constitutional crisis by daring the

Prime Minister openly. It was Indira Gandhi who saw the demise of an active office of President when she got V.V. Giri elected as President against the official Congress candidate N. Sanjeev Reddy. This led to a split in the Congress. Later on, she succeeded in getting Fakhruddin Ali Ahmad installed as the President. He had been Indira Gandhi's loyal colleague and signed the imposition of Emergency in 1975, without any second thoughts. To avert any future constitutional crisis, Mrs Gandhi through the 42nd amendment in Article 74, made it obligatory for the President to act in accordance with the Council of Ministers.

Q20. Discuss the evolution and development of judiciary in India.

Ans. In India, we have a single unified judicial system. The whole system of courts taken together is called judiciary.

The development of judiciary in general can be traced to the growth of modern nation-states. This was the stage when it was assumed that power and administration of justice was prerogative of the state.

During the ancient times, administration of justice was not considered a function of the state as it was based on religious law or dharma. Most of the kings courts dispensed justice according to dharma, 'a set of eternal laws rested upon the individual duty to be performed in four stages of life (ashrama) and status of individual according to his status (varna)'. The king had no true legislative power, the power to make ordinances "on his own initiative and pleasure". Even if a law has been enacted and royally recognised, an individual to whom custom applies may disobey it on the ground that it conflicts the precepts of dharma. At the village level, the local/village/popular courts dispensed justice according to the customary laws.

However, during the medieval times, the king arrogated to himself an important role in administering justice. He was the highest judge in the land.

With the advent of the British rule in India, judicial system on the basis of Anglo-Saxon jurisprudence was introduced in India. The Royal Charter of Charles II of the year 1661 gave the Governor and Council the power to adjudicate both civil and criminal cases according to the laws of England. But it was with the Regulating Act of 1773 that the first Supreme Court came to be established in India. Located at Calcutta, the Supreme Court consisted of Chief Justice and three judges (subsequently it was reduced to two judges) appointed by the Crown and it was made a King's court rather than a Company's court. The court held jurisdiction over "his majesty's subjects" wherever the Supreme Courts were established. Supreme Courts were established in Madras and in Bombay later.

Judicial system during this period consisted of two systems, the Supreme Courts in the Presidencies and the Sadr courts in the provinces. While the former followed the English law and procedure, the latter followed regulation laws and personal laws.

Subsequently, these two systems were merged under the High Courts Act of 1861. This Act replaced the Supreme Courts and the native courts (Sadr Dewani Adalat and Sadr Nizamat Adalat) in the presidency towns of Calcutta, Bombay and Madras with High Courts. The highest court of appeal however was the judicial committee of the Privy Council.

The Federal Court of India was established in Delhi by the Act of 1935. This was to act as an intermediate appellant between the High Courts and the Privy Council in regard to matters involving the interpretation of the Indian constitution. In addition to this appellate jurisdiction, the Federal Court had advisory as well as original jurisdiction in certain other matters. This court continued to function until 26 January 1950, the day the independent India's constitution came into force.

Q21. What are the qualifications required for appointment of a judge of the Supreme Court?

Or

What is the procedure for removing a judge of the Supreme Court?

Or

Explain the powers and functions of the Supreme Court.

Or

How are the judges of the Supreme Court appointed?

Or

Describe the salary and allowances of a Supreme Court judge.

Or

Describe the organisation and jurisdiction of the Supreme Court.

Or

Describe the controversy regarding appointment of the chief justice.

Ans. The entire judicature has been divided into three tiers. At the top there is a Supreme Court, below it is the High Court and the lowest rank is occupied by session's court.

The Supreme Court is the highest court of law. The Constitution says that the law declared by the Supreme Court shall be binding on all small courts within the territory of India. Below the Supreme Court, are the High Courts located in the states. Under each High Court, there are District

Sessions Courts, Subordinate Courts and Courts of Minor Jurisdiction called Small Cause Courts.

Organisation of Supreme Court

The Supreme Court at present consists of one Chief Justice and 25 other judges. In 1950, when the constitution was enacted there were only 8 judges. In 1956, the number was increased to 11, in 1960 to 14, in 1977 to 18 and in 1980 it was increased to 25.

Appointment

Article 124(A) of the Constitution provides that a judge of the Supreme Court will be appointed by the President in consultation with such judges of the Supreme Court and of High Court in the states as the President may deem necessary. In the case of appointment of a judge other than the Chief Justice, the Chief Justice of India may be consulted.

Controversy regarding appointment of Chief Justice

After independence as a matter of convention, the senior most judge of the Supreme Court was appointed as the Chief Justice of India. However, this convention was violated on April 25, 1973 when the claim of three senior most judges– J.M. Shelat, K.S. Hedge and A.N. Grover were superceded and a junior judge Mr. A. N. Ray was appointed as the Chief Justice. Noted legal luminaries criticised this act vehemently as an infringement on the independence of judiciary and an act of political mendicancy. All the three judges resigned in protest. In 1977, this convention was violated once again when the claim of senior most judge, Justice H.R. Khanna was set aside and a junior judge Justice H.M. Beg was appointed as the Chief Justice. Justice Khanna also resigned. His claim was set aside as he had given a controversial judgement on the right to life. In his judgement on the writ of habeas corpus, he while giving his judgement had said that an arrest made illegally and under malafide intention even during emergency can be challenged in the court of law. Justice H.R. Khanna had to pay the price of his integrity and intellect. After 1977, when Janta Party came to power, once again the convention of nominating the senior-most judge as the Chief Justice was restored when V.C. Chandrachud was appointed as Chief Justice of India. In 1993, a full bench of Supreme Court gave a unanimous decision that only the senior-most judge could be appointed as the Chief Justice.

Qualifications for becoming a Supreme Court Judge

(a) He should be a citizen of India.

(b) He should have served as a judge in a High Court for at least five years.

or

He should have been an advocate of one or more High Courts for ten consecutive years.

(c) He should be in the eyes of the President as a distinguished jurist.

Salary and Allowances

A very important element that determines the independence of the judges is the remuneration received by them. The salaries and allowances of the judges are fixed high in order to secure their independence, efficiency and impartiality. Besides, the salary, every judge is entitled to a rent-free official accommodation. The Constitution also provided that the salaries of the judges cannot be changed to their disadvantage, except in times of a Financial Emergency. The administrative expenses of the Supreme Court, the salaries, allowances, etc,. of the judges are charged on the Consolidated Fund of India.

Oath of Office

Before assuming office, each judge is administered oath of office by the President to honour the constitution with loyalty and discharge duties diligently.

Tenure and Removal of Judges

According to Article 124 of the constitution, a Supreme Court judge would hold office till the age of 65 years. If he wants to retire earlier, he should send his resignation letter addressed to the President of India.

The judges of the Supreme Court can be removed if they discharge unconstitutional functions, display unsoundness or on ground of proved incapacity and misbehaviour in performing their functions. The method of removing the judges is quite rigid. A judge can be impeached by the President if both the houses of Parliament pass a resolution supported by a majority of not less than two-third members of Parliament present and voting, and an absolute majority of the total strength of the house. One house moves the proposal while the other sits as a court of appeal. When such a resolution is under consideration, the judge has a right to defend himself either in person or through some representative.

The above prevalent method makes it difficult for a judge to be removed for a ruling political alliance would have to muster a two-thirds majority, which is a difficult proposition for any one single party in Parliament. This ensures the independence of judiciary.

Powers and Functions of Supreme Court

The Supreme Court has vast and enormous jurisdiction. Its powers can be classified under the following headings:

(a) Original Jurisdiction

Under Article 131, original jurisdiction covers all those cases, which can originate directly in the Supreme Court. These include:

- Dispute between central and state government.
- Dispute between central government and one or more states on one side and some states on the other.
- Dispute between state governments.
- Cases related to violation of fundamental rights.

India is a federal state and powers are divided between centre and state. Under such circumstances, disputes are bound to arise between centre and states. Such cases or disputes related to any interpretation on public law between centre and state are settled by the Supreme Court. However, disputes related to Provisions of treaties with former princely states are out of purview of the Supreme Court.

(b) Appellate Jurisdiction

The Supreme Court is the highest court of appeal from all courts in the territory of India. It hears appeals in regard to interpretation of the constitution in civil cases, criminal cases and special appeals.

(i) *Interpretation of the constitution:* According to Article 132, an appeal shall lie in the Supreme Court if the High Court certifies under Article 134 (A) that a case involves a substantial question of law and is fit for appeal in the Supreme Court.

(ii) *Civil Cases:* An appeal shall lie in the Supreme Court from a judgement of a High Court in civil cases, if the High Court certifies that a case is fit for appeal in the Supreme Court as it involves a substantial question of law and in the opinion of High Court needs to be decided by the Supreme Court.

(iii) *Criminal Cases:* In criminal cases, the appellate jurisdiction of the Supreme Court is divided into two parts:

- *Appeal without certification:* This is done in cases where the High Court on appeal reverses an order of acquittal of an accused person by a lower court and sentences him to death or where the High Court withdraws for trial before itself a case in the subordinate court and sentences the accused person to death.

- *Appeal with certification:* If the High Court certifies under Article 134(c) that a case is fit for appeal in the Supreme Court.

(*iv*) *Special Appeal:* Article 132 to 134 provides for regular appeals to Supreme Court from decisions of High Court. However, there still may remain some cases where justice might require interference of the Supreme Court with decision not only of High Court outside the preview of Articles 132-134, but also of any other court or tribunal in the territory of India. This special appeal known as residuary power is conferred upon the Supreme Court by Article 136. According to this article, "Notwithstanding anything in this chapter, the Supreme Court may in its discretion, grant special leave to appeal from any judgement, decree, determination, sentence or order in any cause or matter passed or made by any court or tribunal in the territory of India." Noted constitutional expert M.V. Pylee commenting upon Article 136 wrote, "The reach of Article 136 is indeed formidable. It has become a convenient instrument at the disposal of the court to check arbitrary acts and unjust decision of the ever-increasing number of administrative tribunals which the Union and the states are setting up almost daily in the process of realising the objectives of a socialistic pattern of society."

(c) Advisory Jurisdiction

According to Article 143, if at any time, it appears to the President that a matter of public importance or a question of law has arisen or is likely to arise, and it is expedient to obtain the opinion of the Supreme Court, he may refer the question to the Court for consideration and the Court may after hearing such as it thinks fit, report to the President its opinion thereupon. However, the opinion of Supreme Court is not binding upon the President. Likewise, there is no constitutional compulsion for the court to give its advice. Some of the prominent cases referred to the Supreme Court by the President include the Kerala Education Bill, the Indo-Pak agreement on the Beru Bari, the Delhi Law Act (1912), Presidential Election (1974), Cauevery Dispute Tribunal Case (1992), Sutlej-Yamuna Link Canal Case (2004), etc.

(d) Custodian of Fundamental Rights

Under Article 32 of the Indian constitution, the Supreme Court acts as the guardian of fundamental rights of the citizen of India. The Court can declare a law passed by any legislature null and void if it encroaches upon the fundamental rights guaranteed by the Indian Constitution. The Supreme Court can issue writs in the nature of habeas corpus, mandamus, prohibition, quo warranto and certiorari for the enforcement of fundamental rights.

(e) Judicial Review

A very important function of the Supreme Court is the power of judicial review. Parliament and state legislatures of different states make laws. Any law which contravenes any of the provisions of the constitution is declared ultra vires or unconstitutional by the Supreme Court. Thus, Supreme Court through its power of judicial review is the custodian of the constitution and the highest forum for its interpretation.

(f) To Review its own Judgement

According to Article 137, the Supreme Court has the power to review its own judgement and reverse its earlier decision.

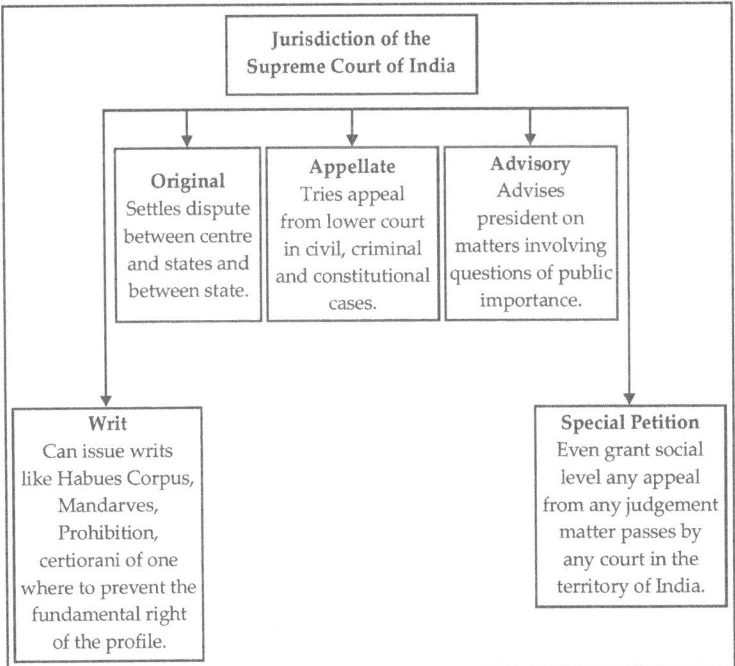

Fig. 3.1

(g) Court of Record

The Supreme Court also acts as a Court of Record. Its decisions are printed and they act as precedents in other cases. The Supreme Court is empowered to punish a person even for contempt of court.

Q22. What are the qualifications required for Chief justice of a state?

Or

Explain the powers and functions of the High Court.

Or

How are the judges of the State High Court appointed?

Or

Describe the salary and allowances of the judges of High Court.

Or

Describe the organisation, composition and jurisdiction of the High Court.

Ans. The Indian constitution provides for an integrated judicial system. At the apex is the Supreme Court of India whose decisions are applicable all over the country. In each state of India, there is a High Court, which exercises power within the territorial jurisdiction of the state concerned. At present, there are 18 High Courts, with four having jurisdiction over more than one state. In India, there is uniformity as far as the appointment and conditions of service of judges and the jurisdictions of High Court is Concerned.

Composition

A High Court consists of a Chief Justice and other such judges as the President may from time to time determine. Since there is no fixed figure, their members vary from state to state.

Appointment

The judges of State High Courts are appointed by the President of India in consultation with the Chief Justice of India, the Governor of the concerned state and the Chief Justice of the concerned High Court. In case of the appointment of the Chief Justice of the High Court, the President shall consult the Chief Justice of India and the Governor of the state concerned.

Qualifications for Chief Justice of a State

(a) He should be a citizen of India

(b) He should have served as a judge of lower court for five years.
or

He should have been an advocate of a High Court for at least ten years.

(c) He should be in the eyes of the President as a distinguished jurist.

Oath

The Chief Justice and other judges of a State High Court are administered oath of office by the Governor of that particular state.

Salary and Allowances

According to the constitutional provisions, the Chief Justice of a High Court and other judges get handsome salaries. In addition, they get certain allowances and a pension after retirement. The salaries and allowances of the High Court Judges are given from the revenue of the State and are non-votable. The salary and allowances can be increased or decreased by an amendment in the Constitution. Salaries of the Judges of the High Courts were revised in 1998.

Tenure

A judge shall hold office till he attains the age of 62 years. However, he may resign his office addressed to the President. The judge of a High Court cannot be dismissed. He can be removed by the President through the process of impeachment, which is similar to those of the judges of the Supreme Court of India.

Transfer of a Judge

The President may after consultation with the Chief Justice of India, transfer a judge from one High Court to another High Court. And in such a case of transfer, the judge shall receive in addition to his salary, compensatory allowances as determined by Parliament by the law.

Powers and Functions of High Court

The High Court of a state has the following powers:

(a) **Original:** The original jurisdiction of the High Court extends to all civil cases, which are in respect of actions of higher value.

(b) **AppellateL** The appellate jurisdiction of the High Court is both civil and criminal. It comes as First or Second Appeal in civil cases. Appeals arise from decisions by district judges and subordinate judges in higher value cases to the High Court. Likewise, decisions come on matters of fact as well as law when a subordinate court inferior to the High Court gives a decision on an appeal from inferior court. In such cases, second appeal lies to High Court. The criminal appellate jurisdiction of the

High Court extends to appeal from the decision of a Sessions judge or an Addition Sessions judge when the sentence of imprisonment exceeds seven years.

(c) **Power of Superintendence:** According to Article 277, every High Court extends the power of superintendence over all courts and tribunals, except those dealing with armed forces operating within its territorial jurisdiction.

(d) **Control over Subordinate Courts:** The High Court is the head of judiciary in a state and is empowered to transfer constitutional cases from lower courts (Article 228). If the High Court is satisfied that a matter involves a question of law and is beyond the jurisdiction of subordinate case, it can withdraw the cased and dispose it off itself.

(e) **Guardian of Fundamental Rights:** According to Article 226, the High Court is empowered to issue writs to any person or authority including the government if it feels that the fundamental rights of any individual are being infringed upon within its jurisdiction. These may include the writs of habeas corpus, mandamus, prohibition, quo warranto and certiorari. Thus, through Article 226 the High Court guarantees the rule of law.

(f) **Court of Record:** The High Court keeps a record of its own cases, which act as a precedent in future cases.

Q23. What do you understand by judiciary at lower level?

Or

What do you understand by subordinate courts?

Ans. The Supreme Court of India is the apex court. It is followed by the State High Courts. At the lowest level, there are the subordinate courts, which comprise of sessions court, district court, judicial magistrate and so on. As far as the appointments to the lower courts are concerned, the Indian judiciary is a career service. Candidates for the State Judicial service sit in competitive examination after at least three years experience before the bar. The successful candidates are provided specialised training before there appointment to the service. The lower courts are therefore staffed with career judges along. They deal with civil and criminal cases of localised nature. Constitutional cases, cases of public law and the power to issue writs for violation of fundamental rights do not come under their jurisdiction.

Q24. What is meant by the term 'Judicial Review' and 'Judicial Reform'?

Ans. Judicial Review: Courts are established to intercept the law and not to make laws. It is the function of the judiciary to say what the law is and to say it fearlessly. The Constitution of India is the supreme law of the land. Any act or order, which is unconstitutional, is void. It is the Supreme Court of India, which decided such questions by the method of Judicial Review. The word "Judicial Review" has nowhere been mentioned in the Constitution. However, the makers of the Constitution gave the power to finally interpret the Constitution to the Supreme Court. It was pointed out in the debates of the Constituent Assembly that the constitutional validity of any central or state law will be determined by the Supreme Court. The Supreme Court can declare a law 'ultra vires' or null and void if it is against the spirit of the Constitution. This act of the Supreme Court is called Judicial Review. It is the Supreme Court, which can interpret the Constitution and has the power of original jurisdiction. The legislature may not possess such wisdom.

Judicial Reforms: Judicial reform is the complete or partial political reform of a country's judiciary. Judicial reform is often done as a part of wider reform of the country's political system or a legal reform. President of the Constitutional Court of the Russian Federation Valery Zorkin give in his article "Twelve Theseses on Legal Reform in Russia first published in Russian magazine «Legislation and Economics», N. 2, 2004 explained correlation between legal and judicial reform:"Complete legal reform should normally include not only judicial reform, but also reform of various aspects of the structural system and content of legislation, legal education, legal awareness by the population, and also the corporate consciousness of the whole legal community. Judicial reform usually aims to improve such things as law courts, procuracies, advocacy (bar), inquest, executory processes, and record keeping.

Legal reform can be the driver for all other reforms, including reform of the economy. A true market economy cannot be created without ensuring both full guarantees of private property and transparent predictability for entrepreneurial activity, on the one hand; and sufficiently reasonable legal control over economic processes, on the other hand. Legal reform should be an integral part of any on-going reform process. Legal reform is a tool for implementing necessary reforms, to balance competing interests, create a dynamic and sustainable economy, and build a sustainable civil society. In modern Russia, aspects and directions of development of judicial reform were formulated in the Judicial Reform

Concept, enacted by the Russian Parliament on October 24, 1991. This document still remains legally valid and applicable.

The separation of powers principle, also proclaimed in the Constitution of the Russian Federation, requires observance of judicial independence. And such independence requires proper funding of the courts and their activities. It is well known that Russian courts remain under-funded. However, the cumulative economic costs suffered by both state and private enterprises as the result of under-performance by various judicial institutions, especially by the trial courts of general jurisdiction and the arbitration courts, is at least twice the order of magnitude as the financial burden carried by the state and society in financing such judicial institutions. The elimination of under-funding of the courts would definitely improve the efficiency of their work and be worthwhile.

Taking into account the specifics of historical developments in Russia, one may assert that without undertaking a large-scale legal reform it would be extremely difficult to succeed concurrently with judicial reform. It is necessary now to start unfolding a full-scale legal reform, which has to be completed by the year 2020. The official public presentation and implementation of such legal reform should become the prime responsibility of executive and legislative authorities. The programme of legal reform needs to be adopted in the form of a legislative act".

Areas of the judicial reform often include; codification of law instead of common law, moving from an inquisitorial system to an adversarial system, establishing stronger judicial independence with judicial councils or changes to appointment procedure, establishing mandatory retirement age for judges or enhancing independence of prosecution.

Q25. What do you understand by bureaucracy? Discuss.

Ans. A bureaucracy is "a body of non-elective government officials" and/or "an administrative policy-making group." Historically, bureaucracy referred to government administration managed by departments staffed with non-elected officials. In modern parlance, bureaucracy refers to the administrative system governing any large institution.

Since being coined, the word "bureaucracy" has developed negative connotations for some. Bureaucracies are criticised for their complexity, their inefficiency, and their inflexibility. The dehumanising effects of excessive bureaucracy were a major theme in the work of Franz Kafka, and were central to his masterpiece The Trial. The elimination of unnecessary bureaucracy is a key concept in modern managerial theory, and has been a central issue in numerous political campaigns.

Others have defended the existence of bureaucracies. The German sociologist Max Weber argued that bureaucracy constitutes the most efficient and rational way in which human activity can be organised, and that systematic processes and organised hierarchies were necessary to maintain order, maximise efficiency and eliminate favouritism. But even Weber saw bureaucracy as a threat to individual freedom, in which the increasing bureaucratisation of human life traps individuals in an "iron cage" of rule-based, rational control.

Q26. Describe the characteristics of bureaucracy in India.

Ans. Bureaucracy is used in a broad as well as narrow sense. In a broad sense, it refers to the totality of personnel from departmental secretaries at the top to the clerks and peons at the bottom. In a narrow sense, it refers to those important public servants who occupy the policy making and supervisory positions in the system of administration.

All state bureaucracies are someway organised on the basis of a definite purpose or functions. This is achieved through the construction of departments, ministries and agencies charged with responsibility for particular policy areas like education, defence, agriculture etc. The number of such departments and agencies varies over time and from state to state. Structurally, a bureaucratic form of organisation exhibits a number of characteristics.

- **Division of Labour:** The work of the department or organisation is divided among the employees in such a way that each employee has only a certain part of the work to perform. In this way, the employee repeatedly performs certain job and becomes efficient at it.
- **Hierarchy:** In every bureaucracy, there is a hierarchy or chain of command, where officials at lower levels are supervised by those at higher levels. The commands or orders of superiors have to be followed by sub-ordinates.
- **Written Documents:** The management of the organisation is based upon written documents or files. Since nothing concerning the office is private, every transaction, decision, and order is recorded which help in efficient decision-making in future.

- **Rules:** Management follows a set of rules, which are made known to all employees of the organisation. Rules are equally applicable to everyone and they prevent any type of arbitrariness.
- **Salaries:** Salaries are fixed for employees and there is a provision for pension, Provident Fund to take care of the employee when he retires from service.
- **Impersonality:** The officials are expected to carry out their duties without allowing themselves to be influenced by their personal likes and dislikes. The employee must treat all clients equally.
- **Rationality:** Bureaucracy represents a rational form of organisation. Decisions are taken on strict evidence and avoid any type of irrationality.
- **Neutrality:** Bureaucracy serves all political parties in power without being biased. It has only committed to work and duty and not to any Party ideology.

Q27. Discuss the nature of Indian bureaucracy during the colonial time as well as at the time of Independence.

Ans. Bureaucracy in some form or the other has existed from times immemorial. In ancient India when monarchy was the predominant form of government, the various categories of courtiers constituted the bureaucracy. Modern bureaucracy in the sense of a body of persons being recruited through an open public competitive examination conducted by an independent, statutory body is credited to People's Republic of China (PRC).

In India, Lord Cornwallis is credited with creating the bureaucracy, as we know it today. The Indian Civil Service (ICS) was the culmination of steps initiated by him. This service as well as branches of colonial bureaucracy, to start with, had Indians only in the lower echelons. They were, in fact, debarred from holding higher positions. From the 1850s onwards, the doors to higher ranks were opened for Indians and many of them made their mark. One can cite names such as that of Netaji Subhash Chandra Bose, K.P.S. Menon Senior, T. N. Kaul among others who distinguished themselves in the ICS. Some of them, in fact, went onto play a crucial role in post-independent India as well.

It should, however, be always remembered that the ICS was essentially a colonial creation designed to serve colonial ends. Though the

Indians in the ICS were occasionally sympathetic to the 'natives' (the Indian masses), by and large they followed the line of their colonial masters. It was for this reason that the nationalist leadership fighting for independence from British rule was highly critical of the role played by the 'steel frame of the British Empire' – the popular name of the ICS (also known as the heaven born service). Jawaharlal Nehru, in particular, was its staunch critic.

The colonial bureaucracy in India largely performed what are called 'maintenance' functions, viz. maintaining law and order, collection of taxes/revenue, etc. The concept of developmental administration was not much heard of then. Fundamentally, the bureaucracy was a policing/tax collecting machinery and very far removed from being a citizen friendly administration. The colonial bureaucracy was repeatedly employed by the British to crush the freedom movement. This was the broad scenario at the time of India's independence.

After attaining freedom from the British rule, the major issue at hand was the type of civilian bureaucracy the newly independent country should have; viz. what kind of structure, method of recruitment and other related questions. There was also the prickly and thorny issue of the fate of the Indian officers in the erstwhile ICS. These matters were resolved the following way; despite their criticism of the ICS, the post-independent leadership decided to let those Indian officers continue in the civilian bureaucracy constituted after August 15, 1947 who still had service years left. However, instead of being absorbed in the newly created Indian Administrative Service (IAS) – the successor to the ICS – quite a few of these officers were directly drafted into the other newly created Central Government service, viz. the IFS (Indian Foreign Service) which was to implement India's non-aligned foreign policy. For instance, KPS Menon Senior and T.N. Kaul joined the foreign service and went onto render distinguished service.

Q28. Write short notes on the following:

(i) Union Public Service Commission (UPSC)

Ans. The Union Public Service Commission (UPSC) is India's central agency authorised to conduct the Civil Services Examination, Engineering Services Examination, Combined Defence Services Examination, National Defence Academy Examination, Naval Academy Examination and Combined Medical Services Examination, Special Class Railway Apprentice, Indian Economic Servce/Indian Statistical Service Examination, Geologists' Examination, Central Armed Police Forces(AC).

The agency's charter is granted by the Constitution of India. Articles 315 to 323 of Part XIV of the constitution, titled Services under the Union and the States, provide for a Public Service Commission for the Union and for each state.

(ii) Special Provisions for Deprived Sections

Ans. It is important to note that as regards recruitment to bureaucratic positions in India, there is provision for reservation of a certain percentage of posts for deprived sections of society. Thus, from the onset of independence, 22.5 per cent of post have been reserved for Scheduled Castes (SCs) and Scheduled Tribes (STs). In addition, since the implementation of the Mandal Commission recommendations, an additional 27 per cent of posts have been reserved for the Other Backward Castes (OBCs).

Also, the various state governments have their own state-wise quotas for government jobs. Some of the Southern Indian States – Karnataka and Tamil Nadu for instance – have always had very high quotas for which there have been historical and socio-political reasons.

(iii) Controversy over the policy of reservation

Ans. The policy of reservation which is based on the principle of affirmative action has been controversial from the beginning. While it has always found favour with the sections for which it is meant, the others have not been too well disposed towards it. While this section somehow reconciled itself towards reservation for the Scheduled Castes and Scheduled Tribes, it found it difficult to accept a similar treatment to the OBCs after the announcement of the Mandal Commission recommendations. This is because it was felt that the OBCs really do not have a history of religion-sanctioned social oppression the way SCs and STs and especially, the SCs have. There is merit in this argument, but as of today, the recommendations have come to stay and the possibility of a change in the *status quo* in extremely remote, if not impossible. In fact, since government jobs are increasingly being reduced in the wake of globalisation, there has been no talk of reserving jobs in the private/corporate sector for the marginalised sections of society. This demand, though not concretised as yet, has further widened the split between those benefited by reservation and those outside the reserved slot.

(iv) State public service commission (SPSC)

Ans. The Royal Commission on the Superior civil Service (popularly known as the Lee Commission) in its report of 1924 categorically argued in favour of the appointment of public service commissions for the states or provinces of India. Unlike the recommendation to have a Union Public Service Commission, the Lee Commission's recommendation to have State Public Service Commissions was remarkably ignored. Instead, the Union Public Service Commission itself was entrusted with the task of recruitment to the provincial civil service.

But the Government of India Act, 1935, in Section 264, provided for the establishment of a public service commission for each province. When the Act came into operation in April 1937, provincial public service commissions were set up in many provinces. Articles 315 to 323 of Part XIV or our Constitution provides for a Public Service Commission for each State. In this connection, it should be mentioned that unlike Britain and the USA, where the civil service commissions are mere creations of the respective legislatures, in India the public service commissions have a constitutional basis and consequently are in a much stronger position. Today, each State has its own Public Service Commission. Regarding recruitment to their services, our Union Territories are helped by the UPSC.

Composition

There is no uniformity regarding the number of members constituting different State Public Service Commissions. The large State of Uttar Pradesh (from the point of view of population) has one Chairman and seven other members while the small State of Assam has one Chairman and only two other members. The Chairman and members of the SPSC are appointed by the Governor on the basis of the advice of the Cabinet. The Constitution makes it clear that at least half the number of members have to be persons who have held office for at least ten years under the Government of India or a State Government.

Each member of the SPSC holds office for a term of six years or until the attainment of the age of sixty years, whichever is earlier. The conditions of service of the members are more or less the same as those of the Union Public Service Commission except that their salary varies from State to State. The expenses of the SPSCs are charged on the consolidated fund of the state.

To ensure the independence of the SPSC, the Constitution debars the Chairman and members from reappointment to the same office. They cannot even undertake any further employment under the Union or the State Government except the chairmanship of any SPSC or the chairmanship or membership of the UPSC. Again, Article 317 provides that the Chairman or any member of the SPSC can be removed from office by the order of the President on the ground of misbehaviour only after the Supreme Court has on inquiry recommended such removal. A Chairman or member would be considered guilty of misbehaviour, if he becomes interested in any government contract or agreement or participates in any way in its profit or in any kind of monetary benefit whatsoever. Article 317 also points out that the President may by order remove the Chairman or any other member if s/he is proved to be an insolvent or is engaged during the term of his/her office in any paid employment or is infirm of body or mind.

Functions

Article 320 or our Constitution prescribes the following functions of the SPSC:

(a) The SPSC shall conduct examinations for appointment to the State service.

(b) If requested by two or more States to assist them in framing and operating schemes of joint recruitment, the SPSC may give its consent. This recruitment is basically meant for services for which candidates possessing special qualifications are required.

(c) The SPSC shall perform any other function in respect with services conferred by the State Legislature.

(d) The SPSC shall give advice on:

  (i) matters relating to methods of recruitment to civil services and civil posts;

  (ii) principles to be followed in making appointments to civil services and posts and in making promotions and transfers from one service to another;

  (iii) all disciplinary matters affecting a person serving under the government of the State in a civil capacity including memorials or petitions relating to such matters;

  (iv) any claim by any person, who is serving or has served under the State Government in a civil capacity; and

  (v) any claim for the award of a pension in respect of injuries sustained by government servants in the discharge of their official duties.

The Governor can make regulations specifying the matters where, either generally or specifically, it will not be necessary for the State

Government to consult the SPSC. Thus, some regulations have been made in Maharashtra decreasing the jurisdiction of the SPSC.

Article 321 empowers the State Legislature to extend the powers of the SPSC by making an Act for the purpose. This provision has been utilised by the Maharashtra Government to extend the powers of the Maharashtra SPSC to the staff of the Secretariat of the Maharashtra State Legislature and certain categories of employees of the Mumbai Municipal Corporation.

In Uttar Pradesh also, certain categories of posts under the Nagar Mahapalikas (municipal corporations) and Zilla Parishads have been brought within the purview of the Uttar Pradesh SPSC.

In performing its tasks, the SPSC takes the assistance of various heads of Departments and other government officials. It also employs suitable persons as examiners, supervisors and invigilators at the examinations conducted by it.

The Chief Minister and the Chief Secretary of any State coordinate the relations of the SPSC with various Departments of the State Government. But in its day-to-day work and statutory responsibilities, it deals directly with the different Departments of the State Government and the various heads of Departments.

According to Article 323, the SPSC submits an annual report on its work to the Governor.

Q29. What do you mean by committed bureaucracy?

Ans. Nehru, India's first Premier believed in a state controlled economy. In his view, civil servants in such a condition were to be neutral participants in the process of development. Later, Premier Indira Gandhi however did not believe in the doctrine of neutrality as it was limited only to giving best to the government of the day. She therefore, advocated the concept of 'committed bureaucracy, which implied belief in the mandate party leaders received from the people. Indira Gandhi wanted a 'committed bureaucracy' and 'committed judiciary' so that these institutions could serve a single party government rather than alternative party governments.

In such a state, the public sector was to create goods and services for society, as it was believed that the private sector would breed inequalities. Thus, India had a highly interventionist state with the private sector being regulated. In such a situation, petty bureaucrats and senior officers became the beneficiaries.

The bureaucratic set up, India had was inherited from the British was efficient and professional. The prestige and standing of the Indian Civil Service (ICS) was exceptional. It was therefore thought that these professional bureaucrats would help in integration and maintenance of law and order in the new state.

However, the ICS, which became Indian Administrative Service (IAS) after Independence continued with its "steel frame" legacy even after Independence. "Steel frame" means that the bureaucracy had immense power to withstand local pressures to maintain law and order. Likewise, bureaucrats considered themselves to be guardians of public interest. It endowed them with a status of superiority and a heaven born status to rule over common masses. The economic strategy implemented after Independence demanded significant bureaucratic reforms as the role of civil servants increased.

During the premiership of Indira Gandhi, the role of the state underwent a dramatic change. Since public sector was dominant and private sector was regulated, bureaucracy became all pervasive. They were unwilling to change and were not influenced by public interest. This made them unresponsive to public needs and demands.

After Independence, the influence of experts and technocrats increased in the bureaucracy. It led to establishment of new research institutes. These may include National Council of Applied Economic Research, Institute of Applied Manpower Research, National Council of Educational Research and Training (NCERT), Indian Institute of Public Administration (IIPA), etc. These institutes are working in close collaboration with Planning Commission to draft, implement and monitor public policy programmes. The need for commitment to public policy programmes has made bureaucracy the backbone of public interest in India. To defend, protect, conserve and promote public policy required a sense of responsibility, commitment and accountability. The search for a committed bureaucracy was, therefore, a necessity.

Q30. Write a short note on the 'Bureaucrat—Politician—Businessman nexus'.

Ans. A parallel – though not always – development was the addition of the businessman to the unholy combine of the politician and the civil servant. In the democratic socialist or the Nehruvian Socialist to be more correct, framework of development that India followed after independence, government permission or licence was required for every small and big thing necessary for setting up a business. The discretionary power rested with the bureaucrat who could grant the licence against favours granted by the concerned businessman or alternatively, withhold the permission on the concerned party's refusal to please the government official. Very often, the bureaucrat and the political boss to whom he reported shared in the spoils, as the ultimate sanctioning authority was the politician. This was the genesis of the notorious 'Licence-Permit-Quota Raj', which in about 20-30 years from independence completely derailed India's socialist pattern of development. The planning process, the mixed economy, all got off track because of the immensely powerful and corrupt troika of the officer-politician-businessman often contemptuously described as the "Babu-Neta-Bania' syndrome.

The ineffective and inefficient mixed economy brought about by the licence-permit-quota raj coupled with the politicisation of the bureaucracy remained the contexts of India's civilian bureaucracy till the onset of globalisation. The globalisation era going back to the 1990s marked another watershed in the world of Indian bureaucracy, just as the 1967 elections had done. It is to this that we turn our attention now.

Q31. What has been the impact of globalisation and liberalisation on the Indian buraucracy?

Ans. The era of globalisation commenced sometime around the mid to the late 1980s. But it was only in the 1990s that it became an official policy of the Government of India. Due to the impact of the liberalisation the monopoly of the Indian state to execute public policies got eroded. Other agencies like the market and civil society organisations emerged important companions of the state. Since bureaucracy is an important segment of the state, erosion in the monopoly of the state also affected it.

Subsequent to the implementation of liberalisation policies, there have been perceptible shifts in the attitude of the bureaucracy. When liberalisation first commenced, a lot of bureaucrats were openly hostile to its as they obviously felt that in a regime of slackening governmental control, the quantum of power wielded by them as well as their importance would come down. This has indeed happened. They have become more transparent and responsive than in the pre-liberalisation era. Apart from end of the state monopoly as the sole policy implementation body, the civil society organisations have played a significant role in this. Especially, the Indian media in the last few years has carried quite a few lead stories on the personal initiatives of the post-90s bureaucrats in the domain of citizen friendly administration. A lot of the comparatively younger bureaucrats have grown up in the new, liberalising India and are, therefore, more amenable to the new ideas of development. However, the change in the nature of bureaucracy is not absolute but it has started.

Q32. Discuss the impact of reservation on Indian bureaucracy.

Ans. India inherited a bureaucracy from the British era, which was elitist in its outlook and social composition. At the time of Independence, Indian bureaucracy consisted largely of the people from the socially and economically privileged background. The ex-untouchable communities like SCs and STs and socially and economically backward classes like the OBCs did not have representation in the initial years of Independence. However, within few years of independence the situation changed. The social composition of Indian bureaucracy came to consist of a large number of SCs and STs. From the 1990s even the OBCs came to form a large section of Indian bureaucracy. It is important to note that in some south Indian states the OBCs recruited into the state bureaucracy since before the independence. This change in the social composition of the Indian bureaucracy occurred due to the policies of reservation introduced for the SCs and STs since the adoption of our Constitution in 1950, and for the OBCs since the 1990s.

Reservation to the OBCs known as the socially and educationally backward classes in the central government jobs and educational institutions was introduced in the 1990s following the implementation of the Mandal Commission Report. The implementation of the reservation for the SCs, STs and OBCs became necessary in order to compensate for the deprivations, which these communities have undergone in the past. The SCs were subjected to untouchability and the STs has suffered due their social and regional isolation. Though the OBCs did not experience untouchability, they were subjected to the other kind's social deprivations and educational backwardness. In order to help their all round development it has become necessary for the state to help them with the policy of affirmative action or protective discrimination. Reservation for them in government jobs and educational institution is one of such policies. It is because of these policies that the composition and nature of Indian bureaucracy has undergone significant changes.

Q33. Discuss some of the controversies/problems associates with the bureaucracy in India.

Ans. The Indian Bureaucracy has had some continuing problems/controversies associated with it from the very beginning. These problems are to be found in bureaucracies worldwide.

Minister versus Civil Servants

The inter-relationship between the political (ministers) and the permanent (government officials) executive in India (as elsewhere) has been complex, to say the least. To a great extent, this is because of the inherent nature of the relationship between the ministers and the civil servants. In any form of government and more so in a democracy, such as India's, the civil servants are subordinate to the ministers. However, this is not always the case. Where the minister is ignorant and incompetent, the officers under him have a field day doing exactly as they please with the minister unable to do a thing. On the other hand, when the minister is powerful the officers are generally too willing to do the minister's bidding; often in contravention of all rules and regulations.

Also, Ministers and bureaucrats in India have often enjoyed a highly mutually beneficial relationship based on a quid pro quo basis; i.e. a relationship based on mutual exchange of favours. The net result of all this has been a highly politicised bureaucracy and this fact, has not changed much even in the post-globalisation era.

Generalists versus Specialists

This again is a controversy that has plagued the bureaucracies the world over. Each country has tried to find its own solution to the problem.

In India, the genesis of the problem can be traced back to the days of Lord Cornwallis who is credited with laying the foundation of the civil services in India. The Britishers needed English knowing Indians and general awareness to man the lower ranks of the bureaucracy. No specialist knowledge was required. This set the precedent for Indians from the pure stream of Arts and Humanities and later on Sciences and Commerce (though not to the same extent) making it to the civil services. Professionals and Specialists (medicos, engineers, etc.) very rarely thought of a career in the bureaucracy. However, this has changed over the years. As governance has become more complex, need has been felt of 'candidates with a more specialised background. This is because civil servants with a generalist background have increasingly been found unequal to the task. The recruiting bodies such as the UPSC have also been encouraging aspirants with a specialist background, viz. medicos, engineers, lawyers, chartered accountants, etc.

The controversy is mainly centred on the fact that one school of opinion holds that a person with a general background (especially in Humanities/Social Sciences) is better suited for the task of civil administration as s/he can take an overall, macro view of the tasks and the issues at hand. The other school, however, holds that in the present globalised era with a lot of emphasis on I.T. (information technology) and on issues of economic and commercial significance, a specialised background is more conducive to effective and productive administration. The solution perhaps lies in effecting a grand mix of the two approaches and in India, this has been attempted. For instance, the department of science and technology has often been headed by professional scientists rather than career bureaucrats, even though one has to mention that the bureaucrats have resented this.

Under-representation of the Minorities

The minorities, especially, the Muslims-India's largest minority – have often complained of their poor representation in the country's premier civil services such as the IAS and the IPS. However, there is no hard core evidence to support that this has been deliberately the case. Poor levels of education and motivation have been a major cause. Solutions such as a separate quota for the minorities have been suggested, but it requires a consensus amongst the political class.

4 Federalism in India

An Overview

Federation is the existence of dual polity. There are two governments in existence, e.g. Government of Federation (in India Union Government) and Government of Unit (in India State Government). These two sets of Government do not subordinate with each other. They cooperate with each other and are independent to each other.

Indian Constitution resembles a federal constitution but in essence, it is not a federal constitution. The unique feature of Indian constitution is the presence of features which are necessary for existence of a federation, at the same time there are provisions which make the Union Government powerful vis-à-vis that of State governments. Hence, Indian constitution can be termed as "Quasi- federal" in nature and Indian Union can be called as "Centralised Federation".

Q1. Explain the concept of federalism.

Ans. Federalism is a type of government in which the power is divided between the national government and other governmental units. It contrasts with a unitary government, in which a central authority holds the power, and a confederation, in which states, for example, are clearly dominant.

While the Constitution addressed only the relationship between the federal government and the states, the American people are under multiple jurisdictions. A person not only pays his or her federal income tax but also may pay state and city income taxes as well. Property taxes are collected by counties and are used to provide law enforcement, build new schools, and maintain local roads.

Throughout the 20th century, the power of the federal government expanded considerably through legislation and court decisions. While much recent political debate has centered on returning power to the states, the relationship between the federal government and the states has been argued over for most of the history of the United States.

Q2. Comment on multiple diversities and nature of a federation.

Ans. It is important to note before Independence India consisted of three different types of regions, i.e., British India, Princely States and Excluded Areas. The British India covered most parts of the country and was under complete rule of the British Crown. The areas under Princely were ruled different 554 Princely States governed by different rulers and rules. The Excluded areas, which form northeast India, were excluded from complete rule of the British Crown. The local traditional leaders were given main role in the administration of these areas with the purpose of protecting their traditions and customs. They were brought together to form a Union of India became Independent of the colonial rule. But at the time of integration these areas inherited different levels of development. The Special Provisions of the Constitution are meant for development of more backward areas in Indian federal structure.

A federation is basically formed on the basis of principles of a contract. It means that the sovereign units-union, states or local units, form a federation on the basis of mutual and voluntary agreement. This kind of voluntary union/federation is possible only in a democratic framework. It also means that the extent of union is limited.

The contracting parties never surrender their complete authority/power. Thus, when two or more sovereign states unite voluntarily, they retain their internal/local autonomy and unite only on matters of common interest. More than a hundred years ago. Therefore, James Bryce declared that 'A federal state is a political contrivance intended to reconcile national unity and power with the maintenance of state rights.

In actual practice, however, not all-federal states have been born through union of sovereign states. Many of them have been products of devolution of powers by a centralised authority of a union government to the lower units. Indian federation is one such example.

The origin of the federal structure of India can be traced back to the colonial period. The Charter of 1833 granted complete authority to the Governor General, who was representative of the East India Company at that time, to look after the affair of the British India. After the transfer of powers to the Queen of England in 1858, he became the representative of the British monarch. The powers of the Governor-General, who later was called Viceroy, defined the nature of the federalism during the colonial time. However, it was the Government of India Act of 1935, which was the first serious attempt to define the nature of federalism in India. The Act of 1935 sought to set up a "Federation of India", explaining the distribution of powers among the Viceroy, the elected provincial governments in the provinces of British India and the princely states. Although the "Federation of India" could not be established because of the reservations of the princely states, an arrangement of sharing of powers between the provincial governments and the Viceroy could be made according to this Act. But the Act provided a limited nature of federalism. The residuary powers were retained by the Viceroy. Besides, the British government had the power to suspend the elected provincial governments.

Q3. Discuss the features of Indian federalism.

Ans. India is a big country characterised by cultural, regional, linguistic and geographical diversities. Such a diverse and vast country cannot be administered and ruled from a single centre. Historically, though India was not a federal state, its various regions enjoyed adequate autonomy from central rule. Keeping in view these factors in mind, the Constitution makers of India opted for the federal form of government.

The Constitution of India displays the following federal features:

(a) The Constitution of India makes the provision for the organisation of two types of governments—the Union Government and the State Governments. The governments at both levels are organised on the basis of Parliamentary System as per the provisions of the Constitution.

(b) The Seventh Schedule of the Constitution makes provision for the division of powers between the Union and the States. It contains three lists:

   (i) The Union List which has 97 subjects of national importance and the Union Parliament has the power to enact laws with respect to these subjects;

   (ii) The State List, which contains 66 subjects of local importance and the State Legislatures have the power to enact laws with respect to these subjects;

   (iii) The Concurrent List, which contains 47 subjects and both the Parliament and State Legislatures can legislate on them. The idea of Concurrent List is inspired by the Constitution of Australia.

(c) As per the requirement of federal system, the Indian Constitution is a written document. It is a rigid Constitution as far as the amendment of federal provisions is concerned.

(d) The Indian Constitution makes provision for an independent and Federal judiciary. The Supreme Court of India acts as a federal court. It has the power to decide the disputes arising either between the Union and the States or between the two or more States under its Original Jurisdiction as mentioned in Article 131 of the Constitution. The Constitution makes various provisions to ensure the independence of judiciary from the Executive and the Legislature both.

Unitary Features of Indian Federation

The unitary features of Indian federation are so striking that a noted scholar Ivor Jennings, has termed it as a 'federation with strong centralising tendencies.' The unitary features of Indian federation are given:

- The Indian federation is an example of 'Indestructible Union with Destructible states.' It means that the Union shall remain intact but the physical existence of states or units can be modified. Accordingly, Article 3 provides that the Parliament may, by law, form the new states by separating or uniting the territory of existing states, increase or diminish the area of any state, and alter the name and boundary of any state. On the other hand, the American federalism is characterised as 'Indestructible Union of Indestructible States'.

- Unlike the American federation, the Indian Constitution provides for a single citizenship. It means that, in India, every person is a citizen of India and they are not entitled for citizenship of any state. The Union Parliament is empowered to enact laws with respect to all matters related to citizenship.
- The Governor of a state, who is the executive head of the state, is appointed by the President and holds office during the pleasure of the President. It should be noted that the Governor is not a nominal head of state, but holds significant powers with respect to the affairs of the state. In fact, the Governor functions as the representative of the Union Government in the state and s/he is not responsible to any authority within the state.
- The provision for single citizenship in India is also considered is the unitary feature of Indian Federalism. In India, every person is a citizen of India.
- Unlike the US Federation, states in India do not have their separate Constitutions. India has a single Constitution, which makes pro vision with respect to both the Union and the States. Also, with the exception of some federal provisions, the states in India do not have any power with respect to the amendment of the Constitution, which is the sole prerogative of the Union Parliament.
- Generally, in federalism, the states or units have equal representation in the second House of Parliament. However, in India, the states do not have equal representation in the Council of States. The representation of states depends on their population; the number of seats allocated to different states is mentioned in the Fourth Schedule of the Constitution. The state of Uttar Pradesh has 31 seats, whereas many states like Nagaland, Manipur, Tripura, etc. have only one seat in the Council of States. For excellent score, read GPH book.

Q4. Write an essay on legislative relations between union and states of India.

Ans. Legislation provides the framework for policy formation and arms the government with the powers to implement the policy. Our constitution provides that every state shall have at least one house, viz. the legislative assembly comprising 66 to 500 members chosen by direct election on the basis of adult suffrage from territorial constituencies. Any state can create a second house, viz. legislative council if it so desires.

This can be done by a resolution of the assembly passed by a special majority (i.e. a majority of total membership of the assembly not being less than two-thirds of the members actually present and voting) followed by an Act of Parliament. By the same process, the existing legislative council can be abolished also. At present, only Bihar, Maharashtra, Karnataka, UP and J&K have two houses.

The Constitution, based on the principle of federalism with a strong and indestructible union, has a scheme of distribution of legislative powers designed to blend the imperatives of diversity with the drive of a common national endeavour.

The Constitution adopts a three-fold distribution of legislative powers by placing them in any of the three lists, namely, Union List, State List and Concurrent List.

The Union List contains subjects of national relevance such as Defence, Atomic Energy, Foreign Affairs, War and Peace, Citizenship, Railways, Income-tax, Excise, etc., over which the Parliament has an exclusive authority to formulate laws.

The State List includes subjects of importance to the States such as Public order, Police, Local Government, Public health, Agriculture, etc., over which the State legislature has an exclusive authority.

The Concurrent List containing subjects of mutual relevance over which both Parliament and State legislatures can legislate but in case of conflict the Union law will prevail.

These include Criminal law and procedure, Family laws, Inter-State trade and Commerce and Communication, Electricity, Newspapers and Books, Education, Stamp duties and so on. Residual powers, like in Canada, but unlike the USA, Australia and Switzerland, are vested in the Parliament.

However, the Union government can legislate on any subject included in the State list, under some specific circumstances:

- If the Rajya Sabha recommends by a two-third majority that such legislation is in national interest;
- If two or more States mutually agree that such a legislation should be made for them;
- In order to implement treaties or international agreements or connections; and
- During the proclamation of emergency made by the President of India, on account of internal disturbance or external

aggression, the Parliament acquires the authority to make laws on all the subjects mentioned in the State List. However, all such laws made by the Parliament become ineffective six months after the Proclamation of Emergency ceases to operate.

- In case of emergency due to the failure of the constitutional machinery in State, the President of India can authorise Parliament to exercise the powers of the State Legislature. All such laws also cease to operate within six months after the Proclamation of Emergency comes to an end.

Article 200 of the Constitution empowers the Governor to reserve a bill passed by the State legislature for consideration by the President of India. This provision has led to a considerable degree of resentment among the State governments, especially due to inordinate delays in communicating the Centre's decision to the State on the bills so reserved.

Article 245 and 246 demarcate the legislative domain, subject to the controlling principle of the supremacy of the Union, which is the basis of the entire system.

Legislative Relations

Distribution of legislative powers described in the VII Schedule of Indian Constitution:

(a) **Union List:** Only Union Parliament is empowered to make laws on the subjects given in the Union List. 98 subjects (after 42nd Constitution Amendment Act, 1976) (few important subjects listed below) Defence, Foreign Relations, Post and Telegraph, International War and Peace, International Trade, Commerce, Citizenship, Coinage, Railway, Reserve Bank, International Debt, Atomic Energy, etc.

(b) **State List:** Only State Legislature is empowered to make laws on the subjects given in the State List. 62 subjects (after 42nd Constitutional Amendment Act, 1976) (few important subjects listed below) Public Health, Roads, Agriculture, Irrigation, Prisons, Local Administration, Distribution of Water, Police, etc.

(c) **Exception:** In the case of Emergency, Union Parliament automatically acquires the power of legislation on the subjects given in the State List

(d) **Concurrent List:** Both, Union Parliament as well as State Legislatures, has the power of legislation on subjects given in the Concurrent List. 52 subjects (After the 42nd Constitutional Amendment Act, 1942) (few important subjects listed below) Marriage, Divorce, News Papers, Trade Unions, Books, Press, Eatable Items, etc.

(e) In case of disagreement, the legislation passed by Union Parliament shall prevail over the law passed by State Legislatures.

(f) **Residuary Powers:** Article 248, Union Parliament shall make laws over the subjects not included in the above given lists. The Indian Constitution gives residuary powers not to the states, but to the Central Government.

Union Parliament's Power to legislate on the Subjects given in the State List:

- On the basis of the resolution passed by the Council of State - Article 249, 2/3 majority, Issues of National Interest.
- On the request of two or more state legislatures -Article 252, Law passed by Union Parliament shall be applicable only to the states, which demanded such legislation.
- Article 253: For the enforcement of International Treaties and Agreements.
- Article 304: Prior approval of President of India on certain Bills.
- Article 352: Supremacy of Union Parliament during National Emergency,
- Article 356: During Constitutional Emergency. Supremacy of Union Parliament over Concurrent List
- Article 248: Residuary Powers are under the control of Union Parliament.
- Article 169: Power of Union Parliament to abolish State Legislative Council.

The Concurrent List gives power to two legislatures, Union as well as State, to legislate on the same subject. In case of conflict or inconsistency, the rule of repugnancy, as contained in Article 254 comes into play to uphold the principle of Union Power. Under this rule, if there is any discrepancy between the State and the Centre over a subject in the Concurrent List, the Union law takes precedence over the state's law.

Problems and prospects of centre state legislative relations

The problems that have attracted attention in the field of Union-State relations have less to do with the need to re-evaluate centre-state relations (state perspective)

- More powers to the state
- Residuary powers to the state
- Reform in the office of Governor
- Not to hold the Bills passed by the State Legislatures
- Delete Articles 356 & 249
- Equal representation of states in council of states (Rajya Sabha)
- Financial Autonomy to States
- Reforms in All India Services
- Participation of states in planning

Q5. Discuss the financial powers of the union and the states.

Ans. No system of federation can be successful unless both the Union and the States have at their disposal adequate financial resources to enable them to discharge their respective responsibilities under the Constitution.

Like the legislative and the executive powers, financial powers are divided between the Union and the states in such a detailed and complicated way that most commentators on the Indian federal system have chosen to use the phrase 'financial relations' rather than 'division of financial power'. This is mainly due to two reasons. Politically speaking the revenues of the Union are far greater than the revenues of the states making the states dependent on federal subsidies. Constitutionally, on the other hand, the Indian Constitution makes a distinction between the power to levy taxes and the power to appropriate them. There is no concurrent jurisdiction in the matter of taxation.

Further, the division of financial powers has been subjected to four amendments; the 3rd (in 1954), the 6th (in 1956), the 46th (in 1982) and the 80th (in 2000). These amendments have enhanced the Union's power to levy taxes but not necessarily to appropriate them. There are three kinds of taxes in the Constitution, as a result:

- Taxes and duties collected and appropriated by the states.
- Taxes and duties collected by the Union on behalf of the states and assigned to them.
- Taxes and duties collected by the Union and distributed among the states according to principles laid down by the Parliament.

Besides these taxes and duties the Union has unlimited power to give grants-in-aid to the states.

The States impose land revenue, agricultural income tax, succession duties and estate duty on agricultural land, taxes on lands and buildings, taxes on mineral rights subject to any limitations imposed by Parliament by law relating to mineral development, excise duties on alcoholic liquors, opium, Indian hemp for non-medicinal purpose, taxes on entry of goods for consumption and sales, taxes on consumption and sale of electricity, sales tax on goods other than newspapers exchanged within the State, taxes on advertisements except those on newspapers, radio or television, taxes on goods transported by roads or inland waterways and vehicles on road, taxes on animals and boats, tolls, taxes on professions, trades, callings and employments, capitation taxes, taxes in luxuries, amusements, betting and gambling and fees in respect of any of the matters in the State List.

The net proceeds of taxes and duties that the Union levies, after being distributed among the states as above, all loans received by the Union and all its receipts in repayment of loans from the Consolidated Fund of India. All revenues, loans and receipts in repayment of loans by a state government form the Consolidated Fund of the State.

Such stamp duties and such duties of excise on medicinal and toilet preparations as are mentioned in the Union list are levied by the Union government but collected and appropriated by the states (Art. 268).

Taxes on sale and purchase of goods other than newspapers and taxes on consignment of goods, where such sale or purchase or consignment takes place in course of inter-State trade and commerce, shall be levied and collected by the Union but assigned to the states according to the principles of distribution formulated by the Parliament (Art. 269).

The other taxes and duties allowed under the Union list-tax on non-agricultural incomes, customs including export duties, excise duty on tobacco and medicinal and toilet preparations containing alcohol, opium and narcotic drugs, corporation tax, taxes on capital value of non-agricultural assets of individuals and companies and capital of companies, estate and succession duties on property other than agricultural land, terminal taxes on goods or passengers carried by railways, sea or air, taxes on railway fares and freights, taxes other than stamp duties on transactions in stock exchanges and futures market—are levied and collected by the Union. A percentage of their proceeds will go to the Union government according to the order of the President (i.e., the Union government) after considering the recommendations of the Finance Commission. The rest will be distributed among the states according to the prescription of the President after considering the recommendations of the Finance Commission (Art. 270).

This leaves the Union with the power to charge fees on any matter relating to the subjects in the Union list for its wholesale appropriation.

Stamp duties other than duties and fees collected by means of judicial stamps and fees imposed on the subjects included in the Concurrent List but not including fees taken in any court are collected concurrently. Taxes on the residual, subjects are exclusively under the Union's jurisdiction.

At the same time, the property of the Union and the purchase and storage of water and electricity by the Union are free from taxation of a state. The property and income of a state is, on the other hand, free from Union taxation. Any tax imposed by a state on a Union property before the commencement of the Constitution would continue to be collected by the state until the Parliament otherwise provides. Further, Parliament, by law, may provide for imposition of tax on a trade or business carried on by a state.

There is a special provision for grant in lieu of export of jute to the states of Assam, Bihar, Orissa and West Bengal (Article 273). All other grants-in-aid are governed by Article 275.

Q6. Discuss the functions of the finance commission.

Ans. Functions of the Finance Commission can be explicitly stated as:

- Distribution of net proceeds of taxes between Centre and the States, to be divided as per their respective contributions to the taxes.
- Determine factors governing Grants-in Aid to the states and the magnitude of the same.
- To make recommendations to president as to the measures needed to augment the Consolidated Fund of a State to supplement the resources of the panchayats and municipalities in the state on the basis of the recommendations made by the Finance Commission of the state.

The President causes the recommendations to be presented to the Parliament (Art. 281). It should, however, be noted that the recommendations are not mandatory. The President, that is, the Union government, is the final authority to decide on such recommendations.

Q7. What do you understand by the planning commission and national development council?

Ans. Unlike the Finance Commission, the Planning Commission is not a statutory body. It was set up by a formal resolution of the Union Cabinet in March 1950. The Planning Commission plays an important role in the formulation of India's economic policies. The Prime Minister is the chairman of the Planning Commission. Some of the important members of the Planning Commission are Union Council of Ministers, Cabinet Secretary and other distinguished persons. It is an extra - constitutional agency and works as an advisory body. It is responsible for the Five Year Plans of the country.

The plans finalised by the Planning Commission are discussed by the National Development Council (NDC). It is the highest reviewing and advisory body in the field of planning. It was constituted in 1952. The member of the NDC are Prime Minister, Chief Ministers of all states, members of Planning Commission and all Union cabinet ministers. It is an intermediary body between the Union, state and local government. Five Year Plans become operational after the approval of the NDC.

Q8. Write short notes on the following:

(i) Article 370 regarding Jammu and Kashmir

Ans. No law passed by the Parliament regarding the state of Jammu and Kashmir can be applied to the state without the Order of President of India in concurrence of the state government. No such conditions exist in the case of other states. In the original Constitution of Jammu and Kashmir, the provisions of Article 370 were described as "temporary" measures. Under the agreement of 1975 signed between Shiekh Abdullah and Indira Gandhi it was agreed upon that Abdullah will give up the demand for plebiscite and special status of Jammu and Kashmir will continue; it would no longer remain a temporary measure. But the agreement could not be implemented owing to the differences and the Order of the President could not be issue. Jammu and Kashmir is the only state in the county having a Constitution of its own within the framework of Indian Union. The important provisions of the Constitution of Jammu and Kashmir can be summarised as follows:

- Territory of Jammu and Kashmir consists of all those areas, which were under the sovereignty of erstwhile ruler. These areas include that territory which is at present under the occupation of Pakistan.
- Out of 123 assembly seats of Jammu and Kashmir, 25 allotted to the Pakistan-occupied portion of Kashmir, remain vacant because the situation is unsuitable for the election there;
- Though the executive and legislative powers of the State government cover the entire state, yet these powers do not apply to those areas, which come under the jurisdiction of Parliament;

- The "permanent residents" of Jammu and Kashmir enjoy all rights, which are guaranteed in the Constitution of the Country.
- A majority of not less than two-thirds of the members of the house can amend the Constitution by passing a bill. But the bill cannot make the changes in provisions relating to the relationship between the state and the Union.

(ii) The VI schedule for the North-East

Ans. The North-Eastern region inhabits 12 per cent of the country's 8.4 crore tribal population and has borders with Bhutan, China, Myanmar and Bangladesh.

According to Article 244 of the Constitution the VI Schedule lays down special provisions for the protection of the interest and cultural identities of the hill tribes of North. The most important provision of the VI Schedule is creation of the Autonomous District Councils. While tribal of some of the North-Eastern states have the Autonomous District Councils, Arunachal Pradesh, Nagaland and greater part of Mizoram do not have this. The Inner Lines Regulation exists for three states, i.e., Arunachal Pradesh, Mizoram and Nagaland, and North Cachar district of Assam.

The modern institution of the Autonomous District Councils are elected bodies. They are controlled by the new generation which has benefited from modern means of education. This placed the new elite in confrontation with the traditional elite who have considered it as an encroachment on their position. In fact, they have been demanding its abrogation. Also a section of the non- tribals have been seeking the removal of the Autonomous District Councils. They argue that the VI Schedule was introduced to protect the interests of the tribals while they would be constituents of Assam. But with the formation of separate states there was no need for the Autonomous District Councils. Besides, there is no clear demarcation of the jurisdiction of the ADCs, which result in overlapping of the jurisdiction of the ADCs, state legislature and the village councils. This causes inconvenience to the people.

Since the British days a system of Inner Line was drawn up under the Bengal Eastern Frontier Regulation, 1873. It prohibits the travel of outsiders into the area beyond the Inner Line without the government's permission. Aimed primarily at protecting the people of the covered area from the exploitation of the plainsmen, this also preserved the British control there and hindered the integration of the people of the hills and plains. The Inner Line is a subject of hot controversy in northeast India.

(iii) The V schedule for scheduled areas

Ans. The main provisions of this schedule are:

PART A

General

(a) Interpretation: In this Schedule, unless the context otherwise requires, the expression "State" does not include the {States of Assam, Meghalaya, Tripura and Mizoram}.

(b) Executive power of a State in Scheduled Areas: Subject to the provision of this Schedule, the executive power of a State extends to the Scheduled Areas therein.

(c) Report by the Governor to the President regarding the administration of Scheduled Areas: The Governor of each State having Scheduled Areas therein shall annually, or whenever so required by the President, make a report to the President regarding the administration of the Scheduled Areas in that State and the executive power of the Union shall extend to the giving of directions to the State as to the administration of the said areas.

PART B

Administration and Control of Scheduled Areas and Scheduled Tribes

(d) Tribes Advisory Council:

- There shall be established in each State having Scheduled Areas therein and, if the President so directs, also in any State having Scheduled Tribes but not Scheduled Areas therein, a Tribes Advisory Council consisting of not more than twenty members of whom, as nearly as may be, three-fourths shall be the representatives of the Scheduled Tribes in the Legislative Assembly of the State:
  Provided that if the number of representatives of the Scheduled Tribes in the Legislative Assembly of the State is less than the number of seats in the Tribes Advisory Council to be filled by such representatives, the remaining seats shall be filled by other members of those tribes.
- It shall be the duty of the Tribes Advisory Council to advise on such matters pertaining to the welfare and advancement of the Scheduled Tribes in the State as may be referred to them by the Governor.
- The Governor may make rules prescribing or regulating, as the case may be- (I) the number of members of the Council, the mode of their appointment and the appointment of the

Chairman of the Council and of the officers and servants thereof; (II) the conduct of its meetings and its procedure in general; and (III) all other incidental matters.

(e) Law applicable to Scheduled Areas:

- Notwithstanding anything in this Constitution, the Governor may by public notification direct that any particular Act of Parliament or of the Legislature of the State shall not apply to a Scheduled Area or any part thereof in the State or shall apply to a Scheduled Area or any part thereof in the State subject to such exceptions and modifications as he may specify in the notification and any direction given under this sub-paragraph may be given so as to have retrospective effect.
- The Governor may make regulations for the peace and good government of any area in a State, which is for the time being a Scheduled Area.

  In particular and without prejudice to the generality of the foregoing power, such regulations may—

  (I) prohibit or restrict the transfer of land by or among members of the Scheduled Tribes in such area;

  (II) regulate the allotment of land to members of the Scheduled Tribes in such area;

  (III) regulate the carrying on of business as money-lender by persons who lend money to members of the Scheduled Tribes in such area.
- In making any such regulation as is referred to in sub-paragraph (ii) of this paragraph, the Governor may repeal or amend any Act of Parliament or of the Legislature of the State or any existing law which is for the time being applicable to the area in question.
- All regulations made under this paragraph shall be submitted forthwith to the President and, until assented to by him, shall have no effect.
- No regulation shall be made under this paragraph unless the Governor making the regulation has, in the case where there is a Tribes Advisory Council for the State, consulted such Council.

PART C

Scheduled Areas

(f) Scheduled Areas:

- In this Constitution, the expression "Scheduled Areas" means such areas as the President may by order declare to be Scheduled Areas.

- The President may at any time by order—
  - (I) direct that the whole or any specified part of a Scheduled Area shall cease to be a Scheduled Area or a part of such an area;
  - (II) increase the area of any Scheduled Area in a State after consultation with the Governor of that State;
  - (III) alter, but only by way of rectification of boundaries, any Scheduled Area;
  - (IV) on any alteration of the boundaries of a State or on the admission into the Union or the establishment of a new State, declare any territory not previously included in any State to be, or to form part of, a Scheduled Area;
  - (V) rescind, in relation to any State or States, any order or orders made under this paragraph, and in consultation with the Governor of the State concerned, make fresh orders redefining the areas which are to be Scheduled Areas; and any such order may contain such incidental and consequential provisions as appear to the President to be necessary and proper, but save as aforesaid, the order made under sub-paragraph (i) of this paragraph shall not be varied by any subsequent order.

PART D

Amendment of the Schedule

(g) Amendment of the Schedule –

- Parliament may from time to time by law amend by way of addition, variation or repeal any of the provisions of this Schedule and, when the Schedule is so amended, any reference to this Schedule in this Constitution shall be construed as a reference to such Schedule as so amended.
- No such law as is mentioned in sub-paragraph (i) of this paragraph shall be deemed to be an amendment of this Constitution for the purposes of article 368.

Q9. Why the Indian constitution makers provides Special provisions for:

(a) Jammu and Kashmir

Ans. Jammu and Kashmir is a constituent State of the Indian Union. It is included in the list of the States of the first Schedule of the Constitution of India. It is the only State in the Indian Union with a Muslim Majority. The

State was acceded to the Dominion of India by Maharaja Hari Singh, who was the ruler of the State in 1947 at the time when India was itself burning in the flames of communal riots. The internal position of the Jammu and Kashmir, was also not far better than India. Communal disturbances and hunger for power in the sub-continent were provocating the religious feelings of community in order to fulfil their long awaited desire to assume political supremacy. The division of the sub-continent on the basis of the religion was creating hindrances in achieving the very objective of "Independence".

Owing to the internal conditions, Maharaja Hari Singh was himself in a dilemma and, therefore, was not in position to take a decision with regard to accession of the state with either of the Dominion-India or Pakistan.

The public opinion of the state was not yet ripe, the invaders spread havoc among the innocent and unarmed people mostly Muslims. The state was helpless. The life and the honour of the people was at stake. Therefore, the great emergency existent in the state perhaps prompted the Maharaja and the leaders of National Conference to appeal to India for urgent help. And later on under these circumstances, the state acceded to the Dominion of India.

After partition of Indian sub-continent, the maintenance of "Unity and Integrity" was the greatest problem. Besides this, State of Jammu and Kashmir was also passing through a phase of grave crisis, therefore, it was necessary that the administration of the state be geared to these unusual conditions until normal life was restored. That is why, the Framers of the Indian Constitution, made some special provisions with respect to the state of Jammu and Kashmir to meet the unique situation.

(b) The North-East

Ans. The VI Schedule of the Constitution of India created Autonomous Districts within Assam in order to preserve tribal autonomy and protect the cultural and economic interests of the hill tribes. The hill regions of North - East India have a history of being governed by different criterion in comparison to the rest of India. While most of India with the exception of the princely states was governed by the standard colonial administration, the hill regions of Assam were ruled by the British indirectly. The British did not interfere with their traditional system of authority. The issues relating to land, inheritance, forest, dispute resolutions, etc., were dealt with according to the customary laws, and through the arbitration of clan and tribal chiefs. They were declared "backward areas" according to the Government of India Act, 1919. The Government of India Act, 1935 turned them into, "excluded" and "partially excluded" areas. There was some difference between the "excluded" and "partially excluded" areas. The former were not represented in the legislature of Assam, though they were located in the province of Assam. The "partially excluded" areas were privileged to have some legislative experience within the state of Assam. The "excluded areas" were administered by the Governor-in- Council as his " reserved" jurisdiction. On the "partially excluded" areas there was some authority of the provincial legislature. Jurisdiction of the courts of British India was limited in such areas.

The British India government placed the hill region of Assam in the "excluded' category because of the expediency of their policy-orientation. Finding the cost of administration not being compensated by the revenue returns, the British found it more expedient not spend on running the administration of this region. Rather the hills were left to be governed by their traditional rule, which did not cost them anything. Besides, the people in this area had been averse to the notion of any outsider ruling over them. Any intrusion or its apprehension into their affairs was met with opposition and hostility.

In order to retain their distinctness, the British mooted a plan to bring all areas of the North-East along with hills of Burma under a "Crown Colony". The plan to create a "Crown colony" was a secret plan and was known as the "Coupland Plan" named after -Reginald Coupland. This suggestion was rejected by the Indian National Congress. But the need to retain the distinctness of this region was recognised by providing special provisions regarding their governance. These provisions were included on the basis of the recommendations of the North-East Frontier (Assam), Tribal and Excluded Area Sub-Committee of the Advisory Committee of the Constituent Assembly of India. The sub-committee was known as Bordoloi sub-committee named after its chairman Gopinath Bordoloi, a member of the Constituent Assembly, and the then Prime Minister of Assam.

The main recommendation of Bordoloi Sub-committee was establishment of the Autonomous District Councils and Regional Councils in for the tribal areas within the state of Assam. With the commencement of the Constitution on January 26, 1950, Autonomous District Councils came into existence in the hill districts of Assam except the Naga Hills (suffering from the separatist violence) and extremely backward Frontier Tracts. After the reorganisation of North-East India there was a restructuring of the District Councils. In 1984, the VI Schedule was extended to Tripura.

(c) The Scheduled Areas

Ans. India has a composite population. The Indian society lacks homogeneity in sop for as there exist numerous religious, cultural and linguistic groups. There are Hindus, Muslims, Christians, Sikhs, Buddhists, Jains and others. The pattern of culture vary from place to place. There are Anglo Indian based on racial religious and linguistic factors. Besides there are sections of people like the Scheduled Castes, The Scheduled Tribes and other backward classes who not only need protection from exploitation but even positive help from the state for amelioration of their miserable lot. Even before India became independent, there was a demand from many of the weaker sections of society for special provisions in the Constitution for the benefit of weaker sections based on the promise that these sections had been socially and economically discriminated against during the British times and therefore special steps were called for to help and improve the condition of these people vis a vis the forward communities. The framers of the Constitution tried level best to safeguard the interest of the various minority groups whether based on religion or language, culture or socio-economic factors so as to give them a sense of security. The scheduled tribes who predominate in certain areas of the country like the North-Eastern region, the large parts of Madhya Pradesh, Bihar, Orissa and certain parts of Gujrat and the hilly regions of most states are those sections of the Indian population who still live in their tribal ways and observe their own peculiar customs and cultural norms. Their primitive way of nomadic habits, love for drink and dance, and habitation in remote and inaccessible areas, less affected by the forces of modernisation, required special treatment from the framers of our Constitution in order to improve their economic and social position. Hence, special provisions were for the development of these tribal groups made and they were classified as scheduled.

Q10. Analyse the politics related to the special provisions.

Ans. Despite the existence of special provisions for different areas, there has been dissatisfaction on their relevance or inefficiency in almost all such regions of the country where such provisions exist. Some oppose these provisions describing them to be inadequate, others oppose them as unnecessary and volatile of the minority rights.

Jammu and Kashmir

The accession of Jammu and Kashmir was opposed by the pro-Pakistan forces known as the "Plebiscite Front". Sheikh Abdullah also joined the movement of "Plebiscite Front". He was incarcerated from 1955 and released in 1964. But he was arrested again in 1965, and externed from the state in 1971. He was released in 1975 following an agreement between Sheikh Abdullah and Indira Gandhi; the "Plebiscite Front" and the Union government. The National Conference led by his son Farooq Abdullah has been demanding that in case of Jammu and Kashmir the pre - 1953 position be restored. That means the central government should have jurisdiction on only three subjects, which were mentioned in the Instrument of Accession-Defence, Communication and Foreign Affairs. Recently the Jammu and Kashmir Legislative Assembly passed a resolution demanding autonomy of the state. This resolution has been rejected by the central government led by the NDA, of which the BJP is the largest party and National Conference is a partner. The BJP is opposed to the continuance of the Article 370.

North-East India

Similarly there are reservations on the VI Schedule from various quarters. In fact, Naga separatists had refused to accept the VI Schedule, as they thought that the VI Schedule was an instrument of the integration of their district with India and Assam.

The introduction of the Autonomous District Councils weakened the position of the erstwhile ruling chiefs of the tribal society. The District Councils are controlled by the new generation of leadership. Therefore, the opposition to the Councils came from them. Thirdly, there are people who feel that the Autonomous District Councils are constrained by limitations; their position should be strengthened. There is overlapping of the jurisdiction of the District Councils, village Councils and the state government. These bodies are also being accused as breeding ground for corruption. Autonomous District Councils are primarily representative bodies, which have legislative power over certain issues like management of unreserved forests, inheritance of property, marriage and social customs, and Governor may. Confer upon these Councils power to try certain suits or offences. The Councils have power to assess and collect land revenue and to impose certain taxes which are specified. It is obligation to get the assent of the Governor for the laws made by the Councils. The non-tribals consider these bodies to be unnecessary. They allege that these are being used by the tribal vested interests to harass them. A large section of them want their abrogation.

Q11. Describe the factors that led to new debates in Union-State relations after the 1967 elections.

Ans. The system of centre's pre-domination and process of centralisation worked without much difficulty or opposition till there was one party's rule at the Centre and in almost all the states and Congress was controlled by a set of leaders who because of their role in the freedom struggle were respected as national leaders. There was also expectation among masses of fulfilment of their hopes of development. From the mid 1960s; however, situation started changing. The charismatic leaders started disappearing from the scene. The planned development's failure to fulfil people's aspiration started becoming clear. There had emerged a powerful middle class with varying political ambitions and conflicting economic interests. As a result of introduction of democracy some land reforms and agricultural development there also rose a rich farmer class interested in protection of their interests at State level.

All this culminated in the change of party system. The Congress started losing its image as a nationalist movement. In addition to the so-called national parties becoming faction-ridden there also emerged new regional parties. In 1967 general elections Congress not only became weak at the central level but also did get the majority party in eight states. With this came up a new debate on Union-state relations. The Non-Congress governments in States, were not prepared to blindly accept the dictates of the centre. Some state governments like those of Kerala, West Bengal and Tamil Nadu, in particular emphasised the need for maintaining intact the principle of state autonomy. The victories on non-Congress parties in several states also intensified factional disputes within Congress and therefore questioning of the control by central leadership.

To begin with debate on union-State relations was limited. By 1972, the Congress party and the Union government regained their predominance. However, the situation was not as before 1967. Now the process of centralisation became more severe.

The Central government adopted increasingly interventionist practices in the States. Not only a more centralised but also personalised process was set in. From 1977 onwards with the change in parties in power and coming of coalition governments at the central level there had been emerging new debates and processes in Union-State relations. But in general, inspite of challenges and new developments. Union governments have continued with the idea of predominance of centre, its right to intervene in State's affairs and misuse of the office of governor and power to impose President's rule. Thus, the general trend has been that of centre encroaching steadily upon the state's domain. This increasing centralisation and intervention of the central government has caused some major tension areas in Union-State relations.

Q12. Discuss the role of Governor which has become a substantial issue of tension between the Centre and states?

Ans. Though the Governor is the executive head of the State and a part of the State Legislature and the administration of the State is carried on in his name, the people of the State or their representatives have no say in the matter of his appointment. While the President is elected by the representatives of the people, namely, the Members of Parliament and the Members of the State Legislatures, the Governor is merely appointed by the President which really means, by the Union Council of Ministers.

Governor has been described as the linchpin of the constitutional apparatus of the State having key role in Union-State relations. The Constitution empowers the Centre to appoint Governors in states to work as Centre's representative and to maintain co-ordination between the Centre and the States. However, in practice, the position and role of Governor has become a substantial issue of tension between the Centre and the States.

Appointment of Governor

The starting point of tension between Union government and states with regard to office of Governor is that centre appoints the Governor as if s/he was just a representative of the centre in the State. In fact ruling part)' at Centre has found the office of Governor as an effective instrument to recapture power for itself. The result is, as Soli Sorabjee puts "It will not be an exaggeration to say that no institution or constitutional office has suffered greater erosion or degradation than the office of the Governor". To make sure that Governors act on behalf of the Central Government the trend of appointing Governor after consulting State Chief Ministers has also been relegated. At present there are some pressures for following this tradition or consulting the Chief Minister before appointing the Governor of that State. So far, it seems, that the Union Government has followed no particular principle and there is no fixed criterion for the appointment of Governors.

The Sarkaria Commission in its report has suggested that a person to be appointed as Governor should satisfy the following criteria; he should be eminent in some walk of life, he should be a person from outside the State, he should not be intimately connected with the local politics of the State and he should be a person who has not taken too great a part in politics generally, and particularly in the recent past. However, even after the submission of the report of the Sarkaria Commission the Governors continue to be appointed from the active politicians of the ruling party and without prior consultation with the Chief Ministers.

Discretionary Powers of Governor

Apart from the normal functions, which the Governor exercises as a constitutional head, he exercises certain discretionary powers. Some of them have been expressly conferred on him while some others flow by necessary implication. As far as the discretionary powers by implication are concerned, these are significant particularly in three matters. One is with regard to the appointment of Chief Minister when neither a single party nor a combination of parties emerges from the election with a clear majority. Related to this is also the question of dismissal of Chief Minister on the loss of majority support or otherwise. The second matter is with regard to making a report to President under Article 356 about his satisfaction that a situation has arisen in which the Government of the State cannot be carried on in accordance with the provisions of the Constitution, thereby recommending the imposition of President's rule. The issue of proclamation of Presidents Rule itself has become a matter of serious tension between union and state governments. The third power is with regard to reservation of bills for the consideration of President.

Reservation of Bills for Consideration of President

Article 200 of the Constitution provides that certain types of bills passed by the State legislature may be reserved by the Governor for the consideration of the President. The President may either give his assent or may direct the Governor to send it back for reconsideration by the State legislature along with his comments. But even after the bill has been passed by the State legislature for the second time the President is not bound to give his assent.

The main purpose of this provision is that the Centre can keep watch on the legislation in the national interest. But Governors, and through them the central Government have used this provision to serve the partisan interests The opposition ruled States have from time to time raised a hue and cry against the misuse of these provisions. This has specially been so in case where the Governor has reserved a bill against the advice of the State Ministry, presumably under the direction of the Central Government. In its memorandum to Sarkaria Commission, the Bharatiya Janata Party alleged that the bills have been reserved for consideration of the President in order to create difficulties for the State governments. The West Bengal government in its reply to the Sarkaria Commission's questionnaire felt that Articles 200 and 201 either should be deleted or Constitution should clarify that the Governor would not act in his discretion but only on the advice of the State Council of Ministers. At the opposition party's conclave held at Srinagar in 1983. The opposition parties demanded that legislatures should be empowered to enact laws on subjects for which they constitutionally have responsibility without having to seek the President's assent. In recent years with regional parties having gained importance and playing an important part in tile connation and continuation of Central Governments the Governors are not using this power extensively. Nevertheless the issue remains one of contention in Union-State relations.

Q13. How have powers under article 356 been misused by central government?

Or

Make a note on Article 356.

Ans. In the Indian Constitution, Article 356 has been used and misused the most number of times. The Article relates to the dismissal of a State Government by the Centre if it feels that there is total anarchy in the State. However, more often than not, it has been misused when the State Government and the Central Government have belonged to different parties. In this regard, two very important questions arise:

- Should Article 356 be deleted?
- If it is retained, should it be in its original form or should amendments be made?

After a lot of debate, the framers of the Constitution decided that there should be an Article enabling the imposition of President's rule if there was a breakdown of constitutional machinery or where the Government was not carrying out its functions in accordance with the Constitution. In fact, B. R. Ambedkar had said in the Constituent Assembly that it should be used as a last resort and hoped that it would be a dead letter. Article 356 has been used over 100 times, mostly for purposes other than what it was intended for. The powers have often been used by obliging Governors to achieve the ulterior motives of the ruling party at the Centre, which seeks to obtain power in that state, striking at the root of the federal system.

As the root cause lies in the conduct of Governors, who sometimes behave like stooges of the Central Government, the remedy lies in amending the provisions of the Constitution relating to their appointment. Instead of vesting powers for appointing Governors with the Union Government, they should be appointed by an independent committee comprising the Speaker, the Prime Minister, the Leader of the Opposition and the Chief Justice of India. If there really is a breakdown of the constitutional machinery of the State, should the people of that State remain helpless? Any government can flout norms and there may be a virtual dictatorship in the State. It is, therefore, the binding duty of the Centre in such instances to ensure that constitutional normalcy is restored in the State. The demand that Article 356 be deleted, therefore, finds no validity.

The next question is if Article 356 is to be retained, should there be amendments to it? It is true that the expressions "Carrying in accordance with the provisions of the constitution" and "Failure in Constitutional machinery" do not permit a precise definition. At the same time, it is difficult to envisage all the circumstances that lead to the failure of the Constitutional machinery or the ways adopted by the State machinery to circumvent provisions of the Constitution. It is, therefore, better to leave the expressions as they are to decide in each case whether there is a failure of the Constitutional machinery or whether the State is unable to carry on in accordance with the Constitutional machinery.

In 1959, Kerala's first-ever Left Government was dismissed invoking Article 356, a questionable promulgation attributed to the then Congress President, Mrs. Indira Gandhi. Ever since, it has ushered new controversies and strains in Centre-State relationship. Yet a clear pattern can be seen emerging out of its usage over the years, leading to some of the following premises:

- It has been freely used to topple politically inconvenient State Governments, and not used even once to dismiss any government that belongs to the same party as the one ruling at the Centre.
- It has been used with fanfare to dismiss State Governments formed by opposition parties following General Elections.
- It has been decisively used to stem excessive violence, terrorist or social, or to end prolonged disturbance.

The State Governments can only oppose the imposition of Article 356 on the first two premises, but they have no locus standing to oppose its imposition in the third.

In spite of occasional grumbling against Article 356, no political party has called for its repeal. There are proposals to circumscribe it, to stave off any wrongful imposition, but that in no way should dilute or take away its uniqueness. The greatest safeguard against unjustified imposition of President's rule is a watchful and impartial President. This proved true when Article 356 was sought to be imposed in Bihar, but could not be done due to the prudent decision of the President K.R. Narayanan.

Q14. What are the areas of conflict between Union and State government on issue of grants?

Ans. For devolution of funds from the Centre to the States, there are four methods: (i) obligatory sharing of Union taxes on income; (ii) permissive sharing of Union excise duties; (iii) assignment of certain Union duties and taxes wholly to the States; (iv) provision for giving financial assistance to the States in the form of grants and loans. With regard to sharing of resources and assignment of certain resources entirely to the States, Articles 280 and 281 provide for the appointment of an independent statutory Finance Commission every fifth year or earlier as the President of India desires. The provision for Finance Commission was in order to regulate, co-ordinate and integrate the finances of the Government of India and the State Governments. Originally, the Finance Commission was intended to cover all the financial transfers from the Centre to States. However, slowly the Planning Commission has also been brought in for the purpose and now it plays a rather important part in devolution of resources from the Centre to the States. Since the Planning commission is a completely central institution and is politically influenced the States have a sense of discrimination in allocation of grants. In addition, provision for grants-in-aid by the Centre is purely a political and arbitrary means of devolution and Centre has been making use of this more and more and that too in a controversial manner.

Centre gives grants-in-aid to States under Article 281 on its discretion for undertaking schemes, meeting natural calamities or for removal of disparities etc. There is a general feeling that the Centre discriminates between States being ruled by different political parties. H.A. Ghani points out that a close scrutiny of the Central relief to the States affected by natural calamities indicates that no well-considered norms were followed in this regard. The central teams pre-occupied by political considerations have always assessed the damage done by droughts, flood, etc. in an adhoc perfunctory manner.

The States, therefore, have sharply questioned the need for the Centre to wield heavy financial clout in the shape of discretionary grants. There are misgivings about the inherent danger of their being used as a political weapon against a State that happen to be out favour with the centre. The States want more resources to be earmarked for statutory devolution so that the trend of increasing allocations through discretionary grants can be curbed.

Q15. How has planning become an area of tension between centre and state?

Ans. It is generally agreed that the process of planning in India has tended to push the political system to greater centralisation due to both the central control over resources for development and the preponderance of the centralised planning machinery. R.K. Hedge points out that the gravest and most harmful consequence of the atrophy of the State's domain in the economic field is in regard to industries and economic planning. For example, the scheme of the Constitution is perfectly clear that industries are essentially a state subject. Only those industries are to be regulated by the centre the control of which by the Union is declared as expedient in the public interest by Parliament. But without an amendment to the constitution industries have been virtually transferred into a Union subject. More that 90 per cent of the organised industries in terms of value put have been brought under the domain of the Union. In practice, the regulation of industrial activity by the Union government has on several occasions inhibited the setting up of new industries. Similarly, it is alleged that in the name of national planning, the Centre for political considerations, has been inordinately delaying viable and important State projects. On the contrary, Centre has been super imposing its schemes on the States which were deemed by State governments to be irrelevant to the conditions prevailing in the State. Owing to this and other reasons the opposition conclave held at Srinagar in October 1983 in a consensus statement said that the present authority of the Planning Commission and Union Ministry of Finance who offer discretionary grants to the States must be drastically reduced.

Q16. Write an essay on Indian Federalism and State autonomy.

Ans. Sixty-three years of Independence have witnessed tremendous changes and there is immediate need to have a fresh look in an introspective spirit at the Centre State relations both in the context of various recommendations of the Sarkaria Commission and formation of three more new states in recent years.

India, as a nation, has been undergoing a radical transformation unprecedented in its scale, sweep and intensity, during the last one-decade since the launching of the package of new economic reforms in mid-1991.

Structural arrangements and clearly defined norms and procedures embodied in the Constitution have provided the guidelines for Indian fledging federalism but it is in the operating dynamics of Centre- State relationship than one sees the true nature of Indian federal equation at three operating levels, viz. political, constitutional and procedural.

The political or politico-constitutional pendulum of Indian federal system has been relentlessly swinging towards a strong Centre for the last five decades and India has become what K. Santhanam called "Centre

Paramount Federation" in view of the paramount need to maintain the unity and integrity of India.

All is not well with the present federal system. Empirical evidence exists to prove that the Union vested with enormous finance powers might use financial leverage to starve the states governed by political parties of other complexion and hue.

There is a need to devise a permanent mechanism, which would ensure a better sharing of economic cake so that the states do not become the perpetual wards of the Centre economically. Recent rise of regionalism cannot be viewed as a threat to our federal system but as a reaction against over-centralisation and demand for a more balanced development of the various states.

The Union and State relations can be made more stable and fair only when the political parties and the people are actively involved at all levels. Union-state relations can be improved when there is greater co-operation and co-ordination between the two for good and effective governance.

Tension Areas of Union-State Relations

Appointment of governors, allocation of resources from Centre to States, deployment of Central Police Forces and imposition of President's rule in the States are some of the main irritants in Centre-State relations. Governors are increasingly becoming constitutional redundancies and are perceived as the whipping boys of the Union Government, doing a command performance wherever different parties are ruling at the Centre and state levels.

Demands of the States

Though the problem is generally termed 'Union-State relationship', there is no unanimity among the States on many issues and hence the dispute is not between Union government on one side and the several State governments on the other.

The non-Congress Chief Ministers held a series of conclaves through the 1980s in Vijayawada, Calcutta and Srinagar, while a proposed conclave in Amritsar was overtaken by the spread of terrorism in the State.

At these forums, the non-Congress Chief Ministers forged strategies for joint actions and articulated their concerns and agendas for federal reforms mostly relating to relief from arbitrary dismissals by the Presidential intervention in the State administration under Article 356 of the Constitution and fiscal autonomy with augmented share in revenue resources and enlarged role in the planning process.

For example, a conference of non-Congress Chief Ministers for the second time in Calcutta on 15 December 1987 deplored the unilateral formulation by the Centre of the terms of reference of the Ninth Finance Commission and appointed a working group chaired by West Bengal Finance Minister Asim Das Gupta to prepare alternative terms of reference keeping in view the needs of the States. The Chief Ministers felt that the unilateral action of the Centre violated the neutral role of the Commission as an inter governmental agency in tune with the spirit of Article 280 of the constitution.

Territorially based ethnic movements, especially in the north-west and the north-east posed serious challenges to Indian federalism in a very acute way in the 1980s under the regimes of Indira Gandhi and Rajiv Gandhi. These movements, especially in Punjab, Assam, Mizoram and Jammu and Kashmir took separatist turns in the form of agitations, terrorist violence, and insurgency.

Extreme pressure was mounted by the separatists inspired and aided from across international borders. In mid-1980s, the Rajiv Gandhi government entered into a series of accords with the major regional parties or movements in Punjab, Assam, Mizoram and Tripura to diffuse the crisis.

The Punjab Accord, between Rajiv Gandhi and the Akali Dal leader Sant Harcharan Singh Longowal, signed in July 1985 proposed the transfer of Chandigarh, the joint capital of Punjab and Haryana, to the former in lieu of the ceding of some Hindi- speaking areas to the latter; the reference of the Anandpur Sahib Resolution of the Akali Dal on greater State autonomy to the Sarkaria Commission on Centre-State Relations; the expansion of the jurisdiction of the Justice Ranganath Mishra Commission inquiring into the November 1984 anti-Sikh riots in Delhi in the wake of Mrs. Gandhi's assassination to include similar disturbances in Bokaro and Kanpur; the enactment of an All-India Gurudwara Act, etc.

The Assam-Accord signed in August 1985 between the Home Secretary R.D. Pradhan and the Assam agitation leaders provided for detection and deletion of the names of foreign intruders into Assam with the base-date for this operation fixed on January 1, 1966. Those migrating to Assam earlier to the date were to be regularised provided their names appeared in the electoral rolls of 1967.

The cut-off point earlier insisted on by the agitationists was to be determined on the basis of the National Register of Citizenship of 1957 and the 1952 electoral rolls. The government had earlier insisted on March 25,

1971, i.e. those who entered Assam from neighbouring East Pakistan(Now Bangladesh) after that date were to be deported, with the ration cards being used as valid document in determining citizenship. Moreover, those who came to Assam after January 1, 1996 (inclusive), up to March 24, 1971, were to be detected in terms of the Foreigners Act 1946 and Foreigners (Tribunal Order, 1964).

The foreigners so detected were to be excluded from the electoral rolls for 10 years. In the meanwhile, they were required to register themselves in respective districts in accordance with Registration of Foreigners Act 1939 and Registration of Foreigners Rules 1930.

The above two movements were in a way diametrically opposed to each other in the sense that the Sikh agitation was fuelled by an intolerant religious fundamentalism seeking to terrorise and drive away the Hindus and moderate Sikhs out of Punjab, while the Assam agitation stemmed from the paranoia of the Assamese threatened to be submerged in their own home by illegal Muslim infiltrators from Bangladesh.

Moreover, Rajiv Gandhi also entered into an accord with the MNF leader Laldenga ending insurgency, granting Statehood to Mizoram, and holding elections leading to the accession of the Mizo rebel as the Chief Minister of newly created State. Further, the political condition in Jammu and Kashmir sharply deteriorated after 1989 leading to a situation even worse than in Punjab and Assam. However, by mid-1990s terrorist violence was brought considerably under control to facilitate Lok Sabha elections in the State in May-June 1996 and Vidhan Sabha elections in September-October the same year. Democratic processes thus returned to the State after more than half a decade with the Congress gaining electorally in the parliamentary elections and the National Conference sweeping the polls in the Assembly elections.

Q17. Why was Sarkaria Commission constituted and what major recommendations has it made?

Ans. In 1983, the Central government appointed a three-member Commission on Centre-state relations under the chairmanship of R S Sarkaria, a retired judge of the Supreme Court. The commission was asked to examine and review the working of existing arrangements between the Centre and states in all spheres and recommend appropriate changes and measures. It was initially given one year to complete its work, but its term was extended four times. The final report was submitted in October 1987, and the summary was later officially released in January 1988.

The Commission did not favour structural changes and regarded the existing constitutional arrangements and principles relating to the institutions basically sound. But, it emphasised on the need for changes in the functional or operational aspects. It observed that federalism is more a functional arrangement for cooperative action than a static institutional concept. It outrightly rejected the demand for curtailing the powers of the Centre and stated that a strong Centre is essential to safeguard the national unity and integrity, which is being threatened by the fissiparous tendencies in the body politic. However, it did not equate strong Centre with centralisation of powers. It observed that over-centralisation leads to blood pressure at the centre and anemia at the pheriphery.

The Commission made 247 recommendations to improve Centre-state relations. The important recommendations are mentioned below:

- A permanent Inter-State Council called the Inter-Governmental Council should be set up under Article 263.
- Article 356 (President's Rule) should be used very sparingly, in extreme cases as a last resort when all the available alternatives fail.
- The institution of All-India Services should be further strengthened and some more such services should be created.
- The residuary powers of taxation should continue to remain with the Parliament, while the other residuary powers should be placed in the Concurrent List.
- When the president withholds his assent to the state bills, the reasons should be communicated to the state government.
- The National Development Council (NDC) should be renamed and reconstituted as the National Economic and Development Council (NEDC).
- The zonal councils should be constituted afresh and reactivated to promote the spirit of federalism.
- The Centre should have powers to deploy its armed forces, even without the consent of states. However, it is desirable that the states should be consulted.
- The Centre should consult the states before making a law on a subject of the Concurrent List.
- The procedure of consulting the chief minister in the appointment of the state governor should be prescribed in the Constitution itself.

- The net proceeds of the corporation tax may be made permissibly shareable with the states.
- The governor cannot dismiss the council of ministers so long as it commands a majority in the assembly.
- The governor's term of five years in a state should not be disturbed except for some extremely compelling reasons.
- No commission of inquiry should be set up against a state minister unless a demand is made by the Parliament.
- The surcharge on income tax should not be levied by the Centre except for a specific purpose and for a strictly limited period.
- The present division of functions between the Finance Commission and the Planning Commission is reasonable and should continue.
- Steps should be taken to uniformly implement the three-language formula in its true spirit.
- No autonomy for radio and television but decentralisation in their operations.
- No change in the role of Rajya Sabha and Centre's power to reorganise the states.
- The commissioner for linguistic minorities should be activated.

Till December 2007, the Central government has implemented 179 (out of 247) recommendations of the Sarkaria Commission. The most important is the establishment of the Inter-State Council in 1990.

Q18. Write a note on Punchhi Commission.

Ans. A new commission on Centre-State Relations was set-up by the Government of India in April 2007 under the Chairmanship of Madan Mohan Punchhi, former Chief Justice of India. It will look into the issues of Centre-State relations keeping in view the sea-changes that have taken place in the polity and economy of India since the Sarkaria Commission had last looked at the issue of Centre-State relations over two decades ago.

The terms of reference of the Commission are as follows:

(1) The Commission will examine and review the working of the existing arrangements between the Union and States as per the Constitution of India, the healthy precedents being followed, various pronouncements of the Courts in regard to powers, functions and responsibilities in all spheres including legislative relations, administrative relations, role of governors, emergency

provisions, financial relations, economic and social planning, Panchayati Raj institutions, sharing of resources including inter-state river water and recommend such changes or other measures as may be appropriate keeping in view the practical difficulties.

(2) In examining and reviewing the working of the existing arrangements between the Union and States and making recommendations as to the changes and measures needed, the Commission will keep in view the social and economic developments that have taken place over the years, particularly over the last two decades and have due regard to the scheme and framework of the Constitution. Such recommendations would also need to address the growing challenges of ensuring good governance for promoting the welfare of the people whilst strengthening the unity and integrity of the country, and of availing emerging opportunities for sustained and rapid economic growth for alleviating poverty and illiteracy in the early decades of the new millennium.

(3) While examining and making its recommendations on the above, the Commission shall have particular regard, but not limit its mandate to the following:-

(a) The role, responsibility and jurisdiction of the Centre *vis-a-vis* States during major and prolonged outbreaks of communal violence, caste violence or any other social conflict leading to prolonged and escalated violence.

(b) The role, responsibility and jurisdiction of the Centre *vis-a-vis* States in the planning and implementation of the mega projects like the inter-linking of rivers, that would normally take 15-20 years for completion and hinge vitally on the support of the States.

(c) The role, responsibility and jurisdiction of the Centre *vis-a-vis* States in promoting effective devolution of powers and autonomy to Panchayati Raj Institutions and Local Bodies including the Autonomous Bodies under the sixth Schedule of the Constitution within a specified period of time.

(d) The role, responsibility and jurisdiction of the Centre *vis-a-vis* States in promoting the concept and practice of independent planning and budgeting at the District level.

(e) The role, responsibility and jurisdiction of the Centre *vis-a-vis* States in linking Central assistance of various kinds with the performance of the States.

(f) The role, responsibility and jurisdiction of the Centre in adopting approaches and policies based on positive discrimination in favour of backward States.

(g) The impact of the recommendations made by the 8th and 12th Finance Commissions on the fiscal relations between the Centre and the States, especially the greater dependence of the States on devolution of funds from the Centre.

(h) The need and relevance of separate taxes on the production and on the sales of goods and services subsequent to the introduction of Value Added Tax regime.

(i) The need for freeing inter-State trade in order to establish a unified and integrated domestic market as also in the context of the reluctance of State Governments to adopt the relevant Sarkaria Commission's recommendation in chapter XVIII of its report.

(j) The need for setting up a Central Law Enforcement Agency empowered to take up suo moto investigation of crimes having inter-State and/or international ramifications with serious implications on national security.

(k) The feasibility of a supporting legislation under Article 355 for the purpose of suo moto deployment of Central forces in the States if and when the situation so demands.

Q19. What is the major problem of state management today?

Or

What do you mean by provincialisation or regionalisation?

Ans. One of the major problems of state management today is the incongruity between the territorial limits and the cultural frontiers of modern states. Modern states are mostly large states and contain several religious, linguistic and ethnic (tribal) groups. In some cases they are mixed as in the United States of America. In some cases they are concentrated in distinct regions as in Canada or Switzerland. When the religious, the linguistic or the tribal groups are concentrated in particular geographical areas, they may be formed into provinces or states and granted local autonomy. This may be called the process of provincialisation or regionalisation.

Even when such provincialisation or regionalisation is possible, there always remain in every province or region sections of population belonging to other cultures. This is particularly true of the border areas of a province or a region.

The problem becomes acute in the countries formerly under colonial rule. The colonial rulers annexed territories whenever and wherever they ruled. While governing such territories they paid little attention to the cultural or ethnic specificities of the people under their rule. Most of the provinced under their rule remained multi-lingual, multi-religious and multi-tribal.

Q20. What do you understand by government in a Multi-cultural state?

Ans. A state where different cultural, linguistic and social groups live is known as a multicultural state. Even the colonial rulers had to deal with people. They could not perpetually ignore the peoples cultural and ethnic aspirations. So they had to adjust the provincial boundaries to the cultural frontiers of the groups they lived under their authority.

In an independent democratic state, such adjustment becomes all the more essential. A government which runs with the consent of the people cannot ignore their aspirations for long. As democracy takes firmer roots, such aspirations also grow. The hitherto neglected sections of the populations realise their own importance, demand new provinces or states, want new borders and secure autonomy.

Q21. Explain cross-cutting cleavage.

Or

What is the most common cross-cutting cleavage?

Ans. Cross-cutting cleavage is a social science term that refers to the structure of two (or more) cleavages, such as race, political, religious divisions, etc., in society. Specifically, it is when groups on a first cleavage overlap among groups on a second cleavage. Formally, members of a group j on a given cleavage x belong to groups on a second cleavage y with members of other groups k, l, m, etc. from the first cleavage x. For example, if a society contained two ethnic groups that had equal proportions of rich and poor it would be cross-cutting. The term's antonym is reinforcing cleavages", which would be the case of one of the ethnic groups being all rich and the other all poor. The term originates from Simmel (1908) in his work Soziologie.

Anthropologists used the term heavily in the first few decades of the 20th century as they brought back descriptions of non-Western societies throughout Asia and Africa.

A Common problem for a colonial government and a free democratic government is what is known as 'Cross-cutting cleavage". This is a problem that India faced throughout the first half of the twentieth century and finally led to the partition of the country. The most common cross-cutting cleavage is between language and religion. People speaking the same language may profess different religions. People professing the same religion may speak different languages.

Q22. Into how many provinces was India divided during the colonial period?

Ans. The British annexed India in stages and by parts. Till they left the country they could not annex the whole of the sub-continent. Consequently, they evolved a variegated style of administration and control.

Till that time India was divided into "British India" and "native India". British India was split into Governor's Provinces and Chief Commissioner's Provinces. Native India was split into two types— (i) 566 princely states of different sizes and in different kinds of subordination to the British rulers, and (ii) "tribal areas" outside the north western and the north eastern borders of British India. Though outside British India the "tribal areas" were very much under the control of the Governor-General of British India, there were several backward districts in British Indian provinces like Assam, Bengal, Bihar and Orissa where distinct tribal groups lived. Several districts were formed with multiple tribal groups. And, as with the provincial boundaries, the district boundaries also cut across several tribal groups. The book you can believe most – GPH book.

Q23. On what basis was Bengal partitioned in 1905? Elaborate.

Ans. The British administration, initially, was organised through what they called "Presidencies" i.e., properties of the President of the Board of Trade of the East India Company. There were three Presidencies Bengal, the largest, Madras and Bombay. As annexation went on the British government constituted new provinces.

The Bengal Presidency comprised today's West Bengal, Bihar, Orissa, a part of Assam and Bangladesh. In 1904, Lord Curzon, Governor-General of British India, decided to split this Presidency for administrative convenience. He put Western Bengal including Bihar and Orissa into one province and joined eastern Bangladesh (roughly, today's Bengali speaking population) into two parts. The government justified its action on the ground of religion. Eastern Bengal was Muslim-majority. Western Bengal was Hindu-majority.

Q24. Into how many types of "states" were the provinces created according to constitution of India in 1950?

Ans. The Constitution of India, in 1950, regrouped the provinces, which existed during the colonial period into "states". It created four kinds of "states" within the federal state of India. The former Governor's provinces were declared Part A states. The Chief Commissioner's Provinces of Ajmer, Coorg and Delhi, along with some of the former princely states that had been taken over for better administration, were made part C states. The other former princely states and groups of princely states became part B states and the extremely backward. Andaman and Nicobar islands were made a Part D state.

Part A states were placed under Governors while Part B states were placed under Rajpramuksh. They would have legislatures. Part A states would have Councils of Ministers responsible to the legislatures while the Part B states would have Executive Councils. Part C and Part D states would be centrally administered. As the Governors and Rajpramukhs would follow the advice of their Councils of Ministers in the Part A and Part B states, they would have the highest amount of autonomy. The centrally-administered states would have the least or no autonomy.

Q25. Write a brief note on linguistic reorganisation of states.

Or

Discuss the factors, which resulted in the formation of linguistic states in South India.

Or

Summaries the process of reorganisation of the North-East India.

Ans. The reorganisation of the states based on language, a major aspect of national consolidation and integration, came to the force almost immediately after independence.

But the leaders thought that, immediately after partition, creation of linguistic states might create further tension So the decision was postponed. But Parliament was given the power to create new states or merge old states or parts of such states or alter their boundaries in future.

Creation of Andhra State

Shortly after the making of the Constitution, the agitation for an Andhra State began. Potti Sriramalu, a respected Andhra Congress leader, fasted unto death demanding creation of Andhra State on the linguistic basis. As a result, on October 1, 1953 the Andhra State was carved out of the State of Madras.

States Reorganisation, 1956

This led to further agitations for linguistic reorganisation. Therefore, the government set up a three-member States Reorganisation Commission in 1953. The commission was supposed to examine the reorganisation of the states of the Indian Union taking into consideration the historical background, the contemporary situation and the language, etc. The Commission consisted of Fazul Ali, H.N. Kurjru and K.M. Pannikar. The Commission recommended creation of new states in south on the basis of language. The Commission submitted its report in 1955. In 1956, the States Reorganisation Act was passed.

The States Reorganisation Act, however, did not make a drastic reorganisation. The former Part B State of Hyderabad was joined with Andhra State to form a larger Andhra Pradesh State. The former Part B State of Mysore turned into a larger State of Karnataka with additional territories transferred from the States of Madras (Tamil Nadu) and Bombay. The former Part B State of Travancore-Cochin was turned into the State of Kerala with new Territories acquired from the State of Madras.

In 1956, these states were reduced into two types - (a) States and (b) Union territories. The autonomy of states was larger than that of the Union territories.

Creation of New States

It will be seen that the states Reorganisation Commission of 1955 did not create any new state. The Commission actually integrated several former Princely States on the basis of language. The Commission was not in favour of many states though it recommended the creation of one new state—Vidarbha—by uniting contiguous territories of Madhya Pradesh and the then State of Bombay. That recommendation was not accepted by the government. On the other hand, Bombay state was enlarged by transfer of territory from Madhya Pradesh.

Creation of new states started shortly thereafter. In 1960 the Bombay state was partitioned into Maharashtra and Gujarat. In 1966 Punjab, A chunk of the territory of the former Punjab state was joined with the Union territory of Himachal Pradesh to constitute it into a State.

There are, at present, a few statehood movements like those for Vidharbha. Gorkhaland, Harit Pradesh and Bhilwara—in different parts of India.

In 2000 a new phase in the politics of creation of new started in India. Three new states were created in this year; Chhattisgarh out of the hill area of Madhya Pradesh, Jharkhand, out of the hill areas of Bihar and Uttarakhand, out of the hill areas of Uttar Pradesh. There was a time the hill areas of Bihar and Madhya Pradesh were dominated by people who are now called Scheduled Tribes. Creation of these states encouraged such demands in several parts of India. Some of these demands were being raised since before the creation of new states in 2000.

All the new states carved out of the old ones since 1972 can therefore, be called 'hill states'.

Reorganisation of North-East India

Meanwhile in northeast India autonomy movements became powerful among peoples of several hills. In 1960, an Interim Government was set up for the Naga Hills. In 1963, the State of Nagaland was created. In 1969, Meghalaya became an autonomous state within Assam. In 1972, Meghalaya became a full-fledged state. Two Union territories – Arunachal Pradesh and Mizoram – were created out of the territories of Assam, while Manipur and Tripura were promoted to full statehood. All the new political entities had populations with large proportions of scheduled tribes. The scheduled tribes themselves are however, many.

Upgradation of Union Territories

No new state was created between 1972 and 2000 but Sikkim joined India in 1974. In 1986, Arunachal Pradesh and Mizoram became full-states. In 1987, Goa was administratively detached from Daman and Diu and made a state while Daman and Diu remained a Union territory.

Q26. Comment on historical background of rural self-government in India.

Ans. Throughout in ancient India, the Village Panchayats were considered as the lowest and basic units of rural local self government. The ancient Panchayats discharged most of the functions affecting the life of the village community and were effective units of administration until the 18th century. In the past, these Panchayats functioned as people's instrument for the management of various village affairs. According to Tinker, the Panchayats "provided a kind of prelude to democracy".

With the advent of British, however, they got relegated to a subservient place in the colonial administrative setup. Even during the British rule, particularly after the Ripon Resolution of 1892, attempts were made to revive these village institutions. Accordingly, Panchayats and local boards were set up in the provinces of British India. In 1907, the British government appointed a Decentralisation Commission to recommend measures for the revival of local-self government. The Commission held that in order to associate people with the local tasks of administration, an attempt should be made to constitute and develop Village Panchayats for the administration of local affairs. The Commission also insisted that the 'tehsil' or 'taluka' boards should exist to fill the gap between the village Panchayat and district boards. The UP Local Self Government Committee also recommended the creation of 'Pargana' committees between the district board and the village Panchayat, thus contemplating three sets of rural authorities. Both Indian Local Self Government Policy Resolution (1915) and Montague-Chelmsford Report (1918) have emphasised the development of self government in India.

The importance of village Panchayats as units of local self-government was further stressed by the Simon Commission in 1930. When provincial autonomy was introduced in 1937 by the Government of India Act of 1935, the popular ministries took up the problem of local self-government and in a number of provinces, committees were appointed to investigate the matter and make recommendations for the reorganisation of local self-government. After Independence, the importance of revitalising the village Panchayats and assigning them a specific role in administration was recognised and it was laid down in our Constitution as a Directive Principle of State Policy stating that, "The State shall take steps to organise village Panchayats and to endow them with such powers and authority as may be necessary to enable them to function as a unit of self government" (Article 40).

Q27. Write a brief note on Panchayati Raj in Post-independence India.

Ans. The term 'Panchayati Raj' refers to a three-tier structure of rural local government in each district. An increased role for local authorities in rural development work was stressed in the First Five Year Plan. The Plan visualised the village Panchayats assuming responsibility for such functions as:

- framing programmes of production for the village;
- framing budget requirements of supplies and finance of carrying out the programmes;
- acting as the channel through which government assistance, other than assistance which is given through agencies like cooperatives reaches the villages

- Securing minimum standards of cultivation to be observed in the village with a view to increasing production;
- bringing wasteland under cultivation;
- arranging for the cultivation of lands not cultivated or managed by the owners;
- making arrangements for cooperative management of land and other resources in the village according to the terms of the prevailing land management legislation, and
- assessing the implementation of reform measures in the village.

In the Second Five Year Plan, Government of India has given attention to "the need for creating a well organised democratic structure of administration within the district." Under the Second Five Year Plan, the scope of Panchayats was extended from that of units of self-government to units of development, and specific measures were recommended for building up active Panchayats in order to secure the broader aims of:

- comprehensive village planning taking into account the needs of the entire village community, in particular, of the weaker sections like tenants, cultivators, landless workers and others;
- bringing about a more just and integrated social structure in rural areas;
- the development of a new type of leadership in the village society; and
- completing the pattern of district administration envisaged in the community development programme.

In January 1957, a study team under the chairmanship of Balwant Rai Mehta was appointed by the Planning Commission to review the working of the community development programme and also to examine the question of reorganisation of district administration to provide the popular organisations between the village and state levels. The study team recommended *inter alia* the setting up of elected and organically linked democratic bodies at the village, block and district levels and the entrustment of all planning and development activities to these bodies. On 12th January 1958, the National Development Council of India endorsed the proposal for democratic decentralisation. Each State was asked to evolve a system of Panchayati Raj to suit its own conditions. Five principles were emphasised:

- There should be three-tier structure of local self governing bodies from village to district levels, with an organic link from the lower to the higher ones.

- There should be a genuine transfer of power and responsibility to these bodies.
- Adequate financial resources should be transferred to these bodies to enable them to discharge their responsibilities.
- All development programmes at these levels should be channelled through these bodies.
- The system evolved should be such as to facilitate further decentralisation of power and responsibility in the future.

Q28. Discuss the main features of the 73rd Amendment Act regarding the disadvantaged groups.

Ans. The 73rd Amendment provides for more democratisation, empowerment of disadvantaged groups and betterment of the functioning of the Panchayats in the country. These Amendment Acts provided a framework and guidelines to all states to formulate their policies regarding the devolution to the Panchayats and the urban bodies. All states were asked to make changes in the provisions regarding the Panchayats.

Salient Features of the Act

The salient features of the 73rd Constitutional Amendment Act are as follows:

After part VIII of the Constitution a separate part IX has been added to the Constitution. A fresh schedule called Eleventh schedule enumerating the powers and functions of PRIs has been incorporated.

There shall be a Gram Sabha in each village exercising such powers and performing such functions at the village level as the legislature of state may provide by law.

Panchayats shall be constituted in every state at the village, intermediate and district levels, thus bringing about uniformity in the PR structure. However, the state having a population not exceeding 20 lakhs have been given the option of not having any Panchayat at the intermediate level.

While the elections in respect of all the members to Panchayats at all levels will be direct, the elections in respect of the post of Chairman at the intermediate and district levels will be indirect. The mode of elections of Chairman to the village level has been left to the State Governments to decide.

Reservation of seats for SCs/STs has been provided in proportion to their population at each level. Not less than one-third of the total membership has been reserved for women and these seats may be allotted by rotation to different constituencies in a Panchayat. Similar reservations have been made in respect of the office of the Chairman also.

A uniform term of five years has been provided for the PRIs and in the event of their supersession, elections to constitute the body should be completed before the expiry of six months from the date of dissolution.

The state legislatures have been given the power to authorise the Panchayats to levy, collect and appropriate suitable local taxes and also provide for making grants-in-aid to the Panchayats from the consolidated fund of the concerned state.

A Finance Commission has to be constituted once in every five years to review the financial position of the Panchayats and to make suitable recommendation to the state on the distribution of funds between the state and local bodies.

With a view to ensuring continuity, it has been provided in the Act that all the Panchayats existing immediately before the commencement of this Amendment Act will continue till the expiry of their duration unless dissolved by a resolution to that effect passed by the state legislature concerned.

The state legislatures should bring in necessary Amendments to the Panchayat Acts within a maximum period of one year from the commencement of this Amendment Act so as to conform to the provision contained in the Constitution.

Thus, it is clear, that a trinity of power, programmes and money is accepted to hold up the weighty business of village self-governance.

In the words of L.C. Jain, "With this constitutional amendment, a beginning has been made. Of course, the Constitution is only a mute document; we now have to amend our own (personal) constitution. But at least, the people will have accountability from their representatives."

Dr. Mahipal is of the view that, "The voice of the weak will begin to be heard with reservations for women and SCs/STs. In the first general election in 1952, many Maharajas and privileged persons were elected to Parliament. Today 45 years later the face of the House has changed, with the poor, SCs and so on represented. This will happen in the villages too, with this Act."

In short, it can be said that so far the 73rd Constitutional Amendment Act, 1992, has only provided the general guidelines for the effective and efficient PRIs in India. It granted the PRIs a constitutional status, some sort of a uniformity by making three-tier system a permanent feature, a regularity by making elections an imperative after the termination of the PRIs after every five years and the State Election Commission to conduct and supervise the elections, more financial autonomy with the constitution of the State Finance Commission, etc.

Q29. Discuss about Panchayats (Extension to the scheduled areas) Act, 1996.

Ans. The Central Act 40 provides the scope of the state legislation regarding extending the provisions of Part IX of the Constitution to the Scheduled Areas. It emphasises, 'A state legislation on the panchayats shall be in consonance with the customary law, social and religious practices and traditional management practices of community resources'.

The Central Act has defined the functions and powers of gram sabha in the scheduled areas. A careful examination reveals that these can be grouped in the following categories:

- Development functions
- Consultative role
- Recommendatory functions
- Statutory powers of the gram sabha

The important features are summarised below:

Development Functions

The development functions and powers assigned to the gram sabha are as follows:

- to approve the plans, programmes and projects for social and economic development before they are taken up for implementation by the village panchayat;
- to identify or select the persons as beneficiaries of poverty alleviation and other programmes;
- to give certification of utilisation of funds by the panchayat for the above programmes.

These powers make the gram sabha a powerful body with regard to implementation of projects for social and economic development of tribals;

- the power to exercise control over institutions and functionaries in all social sectors; and
- the power to control over local plants and resources for such plans including tribal sub-plans.

Consultative Role

Regarding the acquisition of land, the Act has assigned consultative power to the gram sabha. It says, before making acquisition of land in the Scheduled Areas by the authorities concerned for development of projects and before resettling or rehabilitating persons affected by such projects in Scheduled Areas, the gram sabha or the panchayats at the appropriate level (i.e. intermediate and district levels) will be consulted.

Recommendatory Functions

The Central Act has stipulated that the prior recommendations of the gram sabha or the panchayats at the appropriate level will be compulsory in the following matters:

- for grant of prospecting licence or mining lease for minor minerals in the Scheduled Areas; and
- for grant of concession for the exploitation of minor minerals by auction.

Statutory Powers of the Gram Sabha

The Act has prescribed that the State Governments will endow panchayats in the Scheduled Areas with such powers and authorities as considered necessary to enable them to function as institutions of self-governance. With a view to ensuring this, the Act specifies that a state legislature will ensure that the panchayats at the appropriate level and gram sabha in the Scheduled Areas are endowed specifically with following powers:

- the power to enforce prohibition or to regulate or restrict the sale and consumption of any intoxicant;
- the ownership of minor forest produce;
- the power to prevent alienation of land in the Scheduled Areas and to take appropriate action to restore any unlawfully alienated land of a Scheduled Tribe;
- the power to manage village markets by whatever name called; and
- the power to exercise control over money lending to the Scheduled Tribes.

Q30. Write a brief essay on the Panchayati Raj Institutions in the post-73 Amendment era.

Or

What is the composition of a gram panchayat?

Ans. Most of the states covered by the 73rd Amendment Act have passed the conformity Acts and have set up PRIs in the light of the provisions of the Act. Nirmal Mukherjee and Balveer Arora consider the PRIs as the third layer of federalism—an extension of the two-layer federalism between the Centre and states.

Even before the confirmation and implementation of the 73rd Amendment Act five state governments had introduced the PRIs, i.e., western States of Maharastra and Gujarat; eastern state of West Bengal, southern States of Andhra Pradesh and Karnataka.

Though there are slight variations in the nomenclature of the structures of the PRIs. At various levels, the 73rd Amendment provides the common framework for them. We consider the structure of PRIs in UP as one of the examples. The PRIs in UP consist of the following structure:

(a) Gram Panchayat

It consists of the gram sabha and members of the village panchayats directly elected by the electorate, headed by the Pradhans. The body which consists of all adults of the villages is known as gram sabha (village council). The law enjoins the gram sabha to hold general meetings annually. It can make recommendations and suggestions to the gram panchayat on various aspects, statement of account of the gram panchayat on various aspects related to the functioning of the panchayats. The gram panchayats Jurisdiction covers all 29 subjects mentioned in the 11 schedule. The panchayats are supposed to consist of several committees to help it in performing various duties. Therefore, the gram panchayat has a wide sweep of functions, if not powers. Each gram panchayat is expected to function through four committees, viz. Samata Samiti (welfare of women and children and interests of SCs/STs and backward classes). Vikas Samiti (agriculture rural industry and development schemes), Shiksha Samiti (education) and Lok Hita Samiti (Public health, public work). The village panchayat has also a village pradhan, who is elected indirectly by the members of the village panchayat.

Panchayat-Samiti (Kshettra-Samiti)

The Panchayat Samiti constitutes the intermediate tier in the Panchayati Raj system of rural local government in India. It is called by different names in different States. The term of samiti varies from State to State. In Uttar Pradesh, the term of Panchayat-Samiti (Kshettra-Samiti) is of five years. It is generally coterminous with that of the Panchayat. A Kshettra-Samiti consists of ex-officio, associate and co-opted members. All the Pradhans (Sarpanchas) of the village Panchayat in the Samiti area are made ex-officio members of the Kshettra-Samiti. Members of the State Legislature and of Parliament who have been elected from the area covered under the Samiti become the associate members. There is also a provision of co-option of specified number of women and persons from scheduled castes and scheduled tribes as members of the Samiti. The state of Uttar Pradesh provides representation to the cooperative societies. In the Uttar Pradesh, Kshettra-Samiti and Zila-Parishad Adhiniyam 1961 there is provision that every Kshettra-Samiti has a Pramukh (President) and two Up-Pramukh (one senior and one junior Up-Pramukh) who shall be selected by the members of Kshettra-Samiti by a secret ballot.

Functions

Kshettra-Samiti in Uttar Pradesh is the pivot unit of Panchayati Raj system. It is the main executive body charged with the responsibility of implementing community development programmes. Its responsibilities extend to agriculture, animal husbandry, fisheries, health rural sanitation, communications, social education, co-operation, cottage and small scale industries, etc. Besides this, Kshettra-Samitis are charged with preparation and implementation of development plans for the block and acts as an agent of State Government in the performance of tasks which may be specifically assigned to it. It also exercises supervision over Panchayats and provides the necessary technical and financial assistance to them. Finally, it scrutinises budgets of the Panchayats of the area under its control and makes suggestions to them. Thus, the functions of Kshettra-Samiti are to provide civic amenities and fulfilment of development functions.

Functions of Kshettra-Samiti may be classified into two broad areas:

(I) Provision of civil amenities

(II) Fulfilment of development functions

The first category comprises the following functions:

(a) Construction and upkeep of roads.

(b) Supply of drinking water.

(c) Opening of drains and soakage pits.

(d) Establishment of primary health centre and maternity centres.

(e) Provision of medical and health services.

(f) Provision of primary and basic schools, establishment of adult education centres and adult literacy centres.

(g) Establishment of popularisation of libraries.

(h) Establishment of youth organisations, Mahila Mandals, farmers, clubs, etc.

In the second category, the following functions fall within the development programmes:

(a) Execution of all programmes under community development.

(b) Multiplication and distribution of improved seeds.

(c) Procurement, distribution and popularisation of improved manure and fertilisers.

(d) Reclamation of land and conservation of soil.

(e) Providing credit for agricultural purposes.

(f) Providing irrigation facilities by renovating and sinking well, repairing and digging tanks, and maintaining minor irrigation sources and supply channels.

(g) Planting of trees and growing of village forests.

(h) Introducing improved breed of cattle, sheep and poultry.

(i) Introducing improved fodder.

(j) Prevention and cure of disease among cattle.

(k) Dairying and milk supply.

(l) Opening and development of cooperative societies in various fields.

(m) Development of cottage, village and small scale industries.

(n) Establishment and maintenance of production-cum-training centre.

Working Panchayat-Samiti (Kshettra-Samiti) functions through standing committees which are set up for looking after specified aspects of the Samitis' work, like production programmes, education and social welfare, finance and taxation, and public health and sanitation, etc. Members of the Standing Committees are elected by members of the Panchayat Samiti. All State Acts provide that the president (Pramukh) of the Kshettra-Samiti shall be the ex-officio member or chairman of the standing committee. The implementation of the programme is looked after by the Block Development Officer who functions as the Chief Executive Officer of the Panchayat-Samiti and the Block Staff consisting of the executive officer (EOs) and village level workers (VLWs).

Zila Parishad

Zila Parishad is the apex body in the three-tier system of rural local government in India. It is a corporate body at the district level. Zila Parishad generally consists of the representatives of the Panchayat Samiti

(Kshettra Samiti) and some representatives of the weaker sections of the community. The membership of the Zila-Parishad has been designed in such a way as to link it organically with the intermediate tier of Panchayati Raj, namely, the Panchayati Samiti and with the State legislature and the national parliament at the upper level. A Zila Parishad has the following members:

(a) Presidents of Kshettra Samiti in the district.

(b) All members of Parliament of the area.

(c) All members of the State Legislature of the area.

(d) A representative of cooperative society—president of the district cooperative society.

(e) Certain specified number of members of scheduled castes and scheduled tribes.

(f) Some co-opted members possessing experience in administration, public life or rural development.

The Zila Parishad has a membership varying between forty and sixty. In Uttar Pradesh, some members are directly elected to the Zila Parishad. The members of Zila Parishad elected amongst themselves a president called 'Adhyaksha' in Uttar Pradesh. He presides over the meetings of the Zila Parishad and conducts its proceedings. He inspects lower tiers of the Panchayati Raj system and submits inspection report to the Zila Parishad. He exercises administrative supervision and orders of the Zila Parishad and sends his confidential report on the work of the Chief Executive to the Divisional Commissioner.

Functions

Zila Parishad functions through a network of standing committees. In Uttar Pradesh, Zila Parishad has been assigned executive functions in health education and social welfare, etc. In most States (except Maharashtra and Gujarat) the Z.P. functions as a supervisory and coordinating body. In Uttar Pradesh, the Zila Parishad is vested with administrative functions in various fields.

Following functions have been assigned to Zila Parishad:

- It examines and approves the budget of Kshettra Samiti.
- It issues directions to Kshettra Samiti for efficient performance of their functions.
- It coordinates development plans prepared by the Kshettra-Samiti.

- It advises the State Government on all matters relating to development activities in the district.
- It distributes funds, allocated by the State Government, to the Kshettra-Samiti in the district.
- It informs the district collector and the divisional commissioner about irregularities, if any, committed by the Panchayats and Kshettra-Samitis in the district.
- It collects statistics relating to the activities of local authorities in the district.
- It advises the State Government on allocation of work to be made among Panchayats and Kshettra-Samiti in the district and, also, on co-ordination of work between the Samitis and among various Panchayats themselves.
- It exercises such powers and performs such functions as may be conferred by the State Government.

Working: The Zila Parishad is an ex-officio body. A substantial portion of its membership comprises district level officials from the various development departments such as public health, engineering, education, public works, backward classes welfare, etc.

Like Kshettra-Samiti, Zila Parishad also functions through standing committees set up to look after specific items to work like education, planning, industries, etc. The standing committee supervises and controls the imposition and collection of taxes and other dues of the council. It regulates investment of district funds, passes monthly accounts of receipts and expenditure and reviews progress of the various programmes periodically for which it makes a report to the Zila Parishad. It sanctions leave to the Chief Executive Officer upto one month and to other class I and class II officers upto four months. The Pramukh presides over and conducts the meetings of the Zila Parishad. He also sends a report to the Collector (who is chairman of the Committee) regarding the working of the Secretary of Zila Parishad. The Pramukh, thus performs the role of a leader and a supervisor.

Q31. Write short notes on the following:

(a) Urban Local Government

Ans. The urban local bodies, like the rural self-government in villages, discharge the functions regarding education, health, entertainment etc in the cities and towns. In addition, cities have some other problems. The cities are bigger in size than the villages. They have wholesale markets and various industries. They are densely populated. The traffic in cities is heavy. The local self-government bodies have to face problem of road repairs, sanitation, public health and water supply on a much larger scale.

While setting up the local self-governing bodies in the cities, the government classifies the cities based upon the size of population. In the smaller urban areas or cities having population of more than twenty thousand, the municipalities are set up. In larger urban areas of cities with population over 200,000, the municipal corporations are set up. The municipalities and the municipal corporations look after the local affairs of the cities.

Municipal Corporations

The metropolitan cities like Kolkata, Mumbai, Delhi and Chennai are highly populated with a number of problems and requirements like transport facilities, good-quality roads, hospitals, educational institutions. Such big cities are governed by the municipal corporations.

Tenure

In a municipal corporation, the members are elected on the basis of adult franchise for a term of five years. The city is divided into different wards for the purposes of election. The members thus elected are known as the ward councillors or simply councillors. Some of the seats are reserved for the scheduled castes, scheduled tribes, backward class and women. One–third of the seats are reserved for the women.

Composition

The structure and composition of a municipal corporation are mentioned below:

- The whole city is divided into a number of wards for purposes of election. Each ward has an elected councillor.
- The elected councillors form a committee and elect a mayor, who is the head of the corporation. The mayor presides over the meetings of the corporation. A deputy mayor is also appointed who discharges the duty of mayor in his absence. Both these officials are appointed for a term varying between one to two and a half years in different municipal corporations.
- The state government appoints a chief executive officer, or a municipal commissioner, who stays in the office for a period of three to five years. He implements all the decisions of the municipal corporation and prepares the annual budget.

- A number of elderly respected citizens of the city are elected. They are known as the aldermen.
- The corporation comprises the members of the Parliament and the members of the state legislative assembly.
- Some seats are reserved for scheduled castes, scheduled tribes, backward classes and women.

Functions of the Corporation

Various functions of the corporation are enlisted below:

- It provides electricity, drinking water and sanitation.
- It establishes and maintains museums, parks, playgrounds, stadiums, etc.
- It constructs roads and repairs them.
- It builds and maintains primary, secondary and higher secondary schools.
- It makes necessary provisions for adult education and night schools for labourers.
- It issues licences for buildings, shops, industries, vehicles and so on.
- It provides and maintains a good transport system.
- It runs hospitals and health centres for the prevention of epidemics.

Sources of Income

The sources of income of the municipal corporations are as follows:

- Water tax, entertainment taxes from cinema houses, fairs, property tax, pilgrimage tax etc
- Electricity charges
- Parking charges
- Grants from state governments

Municipalities

The municipal councils commonly called the municipalities are set up in the urban areas or cities that have a population of more than 20,000 and up to 5,00,000.

Tenure

A municipality is elected for a period of five years. The membership for the municipality depends on the population of the town or city.

Composition

The structure and composition of a municipality are mentioned below:

- The commissioner, appointed by the state government, is in charge of the general administration of the municipality.
- The members of the municipal committee elect a president and a vice president, who are responsible for carrying out the administrative functions according to the policies approved by the elected members.
- The aldermen are elected by the members of the municipality.
- Some seats are reserved for scheduled castes, scheduled tribes, backward classes and women.

Functions of the Municipalities

Various functions of the municipalities are enlisted below:

- It lays and maintains roads.
- It looks after the drainage facilities and provides safe drinking water.
- It issues licences for new buildings and factories.
- It issues birth and death certificates.
- It provides transport facilities.
- It takes care of educational and cultural activities by setting up primary and secondary schools, promoting adult education and literacy programmes.
- It maintains cremation and burial grounds.

Other Urban Self-governing Bodies

Town Area Committees

The town area committees are the local self-governing bodies operating in small towns or in areas in the process of transition from a rural to an urban area. It is also termed as the notified area committee.

The functions of the town area committee include supply of safe drinking water and electricity, health services, transport, maintenance of roads and sanitation. Its sources of income are taxes on cattle, buildings, factories, shops and octroi.

Cantonment Board

The cantonment boards are a special type of urban local government. They are set up in areas having a considerable population of army personnel. Some of these are seen in cities like Ambala, Delhi, Lucknow, Srinagar, etc.

The main function of the Cantonment Board is to make provisions for maintaining health, cleanliness, recreation and supplying water and electricity to the residents of the area.

The chief source of income for the cantonment board is the grant from the ministry of defence.

Improvement Trusts

It is a development authority set up in large cities like Delhi, Mumbai, Kolkata, and Allahabad to look after the overall improvement of the city in an organised manner.

The local governing bodies, whether urban or rural, encourage active participation of the people in a democracy. Thus, they act as training grounds for the future leaders. Local self government helps the people in expressing and solving their local problems in the best possible way.

(b) 74th Constitutional Amendment

Ans. When the Narasimha Rao government took charges in 1991, it introduced a Constitution Amendment Bill pertaining to municipalities in the Lok Sabha on 16 September 1991. With a few modifications, it was essentially based on the 65th Amendment Bill. It was passed by both the Houses in December 1992. The Bill has since then been ratified by a resolution of at least half the number of State Legislatures. It received the assent of the President on 20 April 1993 and was published in the Gazette on the same day as the Constitution 74th Amendment Acts, 1992.

So far, in the urban area of India, six principal types of local government existed, namely Municipal Corporations, Municipal Councils or Municipalities, Notified Area Committees, Town Area Committees, Cantonment Boards and Township. As a result of the 74th Constitutional Amendment Act, the last four categories now fall under the broad category of Nagar Panchayats. Now the three principal types of local government in urban India are: Municipal Corporations, Municipal Councils or Municipalities and Nagar Panchayats. At present, there are more or less 3600 Municipal Corporations in India. The number of Municipal Councils and Nagar Panchayats in all is around 70,000.

Nagar Panchayats exist in semi-urban, semi-rural areas. These areas have basically rural character; but they have adopted the urban features gradually through a number of years. This type of local government works for both rural and urban population. In a number of States, Nagar Panchayats exist quite successfully.

There are Municipal Councils of Municipalities for the small urban areas or suburbs. But the size of the Municipalities and consequently the size of the population covered by them vary from State to State. This is determined entirely by the government of the state concerned.

The township of some urban areas has such a big size that a number of big industries are developed there. In such large urban areas, Municipal Corporations instead of Municipalities exist.

All States amended the municipalities and corporation Acts in 1994 to give effect to the 74th Constitution Amendment Act. Some State Governments have further amended the laws from time to time to meet the emerging political, legal and administrative problems.

(c) Municipal Finance

Ans. There is no separate list of taxes for municipal bodies. This fall within the discretion of respective state governments. Many bodies like the Local Finance Inquiry Committee (1951) and Taxation Inquiry Commission (1953- 1954) have been set up from time to time to look into the issue of municipal finance. Municipal Revenues are basically of the following types:

Tax Revenue

Major taxes levied by urban local government are the following:

Tax on property including sen ice levy for water supply; Conservancy, drainage, lighting and garbage disposal; Tax on Professions; Tax on vehicles (other than motor vehicles).

The scope of taxation of Municipal Corporations is broader; the Municipal Corporations are generally empowered to impose or increase taxes within the limits laid down in the State Acts. Property tax is one example of such tax. Generally property tax is the largest single source of revenue for municipal bodies in the states where there is no provision for octroi. Property tax is levied on buildings and land on the basis of rental value.

Octroi

Tax on entry of goods into a local area for consumption or sale therein is popularly known as octroi. Octroi is the most traditional tax and a major source of local revalue. It accounts for about 60 to 80 per cent of total revenue of the urban local bodies where it is imposed.

Non-Tax Revenue

Municipal Acts provide for issuance of licences. Every local authority is empowered to charge and collect fees both regulator (for licence issued) and for services provided. A user fee is to be charged for public utilities, parking, entry fees for playground, swimming pools, etc.

Grants-in-Aid

An important element of finance is grants-in-aid. There are two types of grants; a General-Purpose Grant (GPG) and a Specific purpose grant (SPG). The former augments the revenue of the local bodies for discharging their normal functions. The latter is used for specific purposes, e.g., the increase of wage bills due to inflation, education grants, public health, road maintenance, etc. Grants are ad-hoc and discretionary in nature.

Borrowings and Loans

Municipal bodies can borrow from the state government and other agencies under Local Authorities Loans Act. (1914). They can borrow for development activities and for repayment of debt. These borrowings can be for the purposes of: Construction; Provision of relief and relief work during scarcity or famine; Outbreak of any epidemic; Land acquisition; Repayment of outstanding loans.

With the addition of eighteen functions in the Twelfth Schedule after the 74th Amendment, the functional responsibilities of municipalities have increased. They participate in the preparation of plans for local development and in the implementation of development projects, apart from providing civic amenities. Thus they require increased financial allocations.

5 Party System and Elections in India

An Overview

India is a constitutional democracy with a parliamentary system of government, and at the heart of the system is a commitment to hold regular, free and fair elections. Elections in India are events involving political mobilisation and organisational complexity on an amazing scale. Political parties are indispensable to any democratic system and play the most crucial role in the electoral process – in setting up candidates and conducting election campaigns. These elections determine the composition of the government, the membership of the two houses of parliament, the state and union territory legislative assemblies, and the Presidency and vice-presidency. Elections are conducted according to the constitutional provisions, supplemented by laws made by Parliament. The Supreme Court of India has held where the enacted laws are silent or make insufficient provision to deal with a given situation in the conduct of elections, the Election Commission has the residuary powers under the Constitution to act in an appropriate manner.

Q1. Explain the nature of party system in India and identify its various characteristics.

Ans. Rajni Kothari has argued in 'Politics in India' that the party system evolved from an identifiable political centre. This political centre, carved during the nationalist movement that was comprised of the political elite sharing common socio-economic background, i.e. educated, urban, upper-caste people belonging mainly to middle and upper classes.

The common social background of the elite resulted in the homogeneity that became a defining feature of the political centre as well as of the party system. The ruling party and the opposition, both coming from the same social background, shared the social perceptions and converged on many issues. A consensus, therefore, existed within the system around the basic values.

The Indian National Congress was the institutional manifestation of this political centre. Not only, it was an important expression of the nationalist movement but was also a dynamic political organisation that formed the indigenous base for the political system. Accommodating almost all political groups of political importance, it provided a very crucial political space for political negotiations and bargaining.

Characteristics of Indian Party System

In brief, the characteristics of Indian party system can be studied under the following points—

(1) A Multi-party System: Indian political party system happens to be a multi-party system. At present, there are more than 30 national and regional political parties. In 1952, the number of small and national political parties was 52. Since, the formation of political parties in India is highly personalised, it is commented that, there are as many political parties in India as there are political leaders.

(2) Single Party Dominant System: The functioning of Indian party system displays the dominance of one party amongst multitudes of political parties operating in the system. Leaving aside two exceptions of 1977 and 1989 elections, the Congress had been in power at the Centre from 1952 to 1996. After 1996, this feature of Indian party system stands diluted. Now has come the age of alliances or coalitions. Right since 1996 elections, no single party achieved majority. H. D. Deve Gowda, Indra Kumar Gujral, Atal Bihari Vajpayee and Dr. Manmohan Singh are the Prime Ministers who have presided over coalition governments.

(3) Existence of Communal Parties and Caste based Parties: In the Indian political scene, there has been in existence parties based on caste and religion. For example, Akali Dal, Hindu Mahasabha, Muslim League, Muslim Majlis, National Conference, Shiv Sena, etc. Also, we find that certain parties are organised on the basis of the support of certain caste groups. As a consequence, the general public interest is undermined and the sectional, communal and caste interest prevails over the party. Also, it has generated animosity among different castes and communities.

(4) Importance of Regional Parties: India is a land of diverse cultures and traditions. In the midst of national parties having reach over different regions, there are regional parties which have wide support in their respective regions, i.e. Telugu Desam in Andhra Pradesh, DMK and AIDMK in Tamilnadu, AGP in Asam Akali Dal in Punjab and National Conference in J&K, are the examples of some of the regional parties. The regional parties are more pronounced in the South India and the North Eastern part of the country. Usually, their operation and influence is confined to regional politics but in 1990s, these parties have got a foothold in the national politics also. The increasing role and Influence of regional parties in the national politics underlines a new trend in the party system of India.

(5) Factionalism, Defection and Split: Almost all the political parties are suffering or have suffered from factionalism, defections and splits in the course of time. The problem of defection has been sought to be dealt with by 52nd and 91st amendments to the Constitution of India.

(6) Weak Opposition Parties and Lack of Unity among Opposition Parties: To a great extent, the success of Parliamentary democracy depends upon the role of responsible opposition parties, which check and ensure the accountability of the ruling party. But, in India, the opposition parties have been weak and fragile due to multitudes of political parties and lack of unity among political parties. For excellent score, read GPH book.

Q2. Write a short note on Centrality of Congress.

Ans. Due to the unique position of dominance of the Congress party, it was known to be the Central institution of Indian politics. The Centrality of Congress was reflected at various levels:

- At one level, it occupied the most central space of electoral politics, thereby monopolising it and not allowing other parties to seriously challenge its position of power in the centre and the states.
- At another level, its centrality was outlined in its occupation of the pivotal space between the state and society. Representing

diverse interests of society, it remained the most important formal mediating institution of the state. It is, therefore, provided the most crucial space for political negotiations and bargaining.

- At the third level, the centrality of the Congress was reflected in its ideological standpoint. Being an umbrella party, it had space for all kinds of ideological groups. Hence, it pursued a 'centrist' ideology even when it contained ideological viewpoints of the 'left' and 'right'.

Q3. Analyse the changing nature of the party system and explain the emerging patterns.

Or

Discuss the loss of centrality of congress and emerging party system.

Ans. The nature of the Indian polity as well as the party system underwent a substantial change after 1967. This change has been described in varied terms. According to Kothari, this was the beginning of the decline of the dominant party system. While Morris-Jones attributes this to the emergence of 'a market polity', in which the number of opposition parties were brought 'fully into the market place, and competition that had previously occurred within the Congress, was now brought into the realm of inter-party conflict'. A number of new political forces and formations started emerging, making the electoral politics more competitive. All this led gradually to the decline of Congress.

The change in the nature of party system, initially, was much more visible at the state level where the hegemony of the Congress party was challenged through the formation of a number of non-Congress government. The Fourth General election led to the beginning of the politics of coalitions. This election produced truncated majorities of the Congress party. Hence, coalitions were formed in many states with Jana Sangh, SSP, CPI, CPI (M), and a number of regional parties joining the government.

Meanwhile, the Congress also started showing signs of its weakness at the central level. One of the initial indicators of the weakness of the Congress was the changing nature of factionalism and the sharpening of the dissidence within the party. Acute factionalism ultimately led to the split of the Congress in 1969. This split, though an internal affair of the party has far reaching consequences for the Party system of India. One of the major consequences of the split was the decline of the consensual model of Indian politics and of the party system. The old organisational structure of Congress that was relatively more democratic and with greater linkages at the societal levels, was replaced by a more centralised organisational set-up. This new set up was pyramidal in nature. The decision-making within the organisation was personalised and there was no space for democratic dissent. All this had the effect of rendering the Congress organisationally very weak.

The decline of the consensual model of Indian politics was not only a manifestation of the organisational problems of the Congress party but also of the changing nature of the state-society relationship. The homogeneity that earlier characterised the nature of the elite was no more available after the mid-sixties. This was also the time when the new classes had started becoming more assertive, specifically claiming a share in political power. It was the impact of such a changed context of elite politics that the Congress failed to maintain its electoral dominance in a number of states.

By the end of the decade of the seventies, the party system both at the central level as well as at the level of the states was marked by flux. This was due to the fragmentation that was taking place in political parties. It was a process that was to continue for quite some time. Yet, despite the flux, the competitiveness was a distinct feature of the party politics. The number of political parties that entered the electoral arena was also increased. All this meant that the period of the dominance of the single party was already over. A multi-party system, instead, has evolved.

It was in the period starting with the 1989 parliamentary elections that the Congress was displaced from its position of centrality. Such displacement of Congress from the position of the centre has various implications:

- Firstly, Congress has ceased to be the dominant political party. It is no more the single major political party that dominates the political scenario. A number of other political formations have also had their effective presence. For the last two decades, there has been an ascendance of non-Congress political formations. The major non-Congress formations that have been playing a crucial role in Indian politics include the Bharatiya Janata Party (BJP), the Left Parties and a number of other national and regional parties. The central political space, earlier dominated by the Congress party, is now being shared by a number of political parties.

- The loss of centrality of the Congress, in another perspective, implies a decline in its capacity to represent a consensus. It is no more capable of accommodating varying interests. As the nature of state-society relationship has changed and consequently emerging interests have been sharpened, the societal conflicts and contradictions have become more pronounced. The central space needed for defusing such conflict is not available with the Congress. The traditional methods of co-option or bargaining that helped it to deal with the conflicting interests do not work anymore.
- The decline of Congress has not led to the emergence of an alternate national party that could occupy the central space. In other words, the single party dominant system has not been substituted by a two-party system. The rise of the BJP in the early eighties had led some analysts to hope that it might work as an alternate national party and that there might develop a bi-party system with a direct competition of power between the Congress and the BJP. Yet, it could not be possible. While the Congress continued to decline from its position of strength, the BJP could riot to attain the majority on its own.
- Failure of the large national parties like the Congress and the BJP to get majority of seats in Parliament has brought numerous smaller parties to the central stage of Indian politics. The large parties have been depending upon these smaller parties for the formation of governments. Instead of single party majority governments, we have been having minority coalitions. In 1991, the minority government of Congress was installed which attained majority subsequently. The 1996 Parliamentary elections led to the formation of a minority coalition of thirteen parties of the United Front, supported by Congress and the Left Front. This coalition was replaced in 1998 by another coalition led by the Bharatiya Janata Party (BJP). The 1999 Parliamentary elections again resulted in the coalition government of the National Democratic Alliance (NDA) with BJP as the largest member of the coalition.

Q4. Give the meaning of a national and regional party. How are they different?

Ans. India is a multi-party democracy. There are both national and regional parties.

National Parties

The Election Commission grants recognition to political parties in India. There are certain criteria for a party to be recognised as a national party. The party should meet any of the following criteria:

- The party is recognised as a state party in four or more states.
- The candidates of the party secure at least 6 per cent of the total valid votes polled in a minimum of four states and have at least four elected member in the Lok Sabha.
- It secures a minimum of two per cent of the seats in the Lok Sabha, provided the members are drawn from at least three states.

All national parties are given exclusive election symbols, by which they are recognised all over the country. At present, there are six national parties in India, i.e. Indian National Congress (INC), Bharatiya Janta Party (BJP), Bahujan Samaj Party (BSP), Communist Party of India – Marxist (CPI-M), Communist party of India (CPI), and Nationalist congress Party (NCP).

Regional (State) Parties

The parties that work within a region or a state and their influence is limited within the boundaries of a particular region is called a Regional or State Parties. They look after the needs of the people living within the locality and they promote regional interests.

Though the regional parties do not enjoy the same status as the national parties, they play a very important role in the national polity.

- Being based in a particular region, they can focus on the needs of the people in their area and serve them to the fullest.
- As they serve the interests of a state or region, they are able to give single-minded attention to the people and achieve better results. As all members of the party belong to the same area, the problems will be understood better.
- In most cases, the regional parties may have ideological stands different from the parties at the Centre. For this reason, they can serve as a very healthy opposition keeping the Central ministry in check and questioning and arbitrary decisions taken that contravenes the provisions of the Constitution.
- Many regional parties extend support to the party forming a coalition government at the Centre. They lend support to that

party either joining the ministry or from outside, thus, providing stability to the Union Government.

Differences between National and Regional Parties

National Parties	Regional Parties
• Have an all-India outlook as they hold influence over four or more states.	• Restricted to an area of less than four states.
• Have exclusive election symbols through which they are recognised countrywide.	• Have reserved symbols valid only in respective region or states, and invalid in regions beyond them.
• Form the government at the Centre, either by winning a majority on their own or by forming a coalition of parties.	• Form governments at the state level; can have a say at the Centre if they support the ruling party or become part of a coalition government.
• More concerned with national issues as they cater to the needs of the country as a whole.	• More concerned with local issues and try to settle matters in the light of local aspirations.

Q5. Discuss the major national political parties in India.

Ans. Some of the major national parties in our country include the following:

Indian National Congress (I)

It traces its origin to the Indian National Congress founded in 1885. Since then, it has undergone several splits. The seventh General Elections in 1980 saw the faction led by Indira Gandhi returning to power, so the party now came to be called Indian National Congress (Indira) or Congress (I) in short.

The Congress had come to power successively up to the fifth General Elections held in 1971. In 1971, there was a split in the party but it again came to power in the seventh and eighth General Elections. In the ninth General Election, however, the National Front coalition comprising five political parties came to power. The Congress returned to power in the tenth General Elections held in 1991. The 11th General Elections saw the United Front government in power with outside support of Congress. In the 12th and 13th General Elections, held in 1998 and in 1999 respectively, Congress could not win sufficient number of seats to form the government.

However, after the 14th General Elections in 2004, a Congress-led coalition, called the United Progressive Alliance (UPA) formed the government with outside support from the Left parties.

Policies and programmes

The Election Manifesto released by the Congress in 2004 promised the following:

- Reservation of jobs in the private sector for Dalits and tribals.
- Selective privatisation of state-owned companies.
- Reservation of one-third of the Lok Sabha and Assembly seats for women.
- Providing employment to every rural household for at least 100 days every year.
- Increase in budget allocation for education to 6 per cent of the Gross National Product (GNP).
- Revival of the Public Distribution System.
- Revival of the 'sick' Public Sector industries.

Bharatiya Janata Party

Following a spilt in Janata Party in 1989, the erstwhile Jan Sangh was rechristened as Bharatiya Janata Party (BJP). It was the single largest party in the Lok Sabha in 1996, and in the 1999 General Elections, it came close to a majority winning 182 seats. With the help of a few other parties, it formed the National Democratic Alliance (NDA), which came to power at the Centre on 13 October 1999. Atal Bihari Vajpayee headed the coalition government.

Policies and programmes

The NDA's manifesto for 2004 General Elections promised:

- to improve agriculture and water management.
- to enhance growth up to 10 per cent and speed up tax reforms.
- to ensure that the important offices should be occupied by only those who are citizens of India by birth.
- to find an early and amicable solution to the issue of Ram temple in Ayodhya.
- to make all efforts to control the rising population.
- to improve housing facilities.

The Communist Party of India

Like the Indian National Congress, this party was also set up before Independence in the 1920s. The founding members of the party were MN

Roy, Abani Mukherji, Mohammad Ali, Mohammad Shafiq Siddiqui and MPBT Acharya, Evelina Trench Roy and Rosa Fitingof. In 1964, a separate unit of the party started functioning as Communist Party of India (Marxist). The parent party continued to call itself the Communist Party of India. In the 2004 Lok Sabha elections, the CPI bagged 10 seats.

Manifesto of CPI (2004)

- To nationalise units of production and service in order to remove economical and social disparities.
- To oppose both imperialism and capitalism which are the sources of all misery.
- To align with other socialist countries.
- To improve the conditions of the working class.
- To preserve the cottage and small scale industries.
- To nationalise the wholesale trade in most essential commodities.

The Communist Party of India (Marxist)

In the 2004 Lok Sabha elections, the CPI(M) won 44 seats. As of 2008, it also heads governments in three states, i.e. Kerala, Tripura and West Bengal.

Manifesto of CPI(M)

- Rights to work to be made a Fundamental Right and unemployment allowance to the unemployed.
- Equal and fair wage structure for agricultural and industrial workers, uniformity at all levels.
- Nationalisation of all foreign investments and all monopolies. All foreign trade would be brought under public undertaking.
- Distribution of the land of big landlords among the landless workers.
- Establishing close relationship with the socialist countries, Commonwealth and resisting imperialism.

Bahujan Samaj Party

The Bahuajan Samaj Party (BSP) founder Kanshi Ram and General Secretary Mayawati have succeeded to raise the status of the party from the regional level to the national. It bagged 16 Lok Sabha seats in 2004. It also swept the 2007 Assembly elections in Uttar Pradesh and subsequently formed the government. To get success in your studies, read only GPH book.

Q6. Discuss the major regional political parties in India.

Ans. Often, a party is easily identified as a 'regional' party if it propagates the ideology of regionalism or thrives on invocation of regional pride.

Parties like Asom Gana Parishad (AGP) or Telugu Desam Party (TDP) or Dravid Munnetra Kazhagam (DMK) are quickly recognised as regional parties.

The Dravida Munnetra Kazhagam (DMK) and The All India Anna Dravida Munnetra Kazhagam (AIADMK)

The origin of the DMK is traced to the anti-Brahmin movement in the Madras presidency in the early part of the last century. The Congress was seen as an instrument in the hands of the Brahmins to perpetuate their domination in administration and other professions. There was a realisation among the non-Brahmin that for their social advancement, the Bramhanical dominance had to be checked. 'The Non-Brahmin Manifesto of 1916, South Indian Peoples' Association of 1917 and the birth of the Justice Party in 1923-24 to contest election against the Congress Party were the results of such consciousness. EV Ramaswamy Naicker founded the Self-Respect Movement in 1925. This movement touched the masses in a big way. The Justice Party and the Self-Respect Movement merged to create the Dravida Kazhagam under the leadership of Naicker. A section of the youth was alienated because of its opposition to the Congress, anti-north India feeling and the desire to celebrate the independence as a day of mourning. These alienated people broke away from Dravida Kazhagam and formed tile DMK under the leadership of CN Annadurai in 1949. Since its beginning, the focus of DMK has been the interests of the lower castes and classes. It has also donned the mantle of the vanguard of the Tamil identity. The DMK blamed the Aryans, the north Indians for the backwardness of the Tamils. It has been against imposition of Hindi. The DMK entered the Lok Sabha for the first time in 1956. It won the assembly election making Hindi imposition as an election issue. In 1972, the DMK split over the issue of the expulsion from the party of MGR, a Tamil film hero and the party treasurer. This paved the way for the formation of AIADMK in the memory of Annadurai. It followed the principle of electoral alliance with national party and won the 1977 assembly election. It won twelve seats in the 1984 Lok Sabha elections. This did not mean political oblivion for the DMK. Power has kept alternating between the two Tamil parties. The DMK is now being led by M Karunanidhi.

Under the MGR's leadership, the AIADMK followed the policies of assuaging the Tamil pride and populist measures of doling out largesse to the poor. After the death of MGR in 1988, the AIADMK also faced splits. In the 1989 assembly elections, the DMK led by Karunanidhi became victorious. The unification of AIADMK splinter groups under the leadership of Jayalalithaa and an alliance with the Congress Party returned it to power in 1991 assembly election. In 1996 election, the DMK won the election. Jayalalithaa faced many corruption charges but in spite of these charges, her party became victorious in 2001 election to the state assembly.

The Shiromani Akali Dal

The Shiromani Akali Dal (SAD) emerged in the 1920s as a movement of the Sikhs against the corrupt practices of the Mahants in the Gurudwaras. In 1925, the government passed the Sikh Gurudwara Act. This Act gave the right of management and control of Gurudwaras to Shiromani Gurudwara Parbandhak Committee (SGPC). The Akali Dal tried to keep a firm grip over the SGPC arguing that in Sikh tradition, the Church has not been separated from the state. The SAD projected itself as the sole spokesman of the Sikh interest devoted to their upliftment and fighting against injustices done to them first by the British and then by the Indians. The partition and independence in 1947 provided the Sikhs with an opportunity to organise on the territorial lines; there was also dream of a free Punjab with Sikh majority. The SAD leadership wanted a state where Sikh religion would be safer. For the SAD demanded the Punjabi Suba, the central government created a Sikh majority state in November 1966 by separating Haryana from Punjab. Among the other issues raised by the SAD from time to time have been the demands for full regional autonomy to Punjab, protection and promotion of the interests of rich farmers, better deal in distribution of river waters and declaration of Amritsar as a holy city. The main focus of the Anandpur Saheb declaration of 1973 was more autonomy to Punjab. This declaration demanded that the central government should have power only over defence, foreign affairs, communication and currency; rest of the powers should be given to the states. A section of the Akali Dal even supported the idea of secession from the Indian Union. The Operation Blue Star and the anti-Sikh riots in the aftermath of Indira Gandhi's assassination wounded the Sikli psyche. The Rajiv-Longowal Pact could not assuage the hurt feelings of the Sikhs. The SAD split between Badal and Tohra factions both of them putting forward identical demands like the transfer of Chandigarh to Punjab and the release of the Jodhpur detenus. The disintegration of Akali Dal continued as United Akali Dal was born headed by Joginder Singh, the father of Bhindrawale. Similarly, the 1989 Lok Sabha election was fought by Akali Dal (Mann) headed by Simaranjeet Singh Mann. This outfit openly espoused the cause of militancy and won ten out of thirteen seats in Punjab. In 1997, the Akali Dal in alliance with the BJP won the assembly elections. The Akali Dal led by Badal has lost 2002 assembly election and the Congress Party won the election. Captain Amrinder Singh of the Congress Party has become the new Chief Minister. In 2007 election, Akali Dal again won elections and formed government in alliance with the BJP.

The National Conference

The origin of the National Conference can be traced to the political ferment in the state of Jammu and Kashmir in the 1920s and 1930s when a Hindu Maharaja ruled it. An organisation in the name of Anjuman-e-Islamia came up in 1921 with the objective of promoting educational and social welfare of the Muslims. In 1931, the Muslim Conference was born to articulate the interest of the majority community in the state – the Muslims. Under the influence of the nationalist leaders, Sheikh Abdullah opened the doors of Muslim Conference for non-Muslims also in 1939 and the name of the party was also changed to All Jammu and Kashmir National Conference. Later it was again renamed as the National Conference. Sheikh Mohammed Abdullah emerged as the most powerful leader of this party who resisted Pakistani tribal invasion and played a key role in Jammu Kashmir's accession to the Indian Union in 1948. The National Conference (NC) government came to power in the same year. Among the major successes of the National Conference was the abolition of big landed estate and inclusion in the constitution of India article 370 giving Jammu and Kashmir almost a quasi-autonomous position within the Indian polity. In 1965, the National Conference and the Congress Party merged. After his release from prison in 1975, as a part of the Indira-Sheikh accord, Abdullah revived the National Conference. 'The NC formally denounced the two-nation theory, affirmed its faith in secularism, socialism and democracy. In the style of dynastic succession before his death in 1982, he got his son Farooq elected to the Presidentship of the National Conference. After the death of his father, Farooq became Chief Minister. G M Shah the son-in-law of the Sheikh joined hands with the Congress Party in toppling Farooq's government. In 1984 parliamentary election and 1987 assembly election, Farooq led National Conference displayed its continued hold over the Kashmiri people. In 1990, President's rule was imposed in Kashmir and Farooq Abdullah's government was dismissed. The National Conference recaptured political power in the state in 1996 after winning the assembly elections.

The Telugu Desam Party

The Telugu Desam Party (TDP) was established in 1982 by the matinee idol N T Ramarao (NTR) in Andhra Pradesh. In 1983 assembly election, it came to power in state assembly elections. The dramatic rise of the TDP was possible on account of the general disenchantment of the people with the Congress due to the imposition of unpopular Chief Ministers in the state by the central leadership, large-scale corruption and the charismatic leadership of N T Ramarao. The rise of the TDP is also seen as a political ascendance of the Kamma caste at the cost of the Reddies and Brahmins in Andhra politics. Taking a leaf from EV Ramaswamy Naicker in Tamil Nadu, NTR talked of restoration of the Telugu pride, which was eroded under the Congress rule. N T Ramarao felt that there was the need of a regional party to understand the complexities of the problems faced by the state. He supported land reforms, favoured ceiling on urban income, low priced rice and other populist measures. The Telugu Desam has never talked of separation of Andhra from the Indian Union. In 1989, it became part of the National Front government at the centre. It lost assembly elections in the same year and it won only one of the twenty-two Lok Sabha seats. In 1994 and 1999 assembly elections, the party defeated the Congress party. In 1995, Chandrababu Naidu the son-in-law of NTR became the Chief Minister. The electoral alliance with the BJP benefited the TDP in winning the 1999 assembly election and improving its performance in terms of Lok Sabha seats. In the era of coalition politics, the TDP has emerged as a major player even in national politics.

The Assam Gana Parishad

The Assam Gana Parishad (AGP) is a product of a vigourous student movement led by All Assam Students Union (AASU) and its political wing the All Assam Gana Sangram Parishad (ASGPC). The students raised the issue of large-scale migration to Assam by Muslim Bengalis from East Pakistan, which became Bangladesh in 1971 and also by the Nepalese and Biharis. They developed the fear of being swamped in their own land by migrants. They were disenchanted with the central government and the Congress party for treating the migrants as vote banks. The AASU and the AAGSP became the symbol of the aspirations of the Assamese educated middle class. They found the possibility of upward mobility clogged due to Bengali dominance in the bureaucracy and the Marwari dominance in the business. In 1985, the central government signed an accord with AAGSP, which stated that constitutional, legislative and administrative safeguards as may be appropriate shall be provided to protect preserve and promote the cultural, social, linguistic identity and heritage of the Assamese people. The Assam Gana Parishad was formed in 1985. It contested and won the assembly election in 1986 under the leadership of

Prafulla Kumar Mohanta. The AGP and BJP alliance won the 1996 assembly election. In 2001, assembly election in the AGP won only 20 seats while the Congress returned to power winning 71 seats.

The Jharkhand Party

The roots of the Jharkhand Party can be traced to the Adivasi Mahasabha founded in 1938 for the preservation of the ethnic identity and protection and promotion of the economic interest of the Adivasis. According to their understanding, the reason of their social and economical backwardness was firstly the British rule. They also put the blame on the moneylenders and contractors for their exploitation. The government was also to blame for its apathy towards their genuine problems. The Adivasi Mahasabha was transformed into the Jharkhand party in 1950 with the objective of forming a separate state for the tribals. The Party emerged as the main opposition Party in Bihar legislative assembly in 1952, 1957 and 1962 elections. The merger of Jharkhand Party with the Congress Party in 1963 proved to be a big blow to the Jharkhand Movement. Several splinter groups and individuals attempted to reorganise the party to fight strongly to achieve the long cherished goal of separate state but they could not unite them. In the post-1963 phase, there emerged many parties-Jharkhand Party of India, All Jharkhand Party, Hul Jharkhand Party, Jharkhand Mukti Morcha and the Jharkhand & co-ordination Committee. The Jharkhand Mukti Morcha has emerged the main party. In 1980 general elections, it won most of the seats it had contested. The JMM regrouped with the Jharkhand Party to renew the struggle for a separate state. In the year 2000, the state of Jharkhand including the tribal areas of Bihar was created.

The Shiv Sena

The Shiv Sena was founded by Bala Saheb Thakre in 1966. Its base and areas of activities and influence are confined to Maharastra. Ever since its emergence, it has sought to build the regional identity of Marathi People or Marathi Manus on the axis of Marathi language and culture, Maharashtra as a region, economic problems of the Marathi Manus and Hindu religion. While its main agenda has been concerned with the problems of Marathi people, the issues on which it has sought to build Marathi identity has been changing from time to time. In the first few years of its foundation in the late 1960s, the Shiv Sena argued that the economic opportunities in Mumbai were exploited by non-Marathi, South Indian immigrants, especially Tamils. It campaigned against the south Indian immigrants engaged in different occupations in Bombay, especially the unskilled labourers. As a result, a large number of south Indian immigrants had to leave Bombay. During the 1970s, the Shiv Sena focussed its attention on the communists, whom it considered as anti-national. During the late 1980s and early- 1990s, Shiv Sena joined the movement to construct Ram Temple at Ayodhya in Uttar Pradesh. It participated in the Ayodhya movement along with the BJP and its fraternal organisations like the VHP, RSS and Bajranj Dal. The Shiv Sena also mobilised Kar Sevaks, who participated in the demolition of the Babri Masque on December 6, 1992. Thus, while the Shiv Sena has primarily remained a regional party concerned with the intersects of the people of Maharashtra, especially Mumbai, from time to time has sought to build the regional identity on different basis – Marathi culture, against from South India and Hindi belt, against communists, and protection of Hindutva. On March 9, 2006 Raj Thakre, the nephew of the Shiv Sena chief left Shiv Sena and formed Maharashtra Nav Nirvan Sena. Like Shiv Sena — the Maharasthra Nav Nirman Sena also seeks to protect the interests of Marathi Manus and protect the Marathi language, culture and economic interests of the people of Maharashtra. It argues that the migrants especially from Bihar and Uttar Pradesh have appropriated the economic opportunities meant for the local people of Maharashtra. It has launched a violent movement against the migrants from north Indian Hindi speaking states. The rise of the MNS in Maharashtra has challenged the dominance of Shiv Sena as a regional party in the state. Shiv Sens's performance in election has been better in the urban areas than in the rural areas. The Shiv Sena has a strong support base among a section of the Maharashtra, especially Mumbai consisting of the middle classes and the OBCs.

Q7. Describe the Election System in India.

Ans. In India, the elections are normally held after every five years. Elections are held in all constituencies at same time either on same day or within a gap of few days. These are general elections and if an election is held due to vacancy caused by death or resignation of a member then it is called a by-election.

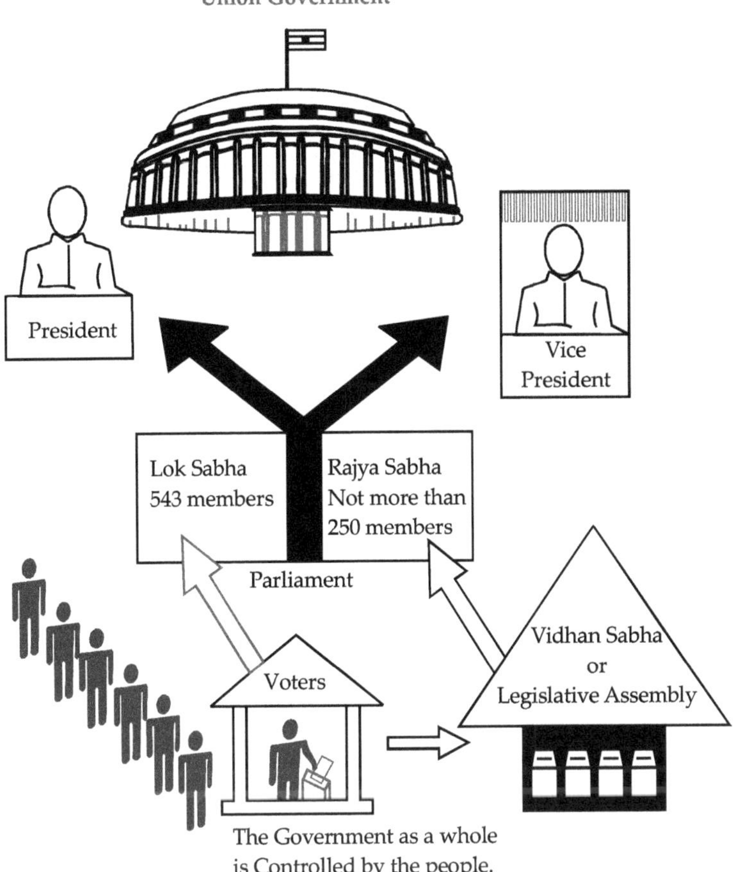

The Government as a whole
is Controlled by the people.

Fig. 5.1

Before the elections, the whole country is divided into constituencies on the basis of population. These are termed as electoral constituencies. The voters living in one area elect one representative. In India, we have 543 Lok Sabha constituencies. The representatives elected from these constituencies are called Member of Parliament or MPs. Each person has one vote one value. Each state is divided into a number of Assembly constituencies. The elected representatives of an assembly constituency are called Member of Legislative Assembly or MLA. Each Parliamentary constituency has several assembly constituencies. The assembly constituencies are further sub-divided into towns and villages. Each village elects member of panchayat while each town elects member of municipality. If we say that a party won 50 seats in a state, it means that it was victorious in 50 assembly constituencies.

Elections to the Lok Sabha and the Vidhan Sabha are carried out using the first-past-the-post electoral system. The country is divided into different geographical areas, known as the constituencies. Different political parties contest the election, though there is no ban on independent candidates for contesting the election. During election, different political parties put up their candidates and people can cast one vote each for a candidate of their own choice to elect their representatives. The candidate, who gets the maximum number of votes, wins the election and gets elected. So election is the means by which the people elect their representatives.

Eligibility to Vote

While there is no maximum age prescribed for the voter, as per the original provisions of the Indian Constitution, all Indian citizens above the age of 21 years are entitled to vote at the time of elections. The minimum voting age of the citizens was reduced to 18 years by the constitution 61st amendment act in the year 1988, by the then Prime Minister, Rajiv Gandhi, which came into effect since 28th of March 1989. Besides to be registered as a voter in any constituency, one should not be disqualified under the law on grounds of non-residence, or a person of unsound mind or disqualified on the grounds of crime or corrupt or illegal practice.

Contestants in Election

All contesting candidates have to make a deposit of ₹10,000 if contesting for the Lok Sabha election and of ₹5,000 if contesting for the Vidhan Sabha elections. This is considered as the security deposit of the candidates. The security deposit for candidates belonging to either the Scheduled caste or the Scheduled tribe community is ₹5,000, if contesting the Lok Sabha election and ₹2,500 for contesting the Vidhan Sabha elections. This security deposit is returned to all those candidates who get more than one-sixth of the total number of valid votes polled in that constituency. All other candidates lose their security deposit.

Further, the nomination must be supported by at least one registered voter of the constituency from which the candidate wishes to contest, in case of the candidate being sponsored by any registered political party and at least by ten registered voters in case of independent candidate.

Q8. What do you mean by the election commission of India?

Ans. The Election Commission of India is a statutory body set up under Article 324 of the Constitution for superintendence, direction and control of the electoral rolls, and conduct elections to the Parliament, State

Legislatures and offices of President and Vice-President of India. The Commission has also to:

- lay down general rules for election,
- determine constituencies and to prepare electoral rolls,
- give recognition to the political parties,
- allot election symbols to political parties and individuals contesting the elections, and
- appoint election tribunals to decide disputes and doubts arising as a result of election to Parliament and State legislatures.

Since its inception in 1950 and till October 1989, the Commission functioned as a single member body consisting of the Chief Election Commissioner. On October 16, 1989, the President of India appointed two more Election Commissioners on the eve of general election to House of the People held in November-December 1989. However, the said two Commissioners ceased to hold office on January 1, 1990 when these two posts of Election Commissioners were abolished. Again, on October 1, 1993, the President appointed two more Election Commissioners. Simultaneously, law [Chief Election Commissioner and other Election Commissioners (Conditions of Service) Act 1991] was also amended to provide that the Chief Election Commissioner and other Election Commissioners will enjoy equal powers and will receive equal salary, allowances and other perquisites. The law further provided that in case of difference of opinion amongst the Chief Election Commissioner and/or two other Election Commissioners, the matters will be decided by the Commission by majority. The validity of that law [renamed in 1993 as the Election Commission (Conditions of Service of Election Commissioners and Transaction of Business) Act 1991] was challenged before the Supreme Court. The Constitution Bench of the Supreme Court, consisting of five judges, however, dismissed the petitions and fully upheld the provisions of the above law by unanimous judgement on July 14, 1995.

The Chief Election Commissioner and Election Commissioners are entitled to the same salary and other facilities, like rent-free accommodation, which are provided to a judge of the Supreme Court. The term of office of the Chief Election Commissioner and other Election Commissioners is six years from the date he assumes office or till the day he attains the age of 65 years, whichever is earlier.

Q9. Explain the election procedure in India.

Or

Mention the stages through which the election process passes.

Ans. The Electoral process in India can be divided into the following main stages:

- **Delimitation of Constituencies:** The whole country in case of Lok Sabha elections and that particular state in the case of Legislative Assembly elections is divided into as many constituencies as there are seats.
- **Preparation of Voter's List:** The voter's list of each constituency is prepared and published. The voter's list contains the names of all those who are eligible to vote.
- **Filing of nomination papers:** Any person (with the necessary qualifications) who wishes to contest elections has to file his nomination papers by the due date. Every candidate has to deposit an amount as 'Security' along with his nomination papers.
- **Scrutiny of nomination papers and withdrawals:** The nomination papers are scrutinised and if the candidate papers are not in order, they are rejected the candidates can also withdraw their names from elections up to a certain date fixed by the EC.
- **Election Campaign:** Through election campaigns, political parties and candidates 'reach out' to the voters with the hope of winning their votes. Posters, pamphlets are printed and distributed. Meetings are held and speeches delivered. Use of electronic media like radio and television is also made by the political parties and candidates. Election campaigns take place for a two-week period between the announcement of final list of candidates and the date of polling.
- **Voting:** The final stage of an election is the day when voters cast their vote. Voters go to the polling booth and cast their votes for the candidate of their choice. Voting is held by secret ballot. These days, electronic voting machines are used for voting.
- **Counting of votes and declaration of results:** After the voting is over, the ballot boxes are sealed and taken to the counting centres. Votes are counted under the supervision of the returning officers. The candidate who gets the highest number of votes is declared elected.

Q10. Discuss about the voter turnout in Indian Elections.

Ans. Though all the eligible voters whose names appear in the electoral rolls in a particular constituency are expected to vote during the time of voting, practically that does not happen and the large number of registered voters who do not vote due to different reasons. The percentage of those who vote is referred to as the polling percentage popularly called the "Turnout of Voters". If we look at the figures of the last 15 Lok Sabha elections held in our country, we would find that the voters turnout has increased to a great extent in the 80's and 90's compared to the elections held during the early days. The lowest voters turnout of only 54.42 per cent was recorded during the first Lok Sabha elections held in the year 1962 and the highest turnout of 64.61 per cent was recorded in the year 1984 when the Lok Sabha election was held following the assassination of the then Prime Minister Mrs. Indira Gandhi.

Q11. What is caste? What are its main features?

Ans. What distinguishes Hindu Society from others is its independent self-sufficient unit called caste, each with a definite unalterable social status deriving its sanction from religion. Birth alone decides a man's status and he cannot change it by effort. In every society, it is true, birth is the principal factor that decides a person's status, and inequalities are not only tolerated but maintained by law; but the essential difference between Hindu Society and others is that while the others are inclined to consider inequalities as superfluous orthodox Hindus believe that inequalities are based on immutable principles.

The word 'caste' is of Portuguese origin. Its Sanskrit equivalent is 'Jati', meaning race. The Hindu social structure is known as Varnashrama Dharma (Social duties based on colour) in Sanskrit, and both these words indicate that caste originated from racial pride and colour prejudice. The Aryans were probably a fairer race than the then inhabitants of India and the caste system originated out of the anxiety of Indo-Aryans to preserve their racial purity.

Meaning of Jati for oneself and for others is not always uniform and consistent among all. It varies from purpose to purpose, for which the tag is used. Jati has a specific social identifying one's place in social order in village society where one interacts everyday with other members of the local community. For instance in a village in central Gujarat its inhabitant, say 'Mr. X' identifies himself as Khant when he interacts with another villager of neighbouring locality who calls himself as Kshatriya when he attends political party meeting at taluka or district place. He would call his caste as OBC (Other Backward Caste) when he visits government office to get loan or subsidy for government sponsored programme or to get scholarship for his son. There is one meaning of Jati for matrimonial and kinship relationship, a different meaning for economic interaction and a third meaning for political purpose. One does not necessarily have the same meaning when one exercises vote for village panchayat than Lok sabha elections.

Thus, it is difficult to give precise meaning of caste applicable in all situations. It is partly a subjective category.

Main features of Caste

According to Prof. Ghurye, the following are the main characteristics of caste:

(1) Segmental Division of Society

Under Caste System, society is divided into several small social groups called castes. Each of these castes is a well-developed social group, the membership that is based on birth. Since membership is based on birth, mobility from one caste to another is impossible. Each caste has its own traditional social status, occupations, customs rules and regulations.

(2) Hierarchy

According to Prof. Ghurye, in each of the linguistics areas, there are about 200 castes which can be graded and arranged into a hierarchy on the basis of their social precedence. At the top of this hierarchy is the touchable caste.

(3) Restriction of Commensurability and Social Intercourse

Every caste imposes restrictions on its members with regard to food drink and social intercourse. The general rule is that the member of caste should accept 'Kachcha food' the food in the preparation of which water is added only from either their own caste of caste ritually higher that their own. They are also required to observe certain restrictions while accepting water from members of other castes.

(4) Differential Civil and Religious Privileges and Disabilities

In a caste society, there is an un-equal distribution of privileges and disabilities among its members. While the higher caste people enjoy all the privilege, the lower caste people suffer from all kinds of disabilities.

(5) Lack of Unrestricted Choice of Occupation

Choice of occupation is not free under Caste System. Each caste or a group of allied castes is traditionally associated with a particular occupation. Occupations are hereditary and the members of a caste are expected to follow their traditional occupation without fail.

(6) Restriction of Marriage

Castes are divided into sub-castes and each sub-caste is an endogamous group. Endogamy, according to some thinkers is the essence of Caste System. Every caste or sub-caste insists that its members should marry within the group.

Q12. How does caste influence voting behaviour?

Ans. Caste has been an important factor in Indian politics. Though recent trends show that its impact is more prominent in the state level politics, it plays a crucial role in shaping up the policy of the governments. Wooing a specific caste has been the principal agenda of many politicians. This has been a retrogressive character of Indian politics and has so far been playing a divisive role.

Role of caste in elections has two dimensions. One is of the parties and candidates and the second is of the voters. The former seeks support of the voters projecting themselves as champions of particular social and economical interests, the latter while exercising their vote in favour of one party or candidate whether people vote on caste consideration.

While nominating candidates parties take into consideration caste of the aspirant candidate and numerical strength of different castes in a constituency. Caste leaders also mobilised their followers on caste lines so that they could show their strength. In the fifties wherever caste associations were able to maintain their unity and did not formally align with any one party they appealed to their members to vote for their caste fellows irrespective of their party affiliation. In Rajasthan, Meenas were asked "Do not give your daughter or your vote to anyone but Meena". Similar slogan was used in Tamilnadu: "the Vanniya vote is not for anyone else". But wherever caste association aligned with a particular party, the caste leaders asked caste members to vote for that party. The Kshatriya leaders of Gujarat in 1952 elections asked Kshatriya voters that it was their Kshatriya dharma to vote for the Congress because it was "the great institution and working for the development of the country". In the subsequent elections as the caste leaders split some Kshatriya leaders appealed, "It is our pledge that the Kshatriya of Gujarat vote for the Congress and not for anyone else". The others appealed that it was the dharma of the Kshatriyas to vote for the Maha Gujarat Janata Parishad (a regional party).

Though there is a trend among the caste members to vote for a particular party, there is never a complete en bloc caste voting. Some castes identify with a particular party as their party, as it was expected that it would protect their interests. Jats in Western UP identified Lok Dal as their party just not only because the leaders of the party were the Jats, but also the party raised the issues concerning the peasants.

In the National Election Survey of the 1972 carried out by Center for the Study of Developing Societies a question was asked, "What were your considerations for voting this candidate/party/symbol?" For a very insignificant number of respondents (less than 1 per cent) candidate's caste was the main consideration. Some of the respondents might have voted for persons who happened to belong to their caste. But it was not caste voting. They voted for the candidate not because s/he was of their caste irrespective of his party and ability. They voted for him/her because s/he was the candidate of the party to which the respondent felt closer for variety of reasons including the feeling that the party would "protect his/her" interests or the party, which had done good work for the people like him/her. Or, they were in touch with the candidate who might have helped them or they feel that he would help them when they need. Their primary consideration is their perception of their interests. In a given alternative parties/candidates, they consider as to who would serve their interests better than others. If the candidate happens to be of their own caste and his/her party is the party, which they identify as theirs, they vote for him/her. If they feel that the candidate belongs to that party which is either not able to serve their interests or hostile or insignificant in electorate politics, they do not vote for that candidate even if he belongs to their caste. That is the reason why several caste leaders lose the elections in the constituency predominantly because of their caste members at one time or another when they change the party or their party loses popularity. Therefore, there is no one to one relationship between candidate's caste and that of the voter's caste.

Q13. Write an essay on political parties based on caste system.

Ans. Several castes join together and launch movements. Non-Brahmin movement in Tamilnadu and Maharashtra are the examples. Jyotirao Phule started Satyashodhak Samaj in 1873 challenging Brahminical hegemony. In Tamilnadu, several peasant castes such as Vellala, Gaunda and Padayachi, trading castes such as Chetri, artisan castes - Tachchan (Carpenter), Kollan (Blacksmith), and Tattan (Goldsmith), individually and jointly initiated non-Brahmin movement. The movement followed several caste associations such as Parayan Mahajan Sabha, Adi-Dravin Mahajan Sabha in the 1890's. In 1916, the Non-Brahmin manifesto was brought out highlighting dominance of the Brahmins in government services and injustice to non-Brahmins who constituted a vast majority. The formation of the Justice party followed in 1916. The party sent a delegation to England in 1919 to present the non-Brahmin case before the joint Parliament Committee, which was responsible for preparing the Government of India Bill. DMK is its offshoot. Two factions Vanniyaakkula Kshatriya Sangam of the Nadars formed Tamilnadu Toilers' Party and Commonwealth Party and fought the 1952 elections. They then bargained with the Congress for positions in the state cabinet. Scheduled Caste Federation was formed in the forties by Dr Ambedkar and the Republican Party formed in 1956 by Dalit leaders. They primarily remained the parties of and by the Dalits. Jharkhand Party formed by Adivasi leaders of Bihar, has primarily remained a party of Adivasis. Bahujan Samaj Party launched by Kanshiram is a party of Dalits aiming at forming alliance of Dalits, minorities and OBCs.

After Independence, some caste associations were formed with political objectives to compete in elections. In Gujarat, some of the leaders of the Kshatriya Sabha contemplated in the early- fifties to form the party of the Kshatriyas. They soon realised that they could not muster enough support to contest elections only on the strength of the Kshatriyas. Similarly, political elite of the Kurmis, Yadavas and Koeris formed the Bihar State Backward caste Association in 1947 to contest elections. The plan did not take-off thanks to the resistance of the Congress leaders belonging to these castes.

Such caste associations are asserted with different leading political parties to see that their caste members get party tickets in elections. These parties initially resisted such pressures because of the counter pressure from the dominant castes that controlled the party. The latter accused the former as castiest or communal. But as the competition among the parties intensify and as the caste association successfully mobilised the members for political activities, all parties began to woo leading aspirants of the caste who could mobilise caste votes. Such political aspirants join different political parties. As they are primarily interested in gaining political positions for themselves rather than serving social or ritual interests of the caste, they either launch a new association or split the existing one. For them, caste association is among several instruments to gain political power.

Some of the political parties identify with certain castes for nomination of the party candidates and mobilisation in elections. Bharatiya Kranti Dal evolved an alliance of four major peasant castes of UP in 1969 elections. The alliance was called AJGAR; that is, Ahirs, Jats, Gurjars and Rajputs. In 1977, in Gujarat the Congress (I) formed KHAM alliance of Kshatriyas, Haryans, Adivasis and Muslims. Lok Dal was identified with Jats in Uttar Pradesh in 1977 and 1980 parliamentary elections. Samajwadi Party in Uttar Pradesh was identified with backward castes in general and Yadavas in particular in 1997 state assembly elections. BJP is generally identified with upper castes and the Congress with the middle and backward castes that reflected in their support base in the eighties in Gujarat and Maharashtra. In the nineties, the BJP has followed the strategy of the Congress of accommodating the backward caste candidates in the elections and successfully getting support of their caste fellows.

There are three consequences of such interaction between caste associations and political parties. One, caste members particularly poor and marginalised who were hitherto remained untouched by the political processes got politicised and began to participate in electoral politics with an expectation that their interests would be served. Second, caste members get split among various political parties weakening hold of the caste. Third, numerically large castes get representation in decision-making bodies and strength of the traditionally dominant castes get weaken. This explains the rise of middle and backward caste representations in most of the state assemblies.

Q14. What is meant by coalition? What are the various forms of coalition politics?

Or

Explain the meaning of coalition. Write the different features of coalition politics.

Ans. The term 'Coalition' is Latin word, which is the verbal substantive of coalescer – co, which means to go or to grow together. The dictionary meaning defines coalition as an act of coalescing, or uniting into one body, a union of persons, states or an alliance. According to W.H. Riker, "Coalition is used for an alliance or temporary union for joint action of various powers of states and also of the union into a single government of distinct parties or member of distinct parties".

Features of Coalition Politics

- Coalitions are made for some material or psychic reward.
- A coalition implies the existence of two or more than two partners.
- Coalition is based on the simple fact of temporary conjunction of specific interest.

- Coalition politics is not a static affair. It is a dynamic affair as coalitions dissolve old cohesion and form new ones.
- In coalitions, compromise is the keystone with rigidity being sidelined.
- Coalition works on the basis of a Common Minimum Programme (CMP).
- Coalition politics is the highest expression of the politics, which means the art of making impossible things possible.
- Pragmatism and not ideology is the hallmark of coalition politics.
- The aim of a coalition adjustment is to seize power, i.e. to stake its claim for the formation of a ministry or for pulling down a ministry.

Forms of Coalition Politics

Constitutional framework and electoral system of a country determines the forms that coalition politics takes. These are three in nature: parliamentary, electoral and governmental.

Parliamentary coalition may occur in a situation when no single party enjoys an overall majority. The party, which is asked to form a government, makes an attempt to rule as a minority government, relying upon an arrangement with other party or parties for its survival. The Janata Dal government led by V.P. Singh in 1989 was such a government. Such a government may seek support from the opposition political parties for different items of legislation or the government may survive merely because the opposition may not like to defeat the government to gain political advantage or not to be deprived of their existing political base. The Congress government led by Narasimha Rao in 1991 was such a government in its early tenure.

Electoral coalitions represent two or more than two political parties who enter into an agreement, which provides for a mutual withdrawal of candidates in an election so that the concerned parties can avoid splitting of votes in the constituencies where they are strong respectively. Such coalitions are difficult to be formed when the parties having strong local base and organisation do not wish to surrender their rights to put up a candidate. Such electoral coalitions have become common in India in recent past in the form of formation of United Front and National Democratic Alliance.

Coalition governments are commonly contrasted with single party government, in which one party holds office. Such government should also be distinguished from non-partisan governments, within which the members of the Council of Ministers do not act as representatives of political parties. Coalition governments are the party governments. The membership of a coalition government is conventionally defined as those parties that are represented in the Cabinet. Some parliamentary governments, however, also consistently co-operate with parties that are not represented in the Cabinet.

At the government level, there can be different types of coalition. The first type is the national government in which most, if not all, of the main parties join together to meet a national emergency arising out of war or economic crisis. The rationale behind the formation of such a government is that national crisis necessitates the suspension of party strife and requires the concentration of all forces in a common direction. The coalition government led by Asquith and Lloyd George during the First World War and by Winston Churchill during Second World War in United Kingdom were the examples of national governments.

Power-sharing coalition governments are formed when two or more than two political parties which are not able to secure majority of their own join together to form a majority government. United Front as well as BJP-led coalition governments in the nineties were such coalition governments. Power-sharing coalition governments strive to implement such policies and programmes as agreed upon among the coalition partners. Continental European countries have experienced such Governments quite often.

Q15. Comparatively analyse the coalition governments.

Ans. In pure or modified two party political systems, such as the United Kingdom; New Zealand and Canada, coalition governments are rare in the peace time. In the countries with multiparty systems, such as Belgium and the Netherlands, almost all the governments have been coalitions. There are other European countries with multiparty system like Denmark and Sweden where the governments alternate between coalitional or single-party, often minority, one. In the normal circumstances, the coalition governments are formed by two to five parties. However, the countries like India in the recent past have seen the coalition government being formed on the basis of as many as eighteen parties, i.e. Vajpayee led Government in 1998. Switzerland is a unique case where all major parties are regularly included in the coalition governments.

Coalition governments are essential features of parliamentary form of governments, but they have been formed also in the countries like

France and Switzerland, which have 'modified' parliamentary or 'semi-presidential' system. In the developed countries, almost all the parties follow centrist ideology. Power sharing is mostly the main basis of the formation of such governments. However, in the developing countries like India and Sri Lanka, the coalition governments have been formed on ideological basis. Some developed countries like Italy, Denmark, France and Sweden have also experienced coalition governments formed on the basis of ideological homogeneity. Despite the widespread presence of coalition governments in both developed and developing countries, there are not sufficient constitutional provisions regarding the process of formulation and dissolution of coalition governments. German constitution is a significant exception, which has provision that make it irresponsible for irresponsible parliamentarians to overthrow a government without being ready to support an alternative. In Sweden, 1974 instrument of government attempts to describe the process of formation of coalition government.

Q16. Discuss the emergence of coalition government in India.

Or

Make a note on coalition politics in India (1947-1990).

Ans. In India, Congress party had a majority for a long time. For nearly 20 years (1947-67), Congress used to win about 45 per cent of the popular vote. No opposition party got more than 6 per cent of the vote. This unquestioned authority of the Congress was however, brought to an end in 1967 general elections. The drought, currency devaluation and growth of non-Congress electorate led Congress to win only by a slant majority of 23 seats. Further, it lost power in six state legislative assemblies. It opened the door for the rise of Indira Gandhi. Through her populist programme like abolition of privy purses and nationalisation of banks, she tried to reach the poor classes. The populist agenda alienated her from Congress party organisation even leading to her expulsion by the veteran old guards of Congress led by Morarji Desai. These plans, however, backfired when Indira Gandhi split the Congress and a majority of the Lok Sabha members supported her. With the outside support of Communists and some other regional parties, she ran a minority government for the first time. However, Indira Gandhi went for a snap poll and swept the elections in 1971 elections as the head of Congress (R) with the other group Congress (O) receiving a severe drubbing. She got 48 per cent popular vote and 68 per cent Lok Sabha seats.

However, within four years, the situation changed once again. The drought situation and increasing prices of oil and food led to political turmoil. When the Allahabad High Court set aside her election, she declared emergency and suspended civil liberties. The entire opposition Company was put behind bars while the powers of judiciary were curtailed through constitutional amendments. For two years, Indira Gandhi ruled as a virtual dictator by imposing an emergency throughout the country. In 1977, Mrs. Gandhi called for surprise elections. The unity of the entire opposition or anti-Congress forces led to the defeat of the Congress. The Janata Party, a strange Conglomeration of forces formed by anti-Congress forces campaigned the emergency ruthlessness of Indira Gandhi. It won 55 per cent of Lok Sabha seats with 41 per cent popular votes.

First Coalition in India (24 March) 1977, 28 March 1979

Representation from constituent groups of the Janata in the Sixth Lok Sabha and Distribution of Seats in the Council of Ministers on the basis of Constituent Groups.

Constituent Groups	Number of MPs	Number of Ministers
(1) Jana Singh	94	11
(2) Bharatiya Lok Dal	71	12
(3) Congress (O)	50	10
(4) Socialist Party	28	4
(5) CFD	28	3
(6) Ex-Congressman (Chandra Shekhar Group)	5	2
(7) Others (Like Akali Dal)	25	2

The accommodative attitude of a several non-Congress groups helped in the formation of Janata Party Coalition government, which lasted for about two years. Several parties like the Bharatiya Jana Sangh, Bharatiya Lok Dal, Congress (O), Socialist Party, CFD, etc. had combined together to form the Janata Party. They had fought the election on a single manifesto and a single symbol. Morarji Desai was chosen as the Prime Minister. He had to maintain a balance in the representation of various units of the coalition. Since this did not happen, power struggle within the coalition started. Decisions could not be imposed on cabinet ministers like Charan Singh and George Fernandes. The divergent concepts of discipline opened the floodgates of defection in 1979 when Janata collapsed like a pack of cards. Thus, the first coalition of India was a failure as it collapsed as fast as it had emerged. In this regard Madhu Dandvate observes, "The Janata Party was apparently a single party, but in reality it was a combination of the Socialist Party, Bharatiya Jana Singh, Congress (O), BLD and the group of dissident Congress man led by Jagjivan Ram and H.

N. Bahuguna. The Janata Government, committed to a common programme, election manifesto. Bread with freedom had caught the imagination of the people and had roused their hopes and aspiration. But temperamental incompatibility of some leaders and fierce inner controversy over the dual loyalty of the Jana Sangh activities to the Janata Party as well as the RSS wrecked the Janata Party and the government and paved the way for the breakup of the Janata Party government which in reality was a coalition government".

Despite failure, the Janata party experiment proved to be the seed for participatory upsurge in the 1990s. The failure of Janata Party helped in the resurgence of Congress (I) which won 353 seats in Lok Sabha while Janata Dal fell to 3 per cent in 1980 elections. The next four years of Indira Gandhi rule were marred with corruption charges as several representatives tried to gain higher positions in government through manipulations.

The sudden assassination of Indira Gandhi and Mr. Rajiv Gandhi had helped congress to gain 76 per cent seats in 1984 elections. Next five years, were however, full of charges of corruption and allegation of kickbacks to public officials in lieu of contracts. By 1989, Congress (I) had lost a specific programme and direction. It won 197 seats in Lok Sabha elections of 1989. Since it did not get a majority, a coalition government led by Janata Dal was formed with outside support of two strange and odd ideological orientations: the BJP and the two Communist parties. It marked the beginning of coalition politics in India.

Fall of Congress

In the elections of 1989, Congress was defeated. Though Congress emerged as the single largest party, it did not get a majority. It thus decided to sit in the opposition. The National Front (NF) supported by two diametrically opposite parties—BJP and Left front formed the government. It marked the end of Congress dominance over the Indian party system. In late 1960, also Congress monopoly had been challenged. But it had been restored under Indira Gandhi. The 1990s saw yet another challenge to Indian Party system. No single party was able to take the space created by the Congress.

It led to the evolution of a multi-party system. A large number of political parties had always contested elections before 1989. But since 1989, several political parties had representatives in Parliament. No political party was able to get majority seats. No single party secured majority since 1989 general election. This development initiated an era of coalitions at the centre in which regional parties played a major role in forming alliances.

Q17. Explain the working and constraint of coalition government in India.

Ans. Working of the coalition government in India

It has been traditionally accepted that the principles of collective responsibility, homogeneity and secrecy have been necessary for effective functioning of Government. Coalition Government formed in India especially at Centre has been found lacking in this respect. The working of the Coalition Government has been affected by the need to secure inter-party Consensus. The heterogeneity of the Coalition partners in terms of their social basis and ideologies often has been resulting into disagreements between the Cabinet ministers on political and departmental matters. This has been hampering the deliberative and decision-making process of the Cabinet. The parties entering into coalition either under the umbrella of United Front or National Democratic Alliance had been confronted with a situation of preserving the unity of Government as well as their separated identity as a partner in the Coalition. The Coalition Governments at centre have been formed, not on the positive basis of ideological or programmatic homogeneity but on the negative basis of capturing power (like BJP led coalition Government in 1998) or to keep Congress and BJP out of power (like United Front Government in 1996). This factor has contributed to the lack of efficacy as well as stability of these Governments. The presence of regional parties in the Coalition has also led to a perception that the national outlook has often sought to be over shadowed by a regional outlook and also that personal or party gains have often received precedence over collective ones. The Steering Committee of the Coalition partners, rather than Cabinet often act as the de-facto deliberative body, thus, undermining the process of Governance. The Governance also has suffered because of the weakened position of the Prime Minister in the coalition Governments formed in the recent years. Prime Minister has been in no position to choose those as ministers in the Council of ministers who do not belong to his own party as they are chosen by their respective party leaders. This has undermined the authority of the Prime Minister more so as he feels constrained even to dismiss them without inviting the wrath of the concerned party.

In the recent past, the coalition governments have been formed on the basis of a common agreement by the coalition partners to implement a Common Minimum Programme (CMP). However, the bickering among the coalition partners has been often obstructive to the process of it's implementation. Moreover, the very fact that the elections in 1996 and 1998 threw up unwieldy, unstable and short-lived coalition government was to a great degree responsible for non-implementation of the CMP.

Constraints of the Coalition Government in India

Formation of coalition governments by an alliance of different political parties has been with a specific purpose. Such purpose was to prevent its rival coalition of parties from getting power because it considers the latter as authoritarian, corrupt, communal or inefficient. In 1977, the purpose of the Janata Party, which was formed due to alliance of several parties, was to prevent Congress party from Congress because it had introduced authoritarian emergency rule in the country. The purpose of the Janata Dal alliance in 1989 was to prevent the Congress from coming to power because it was alleged to be corrupt at that time. The purpose of the non-BJP parties to form coalition governments under the prime ministerships of HD Devegowda, I.K. Gujaral and Manmohan Singh was to prevent the BJP from power, and to protect secularism as the BJP was alleged to be communal. Between 1998 to 2004, the coalition governments at the centre were controlled by an alliance of a large number of political parties, the NDA (National Democratic Alliance) let by the BJP. The purpose of the coalition governments led by the NDA was to provide good and self-governance to the people. The alliance, which has been controlling the central governments since 2004, has been known as the UPA (United Progressive Alliances).

Though different coalition governments claimed to have formed government with a specific idealist agenda, in reality their main purposes have been to prevent the rival alliance from capturing power. Therefore, the coalition governments suffered from several limitations. In order to keep the coalition government intact, the principal party in the coalition had given the conditions of the coalition partners. On several occasion, the demands of the coalition partners were affected by the personal factors and political convenience than the polity issues. The coalition government has been constrained by the fear of instability, internal differences among the coalition partners and by the considerations of power politics than the genuine concerns of good governance. Despite these limitations, however, coalition governments are indicators of expansion of scope of democracy in India.

Q18. Write short notes on the following:

(a) Dynamic relationship of caste

Ans. No social system remains static. Social system changes from time to time with the changing social, economical and political circumstances. This is also true for the caste system. At the empirical level, the caste hierarchy has never been static throughout history. Theoretically, all Jatis are hierarchically placed within a prescribed social status. Some Jatis enjoy high status and some occupy low status. Place of the Jati in the social order in the hierarchy is determined by its ritual status based on the observance of customs for interpersonal relationship. Some scholars believe this value system as the acceptance of one's station in the life is the result of previous birth has consensus among all Hindus including the Untouchables. But it is not true. Though, the upper castes try to maintain their higher status, the middle and lower castes have successfully tried to change their status. Having improved their economic condition, a dominant section of some of the low castes, including the groups, which were at one time treated as untouchables, imitated customs and norms of the upper castes residing in their vicinity. Sociologists call this process as sanskritisation. One also comes across instances of some castes or even individuals who have succeeded in improving their status even without adhering to the norms and rituals of the upper castes. Acquiring political authority facilitates not only power holder, i.e. ruler but also his kin and relatives to enjoy higher social status in caste hierarchy. One can cite instances in history, which show that Shudras and anti-shudras having occupying position of power have acquired status of Kshatriyas even without following the path of sanskritisation.

The process of sanskritisation which was prominent among the lower castes at one point of time, particularly in the 19th and early- 20th century, has been slowed down in the 'sixties' and 'seventies'. Earlier many castes hesitated to be called 'backward' despite the poor economic condition of the members. They feared that they would not be able to improve their social status by identifying themselves as 'backward'. But this is no longer true now, as the State has provided certain benefits to the backward castes. These castes have realised that they could improve their status by improving their economic condition rather than observing rituals followed by the upper castes. Now there is competition among the castes to be called 'backward'. Even some of the Brahmin and Rajput Jatis have approached the Government to be classified as 'backward'. The Kolis of central Gujarat followed the rituals of the Rajputs and struggled for three decades to be acknowledged as Kshatriyas. In the past, they used to feel insulted if they were called Kolis. But now they have started calling themselves as Kolis so that they could get material benefits which is the surest way to improve social status. Social status based on the observance of the rituals has increasingly become redundant.

Traditionally caste members have been forbidden to accept cooked food from persons belonging to the Jatis that they considered lower than theirs. These rules have been weakened, particularly in public spheres in urban areas during the last five decades. In their bid to gain, broad support based on the political elites at district and state level, which do not hesitate to take food with the caste members belonging to lower strata.

Most of the Jatis are endogamous. A few follow hypergamy generally within the caste cluster. The earlier restrictions on marriage have become flexible. Marriage circles are expanding in some cases. With education and urbanisation, instances of inter-caste marriages among the upper and middle castes have somewhat increased though such cases are still exceptions.

(b) Regional Variation Type

Ans. Caste structure in terms of hierarchy and boundary for interaction between the social groups is more or less neat and identifiable at the village level. But it is not so at regional level. And to draw empirically based macro picture of castes at the national level is all the more difficult and hazardous. Caste structure has not developed uniformly in all regions of the sub-continent. Assam has developed a loose caste structure with less rigid hierarchy than that of Uttar Pradesh or Bihar. It is the same regarding observation of caste specific rules.

The number of castes also varies from region to region. Gujarat has a larger number of castes than West Bengal. Different historical experiences have contributed to shaping of the present day socio- political processes in different regions. Moreover, there is and had been uneven economic development in the country and also within the states. Some regions had zamindari and some had ryotwari land tenure system. Generally, Rajputs in Rajasthan or Brahmins in Tamilnadu were enjoying dominance in the farmer and peasant castes like Marathas in Maharashtra and Patidars in Gujarat were dominant castes. All castes do not have uniform numerical strength and spread. Some have a larger number of members and some are very tiny. Some are scattered throughout the region and some are heavily concentrated in a few geographical pockets. Hence, the role and position of caste in relation to politics varies from time to time, area to area and caste to caste.

(c) Stratification within Caste

Ans. Industrialisation and penetration of market economy in rural areas have affected traditional occupation of several castes. In most of the castes, some members have given up their traditional occupation. As early as

1950, F.G. Bailey observed in a village situated in a relatively backward state like Orissa, "Not every person works at his traditional occupation. The distillers do not touch liquor. The Knod potters do not know how to make pots. The fishermen do not fish. The warriors are cultivators. Everywhere, there is a scope for practising a hereditary occupation not all members of caste engage in the work". In the 1950s, Kathleen Gough also observed a similar pattern in Tamilnadu. She noted, "The caste community is no longer homogeneous in occupation and wealth, for caste is today a limiting rather than a determining factor in the choice of the occupation. Exactly half of Kumbarpettai's adult Brahmins are now employed in towns as Government servants, schoolteachers or restraint workers. Of the reminder, some own up to thirty acres of land, others as little as three. One runs a grocery store and one a vegetarian restaurant. Among the non-Brahmins, the fisherman, toddy-tapers, Marathas, Kalians, Koravas and Kuttadis has abandoned their traditional work". Village studies carried out in the fifties and sixties from different parts of the country bear out the same trend. And, diversification of occupation in non-farm sector has increased within most of the castes with the spread of the green revolution.

But there are still several Jatis whose members have more or less similar economic condition. One can find such instances among several Scheduled Castes and numerically "small other backward castes". Such castes have still less than 10 per cent rate of literacy and all the households depend on manual labour for their livelihood. On the other hand, there are number of castes, which are internally stratified. There are three types of economic differentiation within different castes: (1) A caste characterised by sharp polarisation; (2) A caste having a majority of members from upper strata; (3) A caste with a majority members belonging to poor strata. Rajputs and Thakurs of Rajasthan, UP and Gujarat fall in the first category. A few households own large estates and factories and a large number are agricultural labourers. Most of the households of the several upper castes such as Brahmins, Baniyas, Kayasthas are well off. On the other hand, a large number of the backward castes have overwhelming majority households who are small and marginal farmers, tenants and agriculture labourers. Economic stratification affects their cohesiveness on political issues. Dominant stratum projects its interests as the interests of the caste and gives it priority while bargaining with the government.

Social and Political Movements in India

An Overview

More often, political scientists and sociologists do not make a distinction between 'social' and 'political' movements. Sociologists assume, and rightly so, that social movements also include those movements which have a clear objective of bringing about political change.

Social movements are classified on the basis of issues around which participants get mobilised. Some of them are known as the 'forest', 'civil rights', 'anti-untouchability', 'linguistic', 'nationalist' and other such movements. Some others classify movements on the basis of the participants, such as peasants, tribals, students, women, dalits, etc. In many cases the participants and issues go together.

Social movements can be classified on the basis of the socio economic characteristics of the participants and the issues involved: 1. Peasant movements; 2. Tribal movements; 3. Dalit movements; 4. Backward caste movements; 5. Women's movements; 6. Industrial working class movements; 7. Human rights and environmental movements.

These movements are based around certain issues and their theorisations claim to cover all social and economic groups. Though the leadership of these movements in the contemporary times comes from the middle class, they primarily raise the issues affecting the deprived classes and communities.

Q1. Discuss the reforms for women in the 19th and early- 20th centuries.

Or

Why can the 19th century be called the age for women?

Ans. In the 19th and early- 20th centuries there was an improvement in the status of women. We can say that the 19th century was an age for women. Discussions were produced in Europe regarding women's rights and the wrongs done to them, their capacities and potentials. By the end of the century, feminist ideas were in the minds of the "radicals" in England, France, Germany and even Russia. In India, the wrongs against women began to be deplored by social reformers. Such movement of 'for' women, 'by' men originated in Bengal and Maharashtra.

Against Sati

The Indian bourgeois class that was born out of Westernisation sought to reform the society by initiating campaigns against caste, polytheism, idolatry, animism, purda, child-marriage, sati and the like. These, to them, were elements of 'pre-modern' or primitive society. The foreign missionaries had branded these as examples of "Hindu barbarism" thus creating enough grounds for the colonial powers to rule. Ram Mohan Roy and Vidyasagar managed to receive the required administrative and legal support because of this. In 1817, Pandit Mrityunjay Bidyalankar declared that sati had no "Shastric" sanction. One year later Governor william Bentinck prohibited Sati in his province, viz. Bengal. It took 11 years for this prohibition to get extended to other parts of India as the Sati Prohibition Act of 1929.

Widow Remarriage

In 1850s Pandit Ishwar Chandra Vidyasagar, proved from the Shastras that the re-marriage of a widow is allowed. It was a long, difficult journey through debates with orthodox pandits and banter from some of the pillars of the Hindu society. The Vernacular (Bengali) press got filled with songs and satires both in support and against. Such verses appeared in the designs of the woven cloths. They created turmoil in society. Vidyasagar submitted a petition to the Governor General in 1855.

A Widow Remarriage Association had started in Madras in 1871, but was short lived. In 1878, Virasalingam started the Rajamundri Social Reform Association, focussing mainly on widow re-marriage. In 1892, the Young Madras Party or the Hindu Social Reform Association was launched. Aryan Brotherhood Conference, of which Ranade and N.M. Joshi were members, once declared in one of its meetings, "let us no longer live in a fool's paradise in the fond belief that because we have managed to survive so long under our present social arrangement, we will be able to survive forever."

Forty odd years since the Act was passed, there had been 500 widow re-marriages only, though social reform organisations, championing the cause, had mushroomed all over India. The majority of them were child or virgin widows. Widows from the upper caste, who were not virgins, could not and did not- re-marry.

Rehabilitating of the Prostitutes

Jyotiba Phule, Dayanand Saraswati, Karve and women like Pandita Ramabai, Sister Nivedita and Tagore's sister Swarnakumari Devi fought for reforms in anti-woman socio religions customs.

First attempts to reform prostitutes were made in Calcutta by Michael Madhusudan Datta, a member of the young Bengali group, who proposed to rehabilitate them by turning them into actresses, and got the Bengal theatre committee to accede to his proposal. This appears to have been the point at which women began to replace men in playing female roles in commercial theatres: several prostitutes turned actresses, and one of them, Binodini, shot into stardom. Datta's move might have been prompted by an Amrita Bazaar Patrika report appearing in 1869, which created something of a furore in Bengali reformist circles. According to the report, ninety per cent of Calcutta's prostitutes were widows, of whom a large number came from Kulin Brahman familics (Kulin Brahmans practised polygamy). Yet if the report created a furore, the general reaction was to attempt to bury it, rather than act upon it. Though, the dangers of widows turning to prostitution had been darkly hinted at in the campaign for the remarriage of widows, Vidyasagar himself disapproved of Datta's proposal, and resigned from the Bengal theatre committee when Datta gained his way. Whether most reformers were made uncomfortable by the thought that many prostitutes came from their own or similar caste and financial communities, or whether they believed that prostitutes should be punished for their choice of a vocation, the fact was that Datta was one of the very rare reformers to attempt positive rehabilitatory action for prostitutes. Most other reformers were more concerned to show their abhorrence for the practice than with what was to happen to prostitutes themselves.

Arya Samaj

Swami Dayanand, was founder of Arya Samaj, disowned the caste system and prescribed equal treatment to women quoting from the shastras. Arya

Samaj did not impose any duties or obligations on women, which could not be applied to men according to the Hindu law givers. In his representative book "Satyartha Prakash", Dayanand insisted that polygamy, child marriage and the seclusion of women did not exist in Aryan India. He called for compulsory education for boys and girls both and that there should be equal stress on tradition and modernity through the compulsory learning of Sanskrit and English. He rose the age of marriage for girls and boys to 16 and 25, respectively.

But Arya Samajis like Lala Lajpat Rai and Lal Chand opposed higher education for women. They believed that if at all, 'the character of girls' education should be different, because 'the education we give to the girls should not unsex them' Apart from basic literacy, Arithmetic and some poetry, Arya Samaj religious literature, sewing, embroidery, cooking, hygienic, drawing and music were the subjects taught. The Brahma Samaj that started as a protest against idolatry and the backward pulling norms and rituals of Brahminical Hindusim, was not free of this stereotype notion about girls and women. The notion continued till the latter stages of our freedom movement.

Prohibition of Child Marriage

The Brahmo Samaj, the Arya Samaj and many other socio-relgious reform movements worked against child marriage. Ishwar Chandra Vidyasagar did pioneering work on the issue of child marriage and his effort met with success in 1860 when the Indian Penal Code prohibited intercourse with a wife who was below 10 years of age.

Behram Malabari, himself not a Hindu, (a Parsi) started a campaign in support of this Act towards the end of the century. He could manage to convince a good number of lawyers, doctors, teachers and public servants. They believed, that "early marriage weakens the physical strength of a nation; it stunts its full growth and development, it affects the courage and energy of the individuals and brings forth a race of people weak in strength" and determination. In 1891, Tilak had led an agitation against the Act and a modern visionary like Tagore had opposed in words and deed!

Q2. Write a short note on women's first fight for rights during colonial period.

Ans. Madame Cama had the honour of unfurling a 'Vande Mataram' flag at 1907 Congress of the Socialist International at Stuttgart, and, in 1913, Kumudini Mitra, more known as a "terrorist", was invited to the International Women's Suffrage Conference at Budapest, Hungary. Sarojini Naidu waited upon the committee, headed by Montague and Lord chelmsford to demand a series of reforms in the condition of the Indian women. Sarala Debi made representations before the committee on behalf of Bharat Stree Mahamandal. At the sixth National Social conference in 1892, Hardevi Roshanlals, the editor of "Bharat Bhagini" insisted that this platform was 'more important' than Congress, because the former understood that:

- The woman's cause is man's
- They rise or sink together,
- Dwarfed or god-like, bound or free.

Anandibai Joshi was the first woman doctor. She and Kantibai were stoned when they dared wearing shoes and carrying umbrellas on the streets. These were symbols of male and caste authority. Was women's position better than that of the lower castes or the untouchables? In 1882, Tarabai Shinde's book, Stree Purush Tulana generated heated discussions all over. She insisted that the faults, commonly ascribed to women, such as superstition, suspicion, treachery and insolence, could be as much found in men. She suggested to the women that, by the strength of their firm will, they remain always well behaved, pure as fire and unblemished internally and externally. Tarabai also suggested that men would have to hang their heads down in shame.

Mai Bhagawati, an "upadeshika" of the Arya Samaj had the confidence to speak in a large public gathering in Haryana. In 1881, Manorama Majumdar, educated at home by her husband, was appointed dhama pracharika by the Barisal Brahmo Samaj. As expected, lot of heated debate followed questioning the 'wisdom' of carrying the issue of women's equality a little too far. Regular participation in the nationalist campaigns and organisations had generated such a spirit that a group of Brahmo women walked through the streets of Calcutta singing and speaking against the evils of purdah. These are indisputable instances of initiatives or movements "by" women. But Indian National Congress and other political parties were not yet prepared to acknowledge that potential among women. Though the women delegates were allowed to sit on the dias, they were not allowed to speak or vote on the resolutions.

Q3. How did women define "Swaraj" and "Swadhinata" during freedom struggle?

Ans. A discourse on equality began to develop, in the late 1910s and 1920s, amongst women. They used nationalists' arguments to defend their demands for equal rights. Urmila Devi, a militant woman, defined 'swaraj' as self-rule and 'Swadhinata' as the 'strength and power to rule over oneself'. Amiya Debi rightly felt that 'Swadhinata' cannot be given, it has to be taken by force. If it is left to the "well-wishing" men, then women's adhinata (dependence) along will get strengthened. The nationalist leaders, who were the first to call women outside their home and household, believed in complementarity and not sameness, which the revolutionary women demanded. The reformers and the 'givers' believed that women's rights should be recognised because of women's socially useful role as mothers. Women demanded equal rights because, as human beings, they have the same needs, the same desires and the same capacities as men. To get success in your studies, read only GPH book.

Q4. Discuss about the discrimination against women in politics.

Ans. Mahatma Gandhi did not choose any woman in his list of 71 marchers to Dandi. Some women did not accept it. Then Khurshid Naoroji and Margaret Cousins started a protest strongly. But Gandhi remained firm on his decision arguing that he had allocated a greater role to women than the mere breaking of salt laws. Yet, Sarojini naidu joined the march at Dandi at the final stage. She was the first woman to be arrested in Dandi march. After Sarojini Naidu, thousands of women became confident and joined the salt satyagraha. It was happened at first time that women got involved in the struggle for independence. Some famous women, like Kasturba Gandhi, Kamaladebi Chattopadhyay, Nellie Sengupta, Basanti Debi (Roy), Durgabai Deshmukh and Aruna Asaf Ali also participated in this movement.

Q5. Discuss the activities of a few women terrorists.

Ans. Kumudini Mitra had organised a group of educated Brahmin women who liaised between the revolutionaries in hiding. Women got increasingly involved with revolutionary groups, popularly known, feared and revered as "terrorists". In December, 1931, Shanti Ghosh and Suniti Chowdhury shot a district Magistrate, Mr. Stevens, who had harassed women more than the law, perhaps, permitted. Mina Das had atempted to shoot the Governor of Bengal, Stanley Jackson in 1922. They had all acted on their own and the first two were sentenced to transportation for life. Preetilata Wadedar led a raid on a club that the Europeans frequented. The bomb killed one and injured four. Preetilata, clothed in male attire took cyanide to avoid arrest. A paper stating that the raid was an "act of war" was recovered from her person. On the same day pamphlets were distributed exhorting teachers, students and the public to join the campaign against the British rulers and the Europeans.

Sarala Devi and Sister Nivedita were also closely related to, and inspired by the Bengal terrorists.

Q6. Highlight the major issues confronting women's unity.

Ans. Following are the major issues confronting women's unity:

(1) Communalism and Casteism

The issue of communalism was taken up by All India Women's Conference (AIWC) in the thirties. In 1932, both their district branches and the annual conference organised protests against the reservation of separate seats for women in the legislatures applying communal criteria. The Bombay branch, for example, got involved in riot relief and the Andhra Pradesh branch started a campaign against religious prayers in the schools. The organisation was, perhaps, the first to raise demands for uniform civil code so that women cannot be subdued and tortured by religious dictums and caste obligations. They demanded exactly the same law for all women of India- whatever may be their caste or religion.

Unfortunately, by 1940s communal tensions manifested among the members themselves, as a result of the increasingly hostile relations between the congress and the Muslim League. By 1944, most of the Muslim Women Left AIWC. After partition and migration to Pakistan, they formed All Pakistan Women's Conference, thus belying the very purpose of this organisation. The AIWC in India continued to work against communilsim, casteism and patriarchal oppression and started getting members from all religious groups, though the Hindu and the Dalits are many more in number.

Communalism and casteism have taken a horribly violent and ugly form ever since the carving out of the country on communal lines; Intolerance of the lower castes and of the religious and racial minorities has increased by leaps and bounds; mobilisation among women in protest and self-defence has also become stronger and wider. The other modes of oppressions, related to and born out of patriarchy and the concentration of wealth and power in the hands of a few, have also motivated the women's movement in India.

(2) Daily Encounters with Oppression

(a) **Against Alcohol:** In 1972, the voice raised against the alcohol. Bhil women started this movement. Liquor pots were broken by them. The most sustained and successful having been The Anti-Arrack Movement in Nellore in Andhra Pradesh. Alcoholism is understood by women and the men who fight for women's cause, as a major cause behind wife-beating and family violence. Unending or increasing impoverishment of a family is also mainly because of man's income being wasted on this menace. That is why all women's bodies take up alcohol as a major issue, apart from dowry and sexual abuse; in fact all anti-liquor movements gradually get involved in all other problems facing women.

(b) **Against Dowry:** This powerful movement was first organised in Hyderabad in 1975. It used to attract more than 2000 men and women in their demonstrations and the anger had spread to Maharashtra, Karnataka, Madhya Pradesh, Gujarat and even to as far as Punjab and Bengal. But the movement took deep and permanent roots in and around Delhi because the problem was, and is, much more acute and gruesome in this cultural belt. Mahila Dakshata Samiti was the pioneer body in Delhi in this regard. Now its scope, like in case of all other similar organisations, has spread over to all other areas concerning women's oppression and subjugation.

(c) **Against Sexual Abuse:** Rape and other forms of sexual abuse are the most common and frequent of crimes against women and yet, the most unreported. Apart from rapes within the family or due to personal lust or enmity, rapes are quite common occurrence in communal and caste tensions and in police custody. The agitation against rape, for the first time, started against police rape. The rape of Rameeza Bi in police custody became a symbol. The movement is ever-increasing in area, support and anger, yet the upward trend in the number of incidents is not getting checked. Shakti Shalini, Sabal Mahila Sangha, Janwadi Mahila Samiti are some of the striking names in this field. The last named has been organising women in their political battles also. The latest over-riding issue for women of all categories, of course, has been the reservation of seats in the highest decision-making bodies of the land.

A whole new set of personal relationships developed in the feminist movement of friendships which cut across class, caste and cultural barriers, even though, to some extent, these friendships remained unequal. The middle class women, who usually were the leaders or organisers, acted more out of a sense of duty, and the poor from a position of helplessness and gratitude. Yet, the growth of a new sense of 'individuality' was clearly visible.

(d) Human Rights of Women: All rights of women as human beings are human rights. Most important of these include right to equality or right against discrimination; right to freedom; right to dignity and self-respect, and right to life. These human rights of women are violated through different ways - honour killings, dowry and dowry death, denial of equal treatment in life and society, domestic violence, etc. The social movements of women have protected human rights of women. However, they face multiple challenges due to the predominance of the patriarchical values in the society.

(3) Environment and Livelihood

Engels explained that ownership of land and the means of production controls all categories of human relationships and is, therefore, the basis of patriarchy. Even in the age of highly advanced science and technology, food and all that a human being needs come from Nature and environment. We know that from the day one of human existence, women have been the food gatherer and food provider; and therefore, women are the worst affected as a result of environmental degradation and indiscriminate robbing of Nature. That is why; women's movement has been most powerful with regard to their and their family's livelihood and the conservation of Nature. It started with women breaking forest laws in pre-independence India. Chipko and Narmada Bachao movements are good examples in this regard. 'Self-employed Women's Association (SEWA)" is the first known organisation in India and South Asia, which united the women workers in the unorganised and the home-based sectors. This perhaps, is the most successful and sustained women's movement since it got closely tied up with 'Mahila Kosh' or women's cooperative bank. It has inspired many similar movements in Bangladesh, Nepal and elsewhere in South Asia.

Q7. Discuss the various major movements in which women played an important role.

Ans. Women played an important role almost in each and every movement of Indian independence. Some of them are as follows:

Telangana Movement

There was a significant participation of women in the Telangana movement for land and related Eco-political rights. This movement could not be successful without the strong and sustained motivation from the women. This movement was started by people due to the injustices of the British Raj (1941) and their own government (till 1952).

Bodh Gaya Movement

Another landmark movement for land, i.e. livelihood, or economic rights "by" women was the forceful acquisition of the 'patta' by the peasant women, who had collected from in and around Bodh Gaya (Bihar). The men were not putting in enough efforts or resources into the land due to drinking and other bad habits. The unexpected success became a terrific inspiration for all united efforts by women. But, the success here was unique and exceptional; in most other cases success was not in their fate, and Bihar continues to be one of the top States in social injustice and oppression of women.

Dalit Women's Movement

Dalit women got first organised by a self-taught Dalit couple, the Phules in Maharashtra. They (Phule couples) can also be called one of the founders of the movement for women's rights in the 19th Century. At present, Janwadi Mahila Samiti is the strongest supporter of this movement. The Dalit women felt the need to organise themselves separately, both from their men and the other women, mainly because of two reasons: (i) Dalit men, however oppressed themselves, do not stop oppressing their own women; and (ii) The non-Dalit women, however sincere and fail to comprehend the 'double' oppression that a Dalit women invariably suffers.

Adivasi Women's Movement

In the North Cachar hills of Nagaland, a woman named Gudiallo became famous for her part in the civil disobedience movement. Affectionately titled 'Rani' Gudiallo, she had first got involved in the struggle for independence when she was thirteen, joining her cousin, Jadonang, who had started mobilising villagers into satyagraha campaigns in Manipur District in 1925. In 1931, the British arrested Jadonang, summarily tried and sentenced him, and hanged him. Gudiallo now took over the reins of the movement, shifting its base from Manipur district to the North Cachar hills, inhabited by the Zeliagong tribe.

This is one of many such indigenous and spontaneous peoples' movements which used to be strongly discouraged and disowned by the 'mainstream' nationalist politics. This trend and the attitude of deciding what is good and what is necessary for the other or others is the foundation of patriarchy and capitalism (and, of course, imperialism), and continues to this day even after independence. That is why the adivasis, the dalits and the women are continuing to fight their battles even after more than half century of India attaining freedom. At present, the war against environmental degradation is fought mainly by the adivasis or the sons and daughters of Nature, because robbing of nature means robbing of their livelihood and culture.

Movement through Literature, Theatre and other forms of Expression

After independence, there was a bit of a lull in the first few decades in these fields. May be the women took a little time to realise that 1947 did not bring any independence for them. Lately, with the rising strength in the women's movement for equality, there has been a spurt in writings, films and plays by women and on women. Powerful women writers like Arundhuti Roy, are trudging the 'women only' field and taking up the cause of humanism or universal human rights much more forcefully than men. Women are making men realise that their good lies in women's good and that women's good lies in the good of the entire humanity.

Q8. What do you mean by the term Dalit? Discuss the Dalit movement in the colonial period.

Ans. Dalits are those groups of people who have faced social discrimination including the untouchability. They largely belong to the economically disadvantaged groups of our society. They are placed in the Scheduled Caste categories in our constitution. The category of dalits was first used by Jyotiba Phule in the nineteenth century. It was first popularly used by the Dalit Panther in the 1970s. But it has come in currency quite recently – from the 1980s onwards. It has almost replaced the category of harijans used for the dalits or Scheduled Castes.

Movements in Colonial Period

Dalit movements are, in fact, the Harijans/Scheduled Castes movements. The word the "oppressed" is closest to the word "Dalit". As it has been stated earlier, from "Harijan to the "Scheduled Castes" and from the "Scheduled Castes" to "Dalit" mark the process of the emergence of the word "Dalit". Thus, Dalits are the Scheduled Castes (SCs) and they constitute nearly 16 per cent of India's population.

The colonial period saw widespread changes in socio-political scenario of the country. After coming into contact with the idea of equality, a section of caste Hindus started opposing the discrimination against dalit communities. Arya Samaj, Brahma Samaj and Ramakrishna Mission were some such organisations. These organisations condemned caste based discriminations and started some activities for betterment of dalits. However, after initial attachments, the dalits moved away from these organisations mainly because these movements failed to create a radical anti caste unity between the dalits and the middle caste hindus. An important reason for this was that these organisations did never really challenge the 'varna' system which was the basis of caste system. In the meanwhile things were slowly changing for dalits. British started recruiting some of these men in the army which improved their economic condition and instilled some measure of confidence in them. The education policy adopted by the British government was also favourable for social change. While state took over the task of providing education, it also ensured that education was secular and was provided without any discrimination of caste or creed. This opened up educational avenues for these groups. With education arose consciousness about their status which resulted in a number of movements in different parts of the country. Some of these movements were:

- First prominent movement of this kind was led by Jyotiba Phule who was an important social reformer. He laid stress on education and stated that lack of education was at the root of all problems of dalits. In 1848, he started a school for untouchables and another one exclusively for women. In 1873, he founded the Satya Sodhak Samaj whose main aim was to liberate the lower castes from discrimination and oppression
- Sree Narayan Guru was a spiritual leader from the Ezahava community of Kerala. He rejected caste system and the superiority of brahmins. Subsequently, movement by Ezahavas led to Travancore Proclamation which allowed entry of all Hindus in all the temples of Travancore in 1936.
- Adi Dharm movment started in Punjab in 1926. These people claimed that the untouchables were the real inhabitants of India and upper caste people came from outside and enslaved the original people. They believed in non-theistic notion of divinity and believed in equality of men. The movement was active from 1926 to 1946. It worked to bring awareness among the depressed classes in Punjab Due to the efforts of the movement; some of the untouchables were listed in 1931 census as Adi-dharmis and not Hindus.
- Adi Andhra Mahajan Sabha was formed in 1917. It resolved to call untouchables of the region as 'Adi-Andhras' and took up the cause of nominating these people to statutory bodies, to admit their children to common schools and to dig separate wells for drinking water to these classes. The nomenclature of

Adi Andhra was accepted by the government and some of its members were nominated to the Madras Legislative Assembly. The sabha was active till 1940.

- Paraiyar Mahajan Sabha was formed in 1891 by Rettamalai Srinivasan. It became Adi Dravida Mahajan Sabha in 1893. The Sabha took up matters for upliftment of the dalits including reserving posts for them in the public services.
- All Bengal Namsudra Association was formed in 1912. It demanded increasing of franchise by including the depressed classes and reservation of seats in Legislature. The association was instrumental in bringing awareness among untouchables in Bengal.

Dr. Baba Saheb Ambedkar

Dr. Ambedkar was the most important dalit leader in India. He was born on 14th April, 1891 in a mahar family which was considered untouchable. He completed his education in India though during it he was faced with discrimination at every stage. In 1913 he went to United States under a scholarship granted by the Maharaja of Baroda for post graduation at Columbia University. Later he also studied in London School of Economics and also at Gray's Inn for study of law. After his return to India in 1923 he actively involved himself in the works relating to the welfare of depressed classes. He was supported in his activities by Shahuji IV, the rule of Kolhapur. In 1924, he founded Bahishkrat Hitkarini Sabha with the aim of promoting education and culture among the depressed classes and to work for their upliftment. In 1927, he led the famous Mahad Tank Satyagraha for right of untouchables to take water from the main tank. The movement resulted in burning of manusmriti. In 1930, he led a protest for entry of untouchables at Kalaram temple at Nasik.

Due to his prominence as a dalit leader he was invited to the second round table conference wherein he advocated separate electorate for untouchables. The Government announced the Communal Award on these lines. However, this was opposed by Mahatma Gandhi who went on fast in Yerwada jail. Meetings were then arranged between Dr. Ambedkar and Mahatma Gandhi which culminated in the Poona Pact, as per which the depressed classes will not claim separate electorate but will be granted reserved seats in the legislature. He founded the Independent Labour Party in 1936 and All India Schedule Caste Federation in 1942 to contest elections. However, these parties could not taste much electoral success.

The movement led by Dr Ambedkar was somewhat different from the earlier movements. While many of the earlier movements were reformative in the sense that they demanded equality within Hindu religion, his movement rejected the Hindu religion altogether and searched for alternatives. In accordance with these views he adopted Buddhism. Second difference was his stress on sharing of power, both economic and political. It was this thought that he demanded separate electorate for untouchables and despite all the odds was able to obtain reserved seats in the legislature.

Sanskritisation, de-Sanskritisation and reservation

Prof M.N. Srinivas introduced the term sanskritisation in context to Indian society. The term refers to a process whereby people of lower castes collectively try to adopt upper caste practices and beliefs to acquire higher status. It indicates a process of cultural mobility that was taking place in the traditional social system of India.

Through this process, Srinivas found that lower castes in order to raise their position in the caste hierarchy adopted some customs and practices of the Brahmins and gave up some of their own which were considered to be impure by the higher castes.

Sanskritisation has occurred usually in groups who have enjoyed political and economic power but were not ranked high in ritual ranking. Thus after gaining political and/or economic strength these groups tried to imitate certain rights, practices and rituals to gain upward social mobility.

However off late because of reservation and political mobilisation correlated with the caste identities, the trend has reversed. This trend is exactly opposite to sanskritisation, thus can be termed as de-sanskritisation. In the recent past, there has been a increasing tendency among various social groups to project themselves as "backward" in order to accrue the benefits of the reservation. The agitation by Gujjars in Rajasthan to claim the status of Schedule Tribe and by Jats in north western part of the country to include them in the list of backward class truly exemplifies this novel trend.

Q9. Discuss the Dalit movement in the post-colonial period.

Or

What were the basic features of dalit movement in India during the 1950s and 1960s?

Or

Describe the basic features of dalit movement during the 1990s.

Or

Discuss the phases through which the dalit movement has passed.

Ans. Dalit movement in the post – Independence period in India can be divided into three phases, i.e., phase I (1950s – 1960s), phase II (1970s – 1980s); and phase III (1990s onwards).

Phase I (1950s – 1960s)

Implementation of the universal adult franchise, reservation in educational and political institutions, and in jobs for the Schedules Castes as per the provisions of the constitution enabled a large number of them to take advantage of these facilities in the period following independence. Along with these the state in India introduced several programmes for the betterment of the disadvantaged groups of the society, especially the Scheduled Castes and Scheduled Tribes. Though in Most parts of the country the Scheduled Castes could not benefit from the measures introduced by the state due several practical reasons, yet these did help them wherever suitable conditions existed for them. Besides, the political parties, especially Congress party attempted to mobilise them as its vote bank. Despite the difficulties in availing of their right to vote in many parts of the country, politicisation of the dalits took place to a considerable extent. Such process made them conscious of their rights. The policies and strategies of the Congress helped it create its social base which consisted of Dalits as major social group. The politicisation of dalits during this phase took as a constituent of the social base of the political parties, especially the Congress. Meanwhile, there emerged the first generation of dalit leadership borne after independence, which included educated middle class professional as well. This group became critical of dominant political parties and the cultural ethos, especially the Congress and the Hindu belief system. They started feeling that the Congress was using them as the vote bank; the high castes were holding the leadership of this party and not allowing dalits to get the leadership. On the cultural front they felt that the Hindu religion does not provide them a respectable place. Therefore, in order to live respectfully they should discard Hindu religion and convert to Buddhism. The advocates of this opinion were influenced by the ideas of Dr B.R. Ambedkar. They formed Republican Party of India (RPI) based on the ideas and principles of Ambedkar. In the late 1950s and 1960s RPI launched a cultural and political movement in UP and Maharashtra for achieving political and cultural autonomy from the dominant formations. A large number of dalits got converted to Budhhism. The RPI emerged one of the important political parties in the assembly and parliamentary elections held in UP during the 1960s. But the RPI could not remain a force in UP after the 1960s because its main leadership got co-opted into the Congress, a party against whom it had launched movement in the preceding decade.

The Second phase (1970s – 1980s)

This phase was marked by the combination of class and caste struggles. In the rural areas of West Bengal, Bihar and Andhra Pradesh the naxalite movement launched a struggle against the caste and class exploitation. In the cities of Bombay and Pune, the Dalit Panther launched the similar kind of movement.

Dalit Panthers of India

During the 1960s and 1970s, the Dalit Panthers and several groups with a Marxist/Leninist or Maoist orientation, emerged outside the framework of recognised political parties and parliamentary politics to confront the established powers. The Dalit Panthers were formed in the state of Maharashtra in the 1970s ideologically aligning themselves to the Black Panther movement in the United States. During the same period, Dalit literature, painting, and theatre challenged the very premise and nature of established art forms and their depiction of society and religion. Many of these new Dalit artists formed the first generation of the Dalit Panther movement that sought to wage an organised struggle against the varna system. Dalit Panthers visited "atrocity" sites, organised marches and rallies in villages, and raised slogans of direct militant action against their upper-caste aggressors.

The determined stance of the Dalit Panthers served to arouse and unite many Dalits, particularly Dalit youths and students. The defeat of ruling party candidates and the boycott of elections in some areas forced the government to take notice of the movement: Panther leaders were often harassed and removed from districts for speaking out against the government and Hindu religion. They also became frequent targets of police brutality and arbitrary detentions. Disagreements over the future of the movement and the inclusion of other caste groups ultimately led to a dispersal of Dalit Panther leadership. The formed aggressiveness and militancy of the Dalit Panther have for the most part dissipated, through small splinter groups or groups that have adopted the name still survive. In Tamil Nadu, for Example, the Dalit Panther of India have thrived since the 1980s as a nonviolent awareness-raising and organising movement concentrating primarily on women's rights and land issues and claims. They are currently led by a man named Tirumavalavan.

Naxalite Movement in Bihar

The Naxalite movement reached a flashpoint in Musahari block of the Muzaffarpur district in early- 1970s, led to a clash between the Naxalites, the State power and landlords. But soon Jayprakash Narayan, the former revolutionary socialist leader of the Sarvodya Movement initiated measures to bring about changes in agrarian structure. His efforts reduced the intensity of Naxalite activity to a great extent and it seemed the Naxalite movement was losing steam like in West Bengal. But the Naxalites were gaining ground in Central Bihar (now South Bihar) and in Bhojpur district. During this period the Naxalite movement was spreading its tentacles in Patna district too. But its impact was much less compared to other districts.

The movement in Bihar had developed in four phases ever since 1967. In the first phase, the peasants, led by Naxals fought against social and caste exploitation. In the second phase, they moved on to the question of economic exploitation and demanded minimum wages as fixed by the Government under the Bihar Minimum Wages Act. The third phase was related to land disputes. It was for the first time, the landless peasants and landlords/landowning class entered into a direct confrontation with the former demanding occupancy rights over surplus land and land vacated by the government.

The fourth phase was when their demands for payment of minimum wages, free distribution of surplus Government land and enforcement of Bihar Land Ceiling Act and other land reforms were not implemented the landless peasants, with the support of the Naxals, started forcibly grabbing land of the landlords/landowners and clashed with the private armies of the landlords. It may be recalled that the long drawn out struggle against the mahant of Bodh-Gaya launched by the Chhatra Yuva Sangharsh Vahini forcing the mahant to surrender around 300 acres of land which the Government distributed among the Harijan landless peasants of Bodh-Gaya.

Dalit Movement in Karnataka

In Karnataka also dalits organised into the Dalit Sanghasrsh Samiti (DSS). It was an organisation which was set up in 1973 and set up its units in most districts of Karnataka. Like Bihar it also took up caste and class issues and attempted to build an alliance of diverse groups of the exploited classes. It also brought dalits of different persuasions – Marxism, socialism, Ambedkarism, etc, under the banner of a single organisation. During 1974 and 1784 it took up the issues relating to wages of the agricultural labourers, devdasi and reservation. It held study groups to discuss the problems of dalits. The DSS was formed following the resignation of a dalit leader Basavalingappa, who was asked to do so by the chief Minister

Devraj Urs. This leader referred to the literature of the high caste with Bhoosa (cattle fodder). This outraged the students belonging to the high castes, leading to the caste rights between the high castes and dalits. Incensed by consequences of the remarks of the minister the chief minister had asked him to resign. The Bhoosa controversy set a strong anti-caste tendency, which was represented a journal Dalit Voice set up by a journalist Rajshekhar. Dalit Voice attacked Brahmins as "Nazis" and the left movement as "Brahmo –Communist" and termed dalits as "born Marxists". According to the editor of Dalit Voice the main issue in the dalit-OBC mobilisation is not the alliance between the dalits and the OBCs, the leadership of dalits over the OBCs.

Phase III (1990s onwards)

Dalit organisations were propagated in different states of the country in 1990s. The case of Bahujan Samaj Party (BSP) in Uttar Pradesh is most important.

Though the Republican Party of India (RPI) had been influential in Uttar Pradesh like Maharshtra since the 1950s, the rise of the BSP has been the most striking feature of dalit identity and politics in India. It has been able to lead the government in Uttar Pradesh thrice with a dalit woman Mayawati as the chief minister. The BSP was founded on April 14, 1984 by its president Kashi Ram. With the formation of the BSP, Kashi Ram changed the social and cultural organisations into a political party – the BSP. The BSP aimed to mobilise the majority other sections of the society, the Bahujan Samaj, consisting of the dalits, backward class and religious minorities which excluded the high castes like Brahmans, Rajputs, and Banias. The BSP believes that the minority high castes have been using the votes of the majority communities or the Bahujan Samaj. They did not let them become the leaders or the rulers.

The BSP has been able to consolidate its position among dalits mainly for its strategy of electoral alliances and the public policies. The most important case of the BSP's electoral alliance has been in the state of UP, though it has attempted electoral alliances in other states as well. From the 1993 assembly election of UP onwards, the BSP has entered into alliances with the major political formulations like Congress, the BJP and the Samajwadi Party in UP or the Akali Dal and Congress in Punjab, which could help it win the assembly and parliamentary elections or in the post-poll alliance which help it form the government. The first alliance which the BSP made was with the Mulayam Singh Yadav-led Samajwadi Party in UP in 1993 election. This alliance was considered as an example of the unity of the Bahujan Samaj – the BSP identified with the dalits and the Samajwadi Party with the backward classes and the minorities. This alliance, however, continued only till the BSP withdrew support from the Mulayam Singh Yadav-led SP-BSP government in 1995. The fall of Mulayam Singh led-government was followed by its alliance with the BJP, which enabled Mayawati to become the first dalit woman Chief Minister of any state. Immediately after becoming the Chief Minister, Mayawati declared that her party serve the serva samaj; it was shift from her earlier position where she vowed to fight for the Bahujan Samaj. It was beginning of the BSP's change in the electoral or alliance strategy. In the subsequent elections, contrary to original principles, it gave tickets even to the high castes Brahmins, Rajputs, Banias and Kayasthas gave them representation as ministers in her government.

However, during her Chief Ministership, Mayawati introduced special policies for dalits. The most important of these included: – Ambedkar Village Programmes consisting of the special programmes for the welfare of the weaker sections in the villages identified as the Ambedakar Villages on the basis of the substantial dalit population in such villages, and naming of the public institutions after the low caste historical personalities.

Q10. Write a note on 'tribal society and economy'.

Ans. Ralph Linton the legendary and respected anthropologist of mid-20th century has given a definition of the term 'Tribe'. According to him a 'tribe is group of bands occupying a contiguous territory or territories having a feeling of unity deriving from numerous similarities in culture, frequent contacts and a certain community of interests'. Others refer to the tribal society of India as an imperfect segment of the Hindus. Indian tribal society can be underlined as a social group with strict territorial affiliation, possessing characteristics of endogamy, with no specialisation of functions ruled by tribal officers hereditary or otherwise, united in language or dialect recognising social distance with other tribes.

An enormous section of Indian tribal societal population depends on agriculture as their sole way for survival. Some of the agricultural tribes are: Oraons, Mundas, Bhils, Santhals, Baigas, and Hos. The Toda tribe serves as a fabulous illustration of pastoral economy. Their social and economic organisation almost always revolves around buffaloes. They obtain their living through exchange. In some parts of India tribal people are engaged in shifting cultivation. It is known by different names, like, Nagas refer to it as Jhum, Bhuiyas call it Dahi and Koman, Maria of Bastar refer to it as Penda, Khond refer to it as Podu and Saiga call it Bewar.

Many auxiliary occupations, like handicrafts are undertaken in various tribal societies of India. These include basket-making, spinning and weaving. For example, the Tharu tribe depends upon furniture making, manufacturing musical instruments, weapons, ropes and mats. The Korw and Agaria tribes are well known iron-smelters producing tools for local use. Characteristically too Indian tribal society possess their own set of languages, which are unwritten. Hence the degree of communication both in time and space is predictably narrow. At the same time tribal societies demonstrate an outstanding economy of design and have a compactness and self-sufficiency surprisingly lacking in modern city society. According to Indian aboriginal traditions, the tribal societies inhabit and remain within a definitive and common topography. Members of a tribe possess an awareness of mutual unity. The members of a tribe always speak a common language. These members generally marry within their own group, but now due to heightened contact with outsiders there are instances of tribals tying the knot outside as well. A typical Indian tribal societal group believes in ties of blood relationship amongst its members. They have faith in their having descended from a common, real or mythical, forerunner and thus believe in blood relationships with other members. Tribes follow their own political organisation which preserves eternal harmony. Religion is of supreme importance in an Indian tribal society. A tribal political and social organisation is always based upon religion, because they are granted religious sanctity and appreciation. When speaking of Indian tribal society, their variety and usage of novelty in every dance they perform is absolutely one of ecstasy, one of bliss.

Q11. Discuss the social and political movements of tribals.

Or

Discuss the movements of tribals in the pre-colonial and post-colonial periods.

Or

What is the Seng Khasi?

Or

Identify the main trends of the tribal movements in India during 1920-1947.

Ans. Pre-colonial Period

In the pre-colonial period some of the tribes founded states in the territories extending from the north-east, through middle India to western and southern India. Where they did not found states, they were accommodated within regional political system, retaining a great deal of autonomy and freedom. Pre-colonial period can be divided in three phases:

The First Phase (1795-1860)

The rise and establishment of the British rule saw the beginning of the first phase (1795-1860) of the tribal uprisings, which may be described as primary resistance movements. The Santhal insurrection (1855-56) represented a transitional phase marked by the agrarian resistance and revivalism.

In the North-East the sub-phases of tribal rebellions could be similarly demarcated. The Garos and Hajongs who submitted to the British rule to escape the tyranny of their zamindars, came under the influence of the Pagal Panthi. Their chief, Tipu who became the leader of the oppressed peasantry, founded a kingdom and was arrested. The Khasis were engaged in acts of depredations in the plains they raided from 1787 to 1825. The Singphos, Mishmis, Lushais, Khamptis and Daflas raided plains and killed people. The Khasis opposed the construction of the road, and the confederation of Khasi chiefs resisted the British attempt at the occupation of their country, led by Tirot Singh. The British sent out expeditions to punish the Lusahis, Mishmis etc. In middle India, this phase ended with the revolt of Maniram Dewan and Saranga Raja of Assam in 1857.

The Second Phase (1860-1920)

The second phase (1860-1920) coincided with the onset of the intensive period of colonialism, which saw a much deeper penetration of merchant capital, a higher incidence of rent, etc., into tribal and peasant economies. It intensified the exploitation of the tribes. As a result of this, there were not only a larger number of movements, represented by such evocative native terms as mulkui larai, fituri, meli, ulgulan and bhumakal, involving many tribes but also a far more complex type of movement, which represented a curious mix of agrarian, religious and political issues. The Bhakti movement with its tenet of monotheism, vegetarianism, cleanliness, abstention from liquor, etc., was introduced by mendicants (gossainess) artisans and peasants moving into tribal areas. Christianity also arrived and under its impact a new tribal middle classes emerged, which was educated, conscious and self- respecting. Both Christianity and Bhakti movement contributed in this phase to the rise of millenarian movements. The tribal movements demonstrated, in varying degrees, tribal resistance against the assaults on their system and their attempt to prop up its mouldering edifices. They were followed by the socio-religious or revitalisation movements, viz. the Kherwar movement among the Santals (1871-80), the Sardar revivalistic movement among the Mundas and Oraons (1881-90), the Tana bhagat and Haribaba movements in Chhotanagpur, the Bhagat movement in Madhya Pradesh and Bhil revivalism, which were expressive of the tribals urge to create a new order. These two lines of the movement, through the length and breadth of the sub-continent, revealed striking similarities, a basis unity of response to almost the same complex of challenging forces.

The movement led by Birsa Munda (1874-1901) is the best known of the socio-political movements of this phase because the movement sought to establish Munda raj and independence. In its socio-religious aspects, it was like any other Bhagat movement, with the difference that it was also influenced by Christianity, and it used both Hindu and Christian idioms to create the Munda ideology and world view. The rebels attacked police stations and officials, churches and missionaries and though there was an undercurrent of hostility against the dikus, there was no overt attack on them except in a couple of controversial cases. The uprising was quelled, but its lessons were acknowledged in the passing of the Chotanagpur tenancy act. It sought to protect the Munda land system, prohibited transfer of tribal land, recognised tribal right to reclaim land and created a new administrative unit.

The Third Phase (1920-1947)

In the third phase, from 1920 to 1947, we see three trends in tribal movements. The first trend is represented by the impact of the freedom struggle and Mahatma Gandhi on tribes, and participations of some of major tribal groups in the national movement and reconstruction programme. The second trend is represented by the movements centering on land and forest revival and reform of tribal society. The third trend is reflected by the rise of movements seeking autonomy, statehood, separation and independence, led by the tribal middle class.

To the Hindu peasantry steeped in the medieval bhakti tradition, the Mahatma appeared like a bhakti preacher, and to the tribals like a bhagat. We may describe in brief three movements, the Tanabhagat movement among the Oraons, the Haribaba movement among the Hos and allied tribes, and the Rajmohini movement among the Gonds, which reflected the impact of Gandhi.

The best known of Bhagat movements was the Tanabhagat movement which started in the manner of a nativistic movement. On April 21, 1914, an Oraon youth in his 20s, from the Dharmesh, the Supreme God, in a dream, together with the divine power and supernatural gifts necessary for the restoration of the Oraon raj (this sentence to be redone). While the tribes accepted the nationalist programme and joined the mainstream of the national movement, they resisted against their economic and cultural exploitation. Swaraj meant not only freedom from British rule, but also freedom from the oppression of the dikus, money-lenders, zamindars and feudal-overlords.

In the princely states where tribals were more backward, the Praja Mandals launched movements against the feudal order by mobilising the tribals. The tribes who responded particularly to these movements were the Bhils, Gonds, Kharwars, Mundas and Khonds. Most of them had a notion of property, private or communal, in land, which had been threatened by the colonial system and feudal exploitation. The agrarian issues which excited them were the demands for begar or veth (compulsory labour without payment) rasal or magan (free supply of provisions for visiting officers), and exactions other than rent (abwabs).

Two nativistic movements sought to revive the pure and pristine elements of tribal culture. The Seng Khasi, a socio-cultural organisation of the Khasis had been established as early as 1889 to preserve the Khasi way of life. Through its platform the non-Christian Khasis have tried to strengthen the ancient system of clan relationship, which was disturbed by the large-scale conversion of the Khasis to Christianity. The second, the Zeliangrong movement, started as a religio-cultural movement under Jadunang, which assumed a political overtone and became the only movement to have established linkages with the national freedom struggle. Under Gaidinliu it remained strongly nationalistic, promoted tribal solidarity and demanded creation of a separate administrative unit for the Zeliangrong people to be formed out of the territories inhabited by the constituent tribes in the contiguous regions of Manipur, Assam and Nagaland, a demand to which these states did not agree.

Post-colonial Period

The post-colonial period witnessed intensification of the exploitation of resource of the tribal land and the marginalisation, immiseration or pauperisation of the tribal people despite progress in education and employment, representation in politics and share in power, and affluence of a section of tribal middle class. As a result, this period witnessed the rise of a large number of movements centered on the issues of identity, equality, empowerment, self-rule, etc. A survey of tribal movements conducted by the Anthropological Survey of India (ASI) towards the close of 1976 identified 36 ongoing tribal movements. Fourteen of these were concentrated in the northeast. These movements include political movements representing transitions from the politics of insurgency to that of integration, socio-cultural movements seeking new identity, script-based and language related movements. Eastern Indian reported seven movements, the most important of them being the movement for the establishment of a Jharkhand state. There were also mobility movements among the Kurmis re-seeking tribal status. Central India reported the continuation of the bhagat movements and a political movement of sorts among the Gonds. The northern parts of Andhra, which are a part of the central Indian system, witnessed a militant tribal uprising. There were four movements in western India, a bhagat movement among the Bhils, two agrarian movements among tribal peasants and a political movement for autonomy. In the south, where there are small isolated primitive tribes, only an incipient political process could be observed among them.

These and other movements among the tribes could be classified into four types. They are:

- Political movements for autonomy, independence, state formation, and self-rule.
- Movements for control over resources, such as land and forest, or movements directed against land alienation, and displacement, and against restrictions in forest and for forest conservation.
- Cultural movements oriented to Sanskritisation processes, revivalism and movements based on script and language.
- An assortment of other movements.

Political Movements

There been attempts at articulation of the aspirations for political autonomy among the Gonds and Bhils during the period that followed independence. The Raj Gond leaders such as Raja Naresh Singh demanded the formation of a separate state for the adivasis to be carved out of the tribal areas of Chhattisgarh and contiguous districts of Rewa region and Vidarbha, in a memorandum submitted before the States Reorganisation Commission. On 19 May 1963 Narain Singh Ukey, President of the Gondwana Adivasi Seva Mandal reiterated the demand for the formation of the Gondwana state, consisting of the Gond and other tribal regions of the Chhattisgarh and contiguous districts of Vidarbha in Maharshtra to protect them against exploitation. A tribal autonomy movement was reported from south Gujarat. An Adivasi leader (gamit) who represented the tribal area of the Dangs threatened to form a 'Dangi Sena' and ask for a separate state if the problems of the people were not solved. A conference was held at Ahwa in the Dangs in May 1969 which called for the formation of an Adivasi autonomous state.

However, it was in Chotanagpur-Santal Pargana region of Bihar that the movement for political autonomy and formation of a state really developed further. The Adivasi Mahasabha was wound up and merged with a new regional party, the Jharkhand Party, in 1949. Behind it were the experiences of the failure of the militant movements and of the framing of the Constitution of India. The Jharkhand Party was thrown open, at least, in principle, to all residents Chotanagpur. There was thus a transition from ethnicity to regionalism as the formative factor in the movement. The period from 1952 to 1957 was in many ways the peak period for the Jharkhand movement and party, which had emerged as the major party in the Chhotanagpur-Santal pargana region. The second general elections in 1957 had seen it extend its influence to Orissa, where it captured five seats and held the balance of power in the state politics which was plagued by instability. It displayed remarkable unity, laid down the law in the tribal region, could mobilise thousands of people and take out mammoth processions at short notice. The decline of the party, which began in the early- 1960s. The reasons for its decline were the following: involvement of the tribals in the process of development; rivalry between the advanced Christian tribals and backward non-Christian tribals arsing out of competition on education, employment and control on the resources for development; and, shift in the support of the non-Christian tribals from Jharkhand to the Congress and Jana Sangha.

Political Movements in the north-east

Tribal movements in the North-East stand in a category by themselves because of the region's unique geopolitical situation and historical background. Political processes in the North-Eastern hills picked up on the eve of transfer of power when considerable number of tribals and a substantial section of their elite among the Khashis, Mizos, Garos and even among the Nagas agreed to participate in the constitutional system as it emerged and gathered strength later as the secular and democratic system was consolidated. Old tribes assumed new names, small tribes merged with larger tribes, and the tribes combined to form a new ethnic-cum-territorial identity. While the processes up to the formation of the autonomous councils or the state were almost common to all tribes, there were differences on the question of their relationship with the nation-state. A section of the Nagas chose the path of insurgency, followed by the Mizos, the Meiteis, and the Tripuris. Other sections of the same tribes later preferred integration. For example, in Nagaland the Angami, the Ao and the Sema who had played the major role in the beginning of Naga insurgency opted for sedate regional politics. The centre of gravity shifted from the area dominated by these tribes to the areas inhabited by the Konyak and Lotha and now to the international border. The insurgency is now dominated by the Hemis, and the Konyaks and Tangkhuls. In fact there has been a reaction among these minor tribes against the dominated by the Hemis, and the Konyaks and Tangkhuls. There is also a demand for the formation of the remote and underdeveloped Mon and Tuensang districts into a union territory.

Naga Movement

The word "Naga" denotes a conglomeration of hill tribes rather than a single entity. This fact hence contests the real motives of Naga insurgent groups. Some of the major or mattering Naga tribes are the Ao, Rengma, Sumi, Angami, Konyak, Lotha, etc. Among these the dominance of three tribes viz the Ao, Sumi and the Angami is undeniable.

Scattered in the north-eastern part of India, Nagas were once headhunters, as they used to cut off the heads of the enemies and preserve them as trophies. But with the advent of Christianity and education, the Nagas-comprising more than 30 tribes have evolved a rich culture and tradition. Since the Naga tribes have been known for their pride and independent identity, the process of politicisation led to the urge for creation of separate land for Nagas. The Separatist Movement can be traced back to 1918, with the founding of Naga Club in Kohima by a group of erudite Nagas. The Club tendered a memorandum before the Simon Commission which demanded for exclusion of Nagas from the proposed constitutional reform in British administration in India. Although their plea was unsuccessful, the nature of gripes took a drastic change with the emerging of Angami Zapu Phizo, who was considered as one of the most vibrant leaders of Naga separatist movement. During India's struggle for Independence, Phizo had fought on the side of the Indian National Army led by Netaji Subhash Chandra Bose for Japan against the Allies. In 1946, the Naga Club was renamed as Nagaland National Council (NNC). The NNC then asked for as separate sovereign political geography comprising Naga inhabited areas of Nagaland, Assam, Arunachal Pradesh and Myammar (Burma), thus marking the beginning of political conflict between Nagas and the Government of India. On 14th of August 1947, the NNC under Phizo's initiation declared independence of Naga region, thereby resulting in his arrest in 1948 on the charges of instigating a rebellion. But, he was released in 1950, and became the president of NNC. In 1952, he met Pandit Jawaharlal Nehru, the then Prime Minister, and pleaded for Naga Independence, which was rejected. Disappointed with his talks with Nehru, he turned to armed rebellion to sway the Indian government. In 1975, an agreement known as the Shillong Accord was signed between the Indian Government and the NNC. But, some of the NNC hardcore militants were disappointed with the pact, leading to breakage among the armed cadets. This led to the formation of the Nationalist Socialist Council of Nagaland or the NSCN on January 31, 1980 by Isak Chisi Swu, Thuingaleng Muivah and S S Khaplang.

Lamentably, differences shelled out within the outfit later, and on April 30, 1988, the group split into two factions- the NSCN (IM), led by Isak Chisi Swu and Thuingaleng Muivah, and the NSCN (Khaplang), led by Khaplang. Although their philosophies differ, their goals remain the same as both the outfits are fighting for the establishment of a `Greater Nagaland` comprising all Naga-inhabited areas within India and Myanmar.

Agrarian and Forest-Based Movements: In the post-colonial era, the pattern of alienation of tribals' resources such as land shows a marked change. Tribals are being displaced not only by non-tribals but also by the state and other organisations which require land for development. They are now pitted not only against other people but also against the state which they see as the major instrument for displacing them from their land.

The tribals are asking not only for restoration of the land that they lost by invoking the provision of the Andhra Pradesh Scheduled Area Land Transfer Regulations, 1959, which come into force in 1963, but also the transfer of ownership and delivery of possession in regard to the land allotted to them. Of late, they have been organised by CPI (ML) of the People's War Group (PWG). In February 1981 there was an unusual spurt of forced harvesting on lands taken away from them by non-tribals, raiding of houses of moneylenders and decamping with mortgaged valuables. The traditional system of communication was revived to organise the tribals. Signals were exchanged by beating the drum. The Gond durbar held on 6 February 1981 at Keslapur declared that the problems of the tribals had come to a boiling point. The Gonds also prevented the demarcation of land for afforestation. They had earlier reacted strongly to the scheduling of the Lumbadars, a community of traders and moneylenders, as a tribe in 1977, because the Lumbadars always exploited the tribals and their status as a tribe helped them to legitimise their illegal possession of the Gonds' land. On 20 April 1981 a conference was planned by CPI(ML) at Indervalli. The meeting was banned and the tribals were persuaded not to assemble there. However, they took out a procession which came into conflict with a police force. About 15 tribals lost their lives. For excellent score, read GPH book.

Q12. What are the characteristics and consequences of tribal movement in India?

Ans. Basically the tribal movements are identity-based movement. The leadership of the tribal movements has mainly emerged from themselves. The Santal brothers were landless - Birsa Munda was a raiyat or a parja (crop-sharer) and Govind Giri was a hali. The leadership in the third phase that is the post-colonial periods was provided by the members of the upcoming tribal middle class, both in middle India and in the North-East. They were educated people who included priests, catechists, teachers, public servants, rural leaders and professionals who spoke largely in secular idioms. The leadership of the social reform movement was provided by the outsiders such as the Gandhian workers, of the Parja Mandal agitation by outsiders like Motilal Tejawat and of some tribal uprisings such as the Nagesia by even "Baniyas".

The goals of the movement ranged from the restoration of the pre-colonial polity, service tenure (Chuar), and land (Sardar) and right in forest to expulsion of outsiders, end of taxation, social reform, political independenc, or establishment of the tribal raj or participation in constitutional and democratic political apparatus, formation of tribal states, gaining equality and end of exploitation.

The social and ethnic composition of the movements ranged from the movement led by a single tribe to a confederacy of tribes and the castes sub-ordinate to the tribes such as the artisans and service groups. Most of the movements were limited to a tribe but such movements in the first phase such as Kol and Santhal insurrections encompassed many tribal and non-tribal groups. In the third and post-colonial period broad based political parties emerged among the tribes, both in North-East and in middle India. The all India tribal platforms gradually emerged in 1960s.

All tribal movements were limited in scale but they had an immediate impact on policy. Their impact has however to be studied both in the short and long-term perspectives. In the short-run the authorities responded by taking immediate measures to address the tribal concerns, devise measures to protect their resources, facilitate access to the officials etc. In the long-term the colonial policy built up a framework to institutionalise the isolation for tribals, a combination of elements of direct and indirect rule (in princely states, in the North-East, etc., a mix of legal and administrative measures to protect land against alienation to non-tribals, and protect customary rights in forest. There was, however, to be no development of any kind – the missionaries were left free to manage education and health services. It was left to the Gandhian workers and Congress ministries which assumed office in late 1930s to institute inquires into tribals' poverty, indebtedness and backwardness and put in place the first slew of welfare measures.

The results of the uprisings were thus not uniform for whole of tribal India. While in British India they achieved a non-regulation administrative system for tribes and special agrarian laws to protect tribal land, little was done or allowed to be done for them in princely states. However, the political agent did intervene to uphold *status quo* rather than promote change. This ambivalence was typical of the colonial system.

Q13. Discuss the historical relationship between man and the nature, emergence of ecopolitics and debate on development and sustainability.

Ans. Man-Nature Relationship

Human beings live in the realm of nature, they are constantly surrounded by it and interact with it. The most intimate part of nature in relation to man is the biosphere, the thin envelope embracing the earth, its soil cover, and everything else that is alive. Our environment, although outside us, has within us not only its image, as something both actually and imaginatively reflected, but also its material energy and information channels and processes. This presence of nature in an ideal, materialised, energy and information form in man's Self is so organic that when these external natural principles disappear, man himself disappears from life. If we lose nature's image, we lose our life. Industrialisation is also cause for polluting the nature. Vehicles of various kinds are invented to increase the speed of transportation and movement. The adverse effect is poisonous emissions from vehicles causing greenhouse effect in biosphere.

Emergence of Eco-politics

The term eco-politics is of recent origin. Eco-politics is about interrelationship and mutual connection between environmental and political issues. Earlier, the ecological issues were paid attention only if they concerned national defence or collective security such as nuclear fallout or oil scarcity. Over the time, the focus has got extended to issues of development. Eco-politics pleads for a value-based regulation regarding the use of natural resources in a manner that on one hand it prevents narrow unilateral exploitation and on the other hand, ensues equitable distribution of fruits of development.

In the third world or developing countries, conflict on the issue of development takes a different form. Here the divide is between those who wish to protect the environment at all cost and those who are committed to development at any cost. This does not mean that the environmentalists are as such against development but plead for an eco-friendly development. They prefer alternative or sustainable development. Eco-politics results in the process of determining the preferred path of development.

Debate on Development and Sustainability

Development is an extremely nebulous, deceptive and therefore ambiguous concept. It is usually associated with modernisation, industrialisation, urbanisation, science and technology. It essentially connotes change, growth and progress. Industrial revolution epitomised this view of development, resulting in a grave error so far as environmental interests are concerned.

After Second World War, colonialism ended and new nations were born. In order to increase productivity, large industries were set up by employing capital and resource-intensive technology. Unfortunately, this approach resulted in increasing inequalities, poverty and environmental crisis. The Report of the South Commission (1992:38) has observed that, "Inequalities tended to widen, as the economy grew and became more industrialised the gap in income, knowledge and power was growing and large segments of the population experienced no significant improvement in their standard of living". The blind faith in ideology of development through this type of industrialisation caused a huge resource depletion and pollution. The goal of human welfare and meeting basic needs of the people could not be attained by this model of development.

Developing countries consist of poor and the powerless. All efforts for speedy economic development through industrialisation in these countries have given more and more power to the financial and political elites. Degradation of environment has occurred due to both chronic poverty and uneven industrialisation. The general situation is such that the elites pay only lip service to environmental values and actually go on ecological rampaging. Even if they value environment they are often unwilling to part with the profits. Their stock defence and ready excuse is contained in their argument about lack of financial viability and absence of viable technical know-how to clean up (or keep clean the environment). The debate should actually be focussed on the social or environmental cost of production versus mindless plunder of ecology for never ending profits for few. This debate remains unresolved mainly because of an informal alliance between the financial industrial and political-bureaucratic elites. The political system is usually repressive of general and particularly environmental dissent. It is often expressed as well as put down violently. Protests to safeguard the environment are often viewed and dismissed by the elite interest. Thus, the situation in developing countries is sensitive and crucial. Such issues as land degradation, desertification, deforestation and pollution of air, water and soil by industries either remain ignored or inadequately and nominally attended. All in all, the poverty, resulting degradation and insensitive political system make the matters worse. A ray of hope lies in emergence of positive eco-politics by green parties and groups in Europe and micro environment movements by environmental organisations in the developing countries.

Q14. Examine the role of State and judiciary in Environmental issues.

Or

Discuss the major issues addressed by the environment movements in form of the role of the state and judiciary.

Ans. Role of the State

One understanding of state is that it is a neutral space or impartial agency for resolving the conflicts of interest which occur in market and civil society. However, Indian state's performance for last five decades provides contrary evidences. The Indian state has failed to play its role and hence the civil society has to fill the void. Let us first explore the contemporary status of the state. Ever since the ending of cold war, collapse of communism and triumph of advancing capitalism, most nation-states are ruthlessly overrun. There has been an upsurge in global democratic aspirations as a result of the collapse of communism. The forces of free market are linking national economies with global economic systems. Globalisation of politics and economy is taking place. The state is being caught in this process and is under pressures from within and without. It is found that the state or its counterpart in form of a local municipal body have acted in a biased manner in the issue of environmental pollution. The issue of environmental protection is split in two camps. One side is the 'iron triangle' of elitist domination in form of 'bureaucrats-industrialists-politicians' and on the other are the powerless victims of pollution and environmental degradation. Studies have shown that, instead of operating as a mediating and balancing agency, the state functions as a party to the issue against the interests of the people. If we see the history of legislation on pollution, we find that first of all nobody is ready to accept the existence of this issue. The people who are the victims of air or water pollution are left in cold with burden of proof on their shoulders. Whether it is US Steel Mill in Gary Indiana or factories and industries in Vapi Ankleshwar, Nandesari and Baroda in Gujarat, when people go to complain about the impact of pollution in form of holes in the clothes and kitchen vessels or deaths of buffaloes or elephants by drinking polluted water, released stealthily in the nearby open spaces, village ponds, ravines and rivers, the polluting industries' first reaction is there is no such problem. When potato and banana growing farmers of villages in Baroda region of Gujarat complained about crop-destruction due to air pollution, the polluting industry instantly disowned and disclaimed the responsibility The impact of pollution is first felt by the people but the 'iron-triangle' usually opposes its existence. People are ultimately, left with no other option but to launch a movement first to make an issue of the problem. It is the suffering people who find themselves in a strange powerless and helpless situation. Organised existing public power, in form of state and its related structures do not help them. Hence, they launch a movement to exert power resources in their favour by compelling the state first to recognise the existence of issue and then make and implement preventive laws on pollution. The iron-triangle does not stop here but enters the next arena of implementation of legislated policies and laws. It weakens and nullifies the effect by diluting.

Role of Judiciary

The environment movement in India has essentially passed through three phases.

In the first phase, which was the longest phase, legislative hurdles were crossed. That is to say, opposition, obstruction or dilution of pollution laws was done while being framed in legislatures.

In the second phase, opposition to implementation of already made anti-pollution laws was experienced. Here also the iron-triangle operated in favour of the polluters rather than in protecting the interests of the victims of pollution.

In the current phase, as a final recourse to redressal of their grievances against those polluting and jeopardising the increasingly fragile ecosystem, doors of the judiciary are knocked. Eminent legal scholar Upendra Baxi (1991) has observed that, "the growth of environmental jurisprudence in India is a very recent phenomenon. And even now it is confined to a few activist judges, lawyers, law academics and active citizens. Baxi has argued that this is so mainly because "the Constitution itself is environment-blind". The chapter on rights in the Constitution does not explicitly state about protecting the citizens from air and water pollution, deforestation, destruction of wild life and displacements of habitats. Much later 42nd Amendment to the Constitution has added a provision vide Article 48-A instructing the state to make efforts for protecting and improving the environment, forests and wild life. Article 51-A is about the fundamental duty of the citizens to protect and improve the natural environment including forests, lakes, rivers and wild life. The absence of environmental concerns in the Constitution is due to its obsession with development.

However, from 1950-84 neither the state nor the civil society was concerned about systematic and organised degradation and destruction of the environment while pursuing the policy of generating prosperity through massive industrialisation. Judicial activism rose in response to this neglect. In Ratlam Municipal Corporation case, Mr. Justice Krishna Iyer gave a new, progressive and environment-friendly interpretation. He stated that Constitution is "a remedial weapon of versatile use". He further recognised that people's struggle for "social justice" includes environmental justice and "the remedial weapon" must be available to them Anti-power Project stir by Kerala Shastra Sahitya Parishad to protect the fragile Silent Valley ecosystem in 1979 was facilitated by this landmark judicial intervention by Justice Iyer. The apex courts at the state and central level are flooded with petitions seeking protection of environment. This is a major achievement of enlightened judicial process. "Creative interpretations and rulings by the courts in various cases seeking environmental justice or compensation have expanded the scope and role of judiciary in this issue.

Q15. Analyse the impact and nature of Environment Movements.

Ans. Harsh Sethi has divided environmental responses into three types of struggles.:

- In the first type, the struggle addresses the issue of rights of different social strata and communities over using resources.

This type of struggle does not question the development model or the acts of redefining man-nature relations.

- In the second type, we find environmental response which struggles for legal corrections and policy shifts in resource use. At the centre lies concern about destruction and depletion of renewable and non-renewable resources. The normative basis of dominant development model remains unchallenged.
- The third variety of response is substantive and fundamental to the issue. It invokes ecological dimension. It aims at rejecting the dominant development model and redefine man's relationship with the nature. However, it must be stated that the environment struggles do not maintain typological purity once launched. These struggles have resulted centering around different natural resources such as air, wastes, land, forest or sea. Accordingly, they can be referred to as forest-based struggles, land use struggles, anti-big dam struggles, anti-pollution struggles and struggles against destruction of marine resources.

Harsh Sethi has done an analysis of these struggles by focussing on the participants or actors of the struggles, strategies of intervention, issues raised and focussed and finally impact or outcome of struggle in terms of grievance-redressal, policy changes effected and conscientisation. It is found that unlike other struggles, in ecological struggles fairly representative section of society is involved as participants. However, the most adversely affected people constitute the base of the struggle. For example, deforestation stretches the work hours of women in collecting fuel wood and water longer, the tribals lose benefits of forest produce, the fisherman in Goa and Kerala suffer from excessive trawling. The victims are so dispersed and marginalised that for effective raising of voices and redressal of grievances, they require a chain of actors from more vocal and experienced realms of voluntary organisations, media, professionals like scientists, researchers, doctors, engineers, lawyers, technologists, human right groups, sympathetic and concerned policy-makers and bureaucrats. Each of these actors adds strength, vigour, guidance and direction to struggle.

By way of organisational and interventionist strategy, it has become imperative for environment movements that not only to strengthen and hold together the victim-folks in solidarity but also make holes in the opposite camp by skillfully raising doubts about possible benefits being outweighed by collective harm and so on. Most struggles are raised against development projects and therefore, they are likely to be fought back as anti-people, anti-national, anti-development, anti-progress and so on. This is usually countered by careful and systematic analysis of issues at stake and propagation of correct, data-based campaign material in actual resource-use. The limitation of this strategy is that when the issue goes beyond local limit, the original victim-actors are left behind and either the middle class professionals, media or voluntary agency leaders come to the fore. The leadership role and power shifts from local hands to mediating actors. Harsh Sethi has observed this is good strategically but bad ethically. Another aspect of this process is internationalisation of local or national issues as strategy which can harm the movement. In most cases, the central issues of environment movements revolve around fixing tolerance limits on carrying capacity of environment or cost-benefit ratios. Most struggles are of reformist nature. These issues have concomitantly raised interesting interconnections between ecology and feminism as well as ecology and human rights.

Analysing and understanding the impact of movement forms important aspect of the study. The environment movements have by and large remained "diverse and scattered". Their overall impact is uneven. Along with failures there have been successes too.

- The Silent Valley movement's impact was positive, successful and trend setting.
- The Doon Valley environment movement was partly successful. But at many other places, though, the movements are launched, intensified but not successful.
- Bhopal Gas disaster successfully drew the attention of the nation and the world but it has not succeeded in preventing hazardous products and processes (IPT; 1999).

Despite the persistence of struggles, thousands of people are displaced yearly due to large development projects. On the other hand, the movement has made a major contribution to give centrality and public space to the cause of environment protection. This is a historic achievement as never before so much concern, awareness, involvement and participation was witnessed. The government has made many policies on forests, wildlife, wastelands, water, air and soil conservation. But there is a wide gap between the rising concern and actual action by the state. Interestingly, no political party, trade union or peasant organisations have made this to be their issue. The environment movements remain exposed to the dangers of gaps between concern/thoughtand action; fragmented co-optation, manipulation and distortion by government and vested interests.

Q16. Write short notes on following:

(a) Silent Valley Movement

Ans. Silent Valley occupies an area of 8950 hectares at an altitude of 3000 ft. in Palaghat district, Kerala. It is surrounded by the Nilgiri forests to the north and Attappadi forests to the east-together they comprise 40,000 hectares of pristine (i.e. primitive) forest. This tropical rain forest in the Western Ghat is a precious reservoir of genetic diversity which has not been fully exploited. Here plant species and other forms of life have survived for centuries in the forest. It is this gene pool to which man has to turn in future for new materials for agriculture, for life-saving drugs, etc.

The Kerala State Government decided to construct a dam in the Silent Valley for generation of 120 MW (megawatts) of electricity in 1976 at an estimated cost of ₹25 crores (revised in 1984 to ₹51 crores). The proposed dam would-store 270 million cubic feet water in a reservoir spreading over 700 hectares. In order to save the Silent Valley from destruction in the process of Government dam project, the Kerala based NGO, Kerala Sastra Sahitya Parisad (KSSP) launched the Silent Valley Movement, supported by students, teachers and people of Kerala.

Soon the apex policy making bodies NCEPC, DOEn and Switzerland-based IUCN (International Union for Conserva-tion of Nature and Natural Resources) strongly supported the cause of Silent Valley. Finally the Prime Minister (Smt. Indira Gandhi) in 1983 accepted the recommendation of top scientists and environmentalists and declared the Silent Valley as the Bio-sphere Reserve by canceling the Hydel project proposal of the State Government. This is the success story of an environmental movement for protection of an important biosphere reserve.

(b) Chipko Movement

Ans. This is the most famous and powerful people's movement in Garhwal region (Himalayan) of Uttar Pradesh. It originally started as the tribal women's protest against felling of trees by contractors but gained momentum under the leadership of Chandi Prasad Bhatt and Sunder Lal Bahuguna. It coincided with the UN Conference of Human Environment held at Stockholm (1972) which recognised the Chipko movement as a mighty Environment Protection Movement.

The term "Chipko" literally means "hugging". Dasholi Gram Swarajya Mandal (Dasholi village Self-rule Forum) spearheaded the movement in Gopeswar, Chamoli district of UP The DGSM under the leadership of Bhat and Bahuguna started grassroot level movement involving hill women to protect the hill ecosystem. Reckless destruction of hill forests by timber contractors caused landslides and floods in the valley of Alaknanda and Bhagirathi and was destroying the fragile hill ecosystem. A unique feature of the movement was the active participation of hill women villages who were the worst sufferers of deforestation as they had to walk 10-15 km everyday to collect their fuel for cooking. Whenever the contractors with their axmen came for cutting trees, the women hugged the trees and protected them from the axemen. The contractors withdraw from the spot and the forest was saved. Thus the entire Himalayan Garhwal region hill forests were protected from further destruction.

In course of time the Chipko movement spread all along the hill region saving all hill forests and greenery and then moved to the South in Karnataka in 1983 where it named "Appico" movement. Soon it gained international recognition and crossed geographical boundaries to be observed as Chipko Day at New York, USA in April, 1983. A Group of school children assembled at Union Square Park Hugged a big tree, followed by some adults. Environmentalists from France, Germany, Sweden, Switzerland, etc. came to visit the Chipko camps and hailed the Chipko Movement.

Q17. Identify the main features of working class movement in India.

Or

Identify the main issue of the worker's movement in India.

Or

Discuss the Worker's movement during the colonial and post-colonial period.

Ans. According to the labour historians, the span of working class activities in India is divided into four distinct phases. The first phase spans from 1850 to 1890; the second phase from 1890 to 1918; the third phase from 1918 to 1947 and finally the post-independence period. A treatment of the working class movement will follow a brief discussion of some of the essential aspects of the class in colonial and post colonial India.

Workers' Movements in the Colonial Period

The modern working class made its appearance in India in the second half of the 19th century with the growth of modern industries, railways, post and telegraph network, plantation and mining. But the labour movement started in an organised way only after the Second World War. The organised wokers' unions are known as the trade unions. The All India Trade Union Congress (AITUC) was formed in 1920. Its objective was to coordinate activities of all organisations in all the provinces of India to further the interests of the Indian labour in economic, social and political matters. In the second half of the 1920s there was a consolidation of left ideological forces in the country. In 1928 the left wing including the communists succeeded in acquiring dominant position inside the AITUC. The moderates started a new organisation known as All India Trade Union Federation (AITUF). The 1930s was not a favourable period for the growth of trade union movement India. The communists were implicated in the Meerut Conspiracy case and the Bombay Textiles strike of 1929 had failed. A lull marked the activities on the trade union front. The serious economic depression of this period added to the woes of the workers further. It led to large-scale retrenchment. The main focus of the trade union movements during this period was maintaining wages and preventing retrenchment.

The Second World War divided the trade union leaders. The communists argued that with the Nazi attack on the Soviet Union in 1941 the character of the war had changed from imperialist war to people's war. The communists were following the line of the Russian Communist Party and thought that in the changed circumstances it was the duty of the workers to support British war efforts. But the nationalist leaders wanted to strengthen the national movement to overthrow the British rule from India. The ideological rift led to another split in the trade union movement. The mounting cost of living made the workers to realise the need of an organised effort to secure relief. In spite of the government resorting to Defence of India Rules, which prohibited strikes and lockouts, there was a perceptible increase in number of both unions and organised workers.

The Issues and the Types of Collective Actions

The main issues which caused the workers strikes include: wages, bonus, personnel, leave and hours of work, violence and indiscipline, industrial and labour policies, etc. The workers take recourse to various types of collective actions for getting their problems redressed. These are – strikes, satyagrah, hunger strikes, bandhs and hartals, gharaos, demonstrations, mass casual leaves, work to rule, cutting of supply of electricity, etc. The most common form of workers' collective action is the strike. There are examples of the railway, jute, plantation, mine and textiles workers strikes in the pre-Independence period. The centres of the strikes were Nagpur, Ahmedabad, Bombay, Madras, Howrah and Calcutta. In 1920 Gandhi intervened in the strike the textile workers of Ahmedabad and provided leadership to the workers.

Workers' Movements in the Post-colonial Period

(1) The National Level

The high hopes of workers were shattered after independence. There was hardly any improvement on the fronts of better wages and other service conditions. Three central trade union organisations were borne. The Indian National Trade Union Congress (INTUC) started by the Congress party was born in 1947. The Praja Socialist Party started the Hind Mazdoor Sabha (HMS) in 1948. The workers had to struggle hard even to retain what they had achieved earlier. A series of strikes stirred the country. There was highest number of strikes in 1947, i.e., 1811 strikes which involved 1840 thousand workers. The number of strikes and man-days lost had surpassed all the previous records. This declined in the 1950s, but number of strikes and lock-outs increased again in the 1960s-1970s. Some radicalists had formed the United Trade Union Congress (UTUC) in 1949. After 1964 when there was a division in the Communist Party of India and Communist Party of India (Marxist) was borne this led to a split in Communist controlled AITUC as well and in 1970 Centre for Indian Trade Union (CITU) was borne. They are affiliated to the CPI and CMI (M).

According to the provisional figures released by the Chief Labour Commissioner in 1994 Bharatiya Mazdoor Sangh (BMS) which is an affiliate of BJP has acquired a total membership of 31.17 lakh workers has secured the top position. The INTUC a Congress affiliated body with a total membership of 27.06 lakh is on the second position. The third position is enjoyed by CITU affiliated to CPM with a total membership of 17.98 lakh. The fourth position is enjoyed by HMS. According to the provisional figures the hold of Congress affiliated INTUC seems to have weakened. At the same time the hold of organisations like CITU, HMS and AITUC have strengthened.

(2) The Provincial Levels

Another remarkable development of the 1960s was the birth of trade unions of the regional parties like the DMK and AIDMK in Madras. The Shiv Sena was born in Bombay in 1967. It soon set up its labour wing called Bharatiya Kamgar Sena. It was generally believed that the Shiv Sena had the backing of the industrial houses in the Bombay-Pune belt to counter the strong influence of the Communists and Socialists in labour unions. It succeeded in achieving this objective and its trade union established its supremacy in the Bombay region by the mid-1970s. The predominance of the Sena-led union was successfully challenged by Datta Samant, an eminent INTUC leader. When emergency was imposed in 1975 he refused to tone down his militancy. He was arrested and sent to jail. Then he was a Congress MLA. After coming out of jail when the emergency was lifted in 1977 he became even more popular. By the end of the 1970s he became the most powerful trade union leader in the Bombay - Pune belt. In the year 1978 he left both congress and the INTUC to set up an independent union named the Maharastra Girni Kamgar Union (MGKU). He remained one of the most influential trade union leaders in Bombay till he was murdered.

(3) The Trade Unions without Political Affiliations

The 1960s also witnessed the emergence of independent unions or "apolitical". They were independent in the sense that they were not affiliated to any political party or federation. These kinds of "apolitical" trade unions emerged out of the dissatisfaction of the workers with the existing trade unions which were affiliated to the political parties. The leadership of these unions has largely come from the educated middle classes. Engineering Mazdoor Sabha led by R J Mehta is one of the earliest unions of these type-covering workers in engineering, chemicals, printing and allied industries. Datta Samant started a number of unions like Association of Engineering workers, Mumbai General Kamgar Union, Maharashtra Girni Kamgar Union. Shankar Guha Neyogi and A.K.Roy also came into limelight as leaders of independent unions. Neyogi concentrated on contract workers in the iron –ore mines of Dalli Rajhara near Bhilai in Madhya Pradesh into a formidable union. While AITUC and INTUC were concerned with the problems of permanent and better paid workers of the Bhilai Steel Plant, concentrated on casual workers employed in small and medium-scale industries in the region. Niyogi was murdered in 1990. Another example of this type is A.K.Roy who organised coal mine workers in the Dhanbad-Jharia belt of Bihar. Roy's support base was also between contract and casual labour in the coalmines. Roy also received support from a large number of local tribal mine workers because the trade unions operating in these areas did not satisfy them. Another important example of this type was the Self- Employed Women's Association (SEWA) formed by Ela Bhatt. She founded SEWA because she felt that unions in the organised sectors were not sensitive to the problems encountered by female workers. These are not the only examples of independent unions.

One of the most important examples of the movement launched by the union which was unaffiliated to the political parties was the textile workers' strike of 1982 in Mumbai. Dissatisfied with the Rashtriya Mill Mazdoor Sangh (RMMS), affiliated to the INTUC the workers of the textile industry in Mumbai, rallied behind the MGKU-led by Datta Samant.

The workers of the textile workers of Mumbai went on indefinite strike on January 18, 1982. The demands of the workers included higher wages, making the badli (temporary) workers permanent, allowances for leave and travel and payment for house rent. The workers of other sectors than the textile also rallied behind Datta Samant. The Industrialists adopted intransigent attitude towards the strike. The strike created hardships for the workers.

The strike had its repercussion on the rural areas to which the workers belonged. The textile workers also were the poor peasants or small farmers having links both in the cities as well the villages. Datta Samat was able to link the rural issues like the wages of agricultural labourer with those of the textile workers. The strike, however, did not succeed in getting the original demands of the workers accepted. But it helped Datta Samant to emerge as the most influential trade union leader in Bombay.

Q18. Mention the limitations of the trade union movement in India.

Ans. The trade union movement in India suffers from a number of limitations and problems. Important among them are the following:

- **Limited Representations:** Trade unions encompass only a small portion of the total workforce of the country. The extent of unionisation is very limited in the unorganised sectors, particularly in agriculture.
- **Small-Size and Increasing Number:** There has been an increase in the number of trade unions. One reason for this increase has been the break-up of the existing unions into two or more fractions. Besides, new small unions have been taking birth. The small size of unions poses problems of weak financial and administrative position, weakening of collective bargaining power, inter-union rivalry, difficulty in establishing employer-employee rapport, etc.
- **Multiplicity of Unions:** The multiplicity of unions has become a very serious problem. As indicated above, the ever-increasing number of unions reduces the average size of the union, so much so that, in many a situation, no single union has an absolute majority support of the workers. Even when a single union can claim majority, the existence of a number of other unions create serious problems for it. The multiplicity of unions weakens the collective bargaining strength of labour. It also makes employer-employee negotiations and the settlement of issues very difficult. The ideal of "one union for one industry" is likely to remain a dream for a very long time to come.

- **Inter-Union and Intra-Union Rivalries:** Inter-union rivalries are a corollary of the multiplicity of unions. Instances of one union trying to beat another union even at the expense of the interests of labour are not uncommon. Inter-union rivalries tend to be intense when the different unions subscribes to different political ideologies, or when they are controlled by mutually opposing political parties. Such rivalries often undermine the effectiveness of collective bargaining the leads to industrial unrest. Sometimes, intra-union rivalries create problems. The personal aspirations of the members, personality conflicts, personal rivalries, etc., are among the causes of intra-union rivalries.

Q19. Critically examine the Peasant Movements in India.

Ans. Peasants are the people who are engaged in agricultural or related production and peasant moreover is an attempt on their part to effect change in their social, economic and political conditions. About 77 per cent of India's population live in rural areas and agriculture is their main source of livelihood. What is important to note here is that land distribution is unequal. About 55 per cent of the rural population are small and marginal farmers owing five acres of land or less. They own only 11 per cent and the top 13 per cent of farmers own 57 per cent of the cultivated land. Agricultural labourers constitute 27 per cent of rural work-force. In other words, the rural poor who constitute three-fourth of our population are socially oppressed and economically exploited by landlords and rich farmers who are invariably drawn from the ranks of the upper and middle castes. The rural poor generally belong to the backward classes, Scheduled castes and Scheduled tribes.

Despite growth in agricultural production after introduction of new agrarian policies in mid-1960s, the economic conditions of agricultural labourers and small and marginal farmers deteriorated in the last few decades. Only the middle and rich farmers, who were in position to secure loans against land, invest in fertilisers, pesticides and high-yielding seeds could gain benefit from the new policies. It may be pertinent to note here that the land reforms introduced in the first decade after independence were primarily aimed at abolish *zamindars* and other absentee landlords who were not directly involved in cultivation. But this did not remove the landlords and rich farmers who continued to exploit the rural poor.

Different Peasant Movements: The poor peasants who constitute the vast majority have at different times resorted to collective action and protest to express their aspirations and discontent against injustice, for higher wages and better working conditions. These movements were localised and widespread, spontaneous and organised. These movements were generally organised by the Kisan Sabhas and agricultural labour unions of the CPI, CPI (M) and CPI (ML). Thus seven major peasant uprisings in the Indian countryside have been organised in the last four decades.

The Telangana Struggle: The Telangana Struggle (1946-48) in the former Hyderabad state started with the demand for abolition of illegal extractions by the Deshmukhs and Nawabs and later for the cancellation of peasants' debts. The struggle began in the mid-1946 and continued until 1951. Agricultural labourers and poor peasants formed the core support base of the government. In Telangana region of Andhra Pradesh, the condition of small peasants was deplorable. They were compelled to do forced labour by the landlords. Besides, tenants were evicted by landlords because feared tenants acquisition of occupancy rights on their lands. During the mid-forties, village communities were formed in various villages to resist the exploitation and tyranny of the landlords and the Nizam's administration. Sporadic strikes against forced labour and for securing better farm wages, were organised. The landlords, backed by the police, retaliated by firing at workers processions and rallies. These incidents culminated in Telangana insurrection in which the village committees grabbed the land of rich landlords in 300 villages and distributed among the peasants and the labourers. The movement focussed on some programmes which were implemented by the village committees: for example (i) the abolition of forced labour, (ii) the abolition of illegal extractions, etc.

The Tebhaga Movement (1946-47): The Tebhaga uprising in North Bengal in 1946 was a struggle launched by sharecroppers to retain two-thirds of agricultural produce for themselves. It was also in order to reduce the rent they paid to jotedars who generally appropriated from one-half to two-thirds of the agricultural produce as rent. The movement started in Dirajpur district from where it spread to eleven districts under the leadership of the Provincial Kisan Sabha of Bengal. The sharecroppers organised processions and refused to pay any share of the crop to landlords.

Naxalbari Revolt (1967-68): The major peasant mobilisation in the sixties was the Naxalbari revolt between 1967 and 1969 in Naxalbari Srikakulam, Mushahari and Debra-Gopivallabpur. As many as 60 per cent of cultivators in this area were sharecroppers. Village communities were established to conduct the struggle. The main concern of the Naxalbari movement was to propagate the politics of agrarian revolution among the workers and peasants and to form a secret party. The movement decided to (i) seize the lands of jotedars, (ii) seize the lands of the plantation workers who had purchased land from poor peasants, (iii) cultivate these lands and retain all the produce from lands appropriated from the jotedars, but share half of the crop produced on plantation workers' lands. The peasant unions were able to secure temporary 'liberated zones' which they controlled for several weeks under the supervision of the CPI (ML). However, confrontations between the peasants and the landlords, as well as police repression which followed crushed the movement and resulted in the death and arrest of several hundred persons.

Miscellaneous Uprisings: The peasant struggles continued in different parts of the country after the Naxalbari uprising. According to government reports, there were 5424 agrarian agitations between 1967-70. Thus the CPI, CPI (M), SSP and PSP organised agitations in UP and Bihar to highlight the concentration of land in the hands of landlords, former princes, zamindars and monopolists and to grab the land. They also altered the public to the need for radical agrarian reform. These parties were opposed to the ideological and tactical lines of the CPI (ML). However, there was no uniform pattern to the struggle and the nature of mobilisation. For example, the CPI and CPI (M) organised against the big landlords, whereas PSP and the SSP avoided the big landlords. Again, in some places the struggle was organised on class lines, while in other areas, coincided with castes. This land grab movement could not be sustained after a few months because the parties involved in the struggle were not united in their efforts and the state also used repression to crush them. But the impact of this was that several states enacted land ceiling legislations in 1972 and 1973 to distribute surplus land among the landless. This also led the Congress party to raise radical slogan of Garibi Hatao in the 1971 elections to counter the popular appeal of the programmes and action of the opposition. But these slogans have proved to be of no avail because of inequality in the distribution of resource base amongst the rural population.

Rich Peasants' and Farmers' Movements

The last quarter of the twentieth century has seen the movements of a very important social group in the rural areas known as rich peasants, farmers, kulaks or the capitalist farmers in several regions of India. They rallied behind the farmers' organisations in their respective regions. These organisations are - two Bharatiya Kisan Unions (the BKUs) of Punjab and

Uttar Pradesh, Shetkari Sangathana of Maharastra, Khadayata samaj of Gujarat, Karnataka Rajya Raitha Sangha of Karnataka and Vivasayigal of Tamil Nadu. The most prominent leaders of these unions are Bhupindra Singh Mann in Punjab, Mahendra Singh Tikait in UP, Sharad Joshi in Maharashtra and Nandunjappa Swami in Karnataka. These farmers are the most influential and resourceful sections of rural society in their respective regions. They largely belong to the intermediate castes. They have benefited most from the state policies especially the land reforms and the green revolution. They cultivate land with the family labour supported by the hired-labour. They control the maximum resources in the rural society – land, water resources, animals, modern technology like tractors, etc.

The movements of rich farmers unlike the movements of poor peasants are not directed against any rural exploiters. In fact, a large group of them belong to the latter. These are directed against the state and unequal terms of trade.

Their main demands have been – remunerative prices, subsidised inputs, writing off loans, lowering of electricity bills, substantial reduction in water canal charges, representation of the farmers in the Agricultural Price Commission. With the exception of the Maharastra, these movements did not raise the problems of the small producers. Rather, Tikait has demanded scrapping of land ceiling laws and of the Minimum wages Act.

The most common mode of mobilisation in the farmers' or the rich peasants' movements include rallies, satyagrah, road blocaked, gaon bandi (banning the entry of outsiders into the villages) and attack on the public property. Sometimes these result in violence. Their "apolitical" nature, which means they are not being attached to the political parties has been the most effective method of mobilisation, especially in the in the initial phase of the movements.

While the farmers' movements in India shared several common characteristics, e.g., they raised the market-oriented demands, their "apolitical" nature, their direction against the state, patterns of mobilisation, the BKU movement of UP was distinct in terms of leadership and involvement of the traditional institution. Mahendra Singh Tikait, the chief of the Uttar Pradesh BKU is also the hereditary head of the traditional caste organisation known as the Sarva Khap of the farming Jats. His social position enabled him to become the leader of the BKU at a time when the farmers of the UP did not have a leader of that stature in the wake of the death of Charan Singh in 1987. Tikait was able to involve the traditional leaderships or Khaps – chiefs of several farming castes under the banner of the BKU. Besides, the BKU also took up the social issues like dowry in the initial phase of its movement.

The Bharatiya Kisan Union of Mahendra Singh Tikait speaks a language that invokes elements of Charan Singh's discourse on agriculture. Charan Singh used to argue that there was an urban bias in Indian planning and held it accountable for diversion of resources from agriculture. It, however, does not go to the extent of treating industrial and urban India against the rural India unlike the Shetkari Sangathan of Sharad Joshi. The rich peasant organisations do not admit any contradiction between the interests of rich peasants and the poor agrarian classes. They argue that unremunerative prices affect both the rich and the poor peasants. While the Shetkari Sangthana maintains a facade of India and Bharat divide to hide the class divide in agriculture, the BKU conceals it under the cover of existing Bhaichara (brotherhood) and peasant-proprietorship in the western UP

Q20. Identify the impact of Liberalisation on the Workers and Peasant Movements.

Or

What has been the impact of the New Economic Policy on the workers?

Ans. The era of reforms started with the government of P.V. Narsimha Rao. Since, then successive governments have continued with liberalisation agenda. The present government of Atal Bihari Vajpayee is also committed to this agenda. Among the main planks of this New Economic policy are closure of sick and loss making public enterprises, disinvestments from and privatisation of the public sector enterprises. There has been a marked decline in the growth rate of total employment in the organised sector in the 1990s as compared to 1980s. In fact this period is known as a period of jobless growth. Labour laws relating to job security are being changed. Many workers have been pushed out of jobs under the voluntary retirement scheme. A practice of using contract and casual labour in place of regular employees has become widespread. There have been strikes by Trade Unions to protect the interests of workers in State Electricity Boards, ITDC hotels, banks, etc. A National Renewal Fund was created as early as in 1992 to provide a social safety net to the labour force rendered jobless. In 1994 the government of India signed the Uruguay round of the General Agreement on Tariffs and Trade (GATT) at Maracas [Morocco] and became a member of the World Trade Organisation (WTO). This step of the government can be seen as part of the New Economic policy. As per conditions of the GATT, developing countries including India are under obligation to introduce subsidies-discipline. They are being asked to keep subsidies to the farmers up to 10 per cent of their value of output. But cutting down on subsidies is a difficult proposition because no government wants to displease the rich farmers. They continue to get things like irrigation waters and electricity either free or at throwaway prices. Another GATT related problem faced by the farmers is introduction of patenting in agriculture. The farmer is not automatically permitted to use farm-saved-seeds of protected varieties to sow the next crop. He has either to pay compensation for the use of seeds saved by him or obtain the approval of the breeder. As most of the Plant Breeders are the Multi National Corporations (MNCs), their primary intention is maximisation of profit. This leaves the farmers no option but to buy the seeds again. There have been protests against Terminator-Seeds of cotton in Maharashtra and Gujarat. The response of the rich farmers' movements to new developments like the New Economic Policy', India joining WTO has not been undifferentiated. While Sharad Joshi, in the western part of the country has supported the new developments.

Feedback is the breakfast of Champions.

Ken Blanchard

You can Help other students.
"Inform any error or mistake in this book."

We and Universe
will reward you for Your Kind act.

Email at : feedback@gullybaba.com
or
WhatsApp on 9350849407

7

Context of Indian State

An Overview

India is a democratic republic with a system of government legally based on the often-amended 1950 constitution. After independence, it has been the vision of Indian government to adopt some economic reforms. Our govt. adopted "liberalisation and globalisation" both as important weapons to enhance industrialisation and foreign trade. Now India can export and import commodities freely. India has made a tremendous progress in many spheres such as industries, trade, agriculture and finance. India is facing secularism from the forces of communalism. Our society is facing a steady devaluation of the secular ideals, challenged as they are by various social, political and economical developments. Thus, secularism is a part of the commitment to democracy and hence, worth defending and fighting for. The Indian constitution contains civil liberties called Fundamental Rights that are guaranteed to all citizens and include equality before the law and freedom of speech, expression, religion and association. However, crime, repression and terror have become commonly used adjectives for Indian politics.

Q1. What do you understand by the term 'Globalisation'? Outline the basic features of globalisation. What are its approaches?

Ans. 'Globalisation' seems to be a concise term, but it is in fact a manifold and elusive concept for which there is no single definition. According to sociologist Anthony Giddens, 'there are few key terms as frequently used and as poorly conceptualised as globalisation'. Giddens defines globalisation as 'the intensification of worldwide social relations which link distant localities in such a way that local happenings are shaped by events many miles away and vice versa'. The term has been used expansively to include an enormous range of features of contemporary life. Five of them can be considered as crucial to its understanding:

(1) Stretched Social Relations

Globalisation invokes cultural, economical and political networks of relations spread across the world, denser than in any previous periods. Further, they are not confined to merely specific regions. They envelop the whole world.

(2) Intensification of Flows

Globalisation is manifest in the rapid flow of information, capital and goods. They result in networks and interactions that transcend any effective monitoring and control by the nation-states. They beget social interactions that could have little to do with geographical and cultural contiguity. Mobile phones, satellite television and internet, which are based on these flows, do not respect the spatial frameworks that bound communication hitherto.

(3) Increasing Interpenetration

Under globalisation cultures and societies that were hitherto distinct come face-to-face with one another and get interwoven into the ways of social life of others. Differences of language, food, dress and beliefs become constitutive of social make-up.

(4) Global Infrastructure

They are formal and informal institutional arrangements in the economical, political and cultural domains that facilitate networking and flows. Their reach transcends the bounds of nation-state. They facilitate the functioning of a global market. They embody codes and regulations holding transnational interactions in place. They provide the mechanisms of global governance.

(5) Reformulation of Social Relations

Under globalisation, relations between social classes are brought sharply to focus on a global scale. In the earlier phases of capitalism, class relations were primarily defined within the vortex of the nation-state. Globalisation brings about a dense interaction between dominant classes and regions outstripping national cleavages. It throws up new social strata and factions both at the national and global levels. It reformulates inequalities and existing unevenness in economic and power relations.

Characteristics

The above five-fold features inform the following characteristics of the globalising world:

- It is an inter-connected world: It is connected on account of modes of simultaneous communication to any part of the world. It is also a connected world on account of the problems that confront humanity as a whole. Problems such as global climatic changes, the depletion of the ozone layer, drugs, terrorism, pollution of the oceans, etc. are beyond the scope of any particular nation-state.
- Distant actions in one comer of the globe have rapid and significant repercussions in other parts.
- There is the emergence of global social strata sharing certain common cultural features. For instance, English language, Blue Jeans, etc. These features increasingly penetrate national cultures and may attempt to bring about levels of homogenisation of modes of living, thought and interactions.
- Globalisation encapsulates the entire range of social relations. It has its impact on every facet of life. However, the momentum of these relations may not move at a uniform pace.
- Under globalisation power relations come to be articulated increasingly at the global level. New organisations come to be established for the purpose.
- Development of communication technology undermines the authority of the nation-state and poses a threat to its sovereignty.
- It connects localities with the world by passing national boundaries.
- Sometimes individuals and smaller institutions in control of a front-line technology can challenge the power of global organisations by forming alliances. There grows up a new entrepreneurship around such knowledge-based industry.
- The prevailing pattern of globalisation has widened economic inequalities and has worsened the lot of the impoverished. It has threatened the existence of local cultures.

- Globalisation also brings new opportunities. It widens tremendously the range of choices available to people. It breaks down such geographic barriers as town and countryside and metropolis and periphery to access resources and information. One can live locally while being in tune with the global context.
- It is the integration of the global financial markets that often remains the hallmark of globalisation. It involves new forms of financial transactions, assisted by new modes of communication. It has led to the weakening of the national stock markets and tremendous growth in cross border transactions in equities, international bank lending, international bond markets, etc.
- It involves a struggle to dominate global markets and centralisation of power in a few organisations. The rise of the Multinational Corporations (MNCs) and the new role that the International Monetary Fund (IMF), the World Bank and the World Trade Organisation (WTO) have come to play bear witness to it.
- The process of Globalisation has hitherto been accompanied by a strong dose of Americanisation manifest in such symbols as 'Coca-Cola' and 'Macdonald' and has reinforced its influence over the other regions of the world.

Approaches

There are two kinds of globalists, positive/optimistic and negative/pessimistic. The former points out at the benefits of globalisation. Pessimists see it as levelling down differences and promoting homogenisation. They may see it as the dominance of advanced capitalist countries especially United States of America over the rest of the world. They feel that globalisation is going to reinforce deprivation of the vast majority and exasperate conflicts. Its benefits will primarily accrue to those who are already advantaged in the prevailing relations.

- Traditionalists admit that there is intensification of flows and social activity at the global level but they do not see any significant shift in social relations under globalisation. It is not something unprecedented. They assert that there have been moments of great transformation in the past as well that connected the world. They see the continued relevance of the nation-state still. States are throwing up new institutions to face the new demands and requirements they encounter. It is nothing but the continuation of the trends and processes already underway. Traditionalists resist the encroachment of global business in the name of globalisation and its supposed benefits. They also see grave danger to cultures and identities on account of it.

- Transformationalists believe that globalisation has created new economical, political and social circumstances in which states are called upon to operate. It has led to transform state powers. This is a significant shift from the earlier situation. However, they see a major role for nation-states in the emerging context.

They think that globalisation is not a uniform and predictable tendency. Its course is not predetermined. The nation-state and other actors on the scene can play a major role in shaping its course and content.

Q2. Discuss the transformation of the world systems under globalisation.

Ans. The World System can be divided as capitalist system, socialist system and a third variant that went under several names such as mixed economy, democratic socialism, etc. In the capitalist system, the freedom of the market and freedom of choice were privileged; the socialist system stressed on state ownership and control of the means of production and planning in the allocation of resources and distribution of goods; in the mixed economy there was a state sector alongside the private sector. While no society mirrored exactly any of the systems fully, existing societies could be demarcated as tilted to one side or the other.

In the wake of globalisation, state controlled and socialist systems with few exceptions have paved their way to market forces. It has brought increasing interdependence and integration in the global economy as a whole. While trade is moving towards interdependency, a capital flows and investment have led to integration. But, while there is general agreement on the growing interdependency and integration in several aspects of social and economic life, its extent and direction has been deeply contested.

Globalists argue that there has been rapid forging of global bonds as expressed in international trade and investment and they have superseded and supplanted the national economy. Traditionalists, however, do not think that the category of national economy has been supplanted by globalisation. The transformationalists argue that although new forces of intense interdependence and integration inform the world that we are not into a single system yet. They feel that there is the disintegration of local and national economies and the emergence of more mixed, interdependent and highly uneven economies which cannot be encompassed within the fold of a single system. In the globalising world that is underway capitalism definitely holds its sway. There is also no doubt that the present version of globalisation is a triumph of the erstwhile capitalist system worldwide. Analysts, however, are not agreed on:

- to what extent we can characterise the global system as a new phase of capitalism,
- the specific nature of class relations under globalisation and the class blocs that ensue there from, and
- the relation of the market to class struggle.

Q3. What is meant by the regionalisation of the economy?

Ans. Regionalisation is a widespread feature of international trade. Among the eighty (group of) countries, all but ten have more than half their foreign trade concentrated within a single Triad region (America, Asia-Oceania or Eurafrica). This regional polarisation is especially strong in Eurafrica, where the region accounts for more than 75 per cent of foreign trade for most countries therein. The regional polarisation of foreign trade is more limited in America, but still significant, particularly for the US neighbours, Mexico and Canada. Asia-Oceania appears as the region exhibiting the weakest polarisation. However, except for the largest three economies in the region (Japan, China, South Korea), intra-regional trade accounts for around 55 to 60 per cent of total trade.

In order to qualify further these observations, the study uses relative trade intensities (RTIs). The RTI index characterises the intensity of trade relationships between a pair of partners by comparison to the extent of total trade of each of these partners. As such, it refers to the geographical orientation of trade flows, controlling for total trade flows of both partners. This analysis points out to the especially intense trade links of former communist countries between each other and with Western Europe. It also emphasises the relatively intense trade links within Latin America, and between many Southeast Asian countries. Since distance is an obstacle to trade, it does not come as a surprise that countries use to trade more intensively with their neighbours. Therefore, the regionalisation of foreign trade is to some extent a natural pattern, in the sense that countries tend to trade in large part with other countries belonging to the same "region". But there is more to regionalisation than natural neighbouring relationships. Regional trade arrangements (RTAs) might also have contributed to strengthening trade relationships within regions.

Q4. What is meant by liberalisation? What are the its different facets?

Ans. Liberalisation is withdrawal of various restrictions imposed by the government on investment, production, import and export of the country. Liberalisation aims at giving up licensing policy. It favours a competitive market solution to economic issues and a reduced role for the state in economic management. In a wider sense, the term is also used to mean creating accountability of power, periodic elections, multi-party system and an impartial judiciary. These conditions are seen as holding public authority transparent and under scrutiny.

In its primary and stricter meaning, liberalisation proclaims freedom of trade and investment; creation of free trade areas; elimination of government controls on allocation of resources in the domestic economy; progressive removal of restrictions on external trade and payments; expansion of foreign investment, loans and aid and rapid technological progress.

Liberalisation also advocates a balanced budget; reduction in progressive taxation, social security and welfare and a diminished role for the state in economic management. It does not favour subsidies and state protection and resource allocations through administrative means. It suggests that inefficiency, corruption and mismanagement are built into regimes with excessive state control.

Facets of Liberalisation

Liberalisation is a global phenomenon, closely entwined with the process of globalisation. In fact, in its existing version, liberalisation is the enabling condition for the intensive penetration of globalisation into any society. But the contexts in which liberalisation has been carried out and the patterns it has assumed have varied across regions and states.

- In Europe, liberalisation has led to curtailment of public expenditure; cuts in social security and welfare programmes; reduction in progressive taxation; abandonment of full employment policies, curbs on trade unions, flexible labour markets and privatisation of state enterprises. However, liberalisation did not affect highly protected agricultural production, the immigration policy and certain categories of international trade, particularly involving advanced technology.
- In the developing countries, hitherto, the state regulated imports and exports, foreign investment, technology, labour markets and collective bargaining. The state owned and

managed a wide range of industrial, agricultural, marketing and financial enterprises. By mid 1970's, most of these countries were deeply in debt. In them, liberalisation involves the reversal of the previous policies of state directed modernisation and industrialisation. The early phase of liberalisation encompassed stabilisation of the economy through control of public expenditure and increase in tax returns; industrial policy reforms; price liberalisation; control of state expenditure; currency devaluation; reduction and removal of subsidies and capital and financial market reforms. At a later stage, these countries have resorted to privatisation of state enterprises, currency convertibility and integration of the economy in the global economy. To get success in your studies, read GPH book.

Q5. Mark the changing role of nation-state under globalisation.

Ans. The modern world was primarily organised around nation-states as its primary units. Nation-states claimed supreme jurisdiction or sovereignty over a demarcated territorial area. Sovereignty was associated with a political community associated with fixed borders and territories. Under globalisation, there are profound changes in all these conceptions. There are other players in the international arena; the sovereign power of the nation-state has come to be deeply contested; the conception of the political community remains highly fluid and the notions of territories and borders have radically altered in the context of the explosion of communication and states have little capacity to police them as they did in the past. Not everyone, however, is agreed on or prepared to accept the changing role of the State. Globalists think that nation-state has become an anachronism today and there are other institutions, which have effectively taken over or poised to take over the role that it had played hitherto. Traditionalists assert the continued relevance of the nation-state and see the major changes that are underway, as either been authorised or agreed upon by the state or as issues over which nation-states would be competent to exercise its authority, if they so desire. The transformalists agree that nation-state with sovereignty as its attribute is under a cloud today but they argue in response that the nation-state itself is undergoing a profound transformation.

Disagreements on the changed role of the nation state apart, there is no disagreement that they function today in highly altered conditions. Nation-states are increasingly perceived as resources to be employed in negotiations with transnational and international agencies and to keep sub-state actors in control. In such an understanding, sovereignty becomes a bargaining chip in multilateral and transnational negotiations. This reconceptualisation of the role of the state allows room for its continued salience in spite of the profound shift of power to systems of regional and global governance.

There are hosts of issues today where the ability of the state to govern is easily tied to the jurisdiction of individual nation-states. Such problems as environmental pollution, depletion of the ozone layer are simply beyond the control of individual states. No state today can monitor for long and effectively cross border communication. Further, globalisation has reinforced such occupations as drug trade enormously.

Q6. Assess the impact of globalisation on the world.

Or

Enumerate the economical, political and cultural impact of globalisation.

Ans. Globalisation is the new buzzword that has come to dominate the world since the nineties of the last century with the end of the cold war and the break-up of the former Soviet Union and the global trend towards the rolling ball. The frontiers of the state with increased reliance on the market economy and renewed faith in the private capital and resources, a process of structural adjustment spurred by the studies and influences of the World Bank and other International organisations have started in many of the developing countries. Also, Globalisation has brought in new opportunities to developing countries. Greater access to developed country markets and technology transfer hold out promise improved productivity and higher living standard.

We can assess the impact of globalisation under three broad categories, i.e. Economical, Political and Cultural. Such assessments are deeply influenced by the approach one adopts towards globalisation. It allows him to highlight some features and ignore the rest. Some of the most salient features of the impact are highlighted as follows:

Economical Impact

(a) Favourable Impacts:

- It has been beneficial to consumers. It has increased the scale and allocative efficiency of markets for goods and capital in the wake of globalisation.
- It is supposed to have released huge unutilised resources and led to a great economic recovery worldwide.

- It has resulted in the rolling back of the state; undermined parasitism and bureaucracy and has led to a spurt in entrepreneurship and knowledge based industry.
- It has introduced a great deal of flexibility relative to the kind of rigidity that prevailed under the welfare regime and state controlled order. There is, under its aegis, the rise of a flexible mode of production, work processes, labour markets, production, education, patterns of consumption, savings, etc.
- It has set into motion a highly intensified process of mergers and acquisitions of enterprises, promising a global economic order of both scale and quality.
- Globalisation has tightened the rules of the game while at the same time introducing flexibility. There prevailed a great deal of anarchy when national economies dictated the terms. Within the nation-states, liberalisation has enhanced fiscal discipline.
- Globalisation has greatly facilitated the movement of capital and lessened the dependence of developing countries on bilateral and multilateral agencies such as the IMF and World Bank. They can also make their option for FDIs or have an access to global capital markets.
- For several countries, globalisation has been an important mechanism to upgrade their technology and get an access to the global markets.
- Globalisation has led to the appreciation of several technological innovations which closed societies may not have encouraged. In their turn, these technologies have made global flows more intense and rapid.
- Globalisation has linked communities and cultures, and enhanced them.

(b) Unfavourable Impacts:

- Globalisation has greatly increase existing inequalities. Thirty years ago, the gap between the richest fifth of the world's people and the poorest fifth stood at 30 to 1. By 1990, it had widened to 60 to 1 and in 2000, it stands at 74 to 1. In terms of consumption, the richest fifth of the world accounts for 86 per cent of the global produce and the bottom fifth just 1 per cent today. Further, this unevenness operates at various levels reinforcing the disadvantage of the lowliest.

- There appears to be a great deal of evidence to suggest the generalisation that the processes and policies of liberalisation and globalisation have contributed to a significant redistribution of income and wealth from the poor to the rich both nationally and internationally. Between 1975 and 1985, an estimated US$ 165-200 billions were placed by individual investors from the Third World in the international financial markets. There is growing disparity within the developed nations, between the developed nations and the developing nations, the developing nations themselves and among the poor across the world.
- There is a growing prevalence of casual, part-time and informal sectors of employment. In the wake of globalisation, there is a substantial increase worldwide in unemployment and feminisation of the labour force. There are large-scale migrations of people within and across nation-states. But there is a growing tendency among the unemployed to target the migrants as responsible for their flight.
- There has been a cut in welfare programmes due to the decline in public expenditure especially on social services and welfare, reduction in subsidies of goods of mass consumption and decline in real wages.
- There is an increase in the power of foreign investors and creditors, domestic business groups with links to foreign capital and technology. There is a shift of income in favour of capital engaged in international relations.
- While a great deal of attention is paid to formulate rules for the expansion of global markets and capital flows little attention is paid to objectives like labour standards, poverty reduction and human rights.
- The WTO defends its intervention in the name of breaking down tariff barriers, free flow of goods and capital and safeguarding entitlement. But it is perceived by many as market fundamentalism, narrowing down choices before the vast multitude of people rather than expanding them.
- Capital flows and trade have remained highly confined to certain core developed areas of the world. The rest of the world is subjected to a discipline to safeguard the interests of these core economies.

Political Impact

(a) It is argued that the great expansion of liberal democracy worldwide would not have been possible without the promises of globalisation.

(b) It has greatly circumscribed the power of the nation-state. Opponents of the ruling elites and the disadvantaged groups have an access today to a wider world. In fact, several dissident voices and advocacy groups have effectively made use of globalisation to advance their concerns.

(c) There are new institutions of governance today at various levels. They fill an important vacuum by reorganising power at different levels and directing it towards specified ends.

(d) Globalisation has affected class relations enormously. There is a shift of power to capital and to the developed world and transfer of decision-making to an alliance of international financial organisations and corporate capital. There is a decline in the power of the organised working class.

(e) Globalisation has led to new linkages through patterns of migration and created a new elite with a similar life-style in every big city of the world. At the same time, it has created a pool of migrant and local labour at the bottom of the labour market.

(f) Globalisation has radically undermined the spatial and territorial anchoring of power. In its wake, there is the explosion of ethnic and community identities and the avowal of fundamentalism.

(g) It has created global electronic communities of sorts. They allow a diversity of alternative or radical voices to be accessed and heard as they facilitate the grouping of dominant interests.

(h) Globalisation has reinforced inequalities within and between nations in terms of access to information and knowledge. They have spawned new social categories of 'information rich' and 'information poor'.

(i) Neo-liberal ideology has emerged as the reigning ideology under globalisation with its stress on market freedom, private property and accumulation. It has little respect for alternative and hallowed conceptions of the good. It disparages politics overtly while upholding individual enterprise. At the same time, globalisation has led to the construction of a hierarchised world presided over by the US and global capital.

(j) There has emerged an interesting coalition of the traditional 'left', opposed to global corporate capital and the 'right' defending national culture.

(k) Globalisation has led to the rise of new social movements that do not fall within the vortex of traditional class movements, such as of women, peasants, ethnic communities, displaced people, etc.

Cultural Impact

(a) Globalisation has facilitated a phenomenal growth in the global circulation of cultural goods. They include printed matter, music, visual arts, cinema and photography, radio and television. Elements of ethnic cultures are woven through them. However, the ownership of these goods is concentrated in a set of media corporations. Fewer voices can be heard despite the proliferation of the media. Nation-states have little control over them as they are dominated by transnational corporations such as Time Warner, Disney, Viacom, Tele-communications Inc., New Corporation, Sony, Seagram, General electronic, Dutch Philips, etc.

(b) Under globalisation, there has been a great expansion of western and particularly American culture. There has been a great imbalance between cultural flows. Accusations of cultural imposition and domination have been widely heard. Cultures have become vulnerable. For example, vernacular languages in India. However, the extent of such domination and the ability of the local cultures to contest has been a debated issue.

(c) The English language has emerged to a predominant position of being the language of communication within and between global organisations and institutions. It has become the transmission belt for western goods and services.

(d) It is interesting to note that in spite of globalisation, certain institutions such as the press, television and national broadcasting are still anchored in national and the cultural ambiences.

(e) Globalisation involves extensive migrations of people both within and across states. The communication networks make other cultures shape one's way of life very intimately. They strengthen the fabric of cultural pluralism which increasingly confronts tendencies for cultural domination.

Q7. Discuss the various measures adopted by India towards liberalisation.

Or

Enumerate the significant measures adopted by India towards liberalisation.

Ans. Following are the significant measures adopted by India towards liberalisation:

(1) Liberalisation of Industrial Licensing: Main feature of the New Industrial Policy is to adopt a policy of liberalisation in place of controlled economy. Till now, private sector of the economy was functioning under a rigid licensing system. Under 'The New Economy Policy', private sector has been freed to a large extent from licences and other restrictions. As per amendment in the new economic policy in year 2006, with the exceptions of 5 industries, industrial licensing has been abolished for all other industries. Industries for which licences still necessary are: (i) liquor, (ii) cigarette, (iii) defence equipments, (iv) industrial explosives, and (v) dangerous chemicals. Any entrepreneur can float any new company except in above 5 industries without any restriction.

(2) Concessions from Monopolies Act: According to the provisions of Monopolies and Restrictive Trade Practices Act (MRTP Act), all those companies having assets worth more than ₹100 crore used to be declared MRTP firms and were subjected to several restrictions. Now the concept of MRTP has been done away with. These firms are now no longer required to obtain prior approval of the government at the time of taking investment decisions. They are free to expand themselves. Large concessions have been granted to companies falling under MRTP Act. Capital investment limit fixed earlier has been removed. As a result, there would be no restriction on dominant companies and industrial houses for setting up new industries or expansion of industries, taken over and amalgamation. However, under this policy, more emphasis will be laid on checking unfair trade practices to safeguard the interests of the consumers. The newly empowered Monopoly Board will be authorised to investigate any matter *suo motu* (at its own) or on complaints received from individual consumers. In year 2002, MRTP Act has been abolished and in its place a much liberal Competition Act 2002 has been enacted.

(3) Freedom for Expansion and Production to Industries: Under the policy of liberalisation, industries (which are not covered under industrial licensing) are free to expand and produce. They need no prior official approval. Under liberalisation policy, industries have been given the following freedom:

(a) Prior to liberliasation, under the provisions of old policy, at the time of granted licence government used to fix maximum limit of production capacity. No industry could produce beyond this limit. Now, this limit has been removed so as to enable the industry to take full advantage of large-scale production.

(b) Producers are now free to produce anything on the basis of demand in the market. Previously, only those goods could be produced which were mentioned in the licence. It is no larger so now.

(4) Increase in the Investment Limit of Small Industries: Investment limit of the small industries has been raised to ₹5 crore so as to enable them to introduce modernisation. Investment limit of tiny industries or micro enterprises has also been increased to ₹25 lakh.

(5) Freedom to Import Capital Goods and Raw Materials: Under the policy of liberalisation, Indian industries will be free to buy machines and raw material from abroad in order to expand and modernise themselves.

(6) Freedom to Import Technology: New Economic Policy or economic reforms have laid emphasis on the use of high technique to promote modernisation. The objective of the policy is to develop sunrise industries, i.e. computers and electronics. Under new economic reforms, to promote technological dynamism in Indian Industries, government has allowed agreement to import high technology. There is a provision in the new industrial policy that high priority industries need not to seek permission to enter into agreements related to high technology.

(7) Replacing FERA with FEMA: Earlier, for regulation foreign exchange transactions, government had enacted Foreign Exchange Regulation Act (FERA). This act was very restrictive in nature. It involved various checks and controls on transactions involving foreign exchange. Following the economic liberalisation and charged attitude of government towards foreign capital, FERA was replaced with Foreign Exchange Management Act (FEMA) in the year 1999. The Provisions of FEMA are liberal.

(8) Liberalisation of Export and Import Transactions: Government has liberalised its import and export policy. It has made the import of capital goods, raw materials and technology very easy. Quantitative Restrictions on import have been withdrawn. Provisions regarding import quota, import-permit and import-licence have been simplified. The procedures and documents related to import, export have been simplified.

(9) Liberalisation in Taxation Policy: Earlier, tax rates were very high, which was a great hindrance in the path of rapid economic development. High tax rate de-motivate the entrepreneurs in setting up new enterprises or expending the existing enterprise. Following main charges have been made in taxation policy.

(a) Peak Income tax rates have been reduced to 30 per cent.

(b) Custom-duty rates have been drastically reduced from 250 per cent to 10 per cent.

(c) Excise-duty rates have been reduced.

(d) Complex sales tax structure has been replaced with simple value-added-tax.

(10) Liberalisation in Capital Market: Earlier provisions regarding public issue of shares, debentures of companies were very restrictive. Only big companies could fulfil these conditions. But now these provisions have been liberalised. Now companies are given the freedom to fix the price of their public issue. Indian companies have been given the freedom to raise funds from foreign capital markets.

(11) Liberalisation in Banking Sector: Banks play import role in the economic development of any nation. Earlier monetary policy was very restrictive which hindered development of banking sector. Now following main liberalisations have been made in banking sector:

(a) Statutory Liquidity Radio (SLR) has been reduced to 25 per cent.

(b) Bank Rate has been reduced to 6 per cent.

(c) Cash Reserve Ratio (CRR) has been reduced to 6 per cent.

(d) Repo Rate and Reverse Repo Rate have been reduced to 5.25 per cent and 3.75 per cent respectively.

(e) Banks have been given freedom to determine their interest rates within certain limits.

(f) Banks have been given freedom to recruit their employees.

Q8. Evaluate the impact of globalisation on Indian economy.

Ans. Globalisation has both positive and negative effects on Indian Economy. Followings are the main positive and negative effects of globalisation on Indian economy:

(A) Positive Effects of Globalisation

(1) Increase in Foreign Trade: As a result of foreign trade policies adopted in the wake of globalisation, India's share in the world trade has gone up. In 1990-91, India's share in world trade was 0.53 per cent. In 1995-96, it rose to 0.60 per cent. In 2008-09, it further increased to 1.64 per cent.

(2) Increase in Foreign Investment: As a consequence of globalisation, there has been a considerable increase in foreign direct investment as well as foreign portfolio investment.

(a) **Foreign Direct Investment (FDI):** Foreign direct investment is made by foreign companies in order to establish wholly owned companies in another country and to manage them or to purchase shares of companies in another country for the purpose of managing such companies. The main characteristic of foreign direct investment is that native companies are managed by the foreign companies or new companies are set up in India by foreign companies. In this type of investment, it is the foreign investor who takes risk and is solely responsible for profit/loss of such company.

(b) **Portfolio Investment:** Under this type of investment, Foreign Companies/Foreign Institutional Investors (FIIs) buy shares/debentures of native companies, however management and control remain vested with the native/domestic companies themselves.

There is significant increase in foreign investment in India. In the year 1990-91, total foreign investment (FDI and Portfolio investment) was US $ 103 million. In the year 2007-08, amount of foreign investment increased to US $ 62,106 million. Due to global slowdown, inflow of foreign investment in 2008-09 has reduced to US $ 21, 325 million. In 2009-10 (April to Feb.) again inflow of foreign investment has increased to US $ 60,122 million. Because of signification increase in foreign investment, India began to experience a surplus balance of payments and a very remarkable improvement in foreign exchange reserves.

(3) Increase in Foreign Collaborations: Globalisation has promoted collaboration of foreign companies with many Indian companies. These collaboration agreements can be technical collaboration, financial collaboration or both. In financial collaboration, foreign companies provide financial resources, while in technical collaboration modern foreign technology is provided by foreign companies. Foreign companies are setting up many enterprises in India in collaboration with Indian companies.

(4) Increase in Foreign Exchange Reserves: As a result of globalisation of Indian economy, foreign exchange reserves have also increased substantially. In 1991, foreign exchange reserves of India amounted to ₹4,388 crore, which in March 2010 increased to ₹12,72, 666 crore (US $ 279, 71 billion). Thus, there has been an increase of 290 times in foreign exchange reserves of India.

(5) Expansion of Market: Globalisation has expanded the size of market. It has permitted Indian business units to expand their business in the whole world. Now multinational corporations have no national boundaries. Indian companies like Infosys, Tata Consultancy, Wipro Tata Steel, Reliance, etc. are doing their business in many countries.

(6) Technological Development: Globalisation has enabled the inflow of foreign technology, which is very superior and advanced. Now Indian business units use this modern technology.

(7) Brand Development: Globalisation has promoted the use of branded goods. Now not only durable goods are branded but products like garments, juices, snacks, food grains, etc. are also branded. Foreign brands are very popular among Indian consumers. Brand development has led to quality improvement.

(8) Development of Capital Market: Globalisation has helped in development of Indian capital market. Now many foreign investors invest in Indian Capital market. Recently there has been substantial increase in inflow of foreign direct investment and portfolio investment.

(9) Development of Service Sector: Globalisation has helped in growth of service sector. With the entry of foreign companies, tremendous improvement has been witnessed in various services like telecommunication, insurance, banking, etc. Now mobile phones are very cheap and popular in India.

(10) Increase in Employment: Globalisation has promoted employment opportunities. Foreign companies are establishing their production and trading units in India. It has increased employment opportunities for Indians, e.g. many Indians are presently employed in foreign insurance companies, mobile companies, etc.

(11) Reduction in Brain Drain: As a result of globalisation, many multinational corporations have set up their business units in India. These MNCs provide attractive salary package, good working conditions to efficient skilled Indian engineers, managers, professionals, etc. Now Indians get good employment opportunities in India. It has resulted in reduction in brain drain.

(B) Negative Effects of Globalisation

(1) Loss to Domestic Industries: As a consequence of globalisation, foreign competition has increased in India. Now Indian industrial units have to compete with foreign industrial units. Because of better quality and low cost of foreign goods, many Indian industrial units have failed to face competition and have been closed. Small and cottage industries are worst hit by this increased competition.

(2) Unemployment: Foreign companies operating in India use capital-intensive technology. Even some Indian companies use imported capital-intensive technology. With the increasing use of computers and automatic machines, employment avenues are reduced.

(3) Exploitation of Labour: Globalisation is exploiting unskilled workers by giving lower wages, less job security and long working hours. Labourers have to work even in these conditions because bad job and fewer wages are better than no jobs.

(4) Demonstration Effect: With the easy availability of foreign goods, demonstration effect has increased among Indians. Now many consumers are using luxury products by imitating others. It has promoted tendency of wasteful consumption in India. This increasing wasteful expenditure has in turn reducing saving and capital formation.

(5) Increase in Inequalities: Globalisation has increased inequalities in our economy. Gloablisation has benefitted MNCs and big and industrial units but small and cottage industries are adversely hit by it. It has increased income inequalities in India.

(6) Dominance of Foreign Institutions: With globalisation dominance of foreign institutions has increased in India. Globalisation has helped foreign companies in enlarging their market share. For example, in Indian cold drink market, a large share is controlled by Pepsi and Coca-Cola, which are foreign companies.

Q9. Who coined the term secularism and what does it generally imply? Discuss its significance.

Or

Give the characteristics of secularism.

Ans. The term 'secularism' has been derived from the Latin word, Seculum meaning, "this present age" or "this present generation". George Jacob

Holydake was the first man who used the word secularism in the nineteenth century to restructure a pluralistic society based on democracy and tolerance where equal opportunities were to be given to all, irrespective of their caste, creed, colour, race or culture. The real concept of secularism is that the state shall not impose any religion on people and it should pay equal respect to all religions. Strictly speaking, secularism implies an attitude of accepting all religions rather than rejecting any or all religions. According to Holydake, "Secularism may be defined as a system which seeks the development of the physical, moral and intellectual nature of man to the highest possible point as the immediate duty of life, which inculcates the practical sufficiency of natural morality apart from atheism, theism or the Bible, which selects as its methods of promotion of human improvement by material means".

Characteristics of Secularism

- It treats all religions equally, though their paths of realising their goals maybe different.
- It gives freedom to every individual to practise his own religion.
- It implies freedom of worship.
- The perfect toleration of understanding is to be maintained in the field of religion.
- It encourages rational thinking and understanding.
- No one should be politically or socially disqualified for his religious views.
- It encourages values that are more spiritual.
- It develops freedom dogmatic ideas.
- It does not mean a negation of religion but accepts that all religions have equal value.
- It implies that no religion is superior or inferior to other religions.
- Mutual co-existence of all religions without any hatred or bias against anyone.
- Emphasis is given to the material and cultural upliftment of the individual and the society.

Significance

This is important for a country to function democratically. Almost all countries of the world will have more than one religious group living in them. Within these religious groups, there will most likely be one group that is in a majority. If this majority religious group has access to State power, then this power could be quite easily used and financial resources to discriminate against and persecute persons of other religions. This tyranny of the majority could result in the discrimination, coercion and at times even the killing of religious minorities. The majority could quite easily prevent minorities from practicing their religions. Any form of domination based on religion is in violation of the rights that a democratic society guarantees to each and every citizen irrespective of their religion. Therefore, the tyranny of the majority and the violation of Fundamental Rights that can result is one reason why it is important to separate the State and religion in democratic societies.

Another reason that it is important to separate religion from the State in democratic societies because we also need to protect the freedom of individuals to exit from their religion, embrace another religion or have the freedom to interpret religious teachings differently.

Q10. Discuss the provisions of the Article 25-28 and demonstrate how they ensure the secular character of the Indian State.

Ans. Despite the reluctance of the Constituent Assembly to incorporate the word secular, a survey of the provisions of the Constitution suggest the State would be separate from religion and would guarantee religious freedoms to citizens of all faith, while not discriminating against any citizen on the basis of religion. Thus, the Indian Constitution guarantees both individual and collective freedom of religion through the Articles 25-28 in the chapter on Fundamental Rights. Article 15, in the same chapter provides that the state shall not discriminate against anyone on the basis of religion, caste, sex, race and place of birth. Article 16, guarantees that no Indian citizen would be discriminated against in matters of public employment on the basis of religion.

Article 25, guarantees the freedom of conscience and the right to freely propagate, profess and practice any religion. We might be aware of the recent incidents of violent attacks on religious missionaries that challenged the very basis of this right. The unfortunate victims of this violence were the minorities, especially the Christians. The implication seems to be that Hinduism is the most authentic religion of the Indian nation, and the presence of all other religions specially the ones of foreign origin threaten India's nationhood. Such an argument is obviously against the very basic assumptions of a secular state that the Constitution sought to establish in India. Article 27 and 28, further strengthen the individual freedom of religion by banning taxation for the purpose of supporting a particular religion and by banning religious instruction in institutions recognised or aided by the state. Article 28 gives the freedom to all religions to set up trusts and institutions, and acquire property and manage their own affairs.

Q11. Discuss the provisions of Articles 325 and 326.

Ans. Articles 325 and 326 provide for the principle of non-discrimination among citizens in the area of voting and representation on the basis of religion, race or sex. India has no state religion, nor does it give any constitutional recognition to the religion of the majority, besides which is of course the fact that the Government of India has no ecclesiastical department. All these facts taken together demonstrate in ample measure that the Indian Constitution followed very closely the Congress Party and its resolution 1931 made at its Karachi session that the state shall observe neutrality in regard to all religions. A survey of the Constitutional provisions suggest very clearly the framework of a secular state (despite certain anomalies), however, the politics, the nature and the functioning of the Indian state seem to suggest a drift away from this framework. The consensus that Jawaharlal Nehru was able to forge on this and other principles like economic self-reliance, egalitarianism and non-alignment (in the sphere of foreign policy) seems to have broken down.

Q12. Describe the factors responsible for secularism in India.

Or

Indentify the communal challenges to secularism.

Ans. It was expected that with the process of capitalist modernisation, a rationalist discourse would take over and religion would lose control over people's lives. In India, however, the rapid advancement of capitalism has been accompanied by an intensification of communalism. This has happened tragically despite the constitutional provisions for a secular framework and complete institutional backing of the secular forces. Following can be considered as factors responsible for this.

The Character of the National Movement

To investigate this defeat of secularism in the face of organised communal challenges, one would have to examine a variety of factors. Sudipta Kaviraj has suggested in many of her discussions of secularism that one of the gravest mistakes of the Indian bourgeoisie has been its complete neglect of building independence, the nationalist discourse realised the fragility of the new identity based on secular nationhood as against the more familiar identities of caste or religion. After independence however, this nationalist project of building a secular nation lost its popular character and ideological zeal and became merely the ideology of the state. The ruling class failed to realise that the Indian nation was a fragile creation and required constant cultural and political nourishment. Nationalist accounts of history that claimed for India's past, a 'composite culture' were pressed into service, the implication was that it was the evil designs of colonialism that disrupted this harmony.

In this rendering of history, there is a complete denial of the fact that much of the power of Indian nationalism itself came not from a secular idiom but from forces, idioms and symbols of religion, especially from Hinduism. We might also add here the fact that the Congress party conducted its politics in the pre-independence period on the basis of the idea that India was constituted of two distinct communities, i.e. the Hindus and the Muslims.

Akeel Bilgrami has diagnosed the challenge to Indian secularism as a consequence of its non-negotiated, Archimedean character. His argument is that the national movement did not facilitate a creative dialogue between communities which could have ensured the emergence of a negotiated understanding of secularism. The Congress Party, for instance, never undertook such a discussion seriously. Bilgrami is of the opinion that secularism must transcend religious politics from within, and not at the outset itself have a shimmering philosophical existence that is independent of religious and political commitments. Such a negotiated secularism would have, for instance, avoided the resentment towards the minorities because of the special status that they have as a consequence of a non-negotiated secularism.

Not being negotiated, this secularism is becoming increasingly difficult to defend. Hence, it is not really surprising to note that communalism is today no longer an aberration that exists on the fringes of the Indian nation, but as Rajni Kothari points out, it has become a part of the political system.

It is not as if the state has fallen prey to communal forces, rather communalism appears to be the direct outcome of the logic of the Indian state. Although the Indian state made a formal acceptance of the secular agenda, the fact is that apart from the differences between the Gandhians and the Nehruvians in their understanding of secularism, there was a whole section of the political class that was sceptical and even unwilling to accept these secular ideals.

Electoral Politics and the Decline of Democratic Institutions

The unsure commitment to the ideals of secularism at the best of times has meant an unprincipled exploitation of communal fears and sensibilities by all major political parties, including the most important of them, the Congress party. This cynical use of religion was perfected into an electoral strategy in the 1980s leading to disastrous consequences. The Congress, which had long abandoned its popular movement character, now became only a machine to win elections. The party's commitment to pluralism soon degenerated into politics of vote banks where only the numerical strength of the majority and the minority community mattered for electoral purposes.

The sharpening of social and economical conflicts and the intensifying environmental degradation that robbed the ordinary people of their livelihoods made popular discontent a widespread reality. It was becoming clear to the Congress that its earlier slogans of socialism and secularism were fast losing their appeal among the traditional supporters because these slogans remained just that, and had not brought about any significant change in the lives of the poor and marginalised sections of the society, many of whom were traditional Congress supporters. These sections had gradually moved away from the Congress. The party in turn looked for a new constituency and through the 1980s assiduously cultivated the Hindu middle and lower classes that were feeling increasingly threatened by the forces of the various backward caste and subaltern movements. The latter have been gaining in strength and popularity given the fact that the national development project has completely bypassed them. The Congress party's adoption of an openly majoritarian politics was a complete reversal of its historical role as the principle bourgeois adversary of communalism. The Congress, thus, adopted a strategy of downplaying broader social issues and decided to make a direct appeal to the majority community. The strategy was to define the Indian nation increasingly in terms of the majority community, thus, preparing the grounds for communal politics that took the form of cultural nationalism.

Thus, instead of responding to popular discontent and demands, an attempt was made to foist another set of issues by involving sentiments and feelings that engender communal attitudes. Communal politics, in general, and parties like the Bharatiya Janata Party, in particular, have benefited from the collapse of the consensus that the Indian political elite had over secularism, economic self-reliance and non-alignment.

Electoral compulsions made the Congress move away from a pluralistic approach to a techno-bureaucratic-military approach where the state was to be an instrument to crush any challenge from the bottom rather than act as a principal agent of change and transformation.

Apart from the increasing incidents of communal violence, the spread of communal politics and violence to the hitherto unaffected rural areas is yet another major threat to the secular fabric that the Indian state was trying to weave together. These developments provided the ideal conditions for various "Hindu cultural groups" like the Vishwa Hindu Parishad and others that claimed to be engaged in the reconstruction and consolidation of the "Hindu" community to grow. They derive a lot of support from a section of the Indian diaspora as well. These organisations were able to respond to the peculiar fears of the middle class that wanted none of the traditional structures of power and hierarchy challenged while at the same time desiring all the bounties of the modern market place and economy.

One of the serious challenges to secularism in our county is posed by communal riots. In fact, on several occasions, the state agencies and political forces are involved in engineering communal riots. Paul R. Brass in his books *The Production of Hindu-Muslim Violence* and *The Theft of an Idol* have shown that communal violence occurs through an "institutionalised riot system". According to this riot system, there are some political forces-politicians, organisations, intellectuals, etc. who work in a systemic way to mobilise a section of people to indulge in ethnic or communal violence. On several occasions, these forces work in collaboration with the state agencies, i.e. police or government officials. The riots generally take place in some political context and elections form a significant part of such context. As the riots polarise different communities on sectarian lines, they influence elections, result to a considerable extent. Thus, by harming the secularism, the communal riots actually pose a challenge to democracy.

The Nature of Capitalist Development and Character of the Indian Ruling Class

The nature of ruling class politics itself according to Randhir Singh is the related phenomenon like religious revivalism, etc. are that he argues in direct proportion to the depth of the crisis in the Indian polity and the politics of the ruling classes on the one hand, and in inverse proportion to the presence and power of the left and class-based politics of the people, on the other. Thus, he defines the communal challenge to secularism in India as the ideology and practice of politics of the Indian ruling classes in a society with a massive feudal-colonial inheritance, deep religious divisions undergoing its own historically specific form of capitalist development.

The argument is that four decades of development have not altered the deeply uneven nature of Indian society; uneven capitalist development has actually heightened the social tensions. Given the limited nature of opportunities that are available, politics and ideology promoting narrow and exclusivist interests direct this social tension against the minorities. It is indeed a fact that conditions of life have worsened and alienation has increased the dissatisfaction that people feel over the increasing gulf between the rich and the poor instead of being articulated through democratic struggles is being channelised into a revivalist and gaudy religiosity that the media has also supported in ample measures. We only have to look at the major television channels that are competing with one another to host religious extravaganzas. The 1980s witnessed a deliberate attempt to widen the mass base of religious appeal, the large scale and almost commercialised celebrations of certain select festivals is part of the larger strategy to create a more 'universal Hinduism' by replacing the significance of local festivities and rituals.

Q13. To what does Ashish Nandy attribute the failure of Secularism in India?

Ans. Ashish Nandy argues that the ideology and politics of secularism as understood in the western sense have more or less exhausted their possibilities. The western understanding of secularism, he suggests, is essentially opposed to religion and believes that only universal categories can manage the public realm. Religion, thus, is perceived of as a threat to any modern polity by virtue of not being universal. Nandy suggests that secularism as an ideology has failed because it is seen today as being a part of a larger package that consists of a set of standardised ideological products and social processes like development, mega science and national security. Being backed by the might of the state, they appear essentially as violent ideas, because to defend any of these ideas including secularism, the state can justifiably use violence. Nandy is critical of the fact that while the modern nation-state appeals to the believers to keep their private faiths out of public life, it is unable to ensure that the ideologies of secularism, development and nationalism do not themselves begins to act as faiths intolerant of others. The role of the state in such situations is likened by Nandy to that of crusading and inquisitorial role of religious ideologies.

Besides, the proposition that the values derived from the secular ideology of a secular state would somehow be a better guide to political action and to a less violent and richer political life than values and politics based on religious principles. Nandy contends that objectification, scientisation and bureaucratic-rationality, the core principles of a modern nation-state can only breed violence. The elite in such states view statecraft in purely secular and amoral terms, thus, thinking of religion or ethnicity as hurdles to the grand project of nation-building and state formation. Thus, Nandy argues that the western concept of secularism becomes a handy adjunct to a set of legitimating core concepts. Accepting this ideology, his contend leads to the justification and acceptance of domination and violence perpetrated in the name of progress and modernity. It also generates hatred and violence among the believers at having to face a world that is fast moving out of their grip.

This type of secularism has been imposed on those people who never wished to separate religion from politics. This imposition had to be made as a part of the requirements needed to fulfil the creation of a modern nation-state. This, however, has left the ordinary people of India very unhappy who left with no choice in their fight against the brutalities of the nation in the name of modernity turn to the only form of religious political that modernity would permit namely communal politics. Thus, it is secularism as practiced that breeds communalism. Intolerance links the two, replacing the quality of tolerance that characterised the traditional world organised on the basis of religion.

Q14. What is the relationship between democracy and equality?

Ans. *If democracy is defined as the form of government dedicated to the realisation of the values of self-determination, democracy bears a complex relationship to equality.* The idea and principle of democracy cannot be divorced from the principle of equality. Moreover, political democracy cannot be the sufficient basis of ensuring social and economical equality in a condition of glaring inequality of status and position. The idea of social and economical democracy has been getting greater appeal among the people across the globe who have been excluded and deprived on account of their social location and economic position. Therefore, the procedural view of democracy is under question. It is argued that guaranteeing of universal adult franchise is not a sufficient basis of the success of democracy. The formal participation in electoral process is only one indicator of the equal opportunity to participate in the election. This participation may be eclipsed by number of social and economical constraints. In India, the chances of political participation are determined, to a greater extent, by individual's socio-economic position. For instance, the percentage of vote of the dalits, OBCs, minorities and women has been increasing over the years but majority of them still do not participate in the process. Their effective participation cannot be ensured without creating a condition of affectivity. And this affectivity can be advanced through ensuring substantive equality. Mere political equality in terms of equality of opportunity would face disjunction in case of social and economic inequality. Similarly, the ideal of political democracy has to be backed by social and economical democracy. Under this condition, the dichotomy between procedural democracy and substantive democracy ceases to exist. The people would be able to exercise their political rights of citizenship effectively and this would further the ideals of democracy in real terms.

Q15. Discuss the idea of equality in constitution.

Ans. The device of equality, as used in the Indian Constitution, is meaningful to those who need it more urgently. Equality implies that the poor people should approach an economically higher place though the upper placed people may move on to a still upper one, provided the speed of the poor is faster. And for acceleration of speed of the economically lowest, encouragement is necessary. It can be provided through some economic and social measures and particularly by way of reservations.

The Preamble

The Preamble of the Constitution best reflects the vision and intentions of its founding fathers as it establishes equality, justice and liberty as the cardinal principles in regulating the society and state in India and maintaining the unity and integrity of the nation. It judiciously combines the two basic values of equality and justice. The nondiscrimination principle of citizenship rights included in the category of fundamental rights ensures equality before law and equal protection of law, equality of opportunity and equal liberty. The provision of protective discrimination combined with the clauses of group rights, affirmative action and preferential treatment establishes the values of social justice in favour of derived groups and communities. The Constitution ensured equality of opportunity to all irrespective of caste, gender, religion and one's social location. It provided opportunity to equal access in the public domain. It was a major achievement of the dispensation of democratic political order in independent India. However, the formal disjunction between one's social location and opening up of the opportunity structure in public political domain guarantee the equifinality and social justice to the deprived groups of society. In the case of Indian society, which is defined by structured inequality, the social location of individuals and groups has a strong bearing on his/her circumstances and consequent unequal excess to opportunity structure of the public domain. Since social location of individuals has been a major source of privileges and deprivations and determinant of individual circumstances in India, the deliverance of social and economical justice cannot be based only on the principle of merit and equality of opportunity in the public domain.

Fundamental Rights and Directive Principles

This logic of social, economical and political life was well considered by the framers of the Constitution of India. And therefore, the Constitution of India made specific provisions for the socially and economically deprived sections of society along with the generic clauses of equality and liberty to every citizen in India. Whereas the Articles 14, 15 (1) and 16(1) of the Constitution exclusively establish the equality principle, Articles 15(4) and 16(4) incorporate the principle of social justice. If Article 14 proclaims equality before law and equal protection of law, Article 15(1) prohibits discrimination on grounds of race, caste, sex, religion or place of birth. The Article 16(1) further provides equality of opportunity to all. The protective discrimination clauses of Article 15(4) and 16(4) become decisive with regard to protection of rights of socially and economically deprived groups of the hierarchical system. These Articles follow the different principles leading to social justice. Article 15(4) say, "Nothing in this Article shall prevent the State from making any special provision for the advancement of any socially and educationally backward classes of citizens or for the Schedule Caste and Scheduled Tribes". Article 16(4) makes provision that "Nothing in this Article shall prevent the State from making any special provision for the reservation of appointments or posts in favour of any backward class of citizens which, in the opinion of the State is not adequately represented in the services under the State". Both the provisions in the Constitution, however, limited in scope, provide condition for the constitutional protection of the rights of the socially and educationally backward classes and deprived sections of society.

Apart from these protective discrimination clauses in the Constitution, the Directive Principles of the State Policy may be considered as mechanism of realising the goal of social justice and social transformation in the direction of just society. Articles 38 and 46 among others, specifically aim at securing social justice to the deprived sections of population. Article 38 reads that, (i) "the State shall strive to promote the welfare of the people by securing and protecting as effectively as it may a social order in which justice, social, economical and political shall inform all the institutions of the national life", (ii) "the State shall, in particular, strive to minimise the inequalities in income, and endeavour to eliminate inequalities in status, facilities and opportunities, not only amongst individuals but also amongst the groups of people residing in different areas not type in different vocations". Article 46 clearly directs the State that "the State shall promote with special care the educational and economical interests of the weaker sections of the people, and in particular of the Scheduled castes and the Scheduled Tribes, and shall protect them from social injustice and all forms of exploitation".

Other Provisions

Apart from these two Articles of the Directive Principles of State Policy, other Articles of the Constitution which include Articles 330, 332, 335, 338, 340, 341 and 342 specifically advance the goal of realising social justice in independent India. These constitutional provisions have been made after a thoughtful consideration by the members of the Constituent Assembly who were quite conscious and aware about the dynamics of socio-economic order of Indian society. Since caste has been the major identity marker and a source of inequality, the constitutional goal of social justice has been channelised through the category of castes (barring tribes and other groups identified for the protective discrimination). The constitution has recognised the cumulative deprivation of large sections of the population who have been systematically discriminated against on the basis of caste distinction.

Minority Rights

As a means of protection of identity and right of different categories of minorities, the Constitution of India makes special provision of minorities' rights. These rights do not fall in opposition to generic clauses of citizenship rights available to all the citizens in India. These rights in a sense appear as mechanism of advancing substantive democracy. Articles 25 to 30 take special care of the minorities. Whereas Article 25, 26, 27 and 28 ensure religious freedom, the Article 29 and 28 protect and promote their cultural and educational rights.

Q16. Evaluate the participation of women in decision-making bodies.

Ans. Around the world, women's lack of representation in government, especially in high-level executive and legislative bodies, limits their influence over governance and public policies. Arguably, women's participation in decision-making is essential for ensuring their equality and rights. Where women have participated actively in public policy, they have been able to raise the visibility of women's issues and work towards ending gender discrimination. But women have made slow progress in the political arena, even while making impressive gains in other areas such as education, employment and health.

Women's Political Participation: Facts and Figures

In Lok Sabha: Even six decades after Independence, the representation of women in the Lok Sabha do not present an impressive picture. It has not crossed 10 per cent (Table 7.1). In the First Lok Sabha, there were only 22 women constituting 4.4 per cent of the House. It increased marginally over the years except in the Sixth Lok Sabha when the House had only 19 women members.

In the Thirteenth Lok Sabha, there were 49 women members. However, in the Fourteenth Lok Sabha, the strength of women members is 51.

Table 7.1: Number of Women Elected to Lok Sabha

General Elections	No. of Women Elected	Percentage
First	22	4.40
Second	27	5.40
Third	34	6.70
Fourth	31	5.90
Fifth	22	4.20
Sixth	19	3.40
Seventh	28	5.10
Eighth	44	8.10
Ninth	28	5.29
Tenth	39	7.02
Eleventh	40	7.36
Twelfth	44	8.07
Thirteenth	49	9.02
Fourteenth	51	9.51

In Rajya Sabha: Similarly, in the Rajya Sabha, in 1952, the number of women members was merely 15 constituting 6.94 per cent of the membership of the House. Over the years, the percentage of women has increased and now, out of 242 members, 23 are women constituting 9.50 per cent of the House. In the Rajya Sabha, the representation of women has never crossed 12 per cent (Table 7.2).

Table 7.2: Women Members of Rajya Sabha and their Percentage (1952-2008)

Year	Number	Percentage
1952	15	6.94
1954	17	7.79
1956	20	8.62

Contd...

1958	22	09.52
1960	24	10.25
1962	18	07.62
1964	21	08.97
1966	23	09.82
1968	22	09.64
1970	14	05.85
1972	18	07.40
1974	18	07.53
1976	24	10.16
1978	25	10.24
1980	29	11.98
1982	24	10.16
1984	24	10.24
1986	28	11.98
1988	25	10.59
1990	24	10.34
1992	17	07.29
1994	20	08.36
1996	19	07.81
1998	19	07.75
2000	22	09.01
2002	25	10.20
2004	28	11.43
2006	25	10.41
2008	23	09.50

In State Legislatures: Women representation in State legislatures has also been equally dismal. At present, the average percentage of elected women in State Assemblies is 6.94 per cent, the highest being 14.44 per cent in Haryana and the lowest being 1.34 per cent in Karnataka. States like Arunachal Pradesh, Manipur, Mizoram, Nagaland and Union Territory of Puducherry have no representation of women in their Assemblies (Table 7.3).

Table 7.3: Women Members in Legislative Assemblies and their Percentage

Sl. No.	Name of State/UT	Total No. of Seats	Women Members	Percentage
1	Andhra Pradesh	294	28	9.52
2	Arunachal Pradesh	60	0	0.00
3	Assam	126	13	10.32
4	Bihar	243	25	10.29

Contd...

5	Chhattisgarh	90	5	5.56
6	Delhi	70	6	8.57
7	Goa	40	1	2.50
8	Gujarat	182	16	8.79
9	Haryana	90	13	14.44
10	Himachal Pradesh	68	5	7.35
11	Jammu & Kashmir	87	2	2.30
12	Jharkhand	81	5	6.17
13	Karnataka	224	3	1.34
14	Kerala	140	7	5.00
15	Madhya Pradesh	230	19	8.26
16	Maharashtra	288	12	4.17
17	Manipur	60	0	0.00
18	Meghalaya	60	2	3.33
19	Mizoram	40	0	0.00
20	Nagaland	60	0	0.00
21	Orissa	147	11	7.48
22	Punjab	117	7	5.98
23	Puducherry	30	0	0.00
24	Rajasthan	200	13	6.50
25	Sikkim	32	3	9.38
26	Tamil Nadu	234	22	9.40
27	Tripura	60	2	3.33
28	Uttar Pradesh	403	25	6.20
29	Uttarakhand	70	4	5.71
30	West Bengal	294	37	12.59
	Total	4120	286	6.94

It is unfortunate that in India after 58 years of the working of the Constitution, women are still fighting for their empowerment; women's representation in Parliament is merely 8 per cent. It is not surprising that the Global Gender Gap Report 2007 of UNDP had placed India at a disappointing rank of 114 out of 128 countries studied, based on indicators, among others, of political empowerment.

Q17. What do you understand by the term politics?

Ans. Politics, in its broadest sense, is the activity through which people make, preserve and amend the general rules under which they live. Although politics is also an academic subject (sometimes indicated by the use of 'Politics' with a capital P), it is then clearly the study of this activity. Politics is thus inextricably linked to the phenomena of conflict and co-operation. On the one hand, the existence of rival opinions, different wants, competing needs and opposing interests guarantees disagreement about the rules under which people live. On the other hand, people recognise that, in order to influence these rules or to ensure that they are upheld, they must work with others, hence, Hannah Arendt's definition of political power as 'acting in concert'. This is why the heart of politics is often portrayed as a process of conflict resolution, in which rival views or competing interests are reconciled with one another. However, politics in this broad sense is better thought of as a search for conflict resolution then as its achievement, as not all conflicts are, or can be, resolved. Nevertheless, the inescapable presence of diversity (we are not all alike) and scarcity (there is never enough to go around) ensures that politics is an inevitable feature of the human condition. Any attempt to clarify the meaning of 'politics' must nevertheless address two major problems. The first is the mass of associations that the word has when used in everyday language; in other words, politics is a 'loaded' term. Whereas most people think of, say, economics, geography, history and biology simply as academic subjects, few people come to politics without preconceptions. Many, for instance, automatically assume that students and teachers of politics must in some way be biased, finding it difficult to believe that the subject can be approached in an impartial and dispassionate manner. To make matters worse, politics is usually thought of as a 'dirty' word: it conjures up images of trouble, disruption and even violence on the one hand, and deceit, manipulate and lies on the other. There is nothing new about such associations. As long ago as 1775, Samuel Johnson dismissed politics as 'nothing more than a means of rising in the world', while in the nineteenth century, the US historian Henry Adams summed up politics as 'the systematic organisation of hatreds'.

The second and more intractable difficulty is that even respected authorities cannot agree what the subject is about. Politics is defined in such different ways: as the exercise of power, the science of government, the making of collective decisions, the allocation of scarce resources, the practice of deception and manipulation, and so on. The virtue of the definition advanced in this text – 'the making, preserving and amending of general social rules' – is that it is sufficiently broad to encompass most, if not all, of the competing definitions.

	Politics as anAarena	Politics as a Process
Definitions of politics	The art of government public affairs	Compromise and consensus power and the distribution of resources
Approaches to the study of politics	Behaviouralism rational-choice theory institutionalism	Feminism Marxism post-positivist approaches

Fig. 7.1: Approaches to defining Politics

Whether we are dealing with rival concepts or alternative conceptions, it is helpful to distinguish between two broad approaches to defining politics (Hay, 2002; Leftwich, 2004). In the first, politics is associated with an *arena* or location, in which behaviour becomes 'political' where it takes place. In the second, politics is viewed as a *process* or mechanism, in which 'political' behaviour is behaviour that exhibits distinctive characteristics or qualities, and so can take place in any, and perhaps all, social contexts. Each of these broad approaches has spawned alternative definitions of politics.

Q18. Write a note on the criminalisation of politics.

Or

What do you mean by criminalisation of politics?

Ans. Criminalisation of politics in India has attained a stage, where it needs serious attention from the citizens, government and political parties as there is steady decline in values of all sections of our society. Criminalisation of politics has led to immense pressure on functioning of political institution. The worst part of the picture is that "criminal record" becomes an essential qualification for entry into politics. In India, politics is not a social service anymore; instead, it emerged as a lucrative profession or business. Today crime is the shortest access to legislature and parliament in India. Success rate of criminals into electoral process is alluring the young blood of the country. It remains as a source of negative inspiration. It is now believed that the safest haven for criminals is politics and political parties have gone overboard in associating criminals with them more because of their muscle and money power to ensure victory in polls. Criminalisation of politics in India is visualised into two different senses that is discussed as follows:

- In narrow sense, it refers to the direct entry and interference of criminals into state legislatures and parliament of India, and
- In wider sense, it refers to interference of criminals into politics either directly or indirectly like financing any candidate, providing anti-social manpower, booth-capturing, contract killing of rival candidates, providing muscle power services, as well as campaigning or canvassing for any candidate contesting elections.

Since last two decades, the competitive use of anti-social forces for mobilisation of party funds, for management of elections, organising meetings and conference and even recruiting workers at lower levels from among anti-social elements has increased. Political parties from national to regional are taking the services of criminals to win election have become the common practices. Criminals lending outside support in the past was now changed to the criminals themselves entering the electoral arena. These criminals not only become members of the house but even hold the post of ministers. Today we have a new phenomenon in Indian politics called "Tainted Ministers".

Q19. What do you know about terrorism?

Or

Give the definitions of terrorism from various scholars and institutions.

Ans. To begin, it seems appropriate to define the term *terrorism*. Within terrorism lies the word *terror*. **Terror** comes from the Latin *terrere*, which means "frighten" or "tremble". When coupled with the French suffix *isme* (referencing "to practice"), it becomes akin to "practicing the trembling" or "causing the frightening". Trembling and frightening here are synonyms for fear, panic and anxiety—what we would naturally call is terror. In ancient Rome, the terror cimbricus was a state of panic and emergency in response to the coming of the Cimbri tribe killers in 105 BCE. This description of terrorism as being rooted in terror is an example of etymology. Etymology is the study of the origin and evolution of words. From this standpoint, language is organic, changeable, fluctuating, depending on the needs of thinkers and speakers over time and place.

The word terrorism, in and of itself, was coined during the French Revolution's Reign of Terror (1793–1794). In the Reign of Terror a group of rebels, the Jacobins, used the term when self-reflexively portraying their own actions in and explanations of the French Revolution. The Reign of Terror was a campaign of large-scale violence by the French state in which between 16,000 and 40,000 people were killed in a little over a year. It is not surprising, then, that the French National Convention proclaimed in September 1793, "Terror is the order of the day."

While the Reign of Terror was a product of the French government, in modern times, terrorism denotes the killing of humans by non-government political actors for various reasons—usually as a political statement. This interpretation came from Russian radicals in the 1870s. Sergey Nechayev, the founder of People's Retribution in 1869, viewed himself as a terrorist. In the 1880s, German anarchist writer 'Johann Most' helped in promoting the modern gist of the word by giving out "advice for terrorists." Worldwide, many governments are incredibly averse to defining terrorism because they are worried about how an official definition of terrorism would expose the legitimacy of self-proclaimed combats of national liberation. In certain countries, the word has become virtually synonymous with political opponents. For instance, the Chinese call pacific Tibetan Buddhists vicious terrorists. In Zimbabwe, President Robert Mugabe regards the democratic opposition in a similar fashion. Terrorism is a pejorative term. When people employ the term, they characterise their enemies' actions as something evil and lacking human compassion. Terrorism is considered worse than war, torture, or murder. A pejorative term is a term that is fraught with negative and derogatory meanings.

Definitions from Various Scholars and Institutions

Throughout the years, various scholars have attempted to define terrorism. Yet, the term is so loaded with conceptual problems that a totally accepted definition of it still does not exist. The irony is that the recurrent theme of terrorism has become the daily part of the political drama of modern times. One just needs to turn on the TV to hear about it constantly. Below is a list of definitions of terrorism by some of the most distinguished scholars and institutions on the matter:

Walter Laqueur: "Terrorism is the use or the threat of the use of violence, a method of combat, or a strategy to achieve certain targets... It aims to induce a state of fear in the victim, that is ruthless and does not conform with humanitarian rules... Publicity is an essential factor in the terrorist strategy."

Bruce Hoffman: "Terrorism is ineluctably political in aims and motives, violent or equally important, threatens violence, designed to have far-reaching psychological repercussions beyond the immediate victim or target, conducted by an organisation with an identifiable chain of command or conspiratorial cell structure (whose members wear no uniform or identifying insignia), and perpetrated by a sub-national group or non-state entity."

Alex Schmid and Albert Jongman: "Terrorism is an anxiety-inspiring method of repeated violent action, employed by (semi-)clandestine individual, group, or state actors, for idiosyncratic, criminal, or political reasons, whereby, in contrast to assassination, the direct targets of violence are not the main targets. The immediate human victims of violence are generally chosen randomly (targets of opportunity) or selectively (representative or symbolic targets) from a target population, and serve as message generators."

David Rapoport: "Terrorism is the use of violence to provoke consciousness, to evoke certain feelings of sympathy and revulsion."

Yonah Alexander: "Terrorism is the use of violence against random civilian targets in order to intimidate or to create generalised pervasive fear for the purpose of achieving political goals."

Stephen Sloan: The definition of terrorism has evolved over time, but its political, religious, and ideological goals have practically never changed.

Q20. Write short notes on the following:

(a) Political Repression

Ans. Political repression is the persecution of an individual or group for political reasons, particularly for the purpose of restricting or preventing their ability to take part in the political life of a society.

Political repression is sometimes used synonymously with the term political discrimination (also known as politicism). It often is manifested through discriminatory policies, such as human rights violations, surveillance abuse, police brutality, imprisonment, involuntary settlement, stripping of citizen's rights, lustration and violent action or terror such as the murder, summary executions, torture, forced disappearance and other extrajudicial punishment of political activists, dissidents, or general population.

Where political repression is sanctioned and organised by the state, it may constitute state terrorism, genocide, politicide or crimes against humanity. Systemic and violent political repression is a typical feature of dictatorships, totalitarian states and similar regimes. Acts of political repression may be carried out by secret police forces, army, paramilitary groups or death squads. Repressive activities have also been found within democratic contexts as well. This can even include setting up situations where the death of the target of repression is the end result.

If political repression is not carried out with the approval of the state, a section of government may still be responsible. An example is the FBI COINTELPRO operations in the United States between 1956 and 1971.

In some states, "repression" can be an official term used in legislation or the names of government institutions. For example, the Soviet Union had a legal policy of repression of political opposition defined in the penal code and Cuba under Fulgencio Batista had a secret police agency officially named the "Bureau for the Repression of Communist Activities."

(b) Transition in Indian Politics

Ans. From politics of trust to politics of suspicion, the two decades immediately following independence have been characterised by Rajni Kothari as 'decades of trust'. Politics in these decades was determined by a sense of trust between people marked by a mutual concern and understanding about what constituted the 'common good'. Politics was seen as an 'ethical space' where conflicts were resolved amiably and honourably. The seventies, however, marked according to Rajni Kothari, an 'obituary' of the politics of trust of the preceding decades. The 'ethical space' of politics was vitiated by violence, crime, corruption and repression, marking what Kothari calls the 'the virtual elimination of politics'.

What we confront today is not the crisis of politics but its virtual elimination. The last decade has marked the beginning of the Indian State that has not only deprived society of a basic consensus, but which has eschewed any scope of dialogue from it. Rajni Kothari, in his book *Politics and the People: In search of Humane India* mentions that violence, the fear, the repression, the rhetoric of deceit and doublespeak, are symptoms not of crises, but of the end of politics. Indian politics was no longer the democratic space where, through dialogue and interaction, the aspirations and needs of the people could be affirmed and resolved. The 'end of politics' is seen as the period in which the relationship of dialogue among people as well as the people and the state, is ruptured by crime, repression and terror as the means of conflict resolution. Crime, repression and terror make themselves manifest in several forms.

Question Papers

Government and Politics in India: BPSE-212
Sample Question Paper—I

Note: (i) Section I—Any two questions to be answered. (ii) Section II—Any four questions to be answered. (iii) Section III—Any four questions to be answered.

SECTION-I

Answer any two of the following questions in about 500 words each. Each question carries 20 marks.

Q1. Describe and analyse the impact of the first phase of British colonialism in India.

Ans. Refer to Chapter-1, Q.No.-3

Q2. Discuss the various measures adopted by India towards liberalisation.

Ans. Refer to Chapter-7, Q.No.-7

Q3. Write an essay on legislative relations between union and states of India.

Ans. Refer to Chapter-4, Q.No.-4

Q4. Explain the nature of party system in India and identify its various characteristics.

Ans. Refer to Chapter-5, Q.No.-1

SECTION-II

Answer any four of the following questions in about 250 words each. Each question carries 12 marks.

Q5. Highlight the major issues confronting women's unity.

Ans. Refer to Chapter-6, Q.No.-6

Q6. List out the essential features of the Indian Constitution.

Ans. Refer to Chapter-2, Q.No.-5

Q7. Write an essay on the nature of extremist nationalism in colonial India.

Ans. Refer to Chapter-1, Q.No.-11

Q8. Who coined the term secularism and what does it generally imply? Discuss its significance.

Ans. Refer to Chapter-7, Q.No.-9

Q9. Make a brief essay on the Panchayati Raj Institutions in the post-73rd Amendment era.

Ans. Refer to Chapter-4, Q.No.-30

Q10. Describe the organisation, composition and jurisdiction of the High Court.

Ans. Refer to Chapter-3, Q.No.-22

Q11. Discuss the major national political parties in India.

Ans. Refer to Chapter-5, Q.No.-5

Q12. Describe the organisation and jurisdiction of the Supreme Court.

Ans. Refer to Chapter-3, Q.No.-21

SECTION-III

Q13. Write short notes on any two of the following in about 100 words each. Each question carries 6 marks.

(a) Constitutional Government

Ans. Refer to Chapter-2, Q.No.-1

(b) Criminalisation of politics

Ans. Refer to Chapter-7, Q.No.-18

(c) Critique of colonialism

Ans. Refer to Chapter-1, Q.No.-9(ii)

(d) 74th Constitutional Amendment

Ans. Refer to Chapter-4, Q.No.-31(b)

Government and Politics in India: BPSE-212

Sample Question Paper—II

Note: (i) Section I—Any two questions to be answered. (ii) Section II—Any four questions to be answered. (iii) Section III—Any four questions to be answered.

SECTION-I

Answer any two of the following questions in about 500 words each. Each question carries 20 marks.

Q1. Describe the composition, qualification, election procedure, duration, presiding officers and different powers of the Lok Sabha and the Rajya Sabha.

Ans. Refer to Chapter-3, Q.No.-6

Q2. Enumerate the economical, political and cultural impact of globalisation.

Ans. Refer to Chapter-7, Q.No.-6

Q3. Discuss the phases through which the dalit movement has passed.

Ans. Refer to Chapter-6, Q.No.-9

Q4. Discuss the emergency provisions of the Indian Constitution.

Ans. Refer to Chapter-2, Q.No.-6

SECTION-II

Answer any four of the following questions in about 250 words each. Each question carries 12 marks.

Q5. Make a brief note on parliamentary system in India.

Ans. Refer to Chapter-3, Q.No.-4

Q6. What do you know about Panchayats (Extension to the scheduled areas) Act, 1996?

Ans. Refer to Chapter-4, Q.No.-29

Q7. According to the Constitution of India, who are the citizens of India?

Ans. Refer to Chapter-2, Q.No.-17

Q8. Mention the stages through which the election process passes.

Ans. Refer to Chapter-5, Q.No.-9

Q9. Briefly explain reforms movements under colonial rule.

Ans. Refer to Chapter-1, Q.No.-8

Q10. What is meant by liberalisation? What are the its different facets?

Ans. Refer to Chapter-7, Q.No.-4

Q11. Identify the main trends of the tribal movements in India during 1920-1947.

Ans. Refer to Chapter-6, Q.No.-11

Q12. Write an essay on Indian Federalism and State autonomy.

Ans. Refer to Chapter-4, Q.No.-16

SECTION-III

Q13. Write short notes on any two of the following in about 100 words each. Each question carries 6 marks.

(a) Rise of Modern Indian Intelligentsia

Ans. Refer to Chapter-1, Q.No.-20(v)

(b) Speaker of the Lok Sabha

Ans. Refer to Chapter-3, Q.No.-8

(c) Coalition politics in India (1947-1990)

Ans. Refer to Chapter-5, Q.No.-16

(d) Municipal Finance

Ans. Refer to Chapter-4, Q.No.-31(c)

Government and Politics In India: BPSE-212

June, 2014

Note: (i) Section I—Any two questions to be answered. (ii) Section II—Any four questions to be answered. (iii) Section III—Any two parts to be answered.

SECTION-I

Answer any two of the following questions in about 500 words each. Each question carries 20 marks.

Q1. Discuss the impact of colonialism in India's developmental process.

Ans. Refer to Chapter-1, Q.No.-3

Q2. Describe the features of the 73rd Constitutional Amendment Act.

Ans. Refer to Chapter-4, Q.No.-28

Q3. Critically assess the nature of the dalit movement since the 1990s.

Ans. Refer to Chapter-6, Q.No-9

Q4. Evaluate the political impact of globalisation.

Ans. Refer to Chapter-7, Q.No.-6

SECTION-II

Answer any four of the following questions in about 250 words each. Each question carries 12 marks.

Q5. What was the tribal response to colonialism? Explain.

Ans. Refer to Chapter-1, Q.No.-5

Q6. How has the constitution of India sought to balance individual and community rights? Discuss.

Ans. Refer to Chapter-2, Q.No.-19

Q7. Examine the nature of changes which have taken place in the Indian bureaucracy since the 1990s.

Ans. Refer to Chapter-3, Q.No.-31 & 32

Q8. Identify the main features of the 74th Constitutional Amendment Act.

Ans. Refer to Chapter-4, Q.No.-31(b)

Q9. Discuss the nature of relationship between elections and social change.

Ans. Periodic elections voters' turn out and large scale participation of the people have deepened the democracy in India. Reservation of seats for the SCs, the STs at all levels of the legislative bodies-national, state and the local, and with the passage of the 73rd and 74th Constitutional Amendments has enabled even the women and the OBCs to get elected to the seats reserved for them in the village panchayats and municipalities. These sections have not only been elected to various legislative bodies but have become the Chief Ministers, ministers and the President of the country. Political Scientist Ashutosh Varshney has argued that with the entry of the groups like dalits and OBCs into the electoral processes, India has become more democratic. However, women's entry has not been a smooth process. In fact, in large number of cases, especially in the village panchayats, the women elected members are the proxies of male members of their families.

But the democratic essence of the elections get hampered due to the social and economic inequalities, crimes and corruption. Those who do not possess the resources have no connections with the criminals, etc., find it difficult to contest elections or some time vote. Generally the candidates are given tickets by the political parties on the considerations whether the candidates can muster the support of numerically larger casters and communities and possesses enough resources. Even the electorates vote on the caste and communal lines. A large number of elected representative have criminal background have criminal cases registered against them. The relationship between the politicians and criminals exists in the elections at all levels–parliamentary, state legislative assemblies and councils, and panchayats and municipalities. Such nexue became conspicuous, especially since the 1990s. This is a reflection of erosion in the credibility of the democratic values. V N Vohra sub-committee also pointed out that there exists a nexus between criminals, bureaucracy and politicians. Because of the decisive role of the crime, casts, communalism and corruption, the real problems of the people–law and order, development–health, education, basic needs of the people are relegated to the secondary position. Though these issues are also raise by the politicians in every election, it is mainly done as a rhetoric.

Q10. Analyse the nature of farmers' movements in India.

Ans. Refer to Chapter-6, Q.No.-19

Q11. Comment on criminalisation of politics in India.

Ans. Refer to Chapter-7, Q.No.-18

Q12. Describe the nature of relationship between environment and human rights.

Ans. Environmental degradation is indicative of the violation of the rights of the people. It not only deprives of the natural pollution free environment, which is essential for the survival of human beings. It is the result of a vicious circle in which most societies are so badly caught. It is argued that development is undertaken to remove poverty and improve the quality of life of the people. But the mode of development that is followed has turned out to be environmentally disastrous. Instead of reducing proverty, it has increased inequality, deprivation, marginalisation and cause extensive environmental degradation. The growth and expansion of market-driven development strategy, be it socialist or capitalist, is not able "to solve the very problem it creates" (Shiva; 1991 : 342). Management of forest is another area where primacy of growth and basic needs outweigh environmental concerns. The industrialists, politicians and forest bureaucrats have forged a nexus to consume forests without any restraint.

Heavy industrialisation is another potent source of pollution and threat to environment. Unchecked industrialisation has released toxic gases, chemicals, effluents and hazardous substances into air, water and soil. Another dimension of this issue pertains to the occupational hazards on the health and safety of the workers of some specific industries such as chemical, petrochemical, pharmaceutical, pesticides and fertiliser. The workers and the local population are found to be suffering from cancer, respiratory diseases, infertility, corrosion of fingers, toes and holes in the nose (wall separating the nostrils). There is a decline in livelihood prospects from fishing, agricultural and horticultural activities. Such widespread impact has generated anguish among the victims and people's movements were launched.

It shows that developing societies are really caught in choiceless and helpless situation. The market-centered and sensitive strategy of economic development has left us with little scope of amendments. Any alteration in strategy to save the one can maim or kill the other. If livelihood is generated, environment is threatened and if environment is protected, livelihood is threatened. This is a strange predicament. The environment movement in India reflects this predicament and dilemma amply.

SECTION-III

Q13. Write short notes on any two of the following in about 100 words each. Each part carries 6 marks.

(a) The Constituent Assembly

Ans. Refer to Chapter-2, Q.No.-1

(b) The Inter - State Council

Ans. The nature of federalism defines that there are possibilities of difference and tensions between two levels of government. To ensure cooperation between them there can be various mechanisms including the Constitutional. The Indian Constitution provides for such a mechanism through Article 263 making provision for an inter-state council. The Sarkaria Commission in its report recommended that an Inter-State Council charged with duties set out in clauses (b) and (c) of Article 263 should be formed. The then Union government remained lukewarm to the Sarkaria Commission's recommendations in general. Therefore, no efforts were made to establish such a council.

The National Front formed before 1989 elections in its manifesto promised to undertake a comprehensive review of Union-State relations in consultation with all Chief Ministers. In pursuance of this promise the national Front Government established the Inter-State Council through a presidential notification on May 25, 1990. The Council was to consist of the Prime Minister, Chief Ministers of all States, Chief Ministers or Administrators of Unions Territories and six ministers of cabinet rank of the Union Government. The establishment of Inter-State Council is an important step towards cooperation in Union-State relations.

(c) Chipko Movement

Ans. Refer to Chapter-6, Q.No.-16(b)

(d) Inter-State Water Disputes

Ans. The conflicts between Tamil Nadu and Karnataka, Karnataka and Andhra Pradesh, Maharashtra and Andhra Pradesh, between Punjab, Haryana and Rajasthan are important examples of inter-state water disputes. Article 262 of the Constitution provides for parliamentary legislation for the adjudication of inter-state river water disputes and for barring the Courts (including the Supreme Court) in such issues. Yet in some cases, Supreme Court has entertained the cases, particularly on appeals against the awards of tribunals set up to decide the disputes. In view of different political parties in power in disputing states and also at the centre, allegations and counter-allegations on the role of centre are also made various suggestions including constitution of a permanent commission, enactment of laws, etc. are being made, as the issue has become quite conflictual both in terms of centre-state and Inter-State relations.

Government and Politics In India: BPSE-212

December, 2014

Note: (i) Section I—Any two questions to be answered. (ii) Section II—Any four questions to be answered. (iii) Section III—Any two parts to be answered.

SECTION-I

Answer any two of the following questions in about 500 words each. Each question carries 20 marks.

Q1. Identify the main features of Colonialism. Discuss the "Drain Theory" in the context of British Colonialism in India.

Q2. Discuss the role of Mahatma Gandhi in India's freedom struggle.

Q3. Write a note on Fundamental Rights as enshrined in the Constitution of India.

Q4. Discuss the powers and functions of the Supreme Court of India with special reference to its "Judicial Review" power.

SECTION-II

Answer any four of the following questions in about 250 words each. Each question carries 12 marks.

Q5. Describe the main features of the Parliamentary System in India.

Q6. Discuss the Emergency powers of the President of India.

Q7. How does caste influence voting behaviour in India? Explain.

Q8. Analyse the nature of coalition politics in India since the 1990s.

Q9. Examine the factors for the growth of regional parties in Indian politics in recent times.

Q10. Discuss the composition and role of the Election Commission of India.

Q11. Examine the areas of tension between the Centre and the States in India.

Q12. Discuss the major issues before the Women's movement in India.

SECTION-III

Q13. Write short notes on any two of the following in about 100 words each. Each part carries 6 marks.

(a) Chipko Movement

(b) Right to Freedom

(c) Akali Dal

(d) Liberalisation

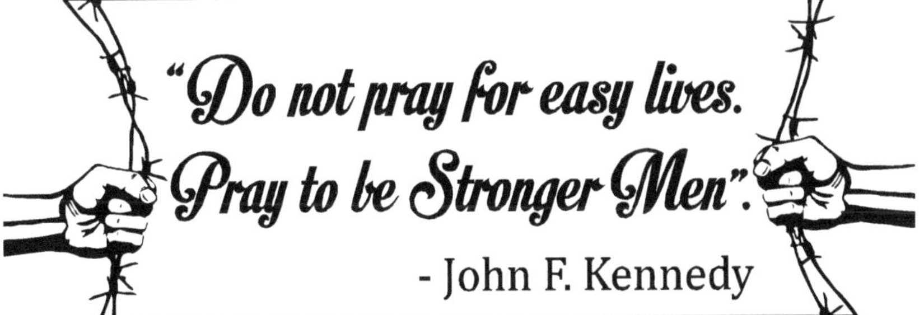

Government and Politics In India: BPSE-212

June, 2015

Note: (i) Section I—Any two questions to be answered. (ii) Section II—Any four questions to be answered. (iii) Section III—Any two parts to be answered.

SECTION-I

Answer any two of the following questions in about 500 words each. Each question carries 20 marks.

Q1. Critically examine the rise of working class during the colonial period in India.

Q2. Discuss the basic features of the India Consitution.

Q3. Evaluate the working of Parliamentary Democracy in India

Q4. Critically examine the emergency powers of the President of India.

SECTION-II

Answer any four of the following questions in about 250 words each. Each question carries 12 marks.

Q5. What were the social evils which the social movements addressed in 19th century India? Elaborate.

Q6. What is citizenship? Who are the citizens of India?

Q7. Discuss the collective responsibility principle of the Parliamentary system in India.

Q8. Write a short note on the bureaucrat-politician-businessman nexus in India.

Q9. Critically examine the changing nature of party system in India.

Q10. Examine the main features of the 73rd Amendment of the Constitution of India.

Q11. Discuss the ideology, programme and social base of the Bharatiya Janata Party (BJP).

Q12. Critically examine the impact of globalisation on social, economic and cultural domains in India.

SECTION-III

Q13. Write short notes on any two of the following in about 100 words each. Each part carries 6 marks.

(a) Quit India Movement

(b) Secularism

(c) Public Interest Litigation (PIL)

(d) Coalition Politics

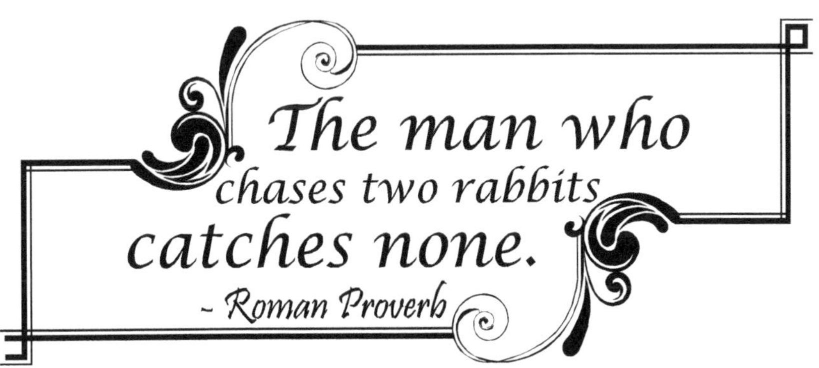

Government and Politics In India: BPSE-212

December, 2015

Note: (i) Section I—Answer any two questions. (ii) Section II—Answer any four questions. (iii) Section III—Answer any two parts.

SECTION-I

Answer any two of the following questions in about 500 words each. Each question carries 20 marks.

Q1. "The Supreme Court of India keeps a check on arbitrary power of the Parliament in amending the Constitution." Discuss.

Q2. Analyse the changing nature of party system in India.

Q3. Identify the trends in the working of Indian federalism.

Q4. "Law making is a long, cumbersome and time-consuming process." Explain.

SECTION-II

Answer any four of the following questions in about 250 words each. Each question carries 12 marks.

Q5. Describe the main features of tribal movements in India.

Q6. What are the main reasons for the rise of the Dalit Panther Movement? Elaborate.

Q7. What is citizenship? What are the provisions related to citizenship in the Indian Constitution?

Q8. Describe the nature of environmental movements in India.

Q9. Describe the provisions and significance of the 73rd Constitutional Amendment.

Q10. **Examine the factors contributing to the rise of regional parties in India.**

Q11. **Describe the parliamentary devices to control the executive in India.**

Q12. **Examine the constitutional provisions for the creation of new states.**

SECTION-III

Q13. **Write short notes on any two of the following in about 100 words each. Each part carries 6 marks.**

(a) **Principle of collective responsibility**

(b) **Naga movement**

(c) **Election Commission of India**

(d) **Sarkaria Commission**

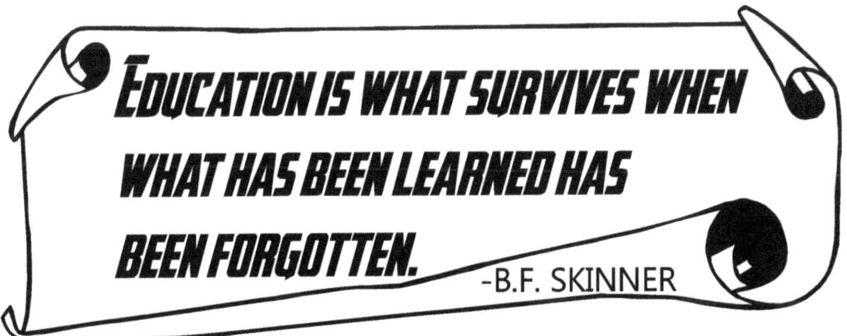

Government and Politics In India: BPSE-212

June, 2016

Note: (i) Section I—Answer any two questions. (ii) Section II—Answer any four questions. (iii) Section III—Answer any two parts.

SECTION-I

Answer any two of the following questions in about 500 words each. Each question carries 20 marks.

Q1. Examine the areas of tensions in Centre-State relations in India.

Q2. What are the provisions in the Indian Constitution which seek to realise the goal of democracy in form and substance? Describe.

Q3. Examine the factors contributing to the rise of regional parties.

Q4. Briefly describe the women's struggle for their rights during the colonial period.

SECTION-II

Answer any four of the following questions in about 250 words each. Each question carries 12 marks.

Q5. What are the reasons for providing special provisions for certain states in the Indian Constitution? Elaborate.

Q6. Comment on the role of Indian Judiciary in environmental protection.

Q7. What are the main recommendations of the Sarkaria Commission? Describe.

Q8. Describe the emergency powers of the President of India.

Q9. Critically examine the legislative procedures in law-making.

Q10. Discuss the characteristics of farmers' movement in India.

Q11. Comment on the changing nature of party system in India.

Q12. How does the Parliament exercise control over the Executive? Explain.

SECTION-III

Q13. Write short notes on any two of the following in about 100 words each. Each part carries 6 marks.

(a) Principle of Collective Responsibility

(b) Parliamentary Privileges

(c) Public Interest Litigation

(d) Election Commission of India

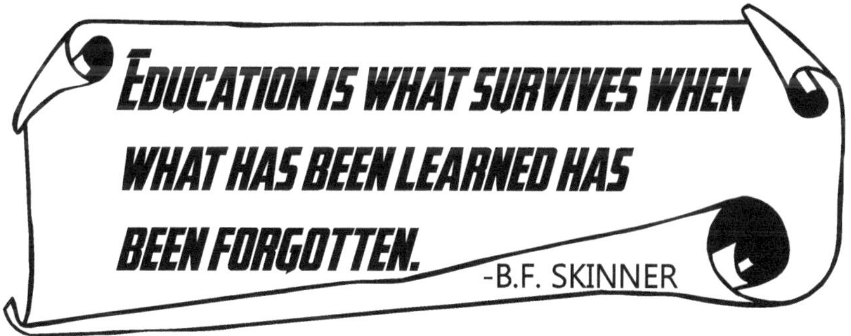

Government and Politics In India: BPSE-212

December, 2016

Note: (i) Section I—Answer any two questions. (ii) Section II—Answer any four questions. (iii) Section III—Answer any two parts.

SECTION-I

Answer any two of the following questions in about 500 words each. Each question carries 20 marks.

Q1. Describe the emergence of major political forces during the colonial period.

Ans. The foundation of the Indian National Congress in 1885 as an all India, secular political party, is widely regarded as a key turning point in formalising opposition to the Raj. It developed from its elite intellectual middle-class confines, and a moderate, loyalist agenda, to become by the inter-war years, a mass organisation. It was an organisation which, despite the tremendous diversity of the sub-continent, was remarkable in achieving broad consensus over the decades.

Yet it was not a homogenous organisation and was often dominated by factionalism and opposing political strategies. This was exemplified by its splintering in 1907 into the so-called 'moderate' and 'extremist' wings, which reunited 10 years later. Another example was the 'pro-changers' (who believed working the constitutional structures to weaken it from within) and 'no-changers' (who wanted to distance themselves from the Raj) during the 1920s.

There was also a split within Congress between those who believed that violence was a justifiable weapon in the fight against imperial oppression (whose most iconic figure was Subhas Chandra Bose, who went on to form the Indian National Army), and those who stressed non-violence.

The towering figure in this latter group was Mahatma Gandhi, who introduced a seismic new idiom of opposition in the shape of non-violent non-cooperation or 'satyagraha' (meaning 'truth' or 'soul' force'). Gandhi oversaw three major nationwide movements which achieved varying degrees of success in 1920-1922, 1930-1934 and in 1942. These mobilised the masses on the one hand, while provoking the authorities into draconian repression. Much to Gandhi's distress, self-restraint among supporters often gave way to violence.

The lack of confidence in the Muslim League among the Muslim population was to be dramatically reversed in the 1946 elections. The intervening years saw the rise of Jinnah and the League to political prominence through the successful exploitation of the wartime insecurities of the British, and the political vacuum created when the Congress ministries (which had unanimously come to power in 1937) resigned en masse to protest at the government's unilateral decision to enter India into the war without consultation.

The rejuvenated League skillfully exploited the communal card. At its Lahore session in 1940, Jinnah made the demand for Pakistan into its rallying cry. The ensuing communal violence, especially after Jinnah declared 'Direct Action Day' in August 1946, put pressure on the British government and Congress to accede to his demands for a separate homeland for Muslims.

The arrival of Lord Louis Mountbatten as India's last viceroy in March 1947, brought with it an agenda to transfer power as quickly and efficiently as possible. The resulting negotiations saw the deadline for British withdrawal brought forward from June 1948 to August 1947.

Q2. Write an essay on the Directive Principles of State Policy.

Ans. Refer to Chapter-2, Q.No.-5

Q3. Describe the basic characteristics of the party system in India.

Ans. Refer to Chapter-5, Q.No.-1

Q4. How has the Reservation Policy in India contributed towards social justice and equality? Discuss.

Ans. Reservation is for the upliftment of the depressed and continuing it for the lifetime of the nation is not good. People for whom this is meant should recognise the efforts the government is putting in for their upliftment and use this opportunity to bring themselves to the mainstream of Indian society. They should understand that Reservation is not a good thing to happen for the society as it is an indication of social inequality and social injustice which do exist in our social setup. We need to diminish this and bring to our country, our nation a society that is free from inequality, injustice and any form of Reservation; but to make this happen people who fall in the category to be benefited from Reservation should come forward and utilise this opportunity to rise and help themselves and the society as a whole to acquire a socially forward, equal and just status.

No political party can afford to initiate any debate on the relevance of reservation policy; leave aside revising the policy. Although the judiciary, in such a scenario, has often been forced to take up a stand against the politicisation of reservations, the caste-based reservation policy is a sensitive issue. The backward classes were classified as the Scheduled castes (SC), Scheduled tribes (ST), and other backward classes. When India became an independent nation, the framers of the Constitution took upon themselves the duty of forwarding interests of the backward classes by having Article 46 in the Constitution. Article 46 stated that the state shall promote with special care the educational and economic interest of the weaker section of the people, also protecting them from social injustice and all forms of exploitation. Article 46 was complimented by the inclusion of many other articles for the empowerment of the backward classes. Since they were the oppressed classes this was thought to be the best mechanism to correct the mistake that was being practiced for many hundreds of years.

But the implementation of reservation or quota system was not carried out smoothly. The Congress government headed by the then Prime Minister Jawahar Lal Nehru felt unable to implement the policies of Planning Commission whose one of the objectives at that time (1951-56) was raising the standard of living of people especially those belonging to backward classes because these policies to some extent infringes upon the fundamental rights provided under Article 14, 15, 16, 21 etc.

Although the reservation policy is an exception to the equality rule, it is still considered an essential element of equality. Equality has many dimensions and one such dimension is the reservation policy for the backward classes. But gradually, there has been bipolarity building up on the issue of reservation which is surely and steadily partitioning the society. The forward class people are feeling pressed and are desperate at the emerging scenario when pie is fast shrinking for them. Nearly half of all government jobs are out of their reach because of the method of social justice adopted by the government. But even after nearly 70 years of independence the people still are having to fall back on reservation, and that shows the success or otherwise, of governments in delivering social justice.

SECTION-II

Answer any four of the following questions in about 250 words each. Each question carries 12 marks.

Q5. How is citizenship acquired in India?

Ans. Refer to Chapter-2, Q.No.-18

Q6. Describe the functions and powers of the Supreme Court of India.

Ans. Refer to Chapter-3, Q.No.-21

Q7. Examine the nature of coalition politics in India since the 1990s.

Ans. Refer to Chapter-5, Q.No.-16

Q8. Discuss the basic characteristics of the Farmers Movement in Independent India.

Ans. Refer to Chapter-6, Q.No.-19

Q9. How does legislature exercise control over the executive in India's Parliamentary system? Explain.

Ans. Refer to Chapter-2, Q.No.-5

Q10. Describe the special provisions meant for North-East India.

Ans. Refer to Chapter-4, Q.No.-9(b)

Q11. Examine the role of women in the environmental movements in India.

Ans. Refer to Chapter-6, Q.No.-6

Q12. What challenges does secularism face in India?

Ans. Refer to Chapter-7, Q.No.-12

SECTION-III

Q13. Write short notes on any two of the following in about 100 words each. Each part carries 6 marks.

(a) Home Rule Movement

Ans. Refer to Chapter-1, Q.No.-11(ii)

(b) Money Bill

Ans. Financial bill may be said to be any bill which relates to revenue and expenditure. But the financial bill is not a money bill. Art. 110 states that no bill is a money bill unless it is certified by the Speaker of the Lok Sabha. A money bill cannot be introduced in the Rajya Sabha. Once a money bill is passed by the Lok Sabha, it is transmitted to the Rajya Sabha. The Rajya Sabha cannot reject a money bill. It must, within a period of fourteen days from the date of receipt of the bill, return the bill to the Lok Sabha which may thereupon either accept or reject all or any of the recommendations. If the Lok Sabha accepts any of the recommendations, the money bill is deemed to have been passed by both Houses.

(c) Regionalism

Ans. The term regionalism refers to that feeling of people of a region in which they display more closeness and faithfulness towards regional identities and interests in comparison to their national identity and national interests. Roots of regionalism is in India's manifold diversity of languages, cultures, ethnic groups, communities, religions and so on, and encouraged by the regional concentration of those identity markers, and fueled by a sense of regional deprivation. For many centuries, India remained the land of many lands, regions, cultures and traditions. Regionalism in India is a multidimensional phenomenon as it is a complex amalgam of geographical, historical, cultural, economic, politico-administrative and psyche factors. It is not possible to indicate exactly any particular factor, which has been solely responsible for the phenomenon of regionalism.

(d) Backward Castes' Associations

Ans. Backward caste associations found in the notion of 'OBC quotas' a good reason to down play their narrow identity and merge it in a broader front which could pressure the state more effectively. In the early 1970s, the All India Kurmi Mahasabha allied with the Koeris and sought a merger of all the 'backward classes'. At its 1972 session, its slogan was 'Pichara Jago Desh Bachao' ("Backwards", wake-up and rescue the country'). One resolution sought to allow non-Kurmis to belong to the association while another asked for the appointment of a Public Service Commission for the Backward Classes.

Government and Politics In India: BPSE-212

June, 2017

Note: (i) Section I—Answer any two questions. (ii) Section II—Answer any four questions. (iii) Section III—Answer any two parts.

SECTION-I

Answer any two of the following questions in about 500 words each. Each question carries 20 marks.

Q1. Describe the vision of Socio-economic and Political justice in India as outlined in the Preamble of the Constitution.

Ans. Refer to Chapter-7, Q.No.-15

Q2. Discuss the Parliament's powers and procedures to amend the Constitution of India.

Ans. Refer to Chapter-3, Q.No.-6

Q3. Compare the ideologies and social bases of the Congress and Bharatiya Janata Party.

Ans. Refer to Chapter-5, Q.No.-5

Q4. Critically analyse the major issues of the environmental movement in India.

Ans. Refer to Chapter-6, Q.No.-16

SECTION-II

Answer any four of the following questions in about 250 words each. Each question carries 12 marks.

Q5. Write a note on the Civil Disobedience Movement.

Ans. Refer to Chapter-1, Q.No.-11(v)

Q6. Analyse the reasons for growing influence of regional parties.

Ans. Refer to Chapter-5, Q.No.-1

Q7. What special powers does the Rajya Sabha enjoy in India?

Ans. Refer to Chapter-3, Q.No.-7

Q8. Discuss the relationship between Caste and Class in India.

Ans. According to some scholars, caste system is essentially a class system. It was essentially so in the early formative years. The classes were: Rajanyas or the Kshatriyas, the aristocracy, the Brahmins, the priests, the Vaishyas, the people at large, mainly peasants and traders, and the Shudras, the service communities. There are various theories of the origin of the system. Some believe that the system was created by the Divine Power for maintaining harmony in society. Accordingly, one gets birth in a particular caste because of one's karma o f the previous birth. Others believe that the system has been evolved in course of time with the development of economic surplus. It came into existence with economic divisions; or the invaders to subjugate the local tribal population created it.

Hindu society was composed of classes such as (1) Brahmin or the priestly class, (2) Kshatriya or the military class and (3) Vaishya or the merchant class and (4) Sudra or the artisan. This was considered as a class system according to B.R. Ambedkar. Among the Hindus, the priestly class maintains social distance from others through a closed policy and becomes a caste by itself.

The other classes undergo differentiation, some into large and some into very minute groups. The natural thing about these sub-divisions is that they have lost the open-door character of the class system and have become self-enclosed units called castes.

The class basis of caste system in India has been highlighted by Cathleen Gough in her reference to conflict and litigation between different castes in a Tanjore village based on economic inequalities Proof Y. Singh is of the view that classes operate within the framework of castes. Commenting on the nexus of caste and class, he writes, "The situation corresponds to a 'prismatic 'model of change where traditional sentiments of caste and kinship undergo adaptive transformation without completely being diffracted into classes or corporate groups.

Q9. What do you understand by the idea of a Committed Bureaucracy?

Ans. Refer to Chapter-3, Q.No.-29

Q10. Describe the factors responsible for the rise of Dalit Panthers.

Ans. Refer to Chapter-6, Q.No.-9

Q11. Write a note on the nexus between crime and politics in India.

Ans. Generally the candidates are given tickets by the political parties on the considerations whether the candidates call muster the support o f numerically larger castes and communities and possesses enough resources. Even the electorates vote on the caste and communal lines. A large number of elected representatives have criminal background or have criminal cases registered against them. The relationship between the politicians and criminals exists in the elections at all levels – parliamentary, state legislative assemblies and councils, and panchayats and municipalities. Such nexus became conspicuous, especially since the 1990s. This is a reflection of erosion in the credibility of the democratic values. V N Vohra sub-committee also pointed out that there exists a nexus between criminals, bureaucracy and politicians. Because of the decisive role o f the crime, caste, communalism and corruption, the real problems of t he people – law and order, development – health, education, basic needs o f the people are relegated to the secondary position. Though these issues are also raise by the politicians in every election, it is mainly done as a rhetoric.

The Sohrabuddin Sheikh fake encounter was a case with strong political repercussions as Sohrabuddin Shaikh, a criminal and alleged terrorist was politically used for ulterior motives by Amit Shah, a close confidant of chief minister Narendra Modi, who himself was allegedly involved in a gigantic extortion racket. The police had initially claimed Sohrabuddin as a terrorist with Lashkar-e-Taiba connections who died while trying to escape from custody. Then, in a media expose by journalist Prashant Dayal, followed by a Supreme Court mediated inquiry conducted by the state CID, the fake encounter was revealed and several top police officers were arrested. This case succinctly proves the vicious nexus of police and government in colluding with rule of law in the country.

Q12. Describe the major reasons behind violence against women.
Ans. Refer to Chapter-6, Q.No.-6

SECTION-III

Q13. Write short notes on any two of the following in about 100 words each. Each part carries 6 marks.

(a) Collective Responsibility
Ans. Refer to Chapter-3, Q.No.-18

(b) Right to Equality
Ans. Article 14, guarantees the Right to Equality before the Law and the Right to Equal Protection of the Laws. In other words, this article ensures that all persons can be tried in a court of law and every person can approach the courts for justice and that no person shall be discriminated

against in the application of laws, nor can any person claim special privileges and favouritism.

Article 15 guarantees protection from discrimination on the basis of 'religion, race, caste, sex or place of birth', and provides for equal access and thus the Right against Discrimination. It also, however, states clearly that the state can make special provisions for the uplift of certain categories of people like socially and culturally backward classes and Scheduled Castes and Scheduled Tribes.

(c) Finance Commission

Ans. Refer to Chapter-4, Q.No.-6

(d) Communalism

Ans. Refer to Chapter-6, Q.No.-6

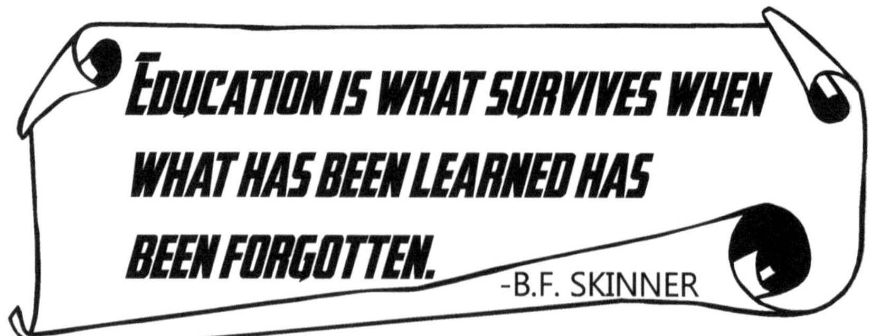

Government and Politics In India: BPSE-212

December, 2017

Note: (i) Section I— Any two questions to be answered. (ii) Section II— Any four questions to be answered. (iii) Section III— Any two short notes to be written.

SECTION-I

Answer any two of the following questions in about 500 words each. Each question carries 20 marks.

Q1. Discuss the role of extremist nationalism in India's National Movement.

Q2. What is meant by Citizenship? How has community been recognised in India's citizenship framework?

Q3. Discuss the relationship between the President and the Prime Minister in India's Parliamentary system.

Q4. What factors are responsible for the emergence and growth of regionalism?

SECTION-II

Answer any four of the following questions in about 250 words each. Each question carries 12 marks.

Q5. What do you understand by Public Interest Litigation? Discuss its uses and abuses.

Q6. Discuss the basic characteristics of the 73rd Constitutional Amendment Act.

Q7. Analyse the role of caste in determining the voting behaviour of the electorate.

Q8. What do you understand by Substantive Democracy? Elaborate.

Q9. Describe the idea of secularism as incorporated in India's Constitution.

Q10. Write a note on the nature and importance of the Dalit Movement.

Q11. Describe the composition and role of the Election Commission of India.

Q12. Write a note on the nature and effects of liberalisation of economy in India.

SECTION-III

Q13. Write short notes on any two of the following in about 100 words each. Each part carries 6 marks.

(a) Right to Equality

(b) Judicial Review

(c) Inter-State Council

(d) Gender Equality

Government and Politics In India: BPSE-212

June, 2018

Note: (i) Section I— Any two questions to be answered. (ii) Section II— Any four questions to be answered. (iii) Section III— Any two parts to be answered.

SECTION-I

Answer any two of the following questions in about 500 words each. Each question carries 20 marks.

Q1. Analyes the nature, importance and role of Directive Principles of State Policy.

Ans. Part IV of the Constitution, titled Directive Principles of State Policy, contains certain non-justiciable rights. These rights, unlike the ones in the preceding section, are not enforceable by courts, but are in the nature of reminders or directives for lawmaking, to usher in conditions in which the rights enumerated in the previous section become more meaningful. However, show a 'simultaneous commitment' to both 'community-ship' and 'citizen-ship', in other words to both the community and the individual citizen. Article 38 for example, directs the State to commit itself to 'promote the welfare of the people' by promoting a 'social order' in which 'justice, social, economic and political, shall inform all the institutions of the national life'. To achieve this, the state is asked to 'strive to minimise inequalities of income' and also 'eliminate inequalities in status, facilities and opportunities'. The significant reminder, however, is that this justice and equality is to be achieved 'not only amongst individuals but also amongst groups of people residing in different areas or engaged in different vocations'. Article 46 likewise instructs the States to 'promote with special care the educational and economic interests of the weaker sections of the people and in particular, of the scheduled Castes and Tribes' and 'protect them from social injustice and all forms of exploitation'. By and large the Directive Principles envisage an active role of the state in providing a range of socially ameliorative or welfare rights ranging from access to an adequate means of livelihood, equal pay for equal work, health arid strength of workers, living wage for workers, provision of just and humane conditions of work, right to work, to education, to public assistance, to equal justice and free legal aid, to adequate nutrition and health, etc.

Article 44 of the Directive Principles enjoins the State to 'secure for all its citizens a uniform civil code throughout the territory of India'. This article needs special attention because it encapsulates the Constitution's 'simultaneous commitment' to individual and community rights. It moreover, provides a window into the tensions which inform citizenship, and its criticism from some quarters, especially the feminists.

The legislative and executive powers of the state are to be exercised under the purview of the Directive Principles of the Indian Constitution.

The Indian Constitution was written immediately after India obtained freedom, and the contributors to the Constitution were well aware of the ruined state of the Indian economy as well as the fragile state of the nation's unity. Thus, they created a set of guidelines under the heading Directive Principles for an inclusive development of the society.

Inspired by the Constitution of Ireland, the Directive Principles contain the very basic philosophy of the Constitution of India, and that is the overall development of the nation through guidelines related to social justice, economic welfare, foreign policy, and legal and administrative matters. The Directive Principles are codified versions of democratic socialist order as conceived by Nehru with an admixture of Gandhian thought.

However, the Directive Principles cannot be enforced in a court of law and the State cannot be sued for non-compliance of the same. This indeed makes the Directive Principles a very interesting and enchanting part of the Constitution because while it does stand for the ideals of the nation, these ideals have not been made mandatory.

Q2. Discuss the powers and functions of the Supreme Court of India and its role as the protector of the Constitution.

Ans. Refer to Chapter-3, Q.No.-21

Role of Supreme Court as the protector of the Constitution

The Supreme Court also has non-exclusive original jurisdiction as the protector of Fundamental Rights. Article 32 of the Constitution gives citizens the right to move the Supreme Court directly for the enforcement of any of the fundamental rights enumerated in Part III of the Constitution. As the guardian of Fundamental Rights, the Supreme Court has the power to issue writs such as Habeas Corpus, Quo Warranto, Prohibition, Certiorari, and Mandamus. Habeas Corpus is a writ issued by the court to bring before the court a person from illegal custody. The court can decide the legality of detention and release the person if detention is found to be illegal. By using the writ of Mandamus, the court may order the public officials to perform their legal duties. Prohibition is a writ to prevent a court or tribunal from doing something in excess of its authority. By the writ of Certiorari, the court may strike off an order passed by any official of the government, local body or a statutory body. Quo warranto is a writ issued to a person who authorisedly occupies a public office to step down from that office. In addition to issuing these writs, the Supreme Court is empowered to issue appropriate directions and orders to the executive.

Q3. Why is the office of Governor considered a tension area in Centre State relations? Explain.

Ans. Refer to Chapter-4, Q.No.-12

Q4. Write an essay on the policy of Reservation and its role in social transformation.

Ans. Refer to Chapter-3, Q.No.-28(iii)

The word "Aarakshan" is a evolution and combination of two parts—Aa + Rakshan, which means reserving something for a specific person or a specific category of persons. In this manner, that thing becomes restricted for other persons. Thus "Aarakshan" carries a wide meaning instead of narrow one which differs according to time and circumstances.

It we look from the historical perspective, we find that during the period of imperial type of governance, the posts of king and his advisers were generally reserved on the basis of heredity. This affected the administrative competence many a times. This had an effect on the medieval history also where higher administrative posts were reserved for Muslims only.

Later on during the British rule, race preference become the basis of reservation where senior administrative posts were reserved for English people only. Although it was decided to adopt the principle of utility, liberalism and neutralism based competence in political and administrative areas, but it was just a hypocracy and in reality the racial preference remained the only option in practice for selection to such posts.

After the independence, in terms of contemporary requirements, stress was given to utility and relevance of reservation. Provisions were made in the constitution as an option to bring the economically and socially backward people to the mainstream which gap had cropped up as a result of British policies.

At present the Hon'ble supreme court of India has submitted detailed explanations on the various issues brought before it from time to time. Based on these explanations provisions of reservations are made for eradicating the social in-equality prevalent in Hindu society (explanation of Supreme Court—Hindustan Times). It has been done with the motive of social upliftment of the castes included in the reservation list.

Keeping in view the earlier circumstances, rules were framed for the backward (dalits) and they were given the rights as available to other people. It was aimed to eradicate the feeling of ups or down from the minds of the people. For this purpose, reservations were made for all the sections of the society in proportion to their population which were also modified from time to time as per the need of the hour. As such constitutional security has been ensured for the welfare and upliftment of certain castes through the system of reservation, where 51% has been reserved for general castes, 27% for other backward classes, 15% for scheduled castes and 7.5% for scheduled tribes.

As such reservation is the need of the hour which cannot be limited to caste, religion or gender only. As on date, economical status is also a big basic of reservation. There was a time when only scheduled castes and scheduled tribes required reservation, but today it requires to be spread to all spheres so that economically backward people from normal castes also get the benefit of reservation. With the passage of time, reservation should be done based on the economic status and merit also in addition caste, gender, religion etc. so that solution could be found for the problems of people belonging to all categories and reservation is beneficial to all in real sense.

SECTION-II

Answer any four of the following questions in about 250 words each. Each question carries 12 marks.

Q5. How does the Parliament exercise its control over the executive?

Ans. Refer to Chapter-2, Q.No.-5

Q6. Describe the characteristics of Party System in India after 1967.

Ans. Refer to Chapter-5, Q.No.-1

Q7. Write a note on the nature of coalition government at the Centre since 1989.

Ans. Refer to Chapter-5, Q.No.-16

Q8. Discuss the socio-political causes responsible for communal politics in India.

Ans. Refer to Chapter-7, Q.No.-12

Q9. Write a note on the nature and role of Farmers' Movement in India.

Ans. Refer to Chapter-6, Q.No.-19

Q10. What do you understand by the nexus between crime and politics?

Ans. Refer to June-2017, Q.No.-11

Q11. What is meant by Globalisation? What impact has it had on India's economy and politics?

Ans. Refer to Chapter-7, Q.No.-1, 6

Q12. Write an essay on the nature and role of Women's Movement.

Ans. Refer to Chapter-6, Q.No.-6, 7

SECTION-III

Q13. Write short notes on any two of the following in about 100 words each. Each part carries 6 marks.

(a) Judicial Review

Ans. Refer to Chapter-3, Q.No.-24

(b) Backwards Assertion

Ans. Under the new dispensation of democratic order, the traditionally backward castes not only challenged the socio-economic and political dominance of the upper castes but also emerged as dominant castes in rural areas and dominant force in the politics of the State. As a consequence, they emerged as visible force in rural power structure, which enforced their significance in the political arena of the state. In many parts of the country, the backward castes emerged as dominant players in politics. The dominant social coalition in politics till the mid sixties was in favour of the upper castes. But the development of the 1950s and 1960s added a new assertiveness among the backward castes. In fact, this change was a product of multiple factors, but primarily a result of the introduction of parliamentary democracy and adult franchise.

(c) Question Hour

Ans. Refer to Chapter-3, Q.No.-14

(d) Chipko Movement

Ans. Refer to Chapter-6, Q.No.-16(b)

Government and Politics In India: BPSE-212

December, 2018

Note: : *(i) Section — I Answer any two questions. (ii) Section II — Answer any four questions. (iii) Section III — Write short notes on any two parts of question no. 13.*

SECTION I

Answer any two of the following questions in about 500 words each. Each question carries 20 marks.

Q1. Analyse the impact of Colonialism on Indian economy and polity.

Q2. Examine the powers and position of the President.

Q3. Write an essay on the changing nature of the Party System in India.

Q4. Write an essay on the impact of globalisation on India's society and economy.

SECTION II

Answer any four of the following questions in about 250 words each. Each question carries 12 marks.

Q5. Describe in brief the composition of the Constituent Assembly.

Q6. Critically examine the nature of Judicial Activism.

Q7. Discuss the role of caste in India's electoral process.

Q8. Describe in brief the role of regional parties in India.

Q9. How does legislature exercise control over the executive?

Q10. Write a note on the importance of the 73rd Constitutional Amendment.

Q11. Describe the nature of Secularism in India and the challenges it faces.

Q12. Discuss the main characteristics and concerns of environmental movements.

SECTION III

Q13. Write short notes on any two of the following in about 100 words each. Each part carries 6 marks.

(a) The Vth Schedule of the Constitution

(b) Right to Freedom of Religion

(c) Backward Caste Associations

(d) The Finance Commission

Government and Politics In India: BPSE-212

June, 2019

Note: : *(i) Section I: Answer any two questions. (ii) Section II: Answer any four questions. (iii) Section III: Answer any two parts.*

Section—I

Answer any two of the following questions in about 500 words each. Each question carries 20 marks.

Q1. Analyse the role of Mahatma Gandhi in India's freedom struggle.

Q2. Explain the differences and the relationship between Fundamental Rights and Directive Principles of State Policy.

Q3. What do you understand by Regionalism? Examine the reasons for the growth of the same.

Q4. How has the reservation policy in India helped the emergence of new social groups? Elaborate.

Section—II

Answer any four of the following questions in about 250 words each. Each question carries 12 marks.

Q5. Write a note on the right to freedom of life and liberty.

Q6. Explain the provisions of the Indian constitution to establish justice and equality.

Q7. What special provisions have been provided in the constitution for the state of Jammu and Kashmir? Explain their importance.

Q8. Describe the characteristics of Tribal Movements in India.

Q9. Describe the causes of emergence and growth of communalism.

Q10. Write a brief note on Public Interest Litigation and its importance.

Q11. Comment on the cultural impact of globalisation.

Q12. Discuss the nature of Indian bureaucracy and its role in development.

Section—III

Q13. Write short notes on any two of the following in about 100 words each. Each part carries 6 marks : (a) Citizenship

(b) Money Bill

(c) Inter-State Council

(d) Liberalization of economy

Government and Politics In India: BPSE-212

December, 2019

Note: : (i) Section I: Answer any two questions. (ii) Section II: Answer any four questions. (iii) Section III: Answer any two parts.

Section – I

Answer any two of the following questions in about 500 words each. Each question carries 20 marks.

Q1. Analyse the extremist nationalism in colonial India.

Ans. Refer to Chapter-1, Q.No.-10 (Page No.-26)

Q2. Discuss the powers and functions of Supreme Court of India with special reference to the power of Judicial review.

Ans. Refer to Chapter-3, Q.No.-21 (Page No.-126) & Refer to June-2018, Q.No.-2 (Page No.-360)

Q3. Why is Indian Federalism some at times criticised as a federal structure with a strong unitary bias?

Ans. Refer to Chapter-4, Q.No.-2, 3 (Page No.-150, 151)

Q4. Discuss the challenges of communalism to Indian democracy.

Ans. Refer to Chapter-7, Q.No.-12 (Page No.-310)

Section – II

Answer any four of the following questions in about 250 words each. Each question carries 12 marks.

Q5. Discuss in brief emergency powers of the President.

Ans. Refer to Chapter-3, Q.No.-6 (Page No.-101)

Q6. Explain the importance of Directive principles as instruments for social-transformation.

Ans. Refer to Chapter-7, Q.No.-15 (Page No.-316)

Q7. Write a note on the functions and role of Election Commission.

Ans. Refer to Chapter-5, Q.No.-8, 9 (Page No.-222, 223)

Q8. What role regional parties have been playing at national level in last two decades or so?

Ans. Refer to Chapter-5, Q.No.-6 (Page No.-214)

Q9. How does globalisation impact State politics in India?

Ans. Refer to Chapter-7, Q.No.-6 (Page No.-297)

Q10. Discuss in brief the nature of Dalit Movement in India.

Ans. Refer to Chapter-6, Q.No.-9 (Page No.-254)

Q11. Briefly discuss the nature of coalition politics in India in 1990s onwards.

Ans. Refer to Chapter-5, Q.No.-14, 16 (Page No.-230, 233)

Q12. What do you understand by the idea of committed bureaucracy?

Ans. Refer to Chapter-3, Q.No.-29 (Page No.-143)

Section – III

Q13. Write short notes on any two of the following in about 100 words each. Each carries 6 marks.

(a) Inter-State council

Ans. Refer to June-2014, Q.No.-13(b) (Page No.-338)

(b) Right to life

Ans. Article 21: "No person shall be deprived of his life or personal liberty except according to procedure established by law" As we have seen earlier, the sight to life and personal liberty has received wide definition in several Supreme Court rulings. The Right to Life covers the right to basic needs such as food, education, health. The right to personal liberty covers freedom from illegal and unnecessary restraint. Denial of information relating to these aspects is often a denial of the right itself.

(c) Criminalisation of politics

Ans. Refer to June-2017, Q.No.-11 (Page No.-354)

(d) Liberalisation

Ans. Refer to Chapter-7, Q.No.-4 (Page No.-295)

www.ingramcontent.com/pod-product-compliance
Ingram Content Group UK Ltd.
Pitfield, Milton Keynes, MK11 3LW, UK
UKHW021709190726
13853UKWH00001B/471

9 789382 688921